ONE MORE WAR TO FIGHT

Union Veterans' Battle for Equality through Reconstruction,
Jim Crow, and the Lost Cause

STEPHEN A. GOLDMAN

ROWMAN & LITTLEFIELD
Lanham • Boulder • New York • London

Published by Rowman & Littlefield
An imprint of The Rowman & Littlefield Publishing Group, Inc.
4501 Forbes Boulevard, Suite 200, Lanham, Maryland 20706
www.rowman.com

86-90 Paul Street, London EC2A 4NE

British Library Cataloguing in Publication Information Available

Library of Congress Cataloging-in-Publication Data Available

ISBN: 978-1-5381-6155-5 (cloth : alk. paper)
ISBN: 978-1-5381-6156-2 (electronic)

♾™ The paper used in this publication meets the minimum requirements of American National
Standard for Information Sciences—Permanence of Paper for Printed Library Materials, ANSI/
NISO Z39.48-1992.

For my father, Abraham M. Goldman, MD, עליה השלום
First Lieutenant and Captain, United States Air Force, 1953–1955
Recipient, National Defense Service Medal

CONTENTS

Foreword

During my tenure as a Historical Specialist for Civil War and Reconstruction at the Library of Congress, I introduced Dr. Goldman to the William Oland Bourne Papers. The collection's many touching and fascinating narratives penned by disabled Northern soldiers and sailors (the "Left-Armed Corps") piqued his interest, the result of which is this examination of the military service and postwar lives of Union veterans.

For the archivist, that is the ultimate reward. Research libraries like to see their holdings acknowledged in credible publications. But in this particular instance, the contribution is reciprocal. The Library of Congress is indebted to Dr. Goldman for saving the Bourne Papers, which at the time of his initial visit were under consideration for declassification and eventual rendering owing to a lack of reader interest.

The essence of Dr. Goldman's study is the lasting influence of military service on individual soldiers, particularly those with combat experience. *One More War to Fight* touches on the root causes of this historic contest, the changing attitudes of Northern servicemen with respect to the Civil War's purpose, the significance of the Veteran Reserve Corps, and the psychological effect of involvement in what, from hindsight, was an "unfinished work" in the cause of freedom and equality for all Americans.

Readers will doubtless grasp the relevance of Dr. Goldman's findings concerning the psychological effect of combat on veterans of subsequent American wars. For men who have experienced combat, whatever the time or place, there is no escape. Whether thrill or pain, the battle is never forgotten. For many, if not most, the effects may not be visible, but they are part of every veteran's psyche.

Perhaps this is why their stories are best told by a trained psychiatrist, particularly this author, who has not only treated those who have been to war but also extensively studied the Civil War and Reconstruction. Dr. Goldman's work offers an innovative look at the most important event in United States history, and not only how, but why, its great impact continues to this day.

John R. Sellers, PhD

Introduction

On September 24, 1864, a hospitalized Army of the Potomac soldier spoke for several hundred thousand men who had put their lives on the line for Union since 1861, and for African American freedom after the preliminary Emancipation Proclamation's issuance in September 1862. Like so many clad in blue, he was outraged by the Democrats' perceived "peace-at-any-price" presidential platform that deemed "the experiment of war" a failure in restoring the Union: "Are they [Copperheads] foolish enough to believe we are not thinking men? . . . when free men rise in arms to defend free institutions, what 'thinking' can be more true, more wise, more patriotic than ours. It is thinking bayonets that compose our army, and it is because they are in the grasp of thinking men that they gather their majesty and power."[1]

Fully aware that it meant further carnage, six weeks later he and his comrades voted overwhelmingly for Abraham Lincoln's re-election. Within one month of the president's April 1865 assassination, the Confederate States of America no longer existed and slavery forever ended with Northern victory, the Thirteenth Amendment's earlier passage, and its later ratification.

Now the United States faced a Reconstruction that would test its resolve in dealing with race, equality, and sectionalism. Abraham Lincoln was gone, but no individual, no matter how extraordinary, is solely responsible for leading a democracy. Others would need to rise to the occasion—would it be only politicians, or would the course more directly involve the people?

Comprising the nation's "terrible swift sword," Union servicemen had been instrumental in achieving the Civil War's two major goals. As it transformed into a titanic struggle for liberation fought by those who profoundly understood what it means to be citizens of a republic, ideological commitment had tightly bound Northern soldiers and sailors. More than the average civilian, they realized just what lay ahead, and that "the unfinished work" promised to be as bitter, divisive, and perilous as the war itself, if not more so.

Coming home irrevocably changed by all they had seen, done, endured, and accomplished, it is not surprising that a sizable proportion of Union citizen servicemen had been politically radicalized. Would that enable white and black Northern veterans in peacetime to sustain their dedication to the causes for which they had battled and bled, and continue the struggle for freedom and opportunity for all Americans? Would the special barrier-shattering brotherhood that forms among those who have risked everything together endure despite the absence of war?

These critical questions are now answered by a book devoted to the political activities and racial views of white Union veterans during Reconstruction and the ensuing decades, and their continued support for the civil rights efforts of black comrades and African Americans overall. Having worked with service personnel from modern wars, I draw upon a psychiatrist's insight into how veterans are inspired by the gift of survival to positively change their society, which in turn fosters greater understanding of the most contentious issue of past times, and ours—race.

I have lost the use of my right arm in this bloody war, and I would freely have sacrificed my life, for home, for law, for right, for Constitution, for freedom, for Government, for humanity.

—PRIVATE ORA D. WALBRIDGE, 104TH ILLINOIS VOLUNTEERS,
SEPTEMBER 11, 1865[2]

One More War to Fight tells the story of how the obligation of Northern servicemen to their beloved country did not end when they left the military but was only just beginning. Exemplifying the powerful warrior identity that motivates veterans in civilian life just as in uniform, Union soldiers and sailors were determined to expand upon the Civil War's results. This commitment fostered outstanding service in the Freedmen's Bureau, bitter opposition to Andrew Johnson's racial policies and Ku Klux Klan atrocities, and grand-scale political activism that spurred Republican gains in the 1866 midterm elections, ratification of the Fourteenth and Fifteenth Amendments, and Ulysses S. Grant's becoming president-elect in 1868.

Then, by studying the words and outstanding work of one-armed Brevet Lieutenant Colonel Joseph Wiley Gelray, the Freedmen's Bureau's foremost investigator of the Klan, we will bear witness to the stunning cruelty, racism, and contempt for the law that underlay the depredations of America's oldest terrorist organization. At the same time, we will see how the Grant administration's strong support of black suffrage established by the Fifteenth Amendment and use of enhanced authority under the 1871 Ku Klux Klan Act crippled the Invisible Empire across the former Confederacy.

Despite such milestone endeavors, Reconstruction was tragically doomed to fail for a combination of reasons we will probe: the need for federal power to maintain its administration, the Freedmen's Bureau shutdown, deep-rooted Southern resistance to any advancements for African Americans, slavery's legacy, and Northern weariness with racial strife.

Yet as Jim Crow took hold on both sides of the Mason-Dixon line, Union veterans individually and collectively maintained their important interconnected roles as potent moral and political forces, particularly through the Grand Army of the Republic (GAR). We will learn how the Left-Armed Corps and other white and black Northern veterans directly fought bigotry and racism in two particular areas—the right to quality public education and social equality. For all the Grand Army's imperfections and professed apolitical nature, the country's most prominent integrated organization in the 1880s remained a stalwart bloc in support of landmark Republican initiatives on behalf of African Americans.

That is why the circumstances leading up to the 1891 showdown over race at the GAR National Encampment, and its significance, will be explored in depth. We will re-live this extraordinary episode in which the Grand Army adamantly refused to accept a color line, an admirable and historic decision emblematic of white Union veterans' staunch and open appreciation for what their black brothers in arms had done during wartime.

With all that, Northern ex-servicemen could not overcome the acceptance of Jim Crow and belief in black inferiority that was pervasive in the 1890s. In a closely related issue, we will observe how a striking number of Union veterans of both races remained steadfast in specifying slavery's destruction alongside maintenance of the Republic as the underlying roots and towering achievements of the Civil War, and strongly resisted any equivalence in the righteousness of each side's fight. In spite of this, reconciliation and a mounting acquiescence to a "Lost Cause" view of the conflict proved insurmountable in both the North and South.

This leads to detailed discussion of the Supreme Court ruling that would set back civil rights for more than half a century, the lack of improvement in racial relations despite black soldiers' service in the Spanish-American War, and the ongoing horrors of lynching. As for controversies that would fester for decades about burial of Union and Confederate dead and festooning of their graves, we will see how they heightened when race became a major bone of contention.

Then, I examine what took place in the new twentieth century as the generation who had gone to war continued toward their final muster. Many white Northern ex-servicemen resolutely continued to manifest racial tolerance, remembrance, and fidelity to why they had fought, often via GAR activities and the Union veteran-centric *National Tribune*. Despite such efforts, their great military and postwar societal triumphs were increasingly consigned to a distant past, and as we shall sadly find, the men of the Union were hardly immune to the prevailing insensitivity and highly prejudiced attitudes characteristic of the race-obsessed period of reconciliation.

This book concludes with a close look at two crucial incendiary events of the early 1900s. After outrageous acts of bigotry against African American soldiers throughout the Jim Crow South seemingly exploded in Brownsville, Texas, in 1906 President Theodore Roosevelt summarily cashiered all 167 troopers of the all-black Twenty-Fifth Infantry and set into motion years of investigations. Despite the leading role played by Ohio senator and Union veteran Joseph B. Foraker, who sought justice for the dishonorably discharged soldiers in the final act of his illustrious political career, the long-standing relationship between the Republican party and people of color was severely affected.

As for how a statue of a fully uniformed Confederate General in Chief Robert E. Lee ended up in the US Capitol, the complete account is now offered. The federal law under which it occurred, the rage of aging Union veterans against such an honor for a man they always considered a traitor, the confrontation between the Grand Army's rank and file and the organization's conservative leadership, and the implications of their decision are all analyzed.

In summary, this book's raison d'être lies in the intertwined, previously untold stories of how Northern veterans, black and white, fought a second war seeking equality for all Americans, thereby creating the model of civic responsibility based on military service that American citizen soldiers, sailors, and marines have emulated in modern times.

Like the most decorated American soldier who was in combat during World War II:

> There's one kind of fighting that has to go on always. You can't ever take a furlough from the fight to preserve human liberties. I think the methods used by the Thomas-Rankin Committee are a challenge to those liberties, and I think we should use every fair and constitutional means to fight those methods.

—LIEUTENANT AUDIE MURPHY, USA, COMMITTEE FOR THE FIRST AMENDMENT RADIO BROADCAST, OCTOBER 26, 1947[3]

And those who fought in Vietnam and later protested against the war:

How do you ask a man to be the last man to die for a mistake?

We have come here . . . because we believe that this body can be responsive to the will of the people, and we believe that the will of the people says that we should be out of Vietnam now.

—Lieutenant John Kerry, USN, Statement before the Senate Foreign Relations Committee, April 22, 1971[4]

The Left-Armed Corps

In the war's immediate aftermath (mid-1865 through early 1866), 268 battle-hardened Northern veterans with lost right-arm function sent writing samples to a national competition designed to encourage training of their uninjured hand for civilian clerical work.

This innovative contest was created by minister and writer William O. Bourne out of his unique experience with those who had been maimed in war. From December 1862 until its closing in July 1865, he served as an unofficial chaplain at Central Park Hospital, a military facility in New York City that specialized in treating debilitated Union servicemen.[5] As described in the foreword, the Bourne Papers had long been under Library of Congress auspices when Dr. Sellers brought them to my attention.

As I worked on the collection, it became apparent that its remarkable material presented an opportunity to perform a pioneering lifelong study of a rare national cohort of Union veterans. With 98 percent of the Left-Armed Corps having entered the service as enlisted personnel and only two men of color, I garnered demographic data from such rich sources as the Bourne Papers, National Archives pension and military service records, local and state archives, newspapers, and books. Then, direct comparison to Northern soldiers in general had to be performed to determine whether the large self-selected group was typical of the white Union enlisted man.

To make this assessment, I primarily utilized the extraordinary database published by the United States Sanitary Commission in 1869,

Benjamin A. Gould's *Investigations in the Military and Anthropological Statistics of American Soldiers*, along with other pertinent volumes like Frederick Phisterer's *Statistical Record of the Armies of the United States*.[6] Year of initial enlistment, true age at first enlistment, length of military service (either continuous or cumulative), country of origin, marital status, geographic distribution (state of initial regiment of enlistment), branch of service, rank at enlistment and discharge, pre-enlistment occupation, and prewar education for the entire Left-Armed Corps were each compared to Northern servicemen overall.

The cohort was found to be exceptionally representative of the white Union common soldier, its members essentially indistinguishable demographically from their two million comrades at enlistment and during wartime service, and with respect to both literacy and education. Constituting a model countrywide sample for research via a classic epidemiological method, I have carried out a longitudinal cohort study of the Left-Armed Corps that spans their lifetimes.

As maimed Union veterans, each was eligible for a service-connected disability pension administered by an embryonic federal bureau that greatly expanded over time. The detailed information contained in their pension files, which as medical records are best reviewed by a trained physician, has greatly benefited my investigation.

Specifically regarding *One More War to Fight*, the cohort offers further advantages. Nine-tenths having entered the war in its first two years, they are ideal for following the evolution of Union veterans' views on slavery, African Americans, freedom, and equality as the conflict's aims changed dramatically, and throughout the postwar decades. Every man was in battle, with most having extensive experience under fire and admirable combat records, as shown by the 42 percent rate of promotion and discharge at a higher rank, including 15 percent with commissions (the latter consistent with the proportion of Union soldiers who served as officers).

While full discussion of the cohort's debilitating injuries await in another book, they play a major role in *One More War to Fight* by enabling explorations into a ground-breaking military organization that arose during the war, another that would have a profound impact during

Reconstruction, and how the Left-Armed Corps exemplified the link between the two.

THE VETERAN RESERVE CORPS

Described by the Indiana Adjutant General "as unusual a fighting force as the United States ever armed and equipped for action,"[7] the Veteran Reserve Corps (VRC) allowed seriously wounded Union soldiers to remain in military service while freeing up able-bodied men for active campaigning.[8] Having come into existence in late April 1863 as the Invalid Corps,[9] its dreadful name was changed within a year to the VRC.[10]

While the work performed by the VRC included hospital-based activities, guarding prisoners, provost-marshal duty, and clerical responsibilities within assorted military departments, it was available for defense in exigent circumstances. One such occasion arose during Confederate General Jubal Early's 1864 summer raid on Washington, when the Ninth Regiment went into action at Fort Stevens and performed as befitted battle-tested veterans.[11]

The VRC, a novel attempt to address the Union's manpower concerns, managed to save the military careers of more than 60,000 soldiers.[12] Its ranks contained some of the North's finest officers and enlisted men, including eighteen members of the Left-Armed Corps, several of whom would go on to serve in the vital Freedmen's Bureau.

"THE LOST CAUSE"

In his 1866 book, *The Lost Cause: A New Southern History of the War of the Confederates*, Edward A. Pollard said "the late Southern Confederacy" had undergone "the most gigantic struggle of the world's history." Through his account of the Confederate States of America's (CSA) "rise and progress," the wartime editor of the *Richmond Examiner* also introduced a new term and concept to American consciousness that soon took hold, and lingers to this day.

Making the case that a "'war of ideas'" was all Southerners had left to wage while "stand[ing] by their principles," Pollard articulated what "would be immeasurably the worst consequence of defeat in this war": "that the South should lose its moral and intellectual distinctiveness as a people, and cease to assert its well-known superiourity in civilization, in political scholarship, and in all the standards of individual character over the people of the North."[13]

On May 1, 1869, the Southern Historical Society was established in New Orleans, with Vice President General Braxton Bragg presiding at the association's first official meeting. Its constitution was adopted and officers were appointed, including General Robert E. Lee (Virginia), General Wade Hampton (South Carolina), and former CSA vice president Alexander H. Stephens (Georgia), among the elected vice presidents of states.

Concerned about "the truth of history," the Society's stated purpose was the "collection, classification, preservation, and final publication . . . of all the documents and facts bearing upon the eventful history of the past few years, illustrating the nature of the struggle from which the country has just emerged, defining and vindicating the principles which lay beneath it."

Three days after running a lengthy story about the Society's formation, the *Memphis Daily Appeal* followed up with a much shorter piece in support of the organization's mission: "Every man who can, should contribute to the noble work of rescuing from oblivion these records of the great struggle. By the testimony of those who have survived the dread ordeal of battle and the vicissitudes of war, the dead are to be judged and the 'Lost Cause' be lifted beyond calumny."[14]

The darker implications of the association's "defining and vindicating the principles" underlying the South's role in the Civil War, concomitant elevation of the "Lost Cause," and the Society's influence all would become starkly evident during Reconstruction. Electing General Jubal A. Early as its new president and now to be headquartered in Richmond, the Society reorganized in August 1873 in White Sulphur Springs, Virginia, with a Southern History Convention immediately following under its sponsorship. Jefferson Davis (who himself would become the Society's president in a few years) was the featured speaker, and the former leader of the Confederacy didn't disappoint: "I am most happy to know the cause for which we have convened. . . . We have been cheated rather than conquered, and could we have foreseen the results of the surrender, we would have been free today. The time has come for us to vindicate the truth for the sake of the unrecorded dead who fought for truth and died in a patriotic cause. These scraps of history do us injustice."[15]

One week later the *Daily Appeal*, reporting that his speech had generated "much comment, some of it very severe and but little of it flattering" and being concerned that Davis "might have been, even unintentionally misrepresented," published an interview he gave to one of its editors. Regarding having "been cheated," Davis insisted a South misled by Northern assurances that it did not intend "to interfere with the institutions of the States" had operated under "the impression . . . that the war was waged for an abstraction, or at most for the preservation of property in slaves."

As a result, had the Confederacy's armies and citizens "known what a surrender would bring," its military "would and could have continued" to fight with full support of its people, the war ongoing "until the invader, weary of what might be regarded an endless struggle, would have retired, and, in the language of General [Winfield] Scott, allowed the 'erring sisters to go in peace.'"[16]

Such revision of history so soon after events had occurred (e.g., Davis completely ignored large-scale enrollment of African American troops [most of whom had once been enslaved] and Abraham Lincoln's re-election on a war platform lauding slavery's destruction and endorsing passage of the Thirteenth Amendment in association with total victory) was not fooling Northerners or Southern Unionists.

In February 1874, the *National Republican*, after lauding a war "in which the slave triumphed . . . class privilege was overthrown and . . . the damnable doctrine that man could hold property in man in this country was forever defeated and overthrown," excoriated the "die hard" Southern Historical Society and White Sulphur Springs conference, whose "movement . . . was denounced in unmeasured terms by the press and . . . the most thoughtful men of the country. The sober, mature judgment of the nation saw in it the seeds of danger and of discord, of disunion and of treason, and as such condemned it. But . . . the men who led in it seem determined to persevere and to vindicate themselves, as they call it, in the eyes of posterity. Posterity will blush for and disown and repudiate them."[17]

If so, how long would that take? In this book, we will see how the Lost Cause flourished in the decades following the Civil War, and its destructive impact on the United States.

THE LEFT-ARMED CORPS AND ALL UNION VETERANS

In this book, I utilize the Left-Armed Corps as a validated, highly characteristic, and uncommonly national (rather than regimental or regional) cohort of white Union veterans. No less prominent are Sergeants Robert A. Pinn and William Hannibal Thomas, the Corps' two Ohio free men of color who fought in the Fifth United States Colored Troops (USCT) Infantry.

While spotlighted, *One More War to Fight* is by no means the Left-Armed Corps' story alone. Many other white Northern soldiers and sailors, and black veterans who withstood so much to serve with distinction in the Civil War, will be heard from and discussed throughout, both solely and as a group, to illustrate the personal and societal impact of their war experience. At the same time, I have taken a chronological approach to best provide a sense of the country in which African American and white Union veterans lived the last several decades of their lives, and how it changed over those years.

No quotation has been edited for spelling, grammar, content, or meaning. The words of Northern veterans and their contemporaries, including racial and religious epithets, are presented verbatim to enable assessment in the context of their times; the one alteration is for length.

To highlight the Left-Armed Corps, all material written by them will be italicized when quoted, in addition to medical or psychiatric information about them of reputable origin (e.g., pension file records; *Medical and Surgical History of the War of the Rebellion*).

Regarding the various military units in which Northern soldiers served, volunteer infantry regiments will be identified by their state and number (e.g., Fifth Ohio), and state cavalry and artillery regiments further identified (e.g., Eighth Illinois Cavalry; First New York Light Artillery; First Maine Heavy Artillery). As for national units, regular army regiments will be identified by branch (e.g., Thirteenth US Infantry; Fifth US Artillery), while USCT infantry regiments will be numerically identified (e.g., Fifth USCT) and USC cavalry or artillery units further identified.

ADDITIONAL INFORMATION ON TOPICS OF INTEREST

In an effort to avoid impeding narrative flow, further information about specific topics (e.g., derivation of the term "Jim Crow") has been placed within a number of endnotes. In order not to miss these interesting details, you should check a chapter's endnotes for such text.

Let us now begin with a nation no longer technically at war with itself, but still divided.

WILLIAM HANNIBAL THOMAS, 1900
Free Person of Color—Ohio, 1860

Sergeant William Hannibal Thomas, Fifth USCT. THE NEW YORK PUBLIC LIBRARY DIGITAL COLLECTIONS.

Shouldering "The Unfinished Work"

Once let the black man get upon his person the brass letter, U.S., let him get an eagle on his button, and a musket on his shoulder and bullets in his pocket, there is no power on earth that can deny that he has earned the right to citizenship.

—FREDERICK DOUGLASS[1]

War exacts such a terrible human and economic price that it is natural to hope the end of hostilities signifies resolution of all underlying causes. Yet throughout history this has rarely been the case, and the American Civil War was no exception. The wretched system that had divided North and South from the country's founding finally sparked a devastating conflict that eliminated slavery as both an institution and source of dispute. Unfortunately, little else about the War of the Rebellion was definitive.

By the summer of 1865, men in blue and gray had stopped shooting at one another, the Confederacy destroyed, but the nation was hardly united. The United States faced unprecedented situations in almost every direction. Reeling from its president's murder and staggering numbers of war dead, millions of African Americans were newly free, and hundreds of thousands of wounded veterans needed care. The linked issues of Reconstruction and equality had to be confronted, and what took place would not only impact Americans of that era, but have repercussions that continue to this day.

The Thirteenth Amendment's evolution clearly shows that slavery's eradication did not mean equality for black Americans. On January 11, 1864, Senator John B. Henderson of Missouri proposed a joint resolution that the Constitution be amended to abolish slavery. With Henderson's resolution still in committee, Massachusetts Senator Charles Sumner upped the ante on February 8 when he submitted another joint resolution amending the initial language to include that "everywhere within the limits of the United States, and of each State or Territory thereof, all persons are equal before the law, so that no person can hold another as a slave." Neither resolution's proposed wording was adopted by the Judiciary Committee, but Sumner's effort to enfold equality into slavery's abolition proved a particular failure.[2] When ratified by Congress, followed by twenty-seven states on December 18, 1865, the entire amendment read:

> SEC. 1. Neither slavery nor involuntary servitude, except as a punishment for crime whereof the party shall have been duly convicted, shall exist within the United States, or any place subject to their jurisdiction.
>
> SEC. 2. Congress shall have power to enforce this article by appropriate legislation.[3]

While equality for all Americans (both in the North and Reconstructed South) would have to wait, it had also become intertwined with employment of black men in the armies and (to a lesser extent) navies of the Union. The famous Douglass quote that opens this chapter encapsulates the hope that successful military performance would prove a compelling factor in the advancement of persons of color. In the wake of such service, historian Dudley T. Cornish concluded that black soldiers "had gradually subdued much of the Negro's worst enemy, white prejudice. As a soldier in the Union Army, the American Negro proved his manhood and established a strong claim to equality of treatment and opportunity."[4]

Black veterans' awareness that recognition of their valor was critical to the fight for full citizenship was exemplified by Fifth USCT Sergeant William Hannibal Thomas's powerful plea for fairness on September 27, 1865:

> [W]e ask no favors in our own behalf, but we _do ask_, if such _devotion_ is not a test of _Loyalty_ and since the evidence is so conclusive, and we have _shared alike_ in the dangers and vicissitudes of the War, ought we not partake of all the immunities pertaining to the rights of The Citizens, even as our _White Brother_. What say you?
>
> Ill Say no more but submit this of mine to the _candid_ and _sincere_ judgement of the _American people_.[5]

There was a basis for cautious optimism regarding what Thomas sought. Cornish's viewpoint has been strongly supported by more recent scholarship, including that of Gary W. Gallagher: "The degree to which much of the loyal white population supported emancipation and praised black soldiers revealed an ability to moderate racial attitudes in pursuit of Union. . . . A number of moderate Republicans joined the party's Radicals in calling for the extension of political rights to black veterans and perhaps to literate African American men more generally."[6]

Immediately following the Civil War, who could be more respected advocates for black civil and political rights than white Union veterans? But would their African American brothers in arms be able to count on such support? Studying regimental newspapers, Chandra Manning found that while "a racial epiphany" was not unanimously undergone by white Northern soldiers, "a fundamental shift in the history of the nation" stemmed from a sizable proportion of them re-evaluating their prewar indifference and "treat[ing] at least fellow soldiers as equals in a shared cause, and to champion increased rights for black Americans."[7]

We will use other untapped contemporary material to begin our further investigation into this crucial question, and the prevailing state of racial attitudes in the United States.

Adjutant General Charles G. Halpine had performed important work in African American enlistment despite harboring deep anti-black intolerance. It is therefore no surprise that in his 1866 volume of collected works, Halpine flatly disagreed with General David Hunter's being "in favor of extending the right of suffrage to every Negro of the South, and disfranchising every white man in the least degree prominent on the rebel side."[8] Yet he still left out an odious poem that would be published posthumously in 1869 by Robert B. Roosevelt, one year after Halpine's death at thirty-nine from an accidental overdose of self-medicated chloroform for insomnia:[9]

SAMBO A BAD EGG.

You're a bad investment, my Sambo,
You're nice, but don't pay, my Sambo,
And so you may go to the—hot place
Befitting each Nix-kom-heraus.
Your skin is nigrific, my Sambo,
And your heels they are long, my Sambo,
And your wool has a horrible odor,
And your shin-bones are Nix-kom-heraus.

Get back to your kennel, my Sambo,
There grovel and rot, my Sambo,
Take off your blue coat and equipments,
For the war was all Nix-kom-heraus.
You had nothing to fight for, my Sambo,
And you gallantly won it, my Sambo,
With your blood and your labors you won it—
Enjoy now your Nix-kom-heraus.

You may work for us white folk, my Sambo,
Black boots and shake carpets, my Sambo,
Steal chickens and do some whitewashing
When our kitchens are Nix-kom-heraus;
But you can not vote with us, my Sambo,
You had nothing to fight for, my Sambo,

In the war, and you gallantly won it—
Hip! hip! for the Nix-kom-heraus.[10]

That Halpine, a Brevet Brigadier General of Volunteers, could be so openly contemptuous of black veterans ("Nix-kom-heraus" essentially translating to "'nothing comes out [of it]'"[11]) and their service is a sign of the times. A review of Roosevelt's volume in *Lippincott's Monthly Magazine* said of this poem, "There were thousands . . . in New York City who entertained prejudices quite as strong, at one time, against the colored race."[12]

Such bigoted views were hardly confined to Gotham. In late August 1865, another Union general officer made a public statement from Doylestown, Pennsylvania, upon accepting nomination as the Democratic candidate for state auditor general. Emphatically opposing the black vote *"as every white man should,"* W. W. H. Davis claimed that *"Nature has erected a barrier against the two races enjoying equal political rights in the same community where they approximate in numbers as in the Southern states."* Using the claimed example of people of color in San Domingo being unable to *"govern a small island in peace,"* Davis asked, *"[W]hat are we to suppose would be the condition of things when the negro comes into competition with the pure Caucasian in the struggle for empire in the South? The founders of our government intended that the white should be the governing race in this country, and it will be a calamitous day for both people when the black man is given the political franchise, and entitled to hold office."*[13]

Like Halpine, Davis's views on black enfranchisement were expected in light of his known animus toward African American troops. It is noteworthy that Davis was defeated at the polls in 1865 and later Congressional campaigns, and would never hold elective office.[14] Yet it is hardly shocking that two highly regarded Union generals felt free to publicly express such blatantly racist views.

In February 1865, Vincent Colyer had been appointed superintendent of the New York Soldiers' Depot as part of the state's efforts "to provide additional means of relief for [its] . . .sick and wounded soldiers."[15] Unlike Halpine and Davis, Colyer had admirably worked on behalf of black soldiers, but also sent a letter to the New York City dailies three months later warning discharged soldiers receiving large sums in "back pay and bounty" to maintain "their guard against the sharpers . . . lying in wait for their victims, at every corner, and in every guise." Colyer said these predators included "prostitutes and their 'pimps'" who got a veteran drunk in order to rob him, a "thief [who] appeared in the guise of a lame soldier, who helped himself to his fellow-soldier's purse while he was buying his railroad ticket," and "five soldiers from New-Orleans [who] were induced, by some Jew clothiers, to pay $80 and $100 each, for suits of clothes not worth $30."[16]

While Colyer's attempt to caution veterans against being cheated was well intentioned, his derogatory reference to "Jew clothiers," a term of common use in the nineteenth century,[17] and equating them to drug-rolling thieves, were anything but. The slurs were not mentioned by Bourne when the letter was reprinted in the June 1865 *Soldier's Friend*, and he described Colyer's missive as "valuable for its facts, and important in its practical bearings on the interests of the soldiers and sailors."[18] But the considerable degree of racism, bigotry, and anti-Semitism that was then acceptable in American society does not mean everyone felt the same way.

When Lieutenant A. O. Abbott published his stunning 1865 exposé of life in Southern prison camps, he noted it was inspired by the enthusiastic response of fellow detainees to readings from a diary and journal he kept during captivity. After thanking fellow officers for secreting portions of the manuscript across enemy lines, crafting the book's appendix, and providing their own experiences, Abbott said: "Should these pages serve to throw any light upon the question 'What shall we do with the Negro?' I shall feel that my labor has not been in vain."[19]

WHITE NORTHERN VETERANS ADVOCATE FOR BLACK EQUALITY

Like Abbott, the Left-Armed Corps, whose opinions on the explosive issue had not been solicited, emphatically showed that it was on the minds of white Northern veterans in the war's aftermath. This national cohort, so characteristic of the Union rank and file, spontaneously and independently expressed concerns for African Americans throughout the contest's duration, revealing collective insight into the challenges of Reconstruction and their commitment to justice for the freedmen.

Over August and September 1865, citizen soldiers' pride and thinking bayonets' understanding of the great work left to be done were shown by these wounded warriors:

> *We have as a people, least now, the doctrine of a Higher Law, than man's own enactment. The dark and gaunt form of slavery, which has tormented our wisest, and best men in many years, has passed away, never to be resurrected. . . . The illiterate freedmen of the South must be taught the value of freedom; they must be instructed and enlightened and thereby prepared for their manifest destiny.*[20] (Sergeant Wm. Penn Sands, Fifth Ohio)

> *I feel proud of the part I have taken in helping to redeem my country from the rule of tyrants and the curse of God. I am happy to see a spirit manifested in the hearts of our people and their rulers to do* Justice *and* Honor *to our poor unfortunates.*[21] (Lieutenant John F. Huntington, 140th New York)

Ezra D. Hilts knew that race and equality, though vexing, had to be addressed for Huntington's goal to be achieved: "*If the black man can improve, so can the white. Nor is there, in the providence of God, any occasion for either subordination or amalgamation. Each may help the other for the good of each. And there is room enough and work enough for all.*"[22]

The First New York Light Artillery corporal turned teacher detailed three leading concerns, and the principles under which they should be decided:

> *The questions of reconstruction, free suffrage, punishment of rebel leaders etc, we trust will be considered from high and just standpoints, that no act may be committed by those in authority not in strict accordance with the best human judgement, and with the immutable laws of justice and of mercy.*

Our work is not yet finished. We must build schoolhouses and educate the masses in the principles of eternal truth and liberty, and this will form a basis of our government as firm as the everlasting hills.[23]

Answering Thomas's burning question one day before he posed it, 121st New York Private Rufus L. Robinson explicitly supported black suffrage: "*It is not sufficient that we have free Institutions, free Speech, and freedom of the Press, we must have freedom at the Ballot Box. We cannot be true to the principles of republicanism while we say to the Colored Man, You have no rights at the ballot-box that we are bound to respect, for we have said to him, Take the musket and gain your freedom. Not till Universal suffrage becomes a law, will our country stand forth in all her greatness and grandeur, United, Disenthralled, and Redeemed.*"[24]

Invoking the political power Union veterans had earned at such a great cost, Third New Jersey Sergeant John Stewart took the moral high ground to demand peacetime advancements consistent with those gained in war: "*may we not fellow Soldiers . . . lay claim to be heard in the Nations Councils, and shall we not as a recognition of our sufferings insist with one heart and one mind that in the reconstruction of the States there shall not be tolerated one principle at varience with the natural rights of any human being.*"[25]

On active duty in Detroit, VRC First Lieutenant Alexander Cameron crafted "*What is Patriotism,*" a remarkable essay that defined it as "*an ardent love of Country, and a desire to advance its interests, and Glory—to make it a model for the nations of the earth in all future time*" through steadfast support of equal rights for all its citizens. Lauding the valor of Northern servicemen, white and black alike, Cameron stated that "*Patriotism is not ungratefull; it delights to honor the men who imperil their lives for their Countrys sake: it stops not to consider into the shade, or color, of the skin of its defenders. . . .*" At the same time, he articulated a growing Union veteran foreboding about how their Confederate foes were generally viewed that would prove all too prescient: "*[Patriotism] will not through a morbid sympathy for traitors, on account of their heroic deeds, raise them to place, and power, it will rather seek for its public servants, among those who have been tried, and not found wanting, at a time when the Republic was encompassed with darkness and danger.*"[26]

Yet another late September 1865 entry that examined the freed-men's future was written by Seventeenth Vermont Sergeant Thomas T. Sanborn within a month of his discharge. With "*slavery* [having been] *annihilated by the flat of the sword*," the conquered South needed "*to be brought into full and complete harmony with the* [nation's] *free institutions.*" But to achieve this, Sanborn knew "*it is not enough merely to acknowledge emancipation and repudiate secession. In passing from the narrow gauge of slavery to broad gauge of freedom . . . the whole dimensions and proportions of car and engine are to be remodeled.*"[27]

As the contest went on, others expressed great support for equality under the law for every American, particularly voting rights and full citizenship. In autumn 1865, Private Henry T. Krahl, late of the Thirteenth US Infantry, tackled the rising "*issues of great and paramount importance*" by standing on the war's terrible toll in furtherance of these goals, along with basic fairness for those newly freed and the men of color who had fought in the nation's behalf:

> *I think all history will show, and our knowledge of human nature teach us, that it would be a most hazardous experiment to cloth a large part of the citizens of a state with freedom and yet deny to them the* rights *and* franchises of citizens.

> *Are we to suppose that 4,000,000 of men made free by the results of a gigantic war, in which they themselves have born no small part, will be satisfied with any thing short of entire citizenship with all its consequent rights?*

> *What better security can we have for the future peace, loyalty and, prosperity of the south than this just measure of universal suffrage? Let the ballot of the loyal black man balance that of the disloyal white.*[28]

In December 1865, another contestant ardently advocated for blacks being given the right to vote. Like Abraham Lincoln and so many other white veterans, Captain Charles Edmonds, who served in Michigan light artillery and infantry regiments, had been impressed by African American soldiers and was standing by his comrades in blue:

Now, the things that must be settled
Are, what kind of Reconstruction
Must the Congress of the Nation
Give, to get the States in motion—

Thus the end of the Rebellion;
Now the question, "What of Sambo?"
Echoes to us, from our Statesmen;
Some are saying "Let us make him
Equal to the Whites in voting".
*   Some say, "No, our country never*
Was intended for the 'Nigger'":
Still they clamor for the Rebels,
And they say they are entitled
To their rights within the Union,
For it is the "Constitution".

I have been a Union Soldier
Fighting, side by side, with Sambo;
We have fought the "Rebs" together;
I, for country, he, for freedom:
Fighting to maintain the Union—
Rebels fighting to destroy it.
*   Now, the Rebels they are conquered,*
And, the time of "Reconstruction"
Has arrived, When we must settle
What, the status of the Rebel;
What the status of poor Sambo.
*   I'm in favor, now of giving*
Hemp, to all the leading Rebels,
Freedom and the right of Voting,
To the true "American Citizens of African
Descent", who have so "nobly dared", so "freely
bled", to aid the Union cause, and to secure

the <u>blessings</u> of <u>liberty</u> to themselves and to
their posterity Forever.[29]

Unlike Halpine, Edmonds employed disparaging racial terms to make savage and salient points. In doing so he advocated a position that in 1861 would have been unthinkable—full freedom and voting rights for African Americans as citizens, and disenfranchisement for Southern whites that fought against the United States.

In this final month for contest submission, two more Left-Armed Corps members devoted their essays to contemplations on black Americans, and equality itself. 121st New York Private Michael J. Fitz James cautioned, *"We must not indulge hatred against our fellow creatures for being black although they differ in dialects, custom and manners in this world."*[30] On behalf of all Union soldiers and their murdered leader, Fitz James concluded with a vow to continue the noble effort begun in war throughout their remaining days: *"We Soldiers know the cause that we hazarded our lives and spilt our blood for. The cause our beloved President was assassinated for. We should maintain and never desist from this cause as long as we live. I hope and trust that God will give us grace to persevere in this to the end."*[31]

On December 15, 1865, First Lieutenant William M. DeCamp composed a wide-ranging meditation comparing white and black men, thus offering a rare contemporaneous glimpse into an enlightened Northern veteran's mindset on race. The former physician immediately established the issue at hand by noting the *"many generations"* that African Americans had no *"legal power to possess and accumulate property, the privelidge of education, and the controll of ones own children,"* which left them with comparatively no *"incentives to action"*:

> *<u>The most inferior Whites</u>, are loudest in their denunciation of Blacks, and insist, that the colored race cannot by any possibility equal them, under any circumstances. Such will frequently ask a more liberal minded opponent, this question. "Do you consider a 'Nigger' as good as you are"? To such I have replied in this manner. "That will depend upon circumstances; it is possible for a Negro to be even*

better than I am." If he can do a harder days work, or can carry a heavy burden, a longer distance, with less fatigue than I can, he is Physically better.

If he can write a better letter, or make a better speech, he is Intellectually better.

If he tells the truth more often, more fully abstains from Profanity, or Obsenity in thought and deed, and can be tempted with a larger amount of money without theft or embezzlement, he is Morally better. If the Negro exhibits more fidelity as a friend, and treats his family more kindly, he is Socially better.[32]

Decamp then asked and answered the leading question point-blank:

Will any sane man, pretend to say, that said white man [who is "extremely vile and heartless"] is superior to an honest, and well behaved back man? In what respect inferior? The idea is absurd![33]

The Twenty-Second Iowa infantryman continued his keenly incisive analysis with frank discussion of a volatile subject at the heart of anti-black prejudice throughout American history:

The advocate of Political equality for the black man is taunted with an equal desire for his Social equality, desire for promiscuous marriage, etc., etc. . . . There is a wide difference between Political equality and Social equality. . . . There is many a white man, whom we would defend in his political rights, and at the same time, we would be very reluctant to make him a social companion, or invite him to our houses and families.

Although the intermarriage of Whites & Blacks is not in accordance with my taste, and I esteem it my priveledge to discourage the same by the mild agencies of remonstrance and argument, yet strictly speaking,

*if a white man chooses to marry a black woman, or the reverse, it is
simply none of my business: nor is it any other mans business; so long as
they behave peacibly, quietly, in violation of no law, and do not intrude
themselves upon the sanctities of other peoples homes & residences.*[34]

Incredibly, in 1865 a maimed Union officer who was asked for a
handwriting sample declared that racial intermarriage, although not
to his preference, should be permissible. Decamp's statement not only
predated the watershed Loving Supreme Court decision by more than
100 years,[35] his summation on African Americans strikes a chord that
resonates with a memorable speech that would be delivered on the steps
of the Lincoln Memorial ninety-eight years later:

*Taking the teachings of Christ, or of Common Sense Justice as our
guide, the Black man should be judged as all other classes of men
are judged, namely, upon their merits, without regard to color.*[36]
(Underlining his)

Although not an official contest entry, on February 24, 1866, Private
Henry C. Allen sent Bourne a poem whose *"lines were suggested by the
vetoing of the Freedmens Bureau Bill by President Johnson."*[37] The former First Massachusetts cavalryman expressed both outrage over the
Reconstruction policies of the man who replaced the Northern soldier's
beloved commander in chief, and misgivings about the meaning of their
collective sacrifices:

*At the "White House", or in Congress,
Traitorous acts, must be put down,
Proud rebellion cannot flourish,
With Union Patriots all around.*

*We have suffered cold and hunger,
We have marched o'er hill and plain;
We have fought in many battles,
Won, and lost, and won again.*

Many noble ones have fallen,
Many wounded yet remain;
Tell me, comrades, true and loyal,
Have our sufferings been in vain?

Must this Union yet be severed,
And "our flag", be rent in twain?
Must the "Freedmen" still be bonded,
In ["slavery"'s crossed out] *wicked, hellish chains?*

Show the rebel hordes and traitors,
Who now ["That dare to" crossed out] *menace;—that we stand*
"Freedom's Banners" floating o'er us
Still, to keep ["protect" crossed out] *our own free land.*[38]

Allen was hardly alone in his early apprehensions.

As seen, the Bourne manuscripts, a completely different data source from the same period, are in categorical agreement with Manning's findings: "in the war's last year, surprising numbers of white Union troops advocated advances (such as legal equality, equal pay for black soldiers, and suffrage) that only the furthest reaches of radical abolitionism broached before the war. . . . The Civil War was revolutionary in many ways, none more so than the radical advances that took place in some Northerners' thinking on race."[39]

EQUAL RIGHTS FOR AFRICAN AMERICANS AND THE FREEDMEN'S BUREAU

Drastic changes in Northern attitudes on race were surely needed, with no issue more illuminating than voting rights. In March 1866, *The Soldier's Friend* described circumstances above the Mason-Dixon line with respect to black suffrage:

> In Massachusetts, Rhode Island, Connecticut, Pennsylvania, North Carolina, South Carolina, and Georgia, all voters must have a property qualification, and in Maine and New Hampshire, paupers are excluded.

The negro is not allowed to vote under any circumstance in any one of the States which composed the Union in 1860 excepting five and in only two States (Vermont and New Hampshire) is a colored person allowed to vote without a property qualification. In New Hampshire there were, in 1860, one hundred and ninety colored voters, and in Vermont, only eighty.

In Massachusetts every voter must, within two years, have paid a State or county tax, unless excluded from taxation.

In Rhode Island a voter must own real estate of one hundred and thirty-four dollars' value, or of the clear yearly value of seven dollars over any ground rent.

A colored person is not allowed to vote in New-York unless he has resided in the State three years, and is a freeholder in value of two hundred and fifty dollars, and has paid taxes thereupon.[40]

That many free men of color who continued in military service could not vote in their own states would have major implications for Reconstruction, in particular enforcement of African American suffrage in the South. It would also make the North vulnerable to legitimate charges of racial hypocrisy.

Significant responsibility for protection of the rights of newly freed slaves fell to an extraordinary organization established by Congress on March 3, 1865, the Bureau of Refugees, Freedmen, and Abandoned Lands, popularly known (and hereafter referred to) as the Freedmen's Bureau. Part of the War Department, the bureau was originally to exist during the Civil War and for one year after, with commitment to "the supervision and management of all abandoned lands, and the control of all subjects relating to refugees and freedmen from rebel states, or from any district of country within the territory embraced in the operations of the army, under such rules and regulations as may be prescribed by the head of the bureau and approved by the President."

The Bureau would be run by a presidentially appointed, Senate-confirmed commissioner paid $3,000 per year, and assigned up to ten clerks by the secretary of war. In addition, with Senate approval, the president could "appoint an assistant commissioner for each of the states declared to be in insurrection, not exceeding ten in number" who would be paid $2,500 annually. Significantly, "any military officer" could be "detailed and assigned to duty under this act without increase of pay or allowances."[41]

Section 4 of the act gave the commissioner, under presidential direction, authority to designate any tract of land under bureau jurisdiction for refugees or freedmen, with every such "male citizen . . . assigned not more than forty acres of such land." The assignee was to be protected in his use of the land for three years at an annual rent of no more than 6 percent of its value as either appraised by state authorities in 1860 or the land's estimated value that year. At the end of three years, or any time during that term, its occupants could buy the land and receive title from the United States.[42]

The act establishing the Freedmen's Bureau was signed by Abraham Lincoln. Upon his death, the critical appointment of its commissioner fell to Andrew Johnson, the newly installed seventeenth president. On the morning of May 10, Major General Oliver O. Howard received an urgent order from General-in-Chief Grant to leave his two army corps under their commanders outside of Richmond and report immediately to the secretary of war, Edwin M. Stanton, in Washington.

Howard had no idea why he was being summoned but did as ordered. When he met with Stanton the next morning, the secretary told Howard he had been Lincoln's choice, but the appointment was delayed until the president felt he could afford to detail him from field duty. With the war's ending, the way was now clear for the job to be offered to Howard, if he wanted it. Permitted time to think it over and discuss with friends, the thirty-four-year-old accepted the position the following day.[43]

Regarding Howard's decision to become the Freedmen's Bureau Commissioner, W. E. B. Du Bois stated that "Any man might well have hesitated to assume charge of such a work, with vast responsibilities, indefinite powers, and limited resources. Probably no one but a soldier would have answered such a call promptly." Du Bois then accurately observed, "indeed no one but a soldier could be called, for Congress had appropriated no money for salaries and expenses."[44]

As for Howard himself, the renowned sociologist and historian thought he was "honest and sincere," "with rather too much faith in human nature, little aptitude for systematic business and intricate detail . . . nevertheless conservative, hard-working, and, above all, acquainted at first-hand with much of the work before him. And of that work it has been truly said, 'No approximately correct history of civilization can ever be written which does not throw out in bold relief, as one of the great landmarks of political and social progress, the organization and adminis-tration of the Freedmen's Bureau.'"[45]

In the same vein, Eric Foner described the bureau's responsibilities as "daunting," for they included "introducing a workable system of free labor in the South, establishing schools for freedmen, providing aid to the destitute, aged, ill and insane, adjudicating disputes among blacks and between the races, and attempting to secure for blacks and white Unionists equal justice from the state and local governments established during Presidential Reconstruction."[46]

While all were critical, the last two were a focus of Howard's Circular No. 5, "Rules and Regulations for Assistant Commissioners," approved by Johnson on June 2, 1865.

One of the general's earliest and most important acts, it attempted to establish the bureau's core principles. In naming locations for assis-tant commissioners' headquarters in the former rebel states, Howard stressed that "Every effort will be made to render the people self-sup-porting," "commissioners are especially to remember that their duties are to enforce . . . the laws of the United States," and emphasized that "Assistant Commissioners will everywhere declare and protect their free-dom, as set forth in the proclamations of the President and the laws of Congress." In fulfilling this tremendous responsibility,

In all places where there is an interruption to civil law, or in which local courts, by reason of old codes, in violation of [federally guaranteed] freedom . . . disregard the negro's right to justice before the laws in not allowing him to give testimony . . . the Assistant Commissioners will adjudicate, either themselves or through officers of their appointment, all difficulties arising between negroes themselves, or between negroes and whites or Indians, except those in military service, so far as recognizable by military authority, and not taken cognizance of by other tribunals, civil or military, of the United States.[47]

In direct contrast to their former status as slaves, free African Americans would now be choosing for whom to work and receiving payment for their efforts, and not be subject to overseers or "acts of cruelty and oppression." In addition, the bureau would safeguard family unity "and all the rights of the family relation," including making provisions for marriages in jurisdictions where there were no laws or statutes concerning the right of people of color to enter into marriage.[48]

Paul A. Cimbala has observed that the bureau's role in education would be coordinating the efforts of numerous benevolent associations. While noting Howard's good faith attempts to establish the bureau's tenor and charge his officers with ensuring legal equality, the commissioner's lack of specifics meant that the bureau's ultimate effectiveness would be dependent upon "who his assistant commissioners were, how they perceived their duty, and who they appointed as their own subordinates."[49] In the historian's view, few if any of them had a realistic concept of what they would be facing, and most "had to learn about freedpeople, intransigent white employers, labor relations, educational requirements, civil rights, and Reconstruction while on the job."[50]

What about the subordinates variously titled as "superintendents, subcommissioners or subassistant commissioners" upon whom the assistant commissioners would rely to administer "the larger divisions or districts of the state organization" and manage those agents on-hand? Cimbala explained that at first the assistant commissioners looked to state commanders who generally had little desire for bureau work, the overall available supply of officers diminishing as more men were discharged from the service.[51]

This discouraging situation took a decided turn for the better when the bureau availed itself of a different pool of shoulder-strapped talent—the Veteran Reserve Corps (VRC). Their relationship is best understood through actions that resulted from the divergent views of President Johnson and Congress. As described by Cimbala, Senator Lyman Trumbull of Illinois, after consultation with Howard, crafted and introduced a bill to increase the bureau's authority and tenure in early January 1866. It passed both houses in February, only to be vetoed by the president,[52] an action that drew Henry C. Allen's previously cited denunciation.

Why had Johnson opposed the bill? According to Foner, he felt the bureau's very existence was unconstitutional and would encourage laziness among the newly emancipated African Americans. These views were compounded by Johnson's decided lack of empathy for the freed people, already demonstrated by his ousting of assistant commissioners perceived as overly sympathetic to their needs. In addition, he mistakenly believed that support for the freedmen was limited to Radical Republicans, and sought to exploit what he saw as divisions within the party to his political advantage.[53]

When an effort to override Johnson's veto narrowly failed in the Senate,[54] the South was heartened by the bureau's apparently bleak future.[55] But Congress responded by ratifying *"An Act to continue in force and to amend 'An Act to establish a Bureau for the Relief of Freedmen and Refugees' and for other Purposes,"* followed swiftly by another veto from Johnson on July 16, 1866. This time, Congress passed the bill over his veto that same day.[56]

Besides continuing the Freedmen's Bureau for an additional two years, the new act contained several provisions that were key to its ongoing work. VRC officers currently serving in the bureau could be retained, and both the need for increased funding and acknowledged importance of its educational efforts were manifest in the act's empowering the commissioner to "seize, hold, use, lease, or sell all buildings and tenements" and any associated lands previously held by the CSA that the federal government had not yet disposed of, with the profits to be used for educational pursuits. In addition, the commissioner was to work with "agents and teachers" that "private benevolent associations" had "duly accredited and appointed," and "hire or provide by lease buildings for purposes of education whenever such association shall, *without cost to the government* [italics mine], provide suitable teachers and means of instruction; and he shall furnish such protection as may be required for the safe conduct of such schools."[57]

The new act reflected two major pieces of legislation recently enacted by Congress. In April, the House overrode Johnson's veto of the Civil Rights Bill of 1866, which conferred citizenship on "all persons born in the United States," excepting Native Americans. As such, citizens were accorded "full and equal benefit of all laws and proceedings for the security of person and property." Later that month a new Homestead Act mandated that "all the public lands" in Alabama, Mississippi, Louisiana, Arkansas, and Florida "be disposed of" in accordance with the Homestead Law of 1862, and "that no distinction or discrimination shall be made in the construction or execution of this act on account of race or color."[58]

That Congress intended these laws to be enforced and African Americans protected in the former Confederacy was made explicit in Section 14 of the July 1866 legislation: "the right to make and enforce contracts, to sue, be parties, and give evidence, to inherit, purchase, lease, sell, hold, and convey real and personal property, and to have full and equal benefit of all laws and proceedings concerning personal liberty, personal security, and the acquisition, enjoyment, and disposition of estate, real and personal, including the constitutional right to bear arms, shall be secured to and enjoyed by all the citizens of such State or district without respect to race or color, or previous condition of slavery."[59]

As to enforcement, until a Confederate state or district was fully restored "in its constitutional relations to the government" and "duly represented in . . . Congress," the president, via the Freedmen's Bureau's Commissioner and officers, and through his secretary of war and the military, would protect the freedom of *all* Americans in such areas, without exception. Further, African Americans would not be subject to any greater "penalty or punishment to which white persons may be liable by law" for any equivalent offence that might be committed.[60]

This astounding second act and its profound implications for Reconstruction were summed up by Du Bois, who saw the legislation as giving "the Freedmen's Bureau its final form,—the form by which it will be known to posterity and judged of men. . . . The government of the unreconstructed South was thus put very largely in the hands of the Freedmen's Bureau."[61]

THE VETERAN RESERVE CORPS AND THE FREEDMEN'S BUREAU

These circumstances pinpoint why the qualities of its commissioner and his subordinates, and their commitment to the bureau's goals and assigned responsibilities, were all-important, as was the Veteran Reserve Corps. Having accepted new commissions, its officers were under different terms of enlistment (and discharge) than their state regiment counterparts.[62] As a result, creation of the VRC not only enabled men of intelligence and dedication to the war's goals to stay in service during active hostilities, it proved an ace-in-the-hole for the Freedmen's Bureau in peacetime. Cimbala made this clear: "As the Bureau matured, the presence of VRC men increased. . . . Indeed, by the end of the Bureau's existence, the majority of the agency's field personnel had had some connection with the VRC."[63]

An outstanding demonstration of the Freedmen's Bureau's reliance on VRC officers to carry out its mission is provided by the Left-Armed Corps. Of its seven members who served in the bureau, four did so as VRC officers, while an eighth man knew Bourne at Central Park Hospital.

First Lieutenant Joseph K. Byers had two stints with the Freedmen's Bureau. While in the VRC he was briefly subcommissioner at Vicksburg, Mississippi, in 1866, and in March 1868 was detailed to the bureau from the army's Forty-Second Infantry Regiment.[64]

Severely wounded as a Twenty-Second USCT First Lieutenant, Charles W. Dodge joined the Twenty-Fourth VRC as a second lieutenant in May 1865, then served the bureau in North Carolina. Starting in January 1866, he, like its other officers, apprenticed children either orphaned or unable to receive adequate support from their parents to adults who would take responsibility for their rearing and overall welfare.[65] Dodge was an assistant superintendent, sub-district of Plymouth from May 1866 to June 1867, then subassistant commissioner at Edenton from July 1867 to August 1868.[66] After his VRC discharge, Dodge spent three months as a civilian bureau agent at Edenton.[67]

Captain George Q. White became the Freedmen's Bureau's chief quartermaster and financial agent for the District of Virginia at Richmond in October 1865. He served in the bureau through April 1869,[68] during which time he was brevetted major of US Volunteers "for faithful services in the Quartermaster's Department"; became a captain in the Forty-Fourth US Infantry (known as Veterans' Reserve, and composed of officers disabled in line of duty)[69] in July 1867; and was made a brevet major, US Army, for meritorious services during the rebellion.[70]

White's bureau service was characteristic of the range and importance of duties performed by district-level officers. Reflective of his logistical skills, he advised other officials about changes in bureau-related "*transportation both of persons and freight*" in a March 1867 general order.[71] Three months later, an agent responded to White's request for information about the final home destinations of teachers leaving from Staunton, Virginia, presumably at the end of their educational efforts. Consistent with the high percentage of teachers from New England who for years worked closely with former slaves, two were from Maine and the other from Vermont.[72] White retired from the army on December 15, 1870,[73] with decades of productive work in other arenas ahead of him.

Benjamin C. Cook was a twenty-two-year-old carpenter when he enlisted in the Fifth Michigan in early August 1861. Promoted to sergeant, he was shot in the foot at Charles City Crossroads, Virginia, on June 30, 1862,[74] only to receive a more serious wound on Gettysburg's second day. After a ball entered at his right wrist and exited near the elbow, one and a half inches of the radius were excised that day in an attempt to salvage the arm. Unfortunately, it continued to worsen with "*alarming symptoms*," leading Cook to appeal for an amputation in order to save his life. Although all fractures of the radius and ulna were below the elbow, his arm was in such terrible condition that an amputation in the lower third of the humerus was performed on July 19, 1863.[75]

Subsequently discharged in October, his military career was far from over despite being disabled.

Cook received his commission as a second lieutenant in the VRC on June 1, 1864, and was serving in its Twenty-Fourth Regiment when he joined the Freedmen's Bureau in April 1866 as assistant sub-assistant commissioner at Richmond, Virginia; he remained in that capacity through December 1868.[76]

Appointed captain by Brevet on July 9, 1866,[77] he was also named military commissioner for Henrico and Chesterfield counties in June 1867.[78] Despite these impressive titles, Cook's experience epitomized the limited actual power the Freedmen's Bureau was able to wield in the reconstructed states on behalf of African Americans.

A bureau file chillingly titled "Records Relating to Murders and Outrages" contains case #47, in which Cook was intimately involved. It concerned Virginia White, a black woman who was shown by affidavits to have been "struck three times with a stick of wood, and shot at twice" on July 15, 1868, by W. H. Brauder, a white man, in Manchester, Virginia. The record further indicates that White was "at the time of the assault going to the well on Brauder's lot for water, which she had been accustomed to do." Within a week, Cook had reviewed the case and sworn statements, and then contacted the current military commander of Chesterfield County to state his opinion that the incident merited "Military interference." The local magistrate not only discharged Brauder, but White was "put under bonds to keep the peace"—incredibly, the case was returned to Cook on August 3 by the military commander, who informed the bureau officer that he "did not consider the case warranted Military interference."[79]

To his credit, Cook did not drop the matter. On October 16, he contacted the assistant commissioner, stating that he had learned the military commander "*failed to consult the plaintiff, or a single witness for the prosecution. Plaintiff states that she has had to keep her bed for several weeks by reason of injuries received &c.*" Within five days another bureau officer was directed "to take statements of witnesses for the prosecution and forward brief of same"; one week later, Lieutenant Hambrick provided "sworn statements of 3 witnesses who corroborate the statements of the plaintiff as to the assault." The next day (October 30, 1868), the full report was forwarded to the assistant adjutant general of the First Military District with a repeat request for the case to be committed to the local military commander "as it appears not to have been thoroughly examined when before referred." The final disposition of the case was not recorded.[80]

Case #71, also reported by Cook, was even worse. On May 8, 1868, in Charles City County, "at a fish fry, after some angry words, [Flemming] Binns threw a piece of iron at [Henry] Smith, causing instant death." Smith was black and Binns, a white man, "was arrested and bailed for the sum of $1,500 in the face of evidence that the murder was willful." The case went to trial in August, with Binns being acquitted. According to Cook, the trial was a travesty—as he reported, "*a most disgraceful scene ensued. The Counsel for the prisoner was drunk, as also was several of the jury. One of them (the jury) actually arose in open court and commenced arguing the case for the prisoner. Witnesses were given the lie by the prisoner. The Court utterly failed to preserve order, and finally adjourned.*" General George Stoneman, who commanded the First Military District of Virginia, received an official copy of Cook's report on September 10, two days after he had filed it.[81]

Elna C. Green provided an informative account of another endeavor in which Cook was an active participant: "Like charity workers throughout the country, Freedmen's Bureau agents were concerned about the role of alcohol in producing poverty. The bureau directed its agents to work to establish temperance organizations among the freedmen and constantly preached the adverse economic impact of drinking." Citing reports Cook submitted in August 1867 and October 1868, the assistant subassistant commissioner apparently was quite pleased with the impact of such actions in Richmond on the freedmen.[82]

While he and other bureau officers deserve benefit of the doubt as to positive motives, this revealing example coupled with Cook's efforts regarding "Murders and Outrages" provides important context for a telling observation by Cimbala on the overall "paternalism" of bureau officials from the North. Irritating to newly emancipated people "who expected the respect and equality that came with freedom," there was "another side to it, one that prompted officers and agents to take seriously their role as guardians. It was in that capacity that Bureau men sought justice for the ex-slaves."[83]

This essential point about bureau officers trying to ensure equality under the law for African Americans is consistent with the findings of Michael B. Chesson, who reported that "The Freedmen's Bureau was the major obstacle to smooth relations between Richmond's commanders and city officials." In this regard, he was particularly skeptical about Cook: "Yet the conservative press's extravagant praise for Cook suggests that he might not have defended freedmen as actively as he could." Chesson went on to note that the officer was among few northerners who remained in Richmond with subsequent success.[84]

The previously described incidents that Cook investigated hardly support questioning of his full commitment to protecting African Americans—quite the contrary. In addition, Chesson reported that "Whatever their personal defects, this trio [Cook and two other subordinates of assistant commissioner, Brevet Brigadier General Orlando Brown] badgered the city council to provide adequate care for impoverished freedmen in Richmond. . . . After more than three years of evasion, the council began to provide general relief in January 1869."[85]

This positive outcome was indicative of Cook's faithful execution of General Brown's September 1867 order that he submit all eligible "pauper negroes" to "the proper civil authorities for care and support." Not only would local authorities need to state in writing for bureau review any instance of being unable to accept this responsibility, Brown instructed his subassistant that: "It will be your duty to report without delay any failures hereafter on the part of the civil authorities to take proper care of such persons. Other freedmen supported by the Government will be cared for as heretofore."[86]

Another former (Thirty-Fifth) USCT officer, Captain James O. Ladd, had been mustered out on June 1, 1866, going to work in the headquarters of the Bureau of Civil Affairs, Department of the South, Charleston, South Carolina. After becoming chief clerk in the adjutant general's office, he was subsequently assigned to the Freedmen's Bureau under the assistant commissioner for South Carolina, Brevet Major General Robert K. Scott. Ladd worked for the Bureau from 1866 to

1867, then left in 1868 to become a bookkeeper for the South Carolina State Treasury Office.[87]

The remaining two members of the Left-Armed Corps who served in the Freedmen's Bureau were among its finest officers. As will be detailed in chapter 4, Joseph Wiley Gelray joined the bureau in 1868 and made an indelible mark as an investigator of the Ku Klux Klan. The other, Second Lieutenant Wm. Augustus MacNulty, who could never have joined the bureau without his great persistence in obtaining a VRC commission, embodied what Howard and Congress envisioned in its officials. Already working for the bureau when he submitted his essay on January 20, 1866, MacNulty unequivocally stated his rationale in a follow-up letter sent to Bourne eleven days later: *"I am at present on duty in the 'Freedmens Bureau' as Asst. Supt. of the SubDist. of Fauquier Va. and am trying in my humble sphere to do all in my power for the amelioration of the condition of the poor yet patient Negro and am bound god being my helper, to see that their rights and privileges as Freemen are not infringed upon by those who would wish to still oppress them."*[88] His skills as a combat soldier with the Tenth New York continued to be recognized with an appointment as brevet first lieutenant from Secretary Stanton for "gallant and meritorious services at the battle of Fredericksburg, Va., to date from March 13, 1865" on May 31, 1866.[89] What about his attributes as a warrior in peacetime?

Eugene Scheel reported that blacks in Warrenton, in response to a public accusation that most preferred vagrancy, started a successful drive to establish a school. When it opened in February 1866, S. Fannie Wood, a white Massachusetts native, became its first teacher under funding from the New England Freedmen's Aid Society of Boston. However, she encountered significant resistance from townspeople, including a threatening anonymous letter and abusive language. Cavalry were brought back for protection, but when they departed after two weeks, "stones pelted her schoolroom. Mayor Charles Bragg apologized for the incidents, and Lt. William Augustus MacNulty, a native of Portland, Maine, and the head of the Freedmen's Bureau in Warrenton, offered to protect Wood." Apparently, no more incidents occurred.[90]

According to Scheel, the assistant superintendent's involvement did not end there. His wife, Abbie (whom he had married in August 1865), became one of the school's day teachers, and when a male replacement teacher was needed for the young adult night school, MacNulty stepped right in: "old-timers in Warrenton told me years ago that his students were amazed that a white soldier in uniform, with only one arm, would go to the trouble of teaching them. MacNulty, a cannoneer [actually, an infantry First Sergeant], had lost his right arm in the Union siege of Fredericksburg."[91]

There was plenty to keep the young officer busy during daylight working hours, as evidenced by available correspondence from bureau records. On May 31, 1866, he sent Assistant Commissioner Brown a report "*in compliance with Par. 6 Circular No. 10 from your Hd. Qrs. the result of turning over to the civil authorities jurisdiction in criminal cases where the freedmen are the party accused or complainants.*" During that month, three blacks had been brought up on charges of "*hog shooting & stealing,*" with MacNulty noting they had received able defense during the hearing. One defendant was discharged, but the other two confessed and were held over for trial, with "*Every opportunity . . . afforded them to introduce evidence if they had so desired.*"[92]

After reporting that the Freedmen's Court had held no sessions during the month, MacNulty stated that

> *No cases of injustice have come under my observation since the turning over of cases to the civil authorities.*
>
> *Justice thus far has been impartially administered.*
>
> *The calendar of crime in this county is very small among the blacks. They are as a group very orderly and industrious.*[93]

On August 31, he sent Brown another monthly report about the outcome of ceding jurisdiction to "*State Authorities in criminal cases over colored persons with reference to the interests of the latter &c.,*" although now from Culpeper Court House, Virginia as the assistant superintendent, counties of Culpeper and Rappahannock. The only black defendant (a woman *"charged with stealing a watch"*) who had been *"tried in the Culpeper County Court"* had been discharged due to lack of *"sufficient evidence"*; this led MacNulty to conclude that *"The Court as far as my observation has extended seems disposed to act impartially."*[94]

He ended with shrewd comments on the bureau's relationship with the courts:

> *I am of the opinion that the Civil Authorities will act impartially toward the Freedmen as a matter of policy if not from a desire to do so.*

> *The different Magistrates do not seem desirous of hearing the complaints of Freedmen for debt &c unless the several cases are by me referred to them. This very possibly arose from a delicacy on their part to act in such cases until I am cognizant of the facts in the case in order that I may be present at the examinations or trials as contemplated in Par. III of the Circular already referred to which has been published in the County papers.*[95]

On June 3, 1867, MacNulty was appointed military commissioner, Culpeper and Rappahannock Counties, in the subdistrict of Fredericksburg, still stationed at Culpeper Court House; he had also been brevetted as captain prior to his new post.[96] Discharged from the VRC on January 1, 1868, he was simultaneously appointed personally by Commissioner Howard as an "agent in a civil capacity of the Bureau" and retained in Culpeper County.[97]

It was in this role that MacNulty on September 24, 1868, initially filed case #72, starkly illustrative of the lethal turn that Reconstruction had taken. A black man, Arthur Lee, *"was taken from his house about 11 or 12 o'clock at night on the night of Sept. 14th, 1868, and was found dead next morning, having been beaten to death."* MacNulty further noted that he and the civil authorities *"are making all efforts in their power to find the murderers, but without avail so far,"* and that he would report any additional information. On October 20, he filed a second report in which he stated, *"that after an examination of a number of persons living in the neighborhood of the murder before the Circuit Court, nothing was elicited."*[98]

Abbie and W. A. MacNulty would both continue their efforts to ensure equality under the law for all Americans after his tenure with the Freedmen's Bureau ended. On December 7, 1870, the Senate confirmed President U. S. Grant's nomination of the decorated one-armed veteran as deputy postmaster at Culpeper,[99] and he would stay in public service for decades to come.

After being discharged from Central Park Hospital, VRC Second Lieutenant Michael Mangan remained in New York City until the war ended, then joined the Freedmen's Bureau in Florida. He eventually served as sub-commissioner at Apalachicola from May 9 to July 31, 1866, and was mustered out of the VRC in September.[100] However, neither his military career nor bureau service were over. Despite having lost his right lower leg at Gettysburg, he accepted appointment as a second lieutenant in the Forty-Fifth US Regiment in March 1867. Becoming unassigned due to physical disability on July 22, 1869, he returned to the Freedmen's Bureau (this time in Kentucky) at the end of September and was on duty there until his retirement on December 31, 1870.[101]

In addition to these eight men who became Freedmen's Bureau officials while on active duty, another Left-Armed Corps member worked on one of the bureau's main goals after being discharged from the army. Corporal Phineas P. Whitehouse of the Sixth New Hampshire ran a school in Muirkirk, Maryland, for both white and black children, along with provision of twice-weekly evening sessions for African American adults. Concerning these last individuals, he wrote Mrs. Edna D. Cheney of the New England Freedmen's Aid Society in March 1867 that *"It is truly encouraging to see these men and women, after working all day, come in and study the reader so attentively."* Whitehouse further noted that *"Both the white and colored pupils manifest a good degree of interest in the school, and all feel proud of the beautiful new school house, the liberal donation of Mr. William E. Coffin, of your city* [Boston]."[102]

Eight months later, his observations were bleaker, yet optimistic:

This section of the state has been one of the darkest portions of the South, and even now, when slavery is wiped away and the colored man begins to hold up his head, many of the bitterest enemies to liberty and progress are looked up to as leaders in social and political circles throughout the State. But the great work of reform is slowly, but steadily and surely advancing.

The colored pupils feel more like children of men and women as they find themselves enjoying the same privileges granted to their white neighbors and they are thus encouraged to press forward and left themselves for the depths of ignorance in which they have been confined.[103]

Du Bois considered the endeavor in which Whitehouse and hundreds of other teachers, numerous Freedmen Aid Societies and the Freedmen's Bureau itself were engaged as the Bureau's crowning achievement, which: "lay in the planting of the free school among Negroes, and the idea of free elementary education among all classes in the South. . . . The opposition to Negro education was bitter in the South, for the South believed an educated Negro to be a dangerous Negro. And the South was not wholly wrong; for education among all kinds of men always has had, and always will have, an element of danger and revolution, of dissatisfaction and discontent."[104]

Typified by the Left-Armed Corps, the Freedmen's Bureau relied heavily upon VRC officers, who by and large proved equal to the formidable task facing them and the nation to be reconstructed.

Private L. Edwin Dudley, Thirteenth Massachusetts. LINCOLN FINANCIAL FOUNDATION COLLECTION.

Getting Political

The 1866 Midterm Elections and Fourteenth Amendment

How extraordinary, and what a tribute to ignorance and religious hypocrisy, is the fact that in the minds of most people, even those of liberals, only murder makes men. The slave pleaded; he was humble; he protected the women of the South, and the world ignored him. The slave killed white men; and behold, he was a man!

—W. E. B. Du Bois[1]

For exploring Northern veterans' opinions of the Freedmen's Bureau and differences between the president and Congress in early Reconstruction, the Soldiers' and Sailors' National Union League is exemplary. Organized in Washington on September 8, 1865, the league consisted of discharged servicemen who wanted to form an organization that would maintain "our best interests" and cultivate "that heroic spirit which led us forth to battle in a sacred cause, and to secure to ourselves a proper recognition of our just claims."[2]

Its fundamental mission established, the league sought preferences in hiring for qualified honorably discharged veterans to federal, state, and municipal government positions; equalization of bounties for soldiers who enlisted in 1861 and 1862 with those paid to later enlistees; assistance to veterans who needed it to "procure employment in the general pursuits of life"; "speedy settlement" by the government of needed claims for veterans, widows, and children of those who had died while in service; and associated amelioration "of the condition of widows and orphans." The league also made a "solemn pledge" to support its members "who, by sickness or other misfortune, are prevented from pursuing their usual avocations [in receiving] such aid as will alleviate their suffering."[3]

The new league quickly proved as good as its word. On October 20, 1865, it unanimously approved a resolution calling for a national Union veterans convention at the end of January 1866 in Washington to pursue its agenda, and asking "all papers throughout the country favorable to our cause" for publicity.[4] One month later, President L. Edwin Dudley wrote the *New York Times* about the convention, urgently requesting representatives from "Each Congressional District, and every organization composed entirely of discharged soldiers and sailors." His notice emphasized uniting as veterans who defended their nation so that "we shall soon see our comrades who have lost a leg or an arm placed in some position which will afford him an honest livelihood."[5]

In 1889, Robert B. Beath noted that while the league was "not organized for political purposes, a large proportion of its members were employed in the different departments in Washington, and were naturally interested in political matters."[6] Dudley, a former private, worked in the Department of the Treasury's Office of Internal Revenue,[7] and it didn't take long for the League to get involved in matters beyond veterans' benefits.

In closing the October 20 meeting, Senator James H. Lane of Kansas stated: "The sentiments uttered by the gallant men who preserved this Government will have more influence in keeping it right than the expression of sentiment from any other direction."[8] Lane's words were visionary. The Soldiers' and Sailors' National Union League, which eventually had more than 1,000 members, was keenly opposed to President Johnson's course of action on Reconstruction and the Freedmen's Bureau.[9] Wielding political power beyond its size, it became embroiled in a unique battle for public opinion via competing conventions that were polar opposites, and very influential.

Though midterm rather than presidential, election stakes were high for the cause of equality in 1866. As explained by Marion Mills Miller, representatives to both the Fortieth Congress and state legislatures, which would select United States senators, were up for re-election. Should "less than a two-thirds majority of Radicals [be] sent to the national legislature," the president could use his veto power to prevent adoption of an opposing Reconstruction policy, even if unable to enforce his own. Not standing a chance of gaining a supportive majority, the Johnson administration nonetheless "trusted to hold matters at a stand-still until a revolution of public sentiment should occur and it would be sustained two years later at the presidential election."[10]

With that in mind, the administration called for a national meeting that was held in Philadelphia on August 14. The Harmony Convention's main object was to avow that each state, including those remaining unre-constructed in the South, should be represented in Congress. Northern and Southern delegates from every state literally made their entrance in matched pairs, linked arm-in-arm.[11]

According to the *Western Reserve Chronicle* of Warren, Ohio, the convention "was composed of out-and-out rebels who fought against the country. . . ; of northern men who sympathized with the rebels; . . . also of a few men seduced from the Union party by the temptations of Executive influence and patronage, and a very few more, perhaps, who were governed by a morbid feeling of magnanimity to a defeated foe. All . . . were governed by hostility to the progressive sentiments of the free north."[12]

Not to be outdone, and to show that the Republican party was not solely sectional, the Radicals quickly called for their own convention in Philadelphia, held two weeks later on September 3.[13] Among the delegates were P. T. Barnum (then serving in the Connecticut General Assembly), Ralph Waldo Emerson, US Senator Charles Sumner of Massachusetts, and Frederick E. Dake of the Soldiers' Union of Washington, DC, and Left-Armed Corps.[14]

As the *Western Reserve Chronicle* observed of this Southern Loyalists' Convention, the City of Brotherly Love witnessed a very different sight in the gathering of sizable Northern state delegations in strong support of representatives from the South, "four hundred true blue Union men, with not a sneaking traitor among them. A large proportion of the Southern delegates were for universal suffrage."

James Speed of Kentucky, who had been chosen the convention's permanent president, declared "'that there was unequal representation as long as one man in the country was unrepresented.'" Speaking of Johnson's Philadelphia convention, he said: "'They do not say in their platform, that any Southern State has abolished slavery, but indicate it has been abolished by military power, and when they have power they will claim compensation for their emancipated slaves.'"[15]

Having resigned as US attorney general in opposition to Johnson's policies, Speed's selection in Philadelphia was a direct challenge to the president.[16] As Miller reported, the main aspects of all convention speeches were the imperative to adopt the Fourteenth Amendment, "and that the Administration would not be permitted to evade this, the great and fundamental political issue of the time."[17]

THE CALL FOR A PRO-ADMINISTRATION SOLDIERS' CONVENTION

Its political concerns heightened, the Johnson administration convened another national meeting, this time almost literally bringing in the big guns. Mindful that the determining factor in the upcoming congressional elections would be the Union soldiers' vote, Miller reported that the invitations sent to army officers of prominence were intended "to show that the sentiment of those who had put down the Rebellion was opposed to coercive measures against the South."[18]

In an August 19 convention call signed by a committee composed of six active duty or former general officers including George Armstrong Custer, Alexander D. McCook, George W. Crook, and Solomon Meredith, "soldiers now or lately in the Union army . . . who approve the restoration policy of the President, and the principles announced by the National Union Convention at Philadelphia" were invited to assemble in Cleveland, Ohio, on September 17.[19]

While regretting the severing of "cherished political associations" and cooperating "with former enemies," the committee nonetheless preferred "to act with those who have been wrong and are now right, rather than with those who were right and now are wrong." Appealing to those who fought to save a government they held "dearer and more sacred than all party ties" and seen to be "again in peril," any "soldiers and sailors agreeing with us in sentiment, and who cannot in person attend" were asked to "send delegates through the action of their societies or of local conventions."[20]Among numerous high-ranking officers who endorsed this call were Major Generals Daniel E. Sickles, William B. Franklin, and Gouverneur K. Warren, with Brigadier Generals W. W. H. Davis and (Brevet) Charles G. Halpine also signees.[21]

Seeking to counteract a statewide Soldiers' Convention held two months earlier in Pittsburgh, which it characterized as veterans "[pledging] to the support of the Radical disunion members of Congress, and . . . opposed to the just and constitutional restoration policy of President Johnson," the Pennsylvania Democratic Soldiers' Convention had met at Harrisburg on August 1. Insisting that "the true sentiments of the great mass of [Pennsylvania's] returned soldiers and sailors" had been "misrepresented," self-proclaimed "authorized representatives" led by Committee on Resolutions member Davis submitted a full slate for general consideration by those in attendance.

All fifteen resolutions were unanimously approved with great applause; while each supported Johnson's Reconstruction policy and castigated Congress and those who backed its plan, one stood out for blatant malice: "we are opposed to negro suffrage, and all legislation that has for its object the raising of the negro to social and political equality with the white man, or to make him the pet of the nation, meets our unqualified disapproval. He and his friends should be satisfied that the war has given his race their boon of freedom, and should not aim to control the destinies of the country."[22]

Those who endorsed the president's positions on Reconstruction and race held high hopes for the upcoming Soldiers' Convention. On August 24, the *Brooklyn Daily Eagle* crowed over an announcement that, after October 1, the Freedmen's Bureau would no longer issue rations to all refugees or blacks, only those orphaned or sick ("Let the darkey and the white take up 'the shovel and the hoe' and cultivate the virgin soil that needs only to be tickled to laugh into harvest.") Predicting that "The Radicals . . . clamorously calling on the 'Boys in Blue' to take a distinctive hand in politics . . . [will result] in a way which will bring [them] no comfort," the *Eagle* then said, "In rallying to the support of the President, the soldiers will find themselves under their old leaders. The Soldiers' Convention is a flank movement on the Radicals, and . . . they had better follow Lee's example, and surrender at discretion."[23]

Apparently its staff either hadn't read or simply chose to ignore an article published across the East River three days earlier by the *New York Tribune* that contained an announcement from the Soldiers' and Sailors' National Union League calling for a convention of its own in Pittsburgh on September 24. Precisely characterizing the Cleveland Convention as an endorsement of Johnson's Reconstruction policy, the league stated its belief "that the soldiers and sailors who take this view of our national affairs are but an insignificant minority of the men who have defended the Republic in the field."[24]

The stage was being set to answer the question that entailed historic implications—where did most Union veterans stand on Reconstruction and equality?

Six days after the call for the Cleveland Convention, the *Tribune* responded with a withering piece that took the general officer signees to task for "the baseness inhering in the platform of the proposed Johnson Soldiers' Convention," and zeroed in on race and deadly brutality against African Americans in the South. Noting that 200,000 black Union soldiers had served in the war, and 28,000 died, "probably One Hundred and Fifty Thousand are still living (though the Rebels have murdered many since Lee and Johnston surrendered). Now, what Mr. Johnson calls 'My Policy' of restoration leaves nearly all of these. . . . Soldiers at the mercy and under the feet of the malignant, chagrined, embittered Rebels whom they helped you to put down."

Making it plain, the newspaper reported that while "the Philadelphia Convention says they *ought* to enjoy all rights of person and property equally with Whites, you know that they *do not*, and if they are left to the mercy of the late Rebels, *never will*." To illustrate this, "NEW-ORLEANS has already shown you how any attempt to help them to the Right of Suffrage will be dealt with at the South," along with "the wholesale destruction of their school-houses, the mobbing and lynching of their teachers, by Rebel 'regulators.'" The *Tribune* concluded by insisting that the generals judge themselves: "Is not the part you are playing toward these Black Union soldiers, your late compatriots in arms, intensely base and treacherous? We merely indicate our opinion of it: will you allow us to compare it with *yours?*"[25]

A MASSACRE IN MEMPHIS

The direct reference to New Orleans and more general allusions to the killing of black veterans and teachers, and associated mob violence, would have struck home with anyone then reading this searing essay. Over May 1 to 3, 1866, a riot in Tennessee had led to what the investigating House Select Committee called an "organized and bloody massacre of the colored people of Memphis, regardless of age, sex, or condition, incited by the teachings of the press, and led on by the sworn officers of the law, comprising the city government, and others."[26]

The riot and subsequent slaughter had been brewing for months, in particular hostilities between stationed black troops and the city's predominantly white Irish police force. It was not coincidental that the very next day following the Third USC Heavy Artillery's being mustered out, an attempt to arrest one of its ex-soldiers lead to a clash between the Memphis police and fifty of his uniformed comrades, with a police officer being killed. When the African American troops obeyed the order of area Commander Stoneman to return to their fort, it appeared the incident was over. However, on the pretense of quelling a soldiers' riot and overall "black insurrection," groups of police, firemen, and citizens terrorized the African American population for two days before General Stoneman declared martial law.[27, 28]

When the dust had settled, forty-six blacks were dead, along with two whites; seventy-five more people were wounded; five African American women had been raped, and another ten "maltreated." In addition, there had been one hundred robberies; ninety-one houses and cabins, four churches, and twelve schoolhouses had been burned, with destruction of total property valued at $130,931.[29]

While the rampage occurred in both the setting and context of Reconstruction, black suffrage was not the incendiary issue it would be in subsequent riots and bloodshed in the South. Here, the very presence and behavior of free African American Union soldiers was resented by most white citizens, who viewed them as a threat to the established social order. In a pointed example, Memphis police responded with physical aggression when soldiers of color refused to step off the sidewalk for them. As Kevin R. Hardwick concluded in his scholarly paper on the events, "The violence of the riot was not random. It was targeted at those black individuals and institutions most symbolic of black empowerment—the soldiers themselves, and the institutions that their presence sheltered."[30, 31]

The House Select Committee (Republican Representatives Elihu Washburne of Illinois and John Martin Broomall of Pennsylvania, with Kentucky Democrat George S. Shanklin dissenting) conclusion was both ominous and prophetic in its judgment that "there will be no safety to loyal men, either white or black . . . [should] the troops be withdrawn":

> [We] believe that the riots and massacres of Memphis are only a specimen of what would take place throughout the entire South should the government fail to afford adequate military protection. Indeed, the Committee believe the sentiment of the South which they observed is not a sentiment of full acquiescence in the results of the war, but that there is among them a lingering hope that their favorite doctrine of secession may yet be vindicated. . . . Though they have been beaten by arms, they assert and maintain that the principle is the same, and hope for its vindication hereafter in some way.[32]

A RIOT IN NEW ORLEANS

Unlike Memphis, what happened three months later in New Orleans was directly related to Reconstruction policy and black enfranchisement. On July 30, a riot broke out when the constitutional convention of 1864 reconvened under a plan of Radical Republicans supported by Louisiana Governor James M. Wells. It involved creation of a new state government, with blacks to be given the vote while certain rebels who went to war against the US government would be disenfranchised. On the day of the convention, twenty-five white delegates arrived, along with two hundred African American supporters, most of them veterans. According to the *Report of the Select Committee on the New Orleans Riot*, "Many of them [black ex-soldiers] had canes and walking sticks, but were otherwise unarmed." As for the opposing municipal police, most of whom were Confederate veterans, Foner reported that some of the officers apparently "conspired to disperse the gathering by force." The *Report* concluded from available evidence that "threats had been made and warnings given of a designed attack."[33, 34]

Shots rang out in the street before the convention met and after it had commenced, and efforts to barricade the hall in anticipation of military support were ineffective as police entered and attacked those inside, black supporters and delegates alike. The *Report*, based on eyewitness testimony, stated in sickening detail what had befallen African Americans "peaceably pursuing their lawful business," as "Men of character and position, some of whom were members and some spectators of the convention, escaped from the hall covered with wounds and blood, and were preserved almost by miracle from death . . . bear[ing] frightful scars more numerous than many soldiers of a dozen well-fought fields can show." But there was worse:

[M]en were shot while waving handkerchiefs in token of surrender and submission; white men and black, with arms uplifted praying for life, were answered by shot and blow from knife and club; the bodies of some were "pounded to a jelly;" a colored man was dragged from under a street-crossing, and killed at a blow; men concealed in outhouses and among piles of lumber were eagerly sought for and slaughtered or maimed without remorse; the dead bodies upon the street were violated by shot, kick, and stab; the face of a man "just breathing his last" was gashed by a knife or razor in the hands of a woman.[35]

Despite some city police having "acted to save and not to destroy life," the *Report* stated that "for several hours, the police and mob, in mutual and bloody emulation, continued the butchery in the hall and on the street." When the riot ended, thirty-four African Americans were dead, along with four whites [one member of the convention and two "loyal citizens" (Radicals) and one "disloyal"]; forty black citizens, four white loyal citizens, and four convention members were severely wounded, with another eighty-eight slightly wounded, along with ten policemen.[36]

Major General Phil Sheridan, then in command of the military division of the Gulf, including Louisiana, was not present during the riot but arrived around midnight on the following day. In testimony before the Select Committee on December 1, 1866, based on his own investigation Sheridan called what had taken place a "massacre," and concluded that if civil authorities had acted appropriately regarding the convention, there would have been no need for military intervention, and no violence. When asked for his opinion as to what would occur if the military and Freedmen's Bureau were withdrawn from New Orleans, Sheridan replied that "although the military do not exercise any actual power, they do exercise a great moral influence, and I believe it is necessary to retain them."[37]

Battle lines both metaphoric and literal were being drawn North and South, and the upcoming conventions showdown would establish where Union veterans stood on issues resulting from the war and the nation's future. Would the administration's gambit result in Northern ex-servicemen falling in line behind some of their former generals in support of the president, or would Union veterans endorse congressional Reconstruction, including black suffrage and the Fourteenth Amendment, and ongoing use of the military in its support?

THE SOLDIERS' AND SAILORS' LEAGUE'S CALL FOR ITS OWN CONVENTION

In the days leading up to the Conventions, indications were inauspicious for the Johnson administration. On August 28 the Ogdensburg, New York, *Daily Journal* noted the generals' call for the Cleveland meeting was poorly received by veterans: "It is in the interest of the Philadelphia movement, but they cannot get many soldiers to surrender. Says the *Tribune*, 'Custer on horses would be of more interest than Custer on statesmanship.'"[38] By marked contrast, the *New York Daily Tribune* reported from Washington on August 20 that the Soldiers' and Sailors' National Union League had already "received several hundred letters from private soldiers residing throughout the country, indorsing the call for the Pittsburgh Soldiers' Convention. It is a good sign to see the rank and file show their colors."[39] The dispatch also made an astute observation: "The Johnson Cleveland call has not the name of a private soldier attached to it. The committee ignore the private soldier, it is only the officers they think of any consequence."[40]

Backing for the Pittsburgh meeting among Union veterans was widespread and growing. From Chicago came news of a large August 28 gathering of soldiers in Peoria that resulted in the unanimous ratification of "strong resolutions," including a statement of full support for the actions of Congress toward the former Confederate States, and another regarding the earlier administration-sponsored convention: "That the present attempt of corrupt politicians to commit the soldiers and sailors of the nation to the Philadelphia Convention merits and meets with our fullest scorn and contempt. That while others may affiliate with the butchers Forrest and Taylor, Wade Hampton and Mosby, and with Jeff Davis when he shall be released from prison, we remember Fort Pillow, Libby Prison and Andersonville, and stand aloof from the degrading spectacle."[41]

Similarly, on September 1, the *Albany Evening Journal* reported, "The call for the Soldiers Convention at Cleveland, instigated by office holders and office seekers, has stirred up the loyal soldiers all over the Union. The Call for a State Convention is being signed by thousands, in Michigan, and so it will be in this State."[42]

The Soldiers' and Sailors' League's appeal for action was galvanizing more than the rank and file. Major General John A. Logan wrote it "'shall have my hearty cooperation for *maintaining the rights of all men*, for which we have just passed through a bloody conflict, and are now fighting a *bitter political one*.'"[43] Taking time from his re-election campaign, US Representative and Major General James A. Garfield of Ohio informed the league that he was "'greatly pleased with your suggestion in regard to a Loyal soldiers' Convention, Such a demonstration ought to be made to show the country that the great mass of heroic soldiers are true to the cause for which they fought.'"[44]

High-ranking officers including Major Generals Joshua L. Chamberlain, George J. Stannard, and Ambrose E. Burnside were selected "to aid in securing a full representation from their respective States" for the convention. In a strange twist of fate, the Kansas representative was Major and US Senator Edmund G. Ross,[45] a Republican who in 1868 would cast a critical vote for acquittal in Johnson's impeachment trial in the Senate.[46]

In Ohio, when the *Western Reserve Chronicle* announced a September 15 meeting for soldiers and sailors to appoint delegates for the Pittsburgh Convention, the newspaper saw the "long list of names appended to the Call" as indicative of Union veterans being "determined to place themselves square on the record against those who affiliate with traitors and copperheads. . . . We have no doubt the meeting will be largely attended." Among those named on the convention announcement was First Sergeant Elisha R. Wise of the Eleventh Pennsylvania and Left-Armed Corps.[47]

THE CLEVELAND SOLDIERS' CONVENTION

When the Cleveland Soldiers' Convention began on September 17, the hoped-for multitudes were nowhere in sight. The city had accommodations for 1,700 people in its hotels, and three sizable halls and a warehouse had been rented for additional lodging. After a highly disappointing 531 delegates showed up, hotels were far from full, and both the halls and warehouse stayed empty throughout.[48]

This was embarrassing enough, but the proceedings proved even worse for Johnson and his supporters. Retired Major General John E. Wool, whose service had begun in the War of 1812, delivered the introductory speech upon nomination by Kentucky Governor Thomas E. Bramlette for the convention's temporary president as "the oldest Major Gen. in the United States, and probably in the world."

Off that dubious designation, Wool praised the president as a "bold and daring friend of the Union," and then lambasted Johnson's opponents, whom he accused of having "a raging thirst for blood and plunder" and being prepared to re-invade the South and "lay waste" to an "already desolated" land: "Another civil war is foreshadowed, unless the freedmen are placed on an equality with their previous masters. . . . These revengeful partisans would leave their country a howling wilderness for the want of more victims to gratify their insatiable cruelty."[49]

That same day, former Confederate officers and enlisted men convened in Memphis to consider resolutions to allay widespread beliefs "industriously and maliciously . . . impressed upon the Northern mind, that a Union or Northern man is not safe, in life, liberty and property, within our limits." A committee chaired by General Nathan Bedford Forrest crafted a message for the Cleveland Convention that was telegraphed to its president under their signatures: "[We] . . . congratulate your convention in your effort to restore peace and quietude to the country . . . express [our] deep sympathy with your patriotic purposes . . . and further assure you that Confederate soldiers are entirely willing to leave the determination of their rights as citizens of States, and of the United States, to the soldiers of the Union. On our part we pledge security of life, person, property and freedom of speech and opinion to all."[50]

By all accounts, the convention responded enthusiastically to the dispatch, with Forrest and his comrades given three cheers. For *The Daily Phoenix* in Columbia, South Carolina, such "courtesies between brave men" contrasted with the "miserable efforts of those who would, if in their power, plunge the country into another civil war." Based on Union soldiers' alleged knowledge of "the gallantry and high bearing of the defeated Confederates," the newspaper made the further astonishing claim that Northern veterans "are as willing to trust the honor and sincerity of the Southern people as the latter are to trust the determination of their rights" to them. The newspaper concluded, "Such is the difference between the true soldier and the sneaking fanatic, who never shouldered a gun or fired a shot in defence of that Union he wishes to keep dissevered."[51]

Focusing on Forrest, Northern newspapers saw it quite differently. To the *Albany Evening Journal* his reception revealed "the true character" of those in attendance, given his record of "persistent violation of the rules of war, and by acts of cruelty toward the people of Tennessee true to the Union cause. But the act of barbarity which closed his military career was the massacre of Fort Pillow, after its surrender." For the New York capital city paper, "that the mention of his name should elicit cheers from those who claim to be honored as defenders of the Union he sought to destroy, almost exceeds the limits of comprehension."[52] The *Fremont Journal* of Sandusky, Ohio, was more succinct, but just as offended: "The Soldiers' Convention of Cleveland greeted the name of Forrest, the butcher of Fort Pillow, with enthusiastic cheers. The fact needs no comment."[53] As we will see in the next chapter, Forrest would become an even greater target for Northern fury and denunciation as Reconstruction progressed.

What had taken place was devastating for Johnson. As the *Evening Telegraph* in Philadelphia stated, "The conservative Soldiers' Convention at Cleveland, for which such great preparations had been made, and from which so much was expected, has proved to be a very slim affair," "a failure" whose sole enthusiasm "was the exchange of congratulations with the Rebel General Forrest, *the hero of the Fort Pillow massacre.*"[54] The *Albany Evening Journal* likewise characterized the convention as a "complete fizzle," from which "the true soldiers of the Union have kept aloof."[55]

THE PITTSBURGH SOLDIERS' AND SAILORS' CONVENTION
One week later, the Pittsburgh Convention would be a dazzling success distinct from the administration's convention in every way. Unlike in Cleveland, turnout was massive—the *Burlington* (Vermont) *Weekly Free Press* put attendance at 20,000,[56] while Miller reported "Pittsburgh was overrun with a vast number of private soldiers (estimated at 25,000)."[57]

Of the throngs packing the city at the Three Rivers Confluence, the *Western Reserve Chronicle* reported "hotels were full to overflowing," with numerous "private houses . . . thrown open for the accommodation of visitors." On Tuesday night, around 3,000 attendees "slept on the steamboats or the levee," along which fires were constructed that veterans gathered around "from down the river, many of whom passed the night signing songs, telling stories and playing cards."

"The Convention reassembled on Wednesday at nine o'clock. There was such a crowd the day before it became necessary to issue tickets to the delegates and station a guard at the door in order that they might obtain admittance to seats. When the seats were filled the guards were taken off, and the crowd rushed in, quickly filling every available space. Thousands went away who could not gain admittance."[58]

Attendee composition also contrasted greatly. The *Free Press* reported Cleveland had attracted only officers, while "The Pittsburgh Convention was a grand representative gathering of the late army of the Union; its temporary chairman a private soldier; and with not a rank or arm of the service that was not represented by numbers of brave, patriotic, fighting men bearing the shot torn banners under which they fought."[59]

The *Chronicle* noted that in addition to numerous major generals (including permanent Chairman Jacob D. Cox, Nathaniel P. Banks, Franz Sigel, John W. Geary, and James Garfield) other participants included "about fifty brigadier generals, many line and staff officers, and fully ten thousand privates from every State in the Union."[60, 61]

In the enlisted group were Left-Armed Corps members Will Warren Jr., one of Indiana's two elected convention vice presidents, and Sergeant Sanborn, who had been appointed a delegate at the Vermont Soldiers' Convention.[62]

When Soldiers' and Sailors' League President Dudley's request for a deserved furlough (using three days of earned leave) to attend the convention had been denied by Treasury, he quit his clerkship. After his letter of resignation was read to the assemblage, he was elected to the chair with booming applause. The *Emporia* (Kansas) *News* further reported that other veterans working in the government had been informed their jobs would be lost if they attended the Pittsburgh Convention, "while furloughs are freely offered to attend the affair at Cleveland, which cheered for Forest [*sic*]."[63]

In a demonstration of both support and the convention's egalitarian nature, Private Amos E. Hardy of Maine and General J. F. Farnsworth of Illinois were appointed a committee of two to lead Dudley to the chair. Hardy, who was then named one of convention's temporary secretaries by Dudley,[64] was yet another Left-Armed Corps veteran, having lost his right arm to a shell at Southside Railroad, Virginia, in October 1864 while serving in the First Maine Heavy Artillery (originally Eighteenth Maine).[65]

The platform accepted at the Pittsburgh Convention could not have differed more with the views articulated just days before in Cleveland. Major General Benjamin Butler had the honor of presenting its principles to great acclaim. Support for the recently passed (but not yet ratified) Fourteenth Amendment was absolute, as "It clearly defines American citizenship and guarantees all his rights to citizens. It places on a just and equal basis the right of representation, making the vote of a man in one State equally potent with the vote of another man in any State."[66]

Other resolutions assailed Johnson for dictatorially implementing a Reconstruction policy in clear opposition to Congress, deeming it "as dangerous as it is unwise," antithetical to the "restoration of peace and unity," and converting "conquered rebels into impudent claimants to rights which they have forfeited, and places which they have desecrated." The platform sought to couple the sacrifices of the nation and its uniformed defenders with a just Reconstruction in which "the Union men of the South, without distinction of race or color . . . [who] are being persecuted by thousands, solely because they are now, and have been, true to the Government" would receive steadfast support from Union veterans.[67]

Once Butler, chairman of the Committee on Resolutions, finished their formal presentation and unanimous acceptance,[68] he reported having been instructed to put forward one more: "Resolved that a National Committee, to form a Soldiers' and Sailors' Union of all who agree with the principles set forth in the resolutions of this Convention, shall be selected by the several delegations here represented, to consist of members from each state and territory, the names to be reported to the Convention in order to perfect an organization, and take such steps as may seem to them necessary for the furtherance of the principles of the great Union party to which we belong."[69] Adopted unanimously, the resolution was an important step in the countrywide formation of the largest and most influential veterans' organization yet seen in American history, the Grand Army of the Republic (GAR).

Miller reported that the ensuing speeches "were in the same tenor. Their burden was 'support the fourteenth Amendment.'" She then cited James G. Blaine, Republican US representative from Maine, who said that the "convention did more to popularize the Fourteenth Amendment than any other instrumentality of the year."[70]

General Stewart L. Woodford, Republican candidate for New York lieutenant governor, delivered one of the convention's finest orations to thunderous applause. After reviewing the war's history, slavery's death, and Reconstruction so far, he got to "His Accidency, the President of the United States."

> If these conditions which the President has imposed are sufficient, why, I may ask you, was that massacre at Memphis? . . . was that horrid butchery at New Orleans? . . . why was it necessary to pass the Civil Rights bill, and stop that suffering with which the reconstructed Legislatures of the South had deluged the land? . . . why is it that Northern men, loyal men, are not safe to-day on Southern land, outside of the picket line? . . . why is it that the black man, simply because he adhered to our banner and wore our uniform, is to be outraged and murdered throughout the Southern States?

> Gentlemen, there will be no reconstruction that is worthy of the name . . . until every man . . . shall find ample protection in all his rights of person and property wherever that banner floats, though it be even in New Orleans.[71]

Correspondents noted the level of enthusiasm kept up throughout the convention, the walls reportedly shaking from cheers for the resolutions and speakers, women waving handkerchiefs, maimed veterans holding their crutches overhead, and a famous raptor making a special visit.[72]

The Eighth Wisconsin's "Old Abe," an eagle who spent three years in the field with his regiment, had been invited to the convention and "was quartered at the St. Charles Hotel with a large number of other warriors not less distinguished than himself."[73] Named after the late president, Old Abe had a group of "Peace Attendants" to care for him, mostly disabled Badger State veterans who included Private William J. Jones of the Sixteenth Wisconsin and Left-Armed Corps.[74] Having been taught that "when he hears great cheering . . . [to] flap his wings and scream," Old Abe's "appearance on the platform was the signal for immense applause."[75]

The day after the formal convention concluded, a mass meeting took place that topped earlier "torch light processions and other demonstrations" deemed exceptional.[76] Convened on Allegheny City (now Pittsburgh's North Side)[77] commons in order to endorse Geary's nomination for Pennsylvania's governor, a huge procession followed speeches by Butler and Banks. Twelve divisions, each under a major general's command, comprised a line of more than 30,000 men nearly ten miles long that took five and a half hours to pass a given point; not surprisingly, the spectacle "exceeded by far anything of the kind that ever took place in this Western Country."[78]

The events of the past few months were simply staggering. In a desperate gamble for their political lives, a sitting American president and his followers counted on support for their Reconstruction program and related racial views from the Union's recently discharged soldiers and sailors. Their assumptions showed a shocking lack of understanding of Northern veterans' collective intelligence, societal savvy, and commitment to the twin ideals of republican democracy and freedom upheld, indeed deepened, through the crucible of war.

They had further blundered by thinking that ex-enlisted personnel would blindly follow the lead of handpicked general officers whose Democratic leanings were antithetical to men who had overwhelmingly voted for Abraham Lincoln just two years before. As the *Lockport* (New York) *Daily Journal* wrote on September 27, "The so-called Soldiers' Convention, at Cleveland, is another signal and significant failure. It was not needed, at this time, to show the impossibility of attaching any great number of genuine Union men to the Johnson cause."[79]

On October 5, the *Burlington Weekly Free Press* showed its scorn for the myopia of Johnson and his operatives like

Gen. [Gordon] Granger, [who] in presenting the Cleveland resolutions to the President, had the face to say: "In them are reflected, as we believe, the true sentiments of the great mass not only of those who were soldiers and sailors of the Union army and navy, but of the patriotic people of the whole country."

A bolder misstatement was never uttered. The soldiers are with Mr. Johnson as much as the people are. How much the people are with him is shown by the figures of the elections in Vermont and Maine, and how far the soldiers are with him is shown by the Pittsburgh Convention.[80]

In celebrating the Pittsburgh Convention's "glorious success," the *Western Reserve Chronicle*, on October 3, flatly stated that Johnson "knows now, if he did not know before, that the soldiers and sailors of this great republic will 'vote as they shot,' that they despise 'my policy,' and are above all bread and butter considerations."[81]

On their own initiative, Union veterans had delivered a ringing repudiation of the administration's concept of Reconstruction under circumstances that were extraordinary. None of the highest-ranking active-duty officers appeared in Pittsburgh, with General of the Army Grant providing the model. When Dudley invited the lieutenant general to the convention, his aide Colonel Adam Badeau answered on Grant's direction one week before it began: "He instructs me to say it is contrary to his habit and to his convictions of duty to attend political meetings of any character whatever, and that he sees with regret the action of any officer of the army taking a conspicuous part in the political dissensions of the day."[82]

The absences of Lieutenant General Sherman and ranking Major Generals Halleck, Meade, Sheridan, and Thomas were thus noticeable but not surprising. John Logan had been the choice to preside over the convention, but was unable to attend, and Jacob Cox took his place;[83] both were inactive major generals.

There were no such scruples regarding the call to, nor attendance at, the Cleveland Convention. The most famous active-duty officer to participate was George A. Custer, and true to his nature, he addressed the matter head-on. The *Lockport Daily Journal* reported that the "gallant and eccentric" cavalryman said in a clear allusion to Grant's position that "there were some who entertained the opinion that a soldier still in the army had no right to discuss political affair; but he had no doubt that if some in the army would discuss political affairs according to the views of those people, there would be no objection made. He intended to act and think as he pleased.'"[84] The New York State paper then stated its own position on the issue: "It would appear from it, that Custar [*sic*] believes Grant to differ with him as to the propriety of *anybody's* joining in this crusade against Union men, so manifestly improper in the beginning, and already proved so utter a failure."[85]

Union veterans clearly didn't need high-ranking officers to tell them how or what to think, or the meaning of their sacrifice. The Soldiers' and Sailors' National Union League was an enlisted man's organization in both leadership and composition, and the Pittsburgh Convention would never have taken place without its instigation and efforts. In turn, Northern veterans were electrified by calls to the Cleveland and Pittsburgh Conventions, with marked activity on local and state levels (including conventions of their own) and tremendous support for the league coming from enlisted ex-servicemen.

What occurred in upstate New York just days before the Pittsburgh conclave was indicative of where Union veterans stood on the most important issue facing postwar America. As reported in the September 24, 1866, *Albany Evening Journal*, "The Democrats called a Soldiers' Convention in Ulster county, and just *seven* attended. At the Republican Union Soldiers' Convention, at the same place, *a thousand* were present."[86]

With little more than one month's notice and subsequent planning, tens of thousands of Union veterans from the rank and file descended upon Pittsburgh in a display of unprecedented political activism that had a major influence on public opinion. Collectively they demonstrated that the measure of a citizen soldier's, sailor's, or marine's time spent in uniform is not solely defined by their deeds in combat—the impact of military service on one's country in peace can be just as crucial, if not more.

In the immediate postwar period, white Northern veterans as a group provided desperately needed moral leadership, whether by actively supporting passage of the Fourteenth Amendment, endorsing Reconstruction as envisioned by the Republican Congress and opposing Johnson's policy, or working in the Freedmen's Bureau as VRC or regular army officers. They exploded the delusional belief that only those who had avoided military service or profiteered from the war supported congressional Reconstruction, black suffrage, or equal rights. Union ex-servicemen also separated respect for the courage of Confederate veterans in battle from strong condemnation of their civilian actions regarding blacks and loyal white citizens in the postwar South.

In recoiling from Union officers' cheering for a commander implicated in one of the war's worst atrocities against African American troops, and deriding the Cleveland Convention's trust that Forrest and his colleagues would ensure protection of the freed peoples' rights, white Northern veterans emphatically answered the question posed by William Hannibal Thomas in September 1865.

Two specific actions that took place at the Pittsburgh Convention further reinforce how far the men of the Union had come in their attitudes toward African Americans. One of the Kansas delegates, a Captain Hinton, offered a resolution declaring "that in justice alike to the living and to the dead, it is our duty to demand at all times the full enfranchisement of those who helped to fight the battle of the Union, and who by the valor and sacrifices of nearly 200,000 men of this race have given ample proof of their capacity to citizenship."

Soon after, a dispatch was read to the convention from Missouri delegates who had been unable to reach Pittsburgh due to "impassible condition of the railroads" in St. Louis. After assuring everyone of their "warm and most earnest support in any measure" that might be adopted in support of Congress, they asked those present "to go further": "We want to fight the political battle that is now being fought on a platform that at least gives to all our comrades, whether white or black the right to the ballot, we ask this as an act of justice to the memory of the gallant colored soldiers who went down in death at Pillow, Wagner, Marshall, and a hundred other hard contested fields, in order that the nation might live."[87]

Such statements and other evidence presented so far testify to the forethought of Frederick Douglass concerning black citizenship. By the same token, they illuminate flaws of perception in the Du Bois statement that heads this chapter. At least for Northern soldiers and sailors, killing other human beings is not what made white men consider adult male African Americans as men for the first time. Proud of their own capabilities as men of war, white veterans appreciated what black soldiers had endured just to serve in the armies of the Union, and their considerable skill, persistence, and bravery when finally given the chance to fight. Black veterans thus received the respect they had earned as fellow professionals from many of their white comrades in arms. Under this solidarity, Union veterans would not tolerate African American troops stationed in the South being abused or worse, as in Memphis, and in the turbulent decades to follow.

That this transformative phenomenon continues in modern times is embodied by Karl Marlantes, who in 2017 stated that he served in Vietnam with an amalgamation of men of various races and ethnicities who needed to rely on one another to survive. The former Marine lieutenant saw this experience as "a racial crucible that played an enormous, if often unappreciated, role in moving America toward real integration."[88]

L. Edwin Dudley told the Pittsburgh Convention that he had "heard it stated less than a month ago that the soldiers of the country were against the policy of Mr. Johnson. My own opinion coincided with that, and my humble efforts of late have been directed to the securing an expression of opinion from the soldiers of the Republic on these questions."[89] His goal was reached in spades in Western Pennsylvania, as was "assist[ing] us in swelling majorities which are certain to be given for all our standard bearers in all the loyal States over those men whom we have defeated in the field and who seek to triumph over us at the polls this fall."[90]

The Pittsburgh Convention, along with the earlier Radical Convention in Philadelphia, would indeed be critical to the election, which according to Foner had become "More than anything else . . . a referendum on the Fourteenth Amendment." The ensuing "disastrous defeat" at the polls for Andrew Johnson not only sustained but strengthened Republican control of Congress, which now could easily defeat a presidential veto.[91] With absolute support for the amendment advocated at both conventions, the activism of tens of thousands of Union veterans and attendant publicity certainly played a role in the results of the vital midterm election.

This initial examination of the Freedmen's Bureau and Reconstruction is concluded with William Hannibal Thomas's "Letter from the Fifth Regiment U.S.C.T." that was published in the November 1865 issue of the *Christian Recorder*:

> *We now turn . . . to the speech of Ex-Gov. Todd [sic], on the reception of the regiment at the capital . . . after having witnessed the undaunted bravery of these troops,—their soldierly bearing and thorough discipline in a hundred instances, he very emphatically says, 'I am opposed to giving the elective franchise to these men.' These are the men whom he very willingly accepted as soldiers. Then they were good enough to go in the place of white men, and thus avoid having a draft. But according to the governor's theory, they were not good enough to vote with the white man.*

> *What absurdity! There is a day of retribution coming, when justice will be meted out to these demagogues and political aspirants. A Cromwell will be found who will secure eternal justice to our oppressed race.*[92]

Thomas proposed that an Executive Committee be formed from individuals in the Fifth and Twenty-Seventh USCT regiments "*who have displayed such decided ministrative abilities on the field of battle*" in order to form an association for black veterans. He then made suggestions for the committee's membership, which included Robert A. Pinn of the Left-Armed Corps and his fellow Medal of Honor awardee, Sergeant Milton M. Holland, and reported that "*upon consultation, these gentlemen are willing to act upon this suggestion.*"[93] Thomas expressed the hope that the organization "*will include all the colored soldiers who have gone out from Ohio in the different branches of the service . . .* [and would] *connect us in the bonds of friendship and grace, and be a guiding star to our future advancement in the cause of liberty and justice.*"[94] There is no evidence such an association was formed, but Robert Pinn and other African American veterans would have a major impact on the cause of equality in the years to come.

Major General of Volunteers John M. Palmer.

CHAPTER 3

Reconstruction and African American Equality

Our work is political also in the sense that we vigorously encourage the veterans to participate in the democratic political life of the country that they fought for.

—JONATHAN SHAY, MD, PhD, *ODYSSEUS IN AMERICA: COMBAT TRAUMA AND THE TRIALS OF HOMECOMING*[1]

I have no regrets that I served my country five years in good faith coming out with only one arm. . . . I look back on my military life with the satisfaction of . . . a duty performed for . . . country, which . . . I love better now than before the war . . . [that] cost life and money in large amounts, but the general good that will grow out of it, in future times, will in the end pay the country as a nation.

—James T. Bicknell, Second Lieutenant, Twenty-Second Massachusetts and Second Battalion, VRC[2]

John M. Palmer had a lot in common with his friend Abraham Lincoln. Both were born poor in Kentucky to a father who detested slavery. After his family relocated to Illinois, Palmer read for the law, and was admitted to the bar in 1839. But unlike his Whig colleague, Palmer joined the Democrats and in 1851 was elected to the State Senate. In 1856 they both switched to the new Republican party, and Palmer placed Lincoln's name in nomination for vice president at the National Convention. Having played a role in creating the victorious Republican ticket in 1860, he met with the president-elect as a delegate to the Peace Convention in February 1861. Palmer told Lincoln that "'I would have to go into the army, in order to prove, after voting for the proposed amendments to the constitution, that I was a sincere anti-slavery man.'"[3]

Upon returning to Carlinville, he was elected colonel of what became the Fourteenth Illinois. Fighting in the West, he was promoted to brigadier general in December 1861, and after running a post in Missouri, became a division leader under Major General John Pope. Promoted to brigade command in the Army of the Mississippi and fighting to the outskirts of Corinth, Palmer fell desperately ill with pneumonia on May 13, 1862, and had to be evacuated. Reaching home in early June, he convalesced until late August.[4]

Among those accompanying Palmer on the arduous trip was his body servant, Martin Taylor, who had been born into slavery. When the general left to rejoin his brigade, Taylor remained with Palmer's family as a house worker. With the state's "black laws" still in effect but generally not imposed, "southern sympathizers" among his neighbors decided to pursue enforcement by organizing a party "to mob the lad." As further described by the Illinois State Historical Society, "The horsemen called at the Palmer home just at day break, but were met at the door by the general's brave daughter, Betty . . . who flourished a pistol and threatened to shoot the first one who entered the house. After a parley the men withdrew and the daughter on searching for the lad found him trembling with fear where he had hidden under the bed in his room."[5]

This did not end with Betty Palmer's act of conscience. In December 1862, her father was indicted in absentia by a Macoupin County (IL) grand jury for "'bringing a negro slave, Martin Taylor,' into the State of Missouri."[6] By then he had retaken divisional command and joined the army of Major General Don Carlos Buell. Palmer's performance at Stone River led to his promotion to Major General of Volunteers, and assignment to occupy Chattanooga. From there he and his men came to the support of Major General George Thomas's beleaguered troops at Chickamauga. After that bitter defeat, Palmer took command of the

Fourteenth Army Corps in late 1863, leading them through the Atlanta campaign until relieved at his personal request in August 1864.[7]

While Palmer had been fighting Rebel armies, his indictment had undergone multiple continuances and "been stricken from the docket, 'with leave to reinstate.'" In the meantime, Martin Taylor had enlisted in the Third USC Heavy Artillery, and after a year of service had returned to Carlinville permanently. When Palmer came home, he insisted on the case being tried—the indictment was reinstated, and trial began December 17, 1864.[8]

In his statement to the jury, Palmer said that unlike Taylor, he didn't know whether the man had been enslaved, "but, unfortunately, we had a [state] statute that prohibited a negro from testifying against a white person. I told them that Martin Taylor was in town, was an honest man, and would tell the truth, and that such a law should be repealed. . . . I proved in addition that I had come home from the army very sick, and that Taylor, with others, had brought me into the state . . . the whole jury found me 'not guilty.'"[9]

Vindicated, Palmer was personally chosen by Lincoln to command the newly created department of their birthplace. Discussing the appointment while being shaved, the president promised his old friend: "'Go to Kentucky, keep your temper, do as you please, and I will sustain you.'" The next time Palmer saw Lincoln was at his funeral, almost three months after the general's tenure in the Bluegrass State had begun.[10]

Once there, Palmer made every effort to protect the rights of African Americans within the limits of current laws and his own sense of justice. In the process, he became the only officer in American military history to be indicted twice for essentially the same "crime," this time "feloniously . . . aid[ing] and assist[ing] a slave named Ellen, a female slave, in an attempt to make her escape from her owner." His indictment subsequently quashed on the basis of Kentucky having ratified the Thirteenth Amendment, Palmer continued to lead the department headquartered in Louisville.

On January 4, 1866, he sent Illinois Senator Lyman Trumbull a copy of a petition signed by the city's black population that he had drafted as a "modest demand for the recognition of the essential rights of the freed people" from the Kentucky legislature. His accompanying letter to the Thirteenth Amendment's coauthor was an eloquent expression of the meaning of freedom; what American citizens, whatever their race, had a right to expect from their government; and the great challenge of Reconstruction:

> [The federal government] has discharged this duty so far through the agency of the military officers and the freedman's bureau, and it may and ought to continue to do so in some effective way until the state governments comprehend them within, and give them the protection of, their general political system. I think a law of congress declaring them to be citizens of the United States, would be a long step in the right direction. . . . The state governments do not govern and protect them as free men, and the states are forbidden by the constitution of the United States to govern them as slaves. They have a natural right resulting from their relations to the government as subjects, or citizens, to demand the benefit of the government, and their interests, as I maintain, are protected by the constitutional guarantee.[11]

Palmer resigned both his commission and command effective April 1, 1866. He left four pending civil lawsuits totaling $70,000 in damage claims, with two of the cases concerning runaway slaves and the others false imprisonment (one involving "numerous outrages perpetrated at will upon negroes in all parts of the states").[12] In November 1866, the Kentucky Court of Appeals handed down a decision "equivalent to a declaration" that Palmer's aiding a fugitive slave's escape was a felony.[13] Two years later he was elected governor of Illinois in a landslide, taking office on January 11, 1869.[14]

John M. Palmer's saga vividly illustrates what America faced in the immediate postwar years and early Reconstruction, but there is even more to the story. In an eerie parallel, Captain Dorus E. Bates of the Second Illinois Cavalry and Left-Armed Corps also owed a great debt to a caring African American. Severely wounded at Vicksburg in May 1863, the essentially helpless officer was carried off the field by a young black man named Rosecrans. Hired by Bates as a servant, he closely attended to the furloughed captain on their trek to Illinois, including applying cold water to the stump of his right arm.[15]

Recuperating in the Pike County town of Pittsfield, Bates experienced as antagonistic a reception to his aide as had Palmer in Carlinville, with another chilling precedent striking closer to home. As recounted by A. S. Chapman, "A short time before this, R. B. Hatch of Griggsville in the same county had been compelled by the force of public sentiment to deport a negro whom he had brought back from the army."[16]

Neither intimidated nor concerned about the feelings of racists, Bates "aroused hostile comment by driving about the region with the colored boy as a driver, till he finally received warning from a committee of citizens to get the boy out of the country."[17] His response to the threat, or rather what a famous writer ascribed to him, would become legendary.

"BANTY TIM"

John G. Nicolay was born in Bavaria, and came to Pittsfield in his teens after his parents died. Through hard work and intelligence, he rapidly rose from printer to publisher, editor, and owner of the Pike County *Free Press*. Having gained statewide political stature through his newspaper, he joined Secretary of State Charles Hatch's office in Springfield and gave up the *Press*. It was at the state capital that he met Abraham Lincoln, who named Nicolay as private secretary during his presidential campaign, and also tabbed John Hay as executive clerk on Nicolay's recommendation.[18]

After an engagement lasting fourteen years, Nicolay married Bates's sister Therena in fall 1865. Not only had John Hay spent time in Pittsfield with his lawyer uncle Milton, who left for Springfield to enter practice with Lincoln, but he and Nicolay were close friends. Hay thus knew Captain Bates and was informed about his exploits during wartime.[19]

In April 1871, John Hay published his "Pike County Ballads" in *Harper's Weekly*, with "Banty Tim" causing an immediate sensation. Within weeks it was reprinted across the nation,[20] and would serve as a litmus test about racial attitudes for decades. While there are elements of Hatch's and particularly Palmer's troubles (of which Hay undoubtedly was aware) in the poem, it is generally accepted that Bates was the leading model for the ballad's Tilmon Joy:[21]

BANTY TIM.

(Remarks of Sergeant Tilmon Joy to the White Man's
    Committee of Spunky Point, Illinois)

I reckon I get your drift, gents—
    You 'low the boy sha'n't stay;
This is a white man's country;
    You're Dimocrats, you say:
And whereas, and seein', and wherefore,
    The times bein' all out o' j'int,
The nigger has got to mosey
    From the limits o' Spunky P'int.

Le's reason the thing a minute;
    I'm an old-fashioned Dimocrat too,
Though I laid my politics out o' the way
    For to keep till the war was through.
But I come back here, allowin'
    To vote as I used to do,
Though it gravels me like the devil to train
    Along o' sich fools as you.

Now dog my cats ef I kin see,
    In all the light of the day,
What you've got to do with the question
    Ef Tim shill go or stay.
And furder than that I give notice,
    Ef one of you tetches the boy,
He kin check his trunks to a warmer clime
    Then he'll find in Illanoy.

Why blame your hearts, jest hear me!
    You know that ungodly day

When our left struck Vicksburg Heights, how ripped
    And torn and tattered we lay,
When the rest retreated I staid behind,
    Fur reasons sufficient to me,—
With a rib caved in, and a leg on a strike,
    I sprawled on that damned glacee.

Lord! how the hot sun went for us,
    And br'iled and blistered and burned!
How the Rebel bullets whizzed round us
    When a cuss in his death-grip turned!
Till along towards dusk I seen a thing
    I could n't believe for a spell:
That nigger—that Tim—was a-crawlin' to me
    Through that fire-proof, gilt-edged hell!

The Rebels seen him as quick as me,
    And the bullets buzzed like bees;
But he jumped for me, and shouldered me,
    Though a shot brought him once to his knees;
But he staggered up, and packed me off,
    With a dozen stumbles and falls,
Till safe in our lines he drapped us both,
    His black hide riddled with balls.

So, my gentle gazelles, thar's my answer,
    And here stays Banty Tim:
He trumped Death's ace for me that day,
    And I'm not goin' back on him!
You may rezoloot till the cows come home,
    But ef one of you tetches the boy,
He'll wrastle his hash to-night in hell,
    Or my name's not Tilmon Joy![22]

How close was the poem to what actually happened with Bates and
Rosecrans? According to the *Quincy* (Illinois) *Herald* of August 7, 1890,
"It is probable that Bates did not use this language exactly, but it was

to the same effect, with the result that the negro remained in Pittsfield unmolested until he returned with his master to the South."[23]

One of the earliest and most severe criticisms of "Banty Tim" originated from another Midwestern state. On April 12, 1871, the *Urbana* (Ohio) *Union* opined that its "writer seems to have imbibed all the vulgarity and blasphemy of the vulgar and blasphemous man for whom he formerly acted as Private Secretary." Calling Hay a "dish-water doggerelist," it berated "this sort of poetry—if bad grammar and blackguardism could be called poetry" as "break[ing] down that delicacy of thought, and feeling, and language, which constitute the refinement and dignity of man."[24] The newspaper's touching concern for America's children came next: "How can we expect our youth to eschew ribaldry and profanity, when our magazines, and newspapers, the most potent of all teachers, countenance the coarsest oaths and obscenity?"[25]

Then the *Union* finally addressed the real bone of contention: "We overlook the slur upon the Democratic party, viz. that it is composed of negro-haters. That organization is not the foe of any race. It denounces the XVth Amendment, not because that measure confers the ballot upon a people with black skins and kinky hair, but because the manner of its adoption was adverse to the Constitution."[26]

Four days earlier the *Syracuse Journal* had reprinted "Banty Tim," noting its "merits and faults—considerable rubbish and a little poetical thought."[27] Most of the newspapers that printed the poem over the next weeks to months did so without commentary, tacitly indicating approval of its content. One example was the *Waverly* (New York) *Advocate* on June 23, its masthead statement of "One Constitution, One Country, One Destiny" quite eloquent on its own.[28]

For those not shocked by Hay's "vulgarity," the dead seriousness of his work's subject matter was apparent. On August 14 the *New York Daily Tribune* included an appraisal of the "Pike County Ballads" by the *London Spectator*. Noting "Banty Tim" in particular, the reviewer realized what lay behind the vernacular: "But the striking feature of these ballads is not only in the grim familiarity of their treatment of guilt, danger, judgment, death, and the supernatural world; they are full of brief, graphic touches, marvelously vivid and picturesque."[29]

Union veterans were prominent among those who "got it." Public recitations of "Banty Tim" began within a few months of its publication, such as that delivered by a member of the Ilion, New York Chismore Grand Army of the Republic Post at their September 1871 meeting.[30] The ballad would be heard at various gatherings for years to come, including an 1884 high school commencement in Wellington, Ohio.[31]

A bit of "doggerel" not only captivated the nation, but also captured its mood at a critical point in history. The issues raised by "Banty Tim," its content, the circumstances surrounding the poem's origin, and the accompanying sectional response reveal the divisions between North and South, president and Congress, white and black that had to be addressed if Reconstruction was to succeed.

One sentence from the December 7, 1867, edition of the *Nashville Union and Dispatch* encapsulates the fear, uncertainty, and yet potential progress of the times, and involves an inspiration for Hay's ballad: "It is said that General John M. Palmer, who will probably be Republican candidate for Governor of Illinois, at the next election, will go into the canvass prepared to stump the State in favor of negro suffrage."[32] The black vote, and all it entailed, would be a major element in the struggle for America's postwar soul.

No one knew that better than Northern soldiers and sailors, ex- or still in uniform. Their support for the Thirteenth and Fourteenth Amendments had been crucial, but the latter was not adopted until July 1868, and did not establish black voting rights.[33] Another amendment to the Constitution was needed for universal male black suffrage—if Union veterans maintained their advocacy for African Americans, it would enhance efforts to ensure ratification by the states.

WHITE AND BLACK UNION VETERANS ENDORSE AFRICAN AMERICAN VOTING RIGHTS

On December 3, 1866, in the nation's capital, a huge procession greeted the returning Republican members of Congress. The numerous organizations represented included the Soldiers' and Sailors' National Union League, National Equal Suffrage Association, and Colored Soldiers' and Sailors' League. Over half of the 6,000 people were African American, and the third point that House Speaker Schuyler Colfax declared "settled beyond all controversy" was "That no person shall be disfranchised on account of race."[34]

In January 1867, Philadelphia hosted the Soldiers' and Sailors' Convention, where black veterans met in response to a resolution passed by the Colored Soldiers' and Sailors' League in Washington on September 1, 1866, eight months after the organization was formed. The League was composed of veterans who "believe[d] that in sustaining the Union with the musket, have now their right to the ballot." The Convention was in full agreement, and planned to "demand for the colored soldiers and sailors . . . equality of rights with their white brethren in arms" and to enlist "influential colored men in different portions of the country" for the fight.[35]

When the African American ex-servicemen reassembled the next day, one of their major resolutions concerned the vote, and its relation to the very essence of democracy. Describing "self-government . . . exercised through the elective franchise" as "the natural and just right of every American," they held that to deprive any man of the ability to "exercise . . . this right is a blasphemous denial of the divine principles upon which just governments are founded."[36]

Proud of their collective military service, the convention also insisted that promotion of deserving active duty "soldiers and seamen" not be barred on the basis of color. Union servicemen who had fought Confederates in their front and Northern bigotry in their rear, they were all too aware of the dangers faced by newly freed blacks in the South. As a result, it was demanded that they "be furnished with the means of protecting themselves by Congress and the President."[37]

The struggle for equality needed to be fought on both sides of the Mason-Dixon line by white and black veterans alike. As shown during the midterm campaigns and elections of 1866, no group in America had greater moral authority, and they were gaining political know-how and power upon which the Republican Congress drew. Yet, the situation concerning suffrage was vexing, particularly in the North, as *The Soldier's Friend* made evident in its July 1868 update as to who could cast a ballot, and where:

MICHIGAN—Every white male citizen.

Maine—Every male citizen.

New Hampshire—Every male inhabitant.

Vermont—Every man.

Massachusetts—Every male citizen.

Rhode Island—Every male citizen.

Connecticut, Indiana, Illinois, Missouri, Iowa, New-Jersey, Ohio, California, Oregon, Nevada, West-Virginia, and Colorado—Every white male citizen.

New-York—Every male citizen, but colored men are required to own $250 worth of taxable property.

Pennsylvania—Every white freeman.

Wisconsin—Every male person.

Minnesota—Every male person.

Kansas—Every white male adult.

Delaware—Every free white male citizen.

Maryland—Every free white male citizen.

Tennessee—Every free white man formerly, but now Negroes vote.

In those States which were engaged in rebellion, and which are governed by the reconstruction laws, Negroes are allowed to vote and hold office.[38]

Three years after Appomattox, neither free man of color in the Left-Armed Corps could vote. A Medal of Honor and right arm ruined by a Rebel bullet did not earn Robert Pinn a ballot in Ohio; his old Fifth USCT compatriot, William H. Thomas, fared no better in Pennsylvania. The same held for Privates John H. Holley (Thirty-Eighth USCT) and John Henry Pinckney (Fourth USCT), both formerly enslaved in Maryland, and whose entries in the autograph books Wm. O. Bourne had kept at Central Park Hospital were written by a white comrade. The one-legged Pinckney was now literate, but still denied the elective franchise in their home state, while it is unlikely that the similarly maimed Holley had the required property to vote in his adopted New York City.[39]

Yet, if they lived in the South, all four could vote and serve in an elected position. Under the Reconstruction Act passed by Congress in 1867, and three subsequent bills to which *The Soldier's Friend* alluded, ten former Confederate states excepting Tennessee (already readmitted after ratifying the Fourteenth Amendment) had been divided into five military districts under a general leading a provisional government. As a requirement for readmission to the Union, each state had to enact a constitution approved by its registered voters that granted suffrage to black men, and ratify the Fourteenth Amendment.[40]

The Freedmen's Bureau and US Army units stood ready to protect the rights of Southern African Americans but had no jurisdiction in the North. In a further cruel irony, many active-duty black soldiers attempting to ensure free elections in the former Confederacy enjoyed no such privileges in their own states. Enactment and ratification of the eventual Fifteenth Amendment was imperative, but existing laws (such as dreaded "black codes") and customs also had to be changed if racial equality was to take hold throughout the United States. The Civil War had been prosecuted successfully from the military standpoint—now it was time to win hearts and minds.

THE GRAND ARMY OF THE REPUBLIC

While two Northern military associations were formed during the war, the largest, most influential, and longest-lived began in April 1866. The first Post of the Grand Army of the Republic (GAR) was founded in Decatur, Illinois, under a Declaration of Principles that specified "preservation of the grand results of the war, the fruits of their [Union servicemen's] labor and toil, so as to benefit the deserving and worthy." One month later, a GAR constitution provided its four-level organizational plan of post ("city, town, township, ward, or precinct"), district ("county"), department ("State"), and national organization. Each would have a commander, adjutant, and quartermaster, with only post officers specified as "presumably" elected.

In July an amendment to the constitution made provisions for more officers, with an assistant commander, surgeon-general, and chaplain at both national and department levels. Posts would have an "Assistant Post Commander, Post Surgeon, Post Chaplain, Officer of the Day and Officer of the Guard," all "elected annually at the last meeting in December."[41]

Within six months, departments had been established in Illinois, Wisconsin, Indiana, Iowa, and Minnesota, along with posts in Ohio, Missouri, Kentucky, Arkansas, District of Columbia, Massachusetts, New York, and Pennsylvania.

At Indianapolis in November, the first National Convention under elected president, Department of Illinois Commander John M. Palmer (the very same) further defined the GAR mission: "to maintain in civil life those great principles for which it stood in arms under the national flag . . . to vindicate everywhere, and at all times, the full and complete rights of every loyal American citizen, against all combinations of force or fraud that may attempt to deny or deprive them of such rights."

This was reiterated by a pledge to wield all legitimate "power and influence," as "individuals or . . . an association," to absolutely protect those who remained loyal in the country's "hour of its agony, in the rebellious States" despite "all manner of losses and injuries, persecutions by force and persecutions under color of law."[42]

The organization's constitution was also amended: "The maintenance of true allegiance to the United States of America, based upon paramount respect for, and fidelity to, the national constitution and laws, manifested by the discountenancing of whatever may tend to weaken loyalty, incite to insurrection, treason or rebellion, or in any manner impairs the efficiency and permanency of our free institutions, together with a defense of universal liberty, equal rights and justice to all men."

"Grand (afterward Department) Commander, Senior and Junior Vice-Grand Commanders" positions were instituted, along with representation at national encampments ("one representative at large from each Department, and one representative for each one thousand members therein"). While retained, districts would not be represented at department encampments, at which "one delegate for every 25 members of the several Posts therein" would be in attendance.

This inaugural meeting further established the GAR structure by electing officers of the national encampment, starting with commander in chief, senior vice–commander in chief, and junior vice–commander in chief, and a national council of administration—at the next national encampment, the district organizations were eliminated.[43]

Early in its existence, the critical issue of where the GAR stood politically came to a head. As Beath reported, in January 1868 the Second National Encampment at Philadelphia heatedly discussed (almost leading to "disruption") a proposed change to "the terms of the Declaration of Principles which would show the Order to be non-partisan." While "one side claim[ed] that the organization should be avowedly political in its objects," "the other, [just] as desirous of upholding 'the rights of the defenders of their country by all moral, social and political means in our control,'" was greatly concerned about a destructive effect of "partisanship" on the GAR, which they felt "could not be maintained while there was any ground for the popular belief that it was a secret organization."

As a result, it was ultimately agreed to add an amendment to the constitution stating that "this Association does not design to make nominations for office or to use its influence as a secret organization for partisan purposes"[44]—the GAR was officially apolitical, and would so insist.

However, its earlier statements could not have been clearer in ideology or intent with respect to Reconstruction. Predominantly white former Union soldiers, sailors, and marines had declared their full support for black suffrage and equality under the law, which would be defended as strongly as if they were still in uniform.

Newspapers in opposition wasted little time in expressing contempt for the new association, along with apparent, unspoken fear. In September 1866, the *Weekly Caucasian* of Lexington, Missouri, called the GAR "the latest dodge of the Radicals for bolstering up their sinking cause. It is a secret organization, into which they are endeavoring to entrap the soldiers. . . . It is simply a branch of the Union League . . . now reorganizing in opposition to the administration of Andrew Johnson."[45]

Ten months later the Republican *New York Tribune* accused the GAR membership of "propos[ing] to keep alive the wrath and bitterness of that dreadful time. They mean to control conventions to nominate men to office to perpetuate in our civil system the bitterness of war." The surprising article concluded with a denunciation of "this new secret association as out of sympathy with the true Republican party, and as inimical to the Constitution and the Union."[46]

Even more frightening to many Northern whites were free black men, particularly combat veterans, pressing for equality. Ex-slave turned whaler William H. Carney, who performed so courageously during the Fifty-Fourth Massachusetts's renowned assault on Fort Wagner that he would be awarded the Medal of Honor, embodied this obligation. In April 1867 he lectured in New York on "'Reconstruction and the Right of Suffrage'" and "advocated the rights of the colored race to the elective franchise, claiming that they had purchased that right by their action in the late war." Unlike the *New York Daily Tribune*, the *Brooklyn Daily Eagle* was dismissive, using the thin crowd to declare African Americans "more apathetic about this question of colored suffrage than are the white people themselves."[47]

Months later, the *Philadelphia Inquirer* clearly sought to allay concerns about black veteran activism. In November the paper stated that the Colored Soldiers' and Sailors' League's sole aim was "relief of widows and orphans of deceased comrades," and further assured its (presumably white) readership that "Neither resistance to law, nor intimidation of the community in which they reside is the object of the brotherhood." Oliver O. Howard's brother Charles, a brigadier general and the Freedmen's Bureau Commissioner's chief of staff, reportedly vouched for the League's "integrity of purpose and . . . patriotic services"; given this assertion, "no fears need be entertained that this harmless Society will be engaged in illegal plots."[48]

In Ohio, the *Athens Messenger*, one month earlier, had provided a classic example of denigration being used to assuage rising trepidation: "Judge Thurman, Democratic candidate for Governor of Ohio, in a speech recently in Portsmouth, took occasion to cast a slur on the colored troops as being of no service in the suppression of the rebellion.

The Judge was somewhat abashed by a colored veteran in the crowd, who retorted that he (Thurman) was too far from the front to decide upon the question."[49]

These reports are consistent with an observation made by Donald R. Shaffer: "Former soldiers who had been free before the Civil War were likely to react more quickly and vociferously throughout the post-war period to perceived assaults on their manhood. Besides being more likely to respond to racist affronts, they also tended to counter them in an organized fashion."[50]

The bigoted attack of a politician who never saw battle was one thing, but what about a famous, disabled Northern general? His longstanding antipathy toward African Americans perhaps even deeper after two years of Reconstruction, no issue enraged W. W. H. Davis more than voting rights. In August 1867, the *Republican Compiler* of Gettysburg reprinted an article Davis wrote for his *Doylestown Democrat* that it felt "every soldier [should] read." If they did, it would have been appalling to discover that one of their own believed the American people were the most "*deceived and swindled*" in history, with Union veterans the biggest patsies of all:

> *Have we got what we fought, and bled and suffered for? . . . Alas, no! . . . For all the blood and treasure we expended we have only the negro to show. We have got him at an enormous price, to be fed out of the public treasury and voted by the Bureau. He is to be made the ruler of the country, and the war has resulted in establishing eleven negro States in the South . . . [missing] . . . a vestige of republican government. . . . Military despotism prevails everywhere. . . . The negro with the ballot in his hands is the only remedy offered to the American people to cure the serious ills that afflict the body politic. . . . Ask for a restoration of the Union and the Constitution, and we are told to wait until the negro is secured in his rights.[51]*

On November 6, 1867, the *Lancaster* (Pennsylvania) *Intelligencer* stated it outright: "The great issue of to-day and of the Presidential election, will be the endorsement of these things [white disenfranchisement and black voting in the South]."[52] In full accord with Davis's views, the newspaper awaited "the verdict with increased confidence. The elections this fall have shown a reaction against the twin brothers, Radicalism and Treason, and we pray to God that 1868 may prove their eternal Waterloo.[53]

Referring to Napoleon's defeat was apt, as two warring veteran organizations formed for the 1866 midterms would influence the 1868 nominating conventions, campaigns, and election for president. In October 1867, the Conservative Soldiers' and Sailors' Union of Washington struck first, calling upon Northern ex-servicemen of like political views "to stand by the conservative elements as the only hope of the government, and to vote down negro suffrage and other radical issues."[54] The emergence of the GAR and its stated principles had likely influenced this announcement.

In February 1868, the Executive Committee appointed by the 1866 Cleveland Soldiers' Convention met and agreed to hold another convention of white soldiers and sailors "opposed to the revolutionary conduct of the Radical party" on July 4 in New York City in order "to take such action as may be considered for the public good."[55] The location and timing coincided with the Democratic National Convention, but the declaration initially did not receive much publicity.

Given what was taking place in Washington, the lack of notice was understandable. Due to conflicting views on Reconstruction, the Republican-controlled Congress and President Andrew Johnson had been at loggerheads throughout his tempestuous term. As Foner explained, "Congress had enjoined the army to carry out a policy its commander-in-chief resolutely opposed." The legislature skirted the issue through its 1867 mandate that all military orders had to come through Grant as general of the army. But then Johnson suspended Secretary of War Stanton in August while Congress was in recess and replaced him with Grant. Emboldened, the president aggressively promoted Southern resistance, only to see Congress void Stanton's suspension under the Tenure of Office Act, with Grant resigning as secretary in response.[56]

When Johnson formally fired Stanton on February 21, 1868, two unprecedented events followed: Stanton barricaded himself into his office, and the president was impeached three days later. Of the eleven articles of impeachment drafted by the House, nine involved Stanton's ousting (thus violating the Tenure of Office Act) and/or accusations of Johnson's attempting to breach the requirement that all army orders be funneled through Grant.[57]

Johnson's trial in the Senate began on March 5, Chief Justice of the Supreme Court Salmon P. Chase presiding. The president was granted extra time to prepare a defense, and the initial enthusiasm and energy of his opposition waned to some degree as the proceedings continued over the next two months. In a surprising development, Johnson nominated Major General John Schofield to replace Stanton as secretary of war on April 25. Schofield was the only remaining military district commander originally appointed under the Reconstruction Acts, Johnson having replaced everyone else in an effort to weaken its enforcement.

As perceptively described by the *Green-Mountain Freeman* of Montpelier, Vermont, Schofield had other attributes. The newspaper felt the timing of his nomination was directly related to Johnson's ongoing trial, with Schofield known to be a friend of Grant's, "and probably unobjectionable in the judgment of a majority of Republican senators." As such, the *Freeman* wondered if the Senate would see this "proposed solution of the War Office imbroglio [as] an 'olive branch'" from "an apparently repentant President," and thus not convict him of the articles of impeachment. The newspaper also asked whether Johnson was admitting that he "had no right to remove or attempt to remove Secretary Stanton, as he did, two months ago?"[58]

Within two days the *Evening Star* of Washington reported that "Impeachment stock from some undefinable cause seems to have a slightly downward tendency to-day," accompanied by talk of "a break" among Republican senators. Public interest remained strong, and tickets to the trial's close on May 12 were in great demand. Four days later, the Senate voted—with thirty-five yeas and nineteen nays (seven Republicans among those deeming him not guilty), Johnson was acquitted by a single vote.[59]

The nation's newspapers reacted along party lines. In the president's home state, the *Nashville Union and Dispatch* lauded the dissenting

Republican senators for saving the GOP from the Radicals, along with the country. The *New York Tribune* pointed out that the Senate vote indicated Johnson "*was* guilty of a high misdemeanor"; while "conced[ing] the right and the duty of each Senator to vote . . . as he saw fit," it sharply noted that Republicans Fessenden, Grimes and Trumbull had done so "mistakenly."[60]

In an unanticipated twist, the Republican National Convention met in Chicago just a few days later. As the Conservative veterans had done, the Executive Committee chosen at the September 1866 Soldiers' and Sailors' Convention in Pittsburgh called for a convention in the Windy City to coincide with the Republican gathering. Five thousand Union ex-servicemen and one eagle marched in procession, Old Abe at its head. General John Logan was voted president, but declined due to his appointment as chair of the Republican Convention's Committee on Resolutions. By acclamation, his nomination of Wisconsin Governor Lucius Fairchild, former general and left-arm amputee, was carried.

In an assemblage characterized by the *Lowell Daily Courier* of Massachusetts as "marked by a good deal of radicalism," Ulysses S. Grant was endorsed for president by the soldiers and sailors. Opposition to Andrew Johnson's acquittal was proclaimed, and they severely criticized any senator who so voted. Other resolutions followed that were in close accord with the GAR's mission and constitution, including: "That in the maintenance of those principles which underlie our Government, and for which we fought during four years of war, we pledge our earnest and active support to the Republican party as the only political organization which in our judgment is true to the principles of loyalty, liberty and equality before the law."

Lest there be any question, General Joseph R. Hawley of Connecticut, president of the Republican National Convention, spoke eloquently in support of giving the government's protection to any Southerners wanting to re-enter the Union as "good citizens." As the *Courier* reported, Hawley then stated that "It made no difference whether that citizen was white or black, he was a citizen. Still he believed that if necessary 2,000,000 boys in blue would come again and protect him in his rights," which drew huge applause.[61]

The Soldiers' and Sailors' Convention delegation was presented to the Republican National Convention the next day. Fairchild introduced the unanimous resolution backing Grant, adding "if you will give us our comrade, as leader in the campaign of 1868, we will bear upon the enemies' works, as we did in the field in 1864." The communication was warmly received "from Republican soldiers and by a Republican Convention."[62]

To no one's surprise, Grant received the National Union Republican party's nomination for president, with House Speaker Colfax his running mate. When the two were formally presented with the convention's proceedings and notified of their nomination at the general's home on the evening of May 29, Hawley quoted Grant's desire to "'save in peace what we won in war.'" The convention's president continued with its statement of principles and purposes, which included: "We mean to make it a solemn and practical reality in the United States that 'all men are created equal,' . . . We believe that there can be no permanent peace save injustice and equal rights, the equality of all men before the law." The nominee expressed his thanks, and said he was "gratified with the harmony and unanimity which seemed to govern the deliberations of the Convention."[63]

Earlier that day, Grant received a committee from the Soldiers' and Sailors' Convention, who provided a copy of its platform in a formal presentation. Noting that he had not sought public office, the general of the army stated that "'it affords me great gratification that I have the support of those who were with me in the war. If I did not feel that I had the confidence of those, I would feel less desirous of accepting the position.'"[64]

THE ELECTION OF 1868 AND THE FIGHT OVER EQUALITY

Grant's nomination and the Republican platform were anathema to the opposition. The *Cambria Freeman* of Ebensburg, Pennsylvania, predicted disaster and defeat for Republicans, quoting the *Lancaster Intelligencer* about their platform and the dread subject of black voting:

> The party, and its nominees, . . . are pledged to negro supremacy in the Southern States. This is followed by a declaration in favor of leaving the question of suffrage to be decided by the people of the loyal States for themselves. . . . That the leaders of the

Republican party expect very soon to make voters of the negroes in every Northern State, if they succeed in electing Grant, no sensible man can doubt.

The truth is that with one-half the Union under negro domination the right to vote and hold office cannot be long denied to that race in any State.

[T]he white men of our section will not vote to subject their own race in the South to the domination of barbarian negroes, with the assurance that the negro equality in the North must speedily follow.[65]

The strong support Grant and black male suffrage had received from Union veterans made the situation even more problematic for the Democrats. Calls for a National Convention of Conservative Soldiers and Sailors to be held in July in New York were renewed, including Pennsylvania's from W. W. H. Davis and other high-ranking former officers.[66] The National Executive Committee then announced on June 4 that this convention would seek to "advise and cooperate with the Democratic party" in finding an appropriate presidential candidate.[67]

The very next day, the *Lowell Daily Courier* offered a sardonic, prophetic retort: "It is not stated whether the call includes rebel soldiers and sailors, but it is probably so, as these are all conservatives."[68]

Both the convention call and subsequent ones issued by veterans in individual Northern states were ridiculed. On June 9, the *National Republican* reported on General Charles F. Manderson's refused selection as a convention delegate: "'I can but ask myself of what mean thing I have been guilty that I should be the recipient of the praise implied by such appointment at the hands of men who have deserted the flag under which they once fought.'"[69] Two days later, the paper printed another withering piece: "The Providence *Journal* wants to know who is 'Colonel Lawrence, of Rhode Island', whose name is attached to the call for a conservative soldiers' and sailors' gathering in New York. Most of the signers of the call were never heard of until their names appeared attached to the convention call."[70]

An item that appeared in the *Albany Evening Journal*'s June 19 edition was the topper. According to the *Chicago Post*, one of the delegates from Ohio was "'General L. C. Hunt of Toledo, *who has been dead six months.*'"[71]

Adding fuel to the fire, the *World* in New York City boasted that the convention would feature "'not the prosperous sutlers and schemers of the national army, but the battle-scarred, war-worn campaigners of the East and West . . . familiar with the ringing volley and rattling charge of Southern rifles.'"[72] This ludicrous remark sparked even greater scrutiny of the National Executive Committee that proved disastrous for the Democrats.

On June 18, the *New York Tribune* reported that of the "eighteen generals and colonels" who signed the convention call, "but four are entitled to wear the rank they assume. The rest were either of a lower rank when they left the service early in the war, or had been discharged for the public good, or had never been in the service at all."[73]

Taunting the *World*, the *Tribune* wondered if "these conservative Generals" when compared to "supporters of Grant, like Sherman, Thomas, Sheridan, Schofield, Howard, Meade . . . and so many others, are carpet knights, prosperous sutlers, or schemers of the National Army?" The newspaper acidly asked, "Why rake up from . . . obscurity [these] discarded failures who pretended to be fighting in the cause of Republicanism, Union and Emancipation?" when such true proponents of Democratic principles as Lee, Beauregard, Johnston and Bragg were available.[74]

Five days later, the *Philadelphia Inquirer* reprinted the signers' list with their "*Real Rank and Service*" as reported by the *New York Commercial Advertiser*. Democratic newspapers had been forced to stop denigrating Republican Union veterans after army records showed several of the "'battle scarred, war-worn campaigners'" were hardly that. Five were either discharged or left the army in 1862 with no combat experience, and a sixth was a lieutenant in a nine-month regiment that was never in battle.[75]

The only substantial refutation came not from a Democratic newspaper, but the *Lowell Daily Courier*. While asserting "It is certain that, in a comparison of records, the soldiers who support Grant are infinitely superior to those who are against him . . . we cannot doubt that among those who are now democrats there are many, who, though not of the highest rank, have done good service in the field." It pinpointed one signatory, General Donahoe, as "Colonel of the Tenth New Hampshire, that he was severely wounded at Fort Harrison, and that he was brevetted Brigadier for gallant conduct in the field. Let every soldier have his due."[76]

Less than a week before the convention, the *Albany Evening Journal* published a last exposé about delegates named at the Kingston, New York, convention, whom they regarded as "fairly representative of the bulk of the Omnibus load of 'Democratic soldiers.'" Three captains and three lieutenants had been on "'a three months' picnic in Maryland in the Spring of 1861'" before returning home; another captain "'resigned before [his regiment] went into service,'" as had a surgeon; three other lieutenants left the service respectively under questionable circumstances, after just three months, and prematurely due to health reasons; and a Democratic New York Assembly member had been "'in three months' service and [the] bounty business.'"[77]

The Democrats had no one but themselves to blame for the fiasco. *The Western New-Yorker* noted that any Union soldier "has a perfect right to vote with and for the men who shot at him in front and reviled him in the rear." However, "because a few soldiers can be found who pursue this utterly illogical course, it does not follow that the soldiers who vote as they shot should be maligned by the Copperhead press. But as this has been done, comparisons of names and services inevitably follow."[78]

Undeterred, Conservative soldiers and sailors prepared to meet in New York City. Now self-identified as "White Boys in Blue," a resolution adopted by the Pennsylvania Convention that chose its delegates well-expressed the faction's overall viewpoint. Focusing solely on the Freedmen's Bureau and the nation's "tax-burdened white citizens," they demanded the bureau's immediate elimination due to "its favoritism to a race which should be taught, as a necessary lesson of freedom, that industry and self-reliance can alone secure their elevation" and "discrimination against the poor of our own race and color." Calling the vital agency a "heavy and constant drain upon the national treasury," the resolution insisted that it was being used by "political adventurers" desirous of "prosper[ing] upon the miseries engendered by oppression."[79]

Two thousand delegates to the Conservative Soldiers' and Sailors' Convention assembled at the Cooper Institute on July 6. Its committee, chaired by Major General Henry W. Slocum, ascended to the Democratic National Convention stage and was presented to Major General William B. Franklin, representing "the conservative soldiers and sailors of our country."

Colonel James R. O'Beirne then gave an address that "arraign[ed] the Republican party" for "destroying the equality of the States," its efforts on behalf of black suffrage and impeachment, "its alleged injustice to the loyal men of the South, who have always been true to the Union," "unjust favor[ing] . . . ex-rebels who have seen fit to aid them politically," and illegally denying Johnson's "constitutional power over the army" while "enabling Gen. Grant to control the southern elections through force and fraud."[80]

Amidst the boilerplate rhetoric was a statement that both encapsulated the Democrats' prime objection to congressional Reconstruction and underscored the Republicans' greatest vulnerability: "The party now in power . . . has forced the Southern States to submit to have their Constitutions and laws framed by ignorant negroes just freed from servitude, while at the north it has denied the negroes, although comparatively educated, the right of suffrage."[81]

When O'Beirne was done, General Thomas Ewing Jr. of Ohio spoke as one of the committee members. Deploring "the dogmas of negro suffrage" and "white disfranchisement," he expressed their strong desire for association with "thousands against whom we fought during the war," as opposed to Republicans, including other Union veterans. Since their convening, he and his comrades "had the pleasure of friendly intercourse with many of the most prominent of the Generals of the Confederate army." After comparing views "as to the present and future policy of this Government" with these "men of honor" and finding agreement, "we will take them by the hand as brothers." Ewing and the Soldiers' and Sailors' Convention then received three cheers.[82]

Over one hundred Rebel officers were delegates to the Democratic Convention, including Generals Wade Hampton (South Carolina), William Preston (Kentucky), and E. Barksdale (Mississippi) of the Platform Committee.[83] Union veterans and Republicans overall were incensed by their Conservative brethren expressing solidarity with former high-ranking Confederate servicemen and government officials, many of whom, like Hampton, had not been pardoned and could not vote in the upcoming election.[84]

It was a situation that bordered on the surreal. The *Schoharie Union* of New York pointed out that the national debt and resultant elevated revenues were mainly due to the Confederacy, yet Rebel officers were contributors to "the Democratic platform which denounces the taxes they made necessary." As it said "'our soldiers and sailors who carried the flag of our country to victory against a gallant and determined foe must ever be gratefully remembered,'" the newspaper wondered as to "*which* soldiers and sailors" and "*which* flag" the platform referred, given that "the convention that puts forth this sentiment was about half Northern copperheads and half Southern Rebels."[85]

The deadlocked Democrats had eventually nominated convention chairman, former New York governor and unannounced candidate Horatio Seymour, pairing him with ex-Union Major General Francis P. Blair Jr. of Missouri. The presidential nominee, aptly described as "a crafty opposer of the war" by one Republican newspaper, had been defeated for gubernatorial re-election in 1864. This loss was attributed in large part to his handling of the New York City draft riot. Despite eyewitness accounts that "Every negro who has been seen by the mob has been either murdered or horribly beaten," the Colored Orphan Asylum targeted for destruction and hundreds of whites "maltreated or killed," Seymour resisted imposition of martial law.

On its second day, he delivered a notorious address to an angry crowd at city hall, calling himself their "friend," said they had acted "under the influence of excitement and a feeling of supposed wrong," promised to protect *their* rights, and reiterated his opposition to the draft.[86]

Seymour's suspect record on race and congressional Reconstruction was trumped by Blair, whose speeches were so inflammatory and racist that the campaign became an anti-Reconstruction, anti–African American crusade for white supremacy. After a call to nullify the Reconstruction Acts, "compel the army to undo its usurpations at the South," and disband "the carpet-bag State governments" for those reorganized by whites, Seymour made it clear just what and whose "restoration" the election was about: "It is to prevent [white] people . . . [and] the government which they created for themselves and for their children . . . [from being] trodden under foot by an inferior and semi-barbarous race. In this contest we shall have the sympathy of every man who is worthy to belong to the white race. What civilized people on earth would refuse to associate themselves in all the rights and honors and dignities of their country such men as Lee and Johnston?"[87]

If their histories and such pronouncements were not burdensome enough, Seymour's nomination had been seconded and strongly supported by Clement L. Vallandigham, back from his Canadian exile, while Nathan Bedford Forrest cast the Tennessee delegation's vote for Blair.[88] Taking a complete view, the *Lowell Daily Courier* stated: "How a soldier who ever entered the service of his country from a sense of patriotism, can support Seymour and Blair passes our comprehension . . . We can appreciate the feelings under which they act, but cannot easily see how such feelings can survive the present revelations which are making concerning the treasonable intentions of the democratic leaders."[89] Their opponents felt the vulnerable Democratic ticket would be easy pickings. In late July, Brooklyn's Twelfth Ward Republicans passed a derisive resolution of thanks to Vallandigham and Forrest "for their unsurpassed efforts in the Democratic Convention in favor of the Republican nominees," namely "their successful nomination[s]" of Seymour and Frank Blair.[90]

Two weeks later, Major General and ex-Democrat Dan Sickles spoke in Saratoga, New York. An active-duty officer constrained to be apolitical ("My sympathies in the Presidential contest are [of] equal impartiality"), the former Congressman still made his views known with his usual flair: "I rejoiced in Gov. Seymour's nomination . . . and I shall rejoice with you most heartily in the election of Grant. I thank Vallandigham, Wade Hampton, General N. B. Forrest, and the *World* newspaper for the unsolicited aid they are giving to insure the election of Grant, and if they only continue in their present work, very little will remain for the Republicans to accomplish."[91]

No delegate was more controversial, nor generated greater backlash, than Nathan Bedford Forrest. Condemnation of his message to the 1866 Cleveland Convention paled in comparison to what ensued after his participation in the 1868 Democratic Convention. His perceived role in the Fort Pillow massacre set him apart from other ex-Confederate military leaders in conservative politics. They were criticized in the press, but only Forrest was consistently called a "butcher."[92] He also tended to make himself the focus of attention, such as a highly publicized oration that drew a lacerating response from the *Syracuse Journal* on August 12: "The rebel General N. B. Forrest, in a speech at Nashville, declared that he 'was willing to forgive all that had been done in the past.' That's rich, he is probably willing to forgive the defenceless negro soldiers of Fort Pillow for allowing themselves to be butchered under his orders."[93]

Forrest continued to be an issue throughout the campaign. In September, former major general and congressman Robert C. Schenck of Ohio, seeking re-election against old foe Vallandigham, invoked Fort Pillow and Forrest's important role at the Democratic Convention. He then asked, "What patriotic man who has stood at the back of the soldiers and helped to maintain them and encouraged them in their holy work, be he democrat or republican, can vote with and follow out the lead of such a man as that?" "'None!'" was the thunderous reply in Dayton.[94]

Then, the *Cincinnati Gazette* broke a story in which the General was accused of another war atrocity. According to an official army letter of April 21, 1864, Major General D. S. Stanley of the Fourth Army Corps reported that after the Union outpost at Murfreesboro, Tennessee, surrendered to Forrest in the summer of 1862, "A mulatto man, who was a servant to one of the officers of the Union forces, was brought to Forrest on horseback. The latter inquired of him, with many oaths, what he was doing there. The mulatto answered that he was a free man, and came out as a servant to an officer, naming the man. Forrest, who was on horseback, deliberately put his hand to his holster, drew out his pistol, and blew the man's brains out."[95]

Stanley's source was a "Rebel citizen of Middle Tennessee, a man of high standing in his community, who had it from his nephew, an Officer serving under Forrest." According to the general, the Confederate officer "denounced the act as one of cold-blooded murder, and declared he would never again serve under Forrest." Stanley believed the story was true beyond "a shadow of doubt, as it can be established any day by living witnesses."[96]

Stanley's letter had been previously published within three weeks of its drafting by the *Gallipolis Journal* in his home state of Ohio.[97] Four years later it received greater exposure, with the article run by other newspapers across the country.[98] Yet, there is no record of Forrest's ever being formally charged with a crime, or even being investigated.

THE RISE OF THE KU KLUX KLAN

Beyond Fort Pillow and the alleged murder at Murfreesboro, an even bigger issue made Forrest a Democratic liability: ascendance of the Ku Klux Klan. While it is unclear exactly when America's oldest terrorist organization was formed (at some point between late December 1865 and June 1866 is generally accepted), the founders were six relatively well-educated Confederate veterans and Pulaski, Tennessee, its birthplace. The Klan's early activities were pranks on other members in the spirit of a social club, but they soon turned to black victims for amusement. Dreading freedmen empowerment, including voting rights, by mid-1867 the Klan and similar groups had progressed to spreading terrible fear among Southern African Americans and their supporters. According to historian Wyn Craig Wade, the Klan had been "fully launched throughout Tennessee as a vigilante army" by the spring of 1868.[99]

Forrest had not been involved in the Klan's founding, but in 1867 he accepted the offer of its highest position, "Grand Wizard." Despite his assumption of leadership and the organization's spread to other Southern states that coincided with his appearances within their borders, Forrest continually denied any role in the Klan, and feigned qualms as to its actual existence. As for any question in this respect, in his pioneering study of the Klan's first five years, Stanley F. Horn concluded that

"General Nathan Bedford Forrest was, beyond any reasonable doubt, the Grand Wizard of the Invisible Empire."[100]

How powerful was the Klan during the presidential election? In late August 1868, Forrest told a reporter from the *Cincinnati Commercial* that the organization existed "not only in Tennessee but all over the South, and its numbers have not been exaggerated." He put membership in the Volunteer State at "over forty thousand," and "in all the Southern States about five hundred and fifty thousand men." After the story appeared, he wrote the *Commercial* with a list of corrections that included having stated the Tennessee Klan statistics were "reported."[101]

On September 2 (the day before his correction letter) Forrest granted a wide-ranging interview to the *New York Herald* at his Memphis office. Both he and the *Herald* acknowledged his great influence within the former Confederacy, despite holding no office and disclaiming any political ambitions. As he stated, "'whenever I have addressed the Southern people it was always at the earnest solicitation of men who had fought in the war and who believe that the generals of the late Confederate army are the faithful exponents of southern public opinion.'"[102]

Queried directly about the Klan, and his reported membership and leadership, the Grand Wizard's response was astounding and chilling:

"I do not belong to the Ku Klux, but . . . I know something about the Klan. I am well satisfied of one thing, and that is that it was not established to kill negroes and commit outrages on republicans. It was originated as an offset to the oath-bound, night-prowling Loyal League politically, and chiefly for the protection of white women from the horrible outrages of the scum of the negro population in certain counties. It was made a vigilance committee to hunt down criminals, black and white, whom the law allowed to slip through its not over careful fingers."

Forrest continued:

" . . . what the law failed to do the Ku Klux performed . . . I guarantee that the Ku Klux have never yet committed one of the

unprovoked outrages with which they are charged by the radicals
. . . Because men disguise themselves and do startling deeds that
does not make them Ku Kluxes. Don't consider me an apologist
for everything that may be done by the Klan, but fair play is a
jewel, and it is but right that the Klan should have its due."[103]

In 1915, D. W. Griffith would use the same odious justification for Klan
violence in his landmark film, *The Birth of a Nation*. Just like Forrest, he
portrayed the murderous Klan as upholders of the law, riding valiantly to
save Southern white womanhood from black predation.[104]

When asked about deprivation of freedmen's rights in Tennessee,
the general provided valuable insights into the mindset of many whites
in the Reconstructed South. First, he claimed that "'There is not the
slightest personal feeling against [the Negro] here, for the whites and
blacks South, having grown up together, do not understand that peculiar
distrust or dislike for one another that I have often noticed North.'"

Pursuing that theme, Forrest insisted that dependence on Southern
whites for work would inevitably lead African Americans to side with
them rather than Northerners come South who are "'of no earthly
benefit'" to blacks, as they are "'fast beginning to find it out.'" While
claiming that "'The white people of Tennessee do not wish to harm the
negro in any respect,'" he made it clear that their insistence on voting
for disfranchisement would backfire among "'those who are his best
friends'" by lessening the prewar, still existing "'good personal feeling,'"
and the "'negro being dependent upon the white man for his bread and
butter would naturally suffer.'"[105]

As for racial equality, Forrest articulated the fury of white supremacists who simply could not conceive of African Americans being "'on the
same [social] footing.'" Insisting that "'No one knows that better than
the negro himself,'" he put the blame solely on "'malicious councils of
bad men from the North'" who were self-servingly inducing blacks to
dream the unthinkable: "'It is bad enough as it is, for a white man to
be compelled to see his former slave, who was always taught to look up
to him as his protector and help, walk freely to the polls and deposit his
ballot, while he himself is deprived of the privilege. Men born and bred

North cannot conceive how hard this is to a southern white man. No man North would stand it, yet it is a subject of wonderment when the people murmur in the south.'"[106]

Forrest concluded with an observation about the "'natural'" inclination of African Americans, who "'if left to themselves . . . [would] side with their masters,'" using the example of his slaves who fled when freed during the war, but whom he claimed had all returned to him. As he was unable to offer them positions, many worked around Memphis, and would "'come to see and advise with me very often. Not one of them but will vote whatever way I desire.'" To emphasize the point, he reported that all but one of forty-two enslaved people who accompanied him to war in 1862 "'remained with me faithfully to the end.'"[107]

As we have already seen, and will to another degree in the next chapter, Forrest had a tenuous relationship with the truth, but there is no doubt about the veracity of his views toward African Americans, and how typical they were among Southern whites. All too real was a shared outrage about being denied the ballot while votes were being cast not by former captives of a racist system based on economic, social, and political self-interest, but perceived ungrateful longtime recipients of purported benevolence—this spelled peril for freed people and their supporters.

Forrest was a polarizing figure who figured to negatively impact Seymour's campaign, but the Republicans were taking no chances. In July, the National Committee proposed to have "Southern friends of Congressional reconstruction" speak on behalf of Grant, including "General Longstreet . . . of Georgia; Senator Alcorn, of Mississippi; Governor Holden and General Barringer, of North Carolina; Governor Smith, of Alabama."[108]

Help was also coming from a familiar corner. Another Soldiers' and Sailors' Convention was set for October 1 to 2, its program determined by the organization's National Republican Executive Committee.[109] By train and boat, thousands of Union veterans flocked to Philadelphia in "an immense turnout" to support Grant and Colfax.[110]

Preparations had been beautifully handled for the meeting of the "Boys in Blue." There was enough food for 20,000 people over two days, and "Engine houses, public halls and factories have been turned into dormitories and volunteer refreshment rooms," just as a few years earlier. War governors, current loyal state governors, former Union and active-duty generals would all be there, with Dan Sickles serving as convention president. Major General Phil Sheridan, "detained by the Indian trouble," would be unable to join the festivities but sent along a note: "'Say to the Boys in Blue that it is as essential to have a political victory this fall as it was to have an Appomattox in sixty-five, and that every man who loves his country should vote for General Grant.'"[111]

Oliver O. Howard and John Pope were also among absent generals who dispatched letters. The Freedmen's Bureau Commissioner fully supported the man "'[who would] lead us on safely to a complete triumph in peace,'" believing that "'to be the earnest hope of every true-hearted Union man, black and white.'" Pope captured the gathering's importance in giving "'with recognized authority, an effectual response to the extraordinary proceedings of the convention of so-called "conservative soldiers and sailors," which . . . fitly illustrated its "conservatism" and . . . consistency by denouncing General GRANT as a renegade, and welcoming [CSA General] Simon BOLIVAR BUCKNER with enthusiastic applause.'"[112]

There were so many delegates and non-veteran attendees that Independence Square was too small for the opening night ceremonies, and the next day's procession was memorable. It included an estimated 30,000 veterans, "enough [from] the Army of the Potomac, and the Army of the Tennessee, to form a full army corps, while there are sailors sufficient to man a fleet of ships of the line. Every branch of the service is represented in the Convention, horse, foot, dragoons, engineers, artillery and the amphibious marines."[113]

Despite violence directed against African Americans and white Republicans in many parts of the South to keep them away from the polls, Grant was elected president by a rather close majority of the popular vote. His slogan, "Let us have peace!" would now be put to the test, along with congressional Reconstruction. In a somber editorial accompanying the election results, the *National Republican* expressed the hopes of those who wished to see the United States move forward after war and sectional discord:

> This land must be one and inseparable, whoever may be its rulers. For this we fought. For this we sacrificed three millions of men, and four thousand millions of treasure. We must be brothers, North and South, East and West, . . . and forget and forgive. . . . Brethren, friends, fellow-citizens. . . . No matter where born, what may be his religion, or the color of his skin.

> This country is working out the great problem of a free government . . . liberty, civil and religious, must be the acknowledged birthright of all. This land must be free. It must be the government for the people and by the people.[114]

For that to occur, the Reconstructed South would need to accept federal authority in such volatile matters as black male suffrage and equal treatment for all African Americans under the law. As for the North, its men of color would have to be accorded the same right to vote as their freedmen brothers, and full overall citizenship for all blacks on par with their white neighbors. As they had already demonstrated, Union veterans would be essential to such efforts.

Brevet Lieutenant Colonel and Forty-Fifth US Regiment Captain Joseph Wiley Gelray. PHOTO COURTESY OF MASSACHUSETTS COMMANDERY OF MOLLUS.

Doing Battle with the Ku Klux Klan and the End of Reconstruction

[I]f something is not done to give the friends of our country protection, and to punish the Ku-Klux Klan in the greater part of Tennessee, another war will result, as practically the negroes are still slaves and the confederacy is a triumphant success . . . the reason it is not more generally known is simply because parties who know the facts are afraid for their lives to report the truth.[1]

While Forrest was denying the Ku Klux Klan had ever carried out any alleged "unprovoked outrages," a regular army officer maimed in the Civil War was gathering evidence that showed the former Confederate general was no mere apologist, but an outright liar. Brevet Lieutenant Colonel and Forty-Fifth Regiment Captain Joseph Wiley Gelray, under special orders from Grant, was among officers (including Left-Armed Corps comrade Joseph K. Byers) detailed to the Freedmen's Bureau in March 1868. They reported forthwith to Oliver O. Howard,[2] with Gelray assigned the critical and perilous task of investigating the Klan in Forrest's domain, the state of Tennessee—his outstanding work led to the devastating statement quoted above.

As leading historians of the Klan have readily agreed, the choice of Gelray was ideal in light of his personal attributes and military experience. Wade rated him the bureau's "most competent, independent inspector," calling Gelray "a highly intelligent, fair-minded, religious, and intrepid soldier."[3] In a similar manner, Horn described the thrice-wounded former printer who lost his right arm at Gettysburg as "a man of rare diplomacy, impartiality and coolness."[4] How Gelray earned such accolades is readily apparent by his remarkable reports and actions in the face of stunning cruelty, racism, and contempt for the law.

On June 19, brevet major general and Freedmen's Bureau assistant commissioner for Tennessee William P. Carlin ordered Gelray to Chapel Hill, Marshall County, to "investigate the present state of feeling between the whites and blacks, and use every effort to restore quiet and peace." The Klan instigated the confrontation by whipping an African American man; his friends, fed up with terrible acts committed by whites over several months without any interference or subsequent penalty from local magistrates, reacted with fury and took up arms to defend themselves. Carlin instructed Gelray to warn the county's white people that unless they suppressed Klan depredations and insisted that the laws be applied equitably, race warfare would break out.[5]

Looking into the so-called "'negro insurrection'" in Murfreesboro, Gelray found that four unarmed African Americans, part of a group that agreed to give up their weapons to the mayor in exchange for protection from angry whites out-numbering them ten to one, had been captured. When a hundred masked Klansmen showed up to take custody of the prisoners "for summary punishment," the sheriff and other townspeople turned them away. At 5:00 a.m., thirteen white men brandishing shotguns demanded that the black prisoners be turned over to them—this was again refused by the sheriff, but he had his deputy take them to the authorities of a neighboring county.

After specifying these events in his June 26 report, Gelray starkly described the terror faced in peacetime by African Americans, loyal whites, Bureau personnel, and an officer of the US Army who had fought in some of history's bloodiest battles. Every day the Klan in Murfreesboro and its environs were threatening *to annihilate the negroes and Union citizens,* with the *county sheriff report*[ing] *that he is entirely powerless to execute the law, or prevent outrages by the Klan.* Loyal *Union men and their families* were petrified by talk of "assassination . . . *as a remedy for imaginary evils, and the most humiliating outrages and insults are heaped upon them daily."* Not surprisingly, Northerners who had relocated to the area *"are leaving as fast as they can get away,"* with those choosing to remain for the time being only doing so to avoid *"great pecuniary loss."*

Concerning the Freedmen's Bureau, its local agent *"is nightly afraid of his life, and was obliged to have another man sleep in his room. He dare not go any distance from the town, night or day,"* and due to personal *"insults and annoyances"* was forced to resign. As for the very African Americans whom the military organization was meant to protect, they *"no longer report outrages perpetrated upon them to the bureau agent, as they have been told by the Ku-Klux Klan that they will be shot if ever seen going to the agent's office."*

When Gelray's presence and mission became known, *"numbers of gentlemen called upon me and freely acknowledged that if something was not done to put down midnight murders and marauders in their midst, that the best people would have to leave the country at any sacrifice; and even ladies pleaded the case of their husbands, saying that they could not sleep at nights for fear of the assassin's blow or the torch of the incendiary."* Everyone who spoke with the Bureau's special investigator beseeched him *"not to use their names, as it would certainly cost them their lives if known."*

Gelray himself was hardly spared: *"I wore my uniform while in Murfreesboro, and I was twice made to go off the sidewalk, (once in front of a church while service was going on,) by young men forming themselves across it to prevent my passing."*[6]

What had four years of war, passage of the Thirteenth and Fourteenth Amendments, creation of the Freedmen's Bureau and congressional Reconstruction accomplished in this region of Tennessee? Gelray provided the honest, horrifying answer:

Many of the freedmen desire again to be in slavery, as they were then secure in life and limb so long as they behaved well, but now they are protected in nothing. They are completely at the mercy of the worst characters of the community, and if they attempt to seek redress their lives are the forfeit of their temerity. It would be less discouraging if there were any grounds of hope for a better state of affairs, but on the contrary, this feeling of antagonism to everything like justice to the negro, or political liberty, is alarmingly on the increase.[7]

Gelray detailed the lengths to which the Klan went to prevent open elections, in particular suppression of the black vote: "*A free expression of our political preferences by ballot is the very foundation of American institutions and all her liberty. When this is not guaranteed and protected, liberty is dead.*" Convinced Klan members "*know no law but that of force,*" he recommended deployment of a cavalry squadron commanded by an able commissioned officer at Murfreesboro to patrol and arrest "*marauders in disguise.*" He candidly expressed fear for his own safety during a ride to Chapel Hill to check on the captured black prisoners that he had been warned against; after stating that African Americans were fully justified in protecting themselves, he assessed their status:

> *Their* [white farmers and planters who employed black share-croppers] *spirit towards the colored laborer is perfectly devilish, and exhibits itself in the most infernal outrages upon their persons and interests that ever was heard of in any community laying the slightest claims to civilization or Christianity . . . But how could these poor colored men get a fair trial when 200 white men, full of bad whiskey, were ready to hang a magistrate, or any body else, in case he did not execute their will in the matter, whether it will be right or wrong?*[8]

Gelray then delivered a verdict and proposed solution that presaged both conditions and federal government measures taken in the South one century later. With blacks and Union whites "*liv*[ing] *in daily and nightly terror of their lives,*" constitutional freedoms such as speech were being suppressed, as "*the best citizens are apparently not in favor of the operations of the Klan, yet they dare not say anything against it except in the most general way.*"

> *In short, if the general government does not make some show of power in these counties, the confederacy, so far as they (the counties and their*

people) are concerned, might as well have been recognized, as there exists no more respect for United States laws, United States officers, or authority among them, than might reasonably be expected in the interior of Africa.[9]

Tennessee's reign of terror continued unabated, with increasing levels of violence. On July 1, James L. Francis, commissioner of registration for Overton County, was taken from his home by at least twelve men, carried a mile and a half away, then shot between twelve and fifteen times. Four days later, J. D. Hale reported the murder to Colonel Alfred L. Hough, stating that "I dont think any real Union man is safe here—we are liable to be killed at any time. This is not only my opinion, but that of every one I meet. . . . Unless some change takes place, we shall be compelled to gather in bands for mutual defence." Hough forwarded Hale's report to Major General George H. Thomas in Louisville, Kentucky, where he was commanding the Department of the Cumberland.[10]

The Freedmen's Bureau continued to look into acts of intimidation and cruelty committed by the Klan. Lieutenant W. H. Brewer took the ghastly deposition of Lewis Powell, a black resident of Hickman County, whose wife was shot dead in the middle of the night by six men on horseback who had first demanded feed for their mounts, then food for themselves. His three daughters, who witnessed their mother's execution, told Powell that the murderers had sworn "to kill every 'nigger on the place, before daylight,' and that 'no damned Union League niggers should rule the country.'"[11]

Gelray followed up his fellow Forty-Fifth Infantry officer's action with a July 27 sworn statement by four African American sharecroppers from Giles County that on the evening of June 30, the Klan had threatened each at their homes with hanging, and beat one man for refusing to reveal where another was hiding. Petrified, they fled their homes for Nashville, seeking protection from the Klan as advised by their employers.

The dreaded night riders had been busy that evening. Pink Harris, another black Giles County citizen who worked as both a teamster and farmer, was shot at by several men in disguise who had surrounded his cabin, one bullet lodging in his side. He likewise fled to Nashville in search of *"protection for his rights and life,"* as Gelray stated in the Harris deposition. According to Harris, it was "generally understood, and believed, that the Ku Klux Klan are preparing to kill, or drive away, all the colored men who were Union men or soldiers in the Federal army, or were ever connected with it in any way."[12]

Yet another bureau official, Captain George E. Judd, declared that "The Ku Klux organization is so extensive, and so well organized and armed, that it is beyond the power of any one to exert any moral influence over them. Powder and ball is the only thing that will put them down." In support of his assertion Judd included a sworn statement from Walter Scott of Cornersville, who had been disarmed by the Klan in April, then was told his days were numbered on July 6. The night before his friend Mint Burks had been awakened and killed, two days after having been told the same thing: "'Mint thought it was a joke, and paid no attention to it.'"[13]

When two more murders were committed in Franklin one month later, Gelray was dispatched to the scene. Within ten days he sent a full investigative report back to Nashville, and the details were sickening. A Jewish storekeeper from Russia named Bierfield was accosted at midnight on August 15 by five Klansmen, from whom he fled into a nearby stable. When a crowd of several hundred who had attended a circus performance that evening were aroused by the disturbance and threatened to interfere, they were ordered at gunpoint to clear off the streets and driven into their homes by no more than fifteen men in masks.

Thus free to do as they pleased, the hunting party soon found Bierfield, and dragged him into the street. When his exertions prevented their efforts to tie him up or put him on a horse, they killed him on the spot. Upon reviewing the physical evidence, Gelray concluded that Bierfield had been shot at close range (four of the five bullets entering his head) while lying down, his face *"burned and blackened by powder."* The only person who intervened on the unfortunate man's behalf was a town magistrate named Burch, who was driven off with lethal threats.

Bierfield had begged for his life, repeatedly invoking his aged, impoverished mother, but it was no use. An incensed Gelray stated: "*A dog, without human speech, that would plead by looks and growls, as Bierfield pleaded in language that all his hearers could understand, would have been spared by any man (I hate to use the word men in reference to these murderers) laying the slightest claim to civilization, Christianity, or humanity.*"[14]

The merchant was not the night's only victim. Two of Bierfield's employees, both black, had been with him when the Klan forced their way in, and were instructed to stand still under penalty of death. They managed to flee the shop during the events taking place outside, but one of the men named Bowman was found dying from a bullet through the back after the killers had fled town. Despite Bowman's telling someone before he expired that the wound was intentional, the coroner's jury deemed his death to be accidental.[15]

What had Bierfield done to bring the Klan's wrath upon himself and, by extension, Bowman? When the masked group found his hiding place, they immediately accused him of complicity in the murder of Jeremiah Ezell, the late-teen brother of a young girl who allegedly had been "brutally outraged" by an African American. As recounted by the *Memphis Daily Appeal*, a man matching the description of the black suspect was found and arrested, only to be taken out of the Franklin jail by a group of disguised men. The next morning his dead body was found on the road six miles away.

In retaliation, a group of African Americans from Franklin and environs arrived in the town and threatened to torch it. A plot to arouse them was "divulged," and soon both whites and blacks were up "in arms.' When the situation cooled, a small group of white men were returning home when they were reportedly ambushed by African Americans, with young Ezell fatally shot.

The *Daily Appeal* reported that the blacks had "acted at the instigation and under the orders" of Bierfield, and printed a letter that supposedly supported the charge—as a result, the paper called his murder "retributive." Gelray's inquest revealed that the accusation was preposterous on multiple counts: Bierfield had vehemently denied any involvement to his murderers; nothing in his background indicated political activities; and investigation of the published letter led Gelray to decide that it was *"undoubtedly a forgery"* (italics his) that could not even be produced, and was probably concocted by a business rival to force Bierfield to leave town. There was another factor of importance: *"He had been known to say that he believed a negro to be as good as a white man, and was in favor of equality before the law to all men."* Gelray concluded: "In short, all the evidence (and I gave everybody an opportunity of giving evidence) *is in proof of the Bierfield and Bowman tragedy being a cool, deliberate, and brutal* murder, without palliation or justification from any point of view"[16] (italics his).

Gelray, thwarted in his efforts to obtain justice for either man, or even Ezell through investigation of the letter he believed to be forged, was "forced to the disagreeable conclusion that there is *no intention or desire on the part of the civil authorities or the community at large to bring the murderers to justice"* (italics his). Beyond ever-present fear, he found *"the most shocking part . . . is that some of those who are considered good citizens, and actual leaders of good society, and moulders of public opinion, are active with both tongue and pen in defending and justifying the Ku-Klux Klan in these most horrible outrages against law and nature."*[17]

Gelray, having seen his report on what had taken place at Waynesboro *"published in the Nashville papers,"* took *"the liberty of particularizing and giving my individual opinions . . . , which ordinarily and militarily speaking would be inexcusable,"* in this latest report to Carlin. The Bureau inspector did so for a very good reason: *"I have thought it possible that you might publish this, and as those who know me well know that I am entirely unbiased by party politics or hope of reward from any individual, party or organization, and conscious of the purity of the motives, I beg to be excused for indulging the hope that what I have said may be accepted by both parties in the spirit in which it is offered, and as coming from an unprejudiced source."*[18]

Gelray had indeed become part of the events he was charged to probe. The *"troubles at Waynesboro"* was an assignment received immediately after finishing in Franklin. He skillfully brokered an admittedly fragile peace between the Klan and black furnace workers, their white Union supporters and the Wayne County sheriff, with no further violence or threats.[19]

On August 22, the *Public Ledger* of Memphis published an item from the *Nashville Banner* that characterized his inquiry into the Franklin murders as a "sham," and belittled "these sagacious detectives" for calling the purported letter a forgery.[20] What about the Grand Wizard himself? Just days after Bierfield's murder (and Bowman's, which he did not mention) Forrest told the *Cincinnati Commercial*: "'I sent a man up there especially to investigate the case, and report to me, and I have his letter here now, in which he states that they [Ku Klux Klan] have nothing to do with it as an organization.'"[21]

Forrest's pathetic "inquest," interviews and speeches elicited scorn from numerous Northern newspapers, such as Ohio's *Jackson Standard*. Ridiculing the statement of "Gen. Negro Butcher" that if troops backed by federal forces were called out under Tennessee's Militia law, he advocated "giving no quarter," the paper noted: "We have always regarded it as a disgrace to the United States Government that Forrest was not shot or hung."[22] Southern accounts of violent acts committed by the Klan were being reprinted all across the North,[23] as a Massachusetts newspaper warned its subscribers not to "treat the stories of the Klan as figments of the imagination." In one of its own citizens, the *Lowell Daily Courier* had a trusted source: "[Colonel Gelray] says the Ku-Klux Klan is an exceedingly dangerous organization. . . . This is but a corroboration of all we have heard, and it adds to the satisfaction experienced at the assurances given to General Thomas that he will be afforded every facility to keep the peace in Tennessee."[24]

Ordinary Americans were not the only ones reading Forrest's interviews with apprehension. Wade reported that Congressmen were increasingly concerned over Klan activities: "There was no doubt about it—the Ku-Klux was growing and spreading. But the focal point remained in Tennessee, where the Klan's nocturnal raids were already an uninterrupted nightmare."[25] Gelray's first-rate investigative work and related efforts by his Freedmen's Bureau colleagues made the situation in Tennessee crystal clear, and their advocacy for direct military action was a factor in President Johnson's unenthusiastic order to George Thomas that civilian authority be supported by the army.[26]

But the neutered Johnson was departing the national stage, and six days before Grant took office on March 4, 1869, Congress provided an apparent boost with its approval of the Fifteenth Amendment. Its simple yet revolutionary text read:

> SECTION 1. The right of citizens of the United States to vote shall not be denied or abridged by the United States or by any State on account of race, color, or previous condition of servitude.
>
> SEC. 2. The Congress shall have power to enforce this article by appropriate legislation.[27]

In his inaugural address, the eighteenth president stressed its significance: "The question of suffrage is one which is likely to agitate the public so long as a portion of the citizens of the nation are excluded from its privileges in any State. It seems to me very desirable that this question . . . be settled now, and I . . . hope and express the desire that it may be by . . . [its] ratification."[28]

The Fifteenth Amendment was ratified on February 3, 1870,[29] making black suffrage the law of the land, North and South. Grant gave the amendment his heartfelt support, calling it "the most important event that has occurred since the nation came into life."[30]

GRANT BATTLES THE KLAN

Despite the change of administration, the Klan's terror campaign continued across those states undergoing Reconstruction. According to Wade, from 1868 through 1871, "no black Republican, carpetbagger or scalawag was safe in the rural south."[31] This is consistent with Horn's observation that the country's first widespread interest in the Klan was fostered via Grant's Annual Message to Congress in December 1870. Pressured by the governor of North Carolina, whose state was particularly affected, the president stressed denial of "free exercise of the elective franchise" through "violence and intimidation" in several former Confederate states.

After Grant responded to a Senate resolution asking for information regarding "disloyal or evil-designed organizations" with thousands of instances of alleged wrongdoing, including killings, in the Tar Heel State and other parts of the South, a Senate select committee went to North Carolina to investigate. In March 1871, it reported that the Klan clearly existed (why that was in question after the Freedmen Bureau's stellar work is incomprehensible), and confirmed both the extent and intensity of terrorizing violence in not only North Carolina but other states. As a result, the committee recommended a larger investigation throughout the South.[32]

In Vermont, the *St. Johnsbury Caledonian* captured the situation in Gelray-like prose: "The war upon the colored people . . . is as vindictive and barbarous to-day as at any time during the Rebellion or since. The ku-klux are setting the laws at defiance . . . and carrying on their bloody and savage operations with as much impunity as though there was no government and no hand of justice to arrest them in their course."[33]

Congress had sought to protect full voting rights nationwide under the Fifteenth Amendment through the Enforcement Acts in 1870 and 1871. When they proved woefully inadequate in reducing violence in the South, the House and Senate passed the Ku Klux Klan Act (or Third Enforcement Act) in April 1871. This landmark legislation was enacted to enforce the Fourteenth Amendment's provisions guaranteeing all American citizens due and equal protection under the law. Criminal penalties (fines and/or imprisonment) under federal jurisdiction were specified for such crimes as preventing an individual from holding office, carrying out the duties of a federal position, testifying in court or serving as a juror or voting, or depriving any person or group of equal legal protection.

If any state was "unable to protect, or shall, from any cause, fail in or refuse protection of the people in such rights," the president was given full authority to employ militia or any branch of the armed forces as deemed necessary. Further, the president could suspend the writ of *habeas corpus* in the event of rebellion or organized armed defiance of constituted state or federal authorities under the act's provisions.[34]

In sum, the act established the federal government's authority to protect any American citizen against threats or actual violence intended to prevent exercise of rights guaranteed under the Constitution. While safeguarding voting privileges was a major component, other basic rights would be likewise defended. In combination with the Fifteenth Amendment, the Act took dead aim at the Klan, its membership's shield against facing indictment and trial for their crimes limited to local and state sympathizers now that the federal government was empowered to bring them to justice. Also gone with the Fifteenth Amendment's ratification was the basis for accusations of hypocrisy due to the lack of full voting rights for African American men in the North.[35]

It didn't take long for the president's new powers to be used in the war against the Klan. Just weeks before the act's passage, Grant sent federal troops to South Carolina in response to pleas for assistance from Governor Robert K. Scott, an ex-Union general and Freedmen's Bureau assistant commissioner. In October, having given the Klan fair warning, the writ of *habeas corpus* was suspended by Grant in the state's northern region. An unprecedented peacetime action, it led to wholesale arrest, incarceration, or flight of the night riders; trials in the US District Court then ensued. Historians credit the sustained aggressive enforcement policy of the Grant administration with not only decimating the Klan's power in South Carolina, but across the entire South, by 1872.[36]

However, Foner, Wade, and Charles Lane all offered cautionary notes as to the tragic fate of Reconstruction even in light of the successful campaign against the Klan:

> National power had achieved what most Southern governments had been unable, and Southern white public opinion unwilling, to accomplish: acquiescence in the rule of law. Yet the need for outside intervention was a humiliating confession of weakness for the Reconstruction regimes. (Foner)[37]

> Yet Grant's attack on the Klan triggered a political backlash which ultimately spread to the Republicans' own ranks. The reaction was strongest in the South, of course, but for many Northern whites, the struggle with the Klan simply underscored

the fact that Reconstruction, for all its initial promise, had turned into a long, violent slog. (Lane)[38]

Over the next four years, the Republican ardor for civil rights would cool, Reconstruction itself would be "frozen out," and prospects for racial justice would be put on ice for nearly a century. (Wade)[39]

Compounding African Americans' precarious circumstances in the South was the loss of the foremost federal body devoted to their welfare. In July 1868, Congress extended the Freedmen's Bureau existence for one year while ordering operations to be discontinued in any state upon readmission to the Union, unless the secretary of war, in consultation with the bureau commissioner and fully considering "the condition of freedmen's affairs in such State," thought its services were still needed. The bureau's education division would continue its work until a state made "suitable provision" for educating freedmen's children.[40] Three weeks later, another act discontinued bureau operations as of January 1, 1869, excepting its educational efforts and "collection and payment" of money due to "soldiers, sailors, and marines, or their heirs."[41]

As a result, the critical field endeavors of assistant commissioners and their officers (like W. A. MacNulty) ceased in early 1869, and in February 1870 the War Department took on the financial claims, along with administering hospitals and asylums that had been under bureau authority. All educational work and personnel were transferred to a new Bureau of Education within the Department of the Interior in the summer of 1870. On June 30, 1872, the Freedmen's Bureau officially shut its doors.[42]

In 1901, W. E. B. Du Bois paid tribute to the under-funded, under-manned, and unprecedented organization that had tried to accomplish so much with so little: "at last there arose in the South a government of men called the Freedmen's Bureau, which lasted, legally, from 1865 to 1872, but in a sense from 1861 to 1876, and which sought to settle the Negro problems in the United States of America."[43]

One of those men, Joseph W. Gelray, retired from the army in December 1870,[44] having done all he could to warn his fellow citizens about homegrown terrorists, and protect those in danger.

THE COLFAX MASSACRE

The Colfax Massacre of 1873, and its aftermath, exemplified what destroyed Reconstruction. Begun on Easter Sunday in Colfax, county seat of Louisiana's Grant Parish, one of the era's deadliest racial confrontations was described by James R. Beckwith, US attorney in New Orleans, in an April 17 report to Attorney General George H. Williams. Relying on what Deputy Marshal DeKlyne found after "arriv[ing] there the day after the massacre," Beckwith stated that

> The details are horrible. The Democrat whites of Grant parish attempted to oust the incumbent parish officers by force and failed, the Sheriff protecting the officers with a colored posse.—Several days afterwards recruits from other parishes to the number of three hundred, came to the assistance of the assailants, when they demanded the surrender of the colored posse. This they refused, and an attack made and the negroes driven into the Court House.

> The Court House was then fired, and the negroes slaughtered as they left the burning building, after resistance ceased. Sixty-five negroes, terribly mutilated, were found dead near the ruins of the Court House. Thirty known to have been taken prisoners, are said to have been shot after the surrender, and thrown into the river. Two of the assailants were wounded. The slaughter is greater than it was in the riot of 1866 in this city.[45]

That same day, Stephen B. Packard, US marshal for Louisiana and chairman of the state's Republican Party,[46] submitted his own report to Williams that provided further information. DeKlyne had departed for Colfax "with several warrants of arrest for parties in the parishes of Grant and Rapides," and the African American posse that held the Court House was under the command of the white Sheriff Shaw, who had been appointed by Republican Governor William P. Kellog. They were opposed by whites led by former Sheriff Nash who had been "super-ceeded by Shaw," now reported missing and presumed dead, although he had actually survived.

The "Armed bodies of whites . . . still scouring the country . . . consisted of organized parties from" Grant and five other parishes who "possess[ed] a six pounder cannon, taken, or some alleged loaned, from the Red River steamer *John T. Moore* fifteen months since." As to law enforcement, Packard emphasized that US soldiers were "required to execute warrants in this parish, when a prominent white Republican was murdered. Nash and others connected with this butchery were then arrested. No warrants have yet been issued for parties connected with this last outbreak. When the circumstances of this massacre are fully known, it will be found to be only equalled by that of Fort Pillow."[47]

Both men were right—the events in Colfax were even bloodier than the 1866 riot in New Orleans, and rivaled the wartime slaughter of surrendered black soldiers. In further dreadful parallel to Fort Pillow, many of the slain African Americans were veterans.

In his book on the Colfax Massacre, Lane meticulously told how Beckwith courageously sought justice for those murdered despite little financial, military or departmental support. He indicted ninety-eight men for civil rights violations under the 1870 Enforcement Act and its later amendments, with capital punishment to be imposed on conviction of counts involving murder. Due to various obstacles preventing the arrest of most of those charged, only nine stood trial.

Over two trials they all were acquitted of murder, but in June 1874, Beckwith obtained convictions of three defendants for conspiracy to violate the civil rights of the African American victims, with ten years' imprisonment and $5,000 fines awaiting each man. Yet even this small but significant victory was fleeting, as US Supreme Court associate justice Joseph P. Bradley, riding the region's federal court circuit, soon overturned the convictions due to lack of specification in the indictments of a racial basis for the conspiracy.[48]

The implications of Bradley's ruling, particularly in the face of evident waning of Northern patience with the seemingly endless problems of blacks in the Deep South, were dire. If the Enforcement Acts and the

Fourteenth and Fifteenth Amendments could not guarantee prosecution and conviction of those who used violence against African Americans and their white Republican supporters, it would be open season for racists with no reason to fear the law. That is just what happened in Louisiana, as the newly formed supremacist White League carried on a campaign of intimidation and murder until forced to temporarily desist upon arrival of federal troops. Now it would be up to the US Supreme Court to decide whether laws passed by Congress and amendments ratified by the states would protect the civil rights of all American citizens.[49]

While the Court deliberated for twelve months, the death knell for Reconstruction could be heard in Mississippi. With African Americans comprising a slight population majority, considerable racial progress had been achieved there before Bradley's action. The black vote and an active Republican party led to stunning results at the polls in 1873. Republican Adelbert Ames, elected senator by the Mississippi legislature on the state's readmission in 1870, was swept into the governor's mansion, while men of color took possession of a significant proportion of statewide seats and reinforced their strength in local offices. When the new legislature convened, African Americans were selected as Speaker of the House and US senator.[50]

These heady accomplishments would be short-lived. The strict federal enforcement policy, which had been a notable success in protecting the rights of black Mississippians and their supporters, was greatly curtailed in the wake of Bradley's ruling.

Having closely watched the government's effective campaign against the Klan, the White League adopted a deadly new strategy that led to the Vicksburg Massacre of late 1874. A campaign of intimidation had kept blacks from the city's polling places in August, thus defeating the Republican municipal government; Democratic victories in other parts of the state followed in the fall. Buoyed by these results, armed gangs returned to Vicksburg in December to oust its black sheriff, Peter Crosby, and associated officials. When Crosby was forced to flee and a group of supportive African Americans arrived in response, all hell broke loose. By the time federal troops were dispatched to restore order and reinstate Crosby, an estimated three hundred blacks had been killed.[51]

An astute *New York Daily Tribune* correspondent in 1880 explained how Mississippi's Republican government was subsequently overthrown. Instead of hooded Klan night riders, the White League "substitute[d] open daylight attacks upon Republican gatherings by well-armed and disciplined military companies." Throughout spring 1875, "large shipments of arms . . . mainly repeating rifles of the best patterns" arrived in the state, then "found their way, without much attempt at secrecy, into the hands of companies formed in advance of their reception," with "scarcely a county . . . that did not have one or more of these companies before the first of July. They were all organized without the authority of the Governor, and therefore in defiance of State law. Their officers were men who had served as officers in the Confederate Army and the rank and file was made up of veteran rebel soldiers."[52]

Rural blacks, most without military experience and armed mainly with pistols and shotguns, were no match for combat veterans with the latest weaponry. This was tragically shown in yet another massacre, this time at Clinton, just ten miles from the state capital. When a major meeting of Republicans for the upcoming elections convened in early September, they were "attacked by a large body of armed Democrats. For the first and only time in the course of the bloody campaign of 1875 the Republicans resisted. They were dispersed and hunted for days in the woods, and killed wherever found. In all, 107 men were killed in the affair, of whom six were white Democrats and the rest colored Republicans."[53]

Governor Ames, a West Point graduate from Maine, was himself a Medal of Honor recipient who rose to brigadier general during the war, transferred to the regular army and resigned as a lieutenant colonel in 1870.[54] He now perceived "that a rebellion was on foot, if not against the National Government, at least against the State."

The governor wrote Grant about the situation and asked for military assistance. Simultaneously, Attorney General Edwards Pierrepont was receiving a barrage of telegrams from Mississippi's leading Democrat, Colonel J. Z. George, "assuring him that perfect peace prevailed throughout the State, and that there was no danger of disturbance 'unless incited by the State authorities.'" This "perfect peace" stemmed from the menace of rifle barrels deployed against any Republicans daring to assemble.[55]

On September 11, Ames sent a lengthy reply to Pierrepont's request for information, a telegram being insufficient. In an extraordinary letter, he spelled out the intertwined racial and political state of affairs, and its relationship to the violence: "the race feeling is so intense that protection for the colored by the white organizations is despaired of. . . . This state has been opposed to organizing a militia of colored men. It has been believed by them that it would develop a war of the races, which would extend beyond the border of this state."[56]

Ames was all too "aware of the reluctance of the people of the country to national interference in state affairs, though if there be no violation of the law there can be no interference." With savvy and principled acceptance of responsibility, he offered Grant and the Republican party a political out in order to ensure equal rights for all Mississippians: "As the governor of the state, I made a demand which cannot well be refused. Let the odium in all its magnitude descend upon me. I can not escape the conscious discharge of my duty towards a class of American citizens whose only offense consists in their color, and whom I am powerless to protect."[57]

Pierrepont forwarded this latest correspondence from Ames and all prior communication to Grant, providing the president with his own take on the situation. Incredibly, the attorney general thought federal intervention in Mississippi was not indicated either by the Constitution or applicable statutes, and just as inexplicable was Grant's lack of direct contact with Ames. Instead, the vacationing president telegraphed Pierrepont from Long Branch, New Jersey:

> "The whole public are tired out with these annual Autumnal outbreaks in the South, and the great majority are ready now to condemn any interference on the part of the Government. I heartily wish that peace and good order may be restored without issuing the proclamation; but if it is not, the proclamation must be issued; and if it is, I shall instruct the commander of the forces to have no child's play. If there is a necessity for military interference, there is justice in such interference as shall deter evil doers."

Grant added his suggestion that Ames be implored "'to strengthen his own position by exhausting his own resources in restoring order before he receives Government aid . . . Gov. Ames and his advisers can be made perfectly secure, as many of the troops in Mississippi as he deems necessary may be sent to Jackson.'"[58]

Upon receiving this dispatch, Pierrepont responded to Ames on September 14. Including portions of Grant's cable to "best convey to you his ideas" with which the attorney general and entire Cabinet professed "full accord," it was obvious that the administration somehow still did not grasp the situation: "We cannot understand why you do not strengthen yourself in the way the President suggests; nor do we see why you do not call the Legislature together, and obtain from them whatever powers, money, and arms you need."

Insisting that Ames had made "no suggestion even that there is any insurrection against the Government of the State," Pierrepont urged the governor to demonstrate to America that Mississippi's predominantly Republican citizens "have the courage and the manhood to fight for their rights, and to destroy the bloody ruffians who murder the innocent and unoffending freedmen." He left Ames with the promise that should there be "such resistance to your State authorities as you cannot by all the means at your command suppress, the President will swiftly aid you in crushing these lawless traitors to human rights."[59]

At the request of Blanche K. Bruce of Mississippi, a former slave and the first elected African American to serve a full term in the Senate,[60] Grant gave permission for Pierrepont's publication of his letter to Ames, which began on September 17.[61] As newspapers across the country reprinted the attorney general's communication, the impact was catastrophic for Mississippi, and Reconstruction in general.

While Grant's perception as to Northern exhaustion with fifteen years of fighting for race-related issues was undoubtedly accurate, his choice of language was ruinous. Democratic-leaning papers seized upon "annual Autumnal outbreaks" as a way to trivialize the terrorist campaigns of violence, intimidation and murder of African Americans and white Republicans carried out since 1866, and which had escalated over the past two years. This was not unexpected in the South, but a number of Northern publications were hardly more sympathetic.

The *Daily Register* of Hudson, New York, was typical in seeing the "outbreaks" as "nothing more or less than infamous dodges and fulminations of unscrupulous Radical tricksters and political shysters, of which this Ames is a true representative." As for Grant's statement on federal "interference," the newspaper said Northerners were "heartily tired of such *sham* 'outbreaks' as those gotten up in Louisiana, Alabama, Arkansas, and Mississippi . . . With them the 'war of race' is utterly played out."[62]

Even among newspapers favorable toward Ames and infuriated by the open warfare on African Americans, many supported the administration's position. One day after release of Pierrepont's letter, the *Daily Graphic* in New York City confirmed its viewpoint in stating Northerners did not wish Southern outrages to be "used as electioneering capital," with "bloody shirt" waving having increasingly frightened voters "the wrong way." The paper saw "public sentiment favor[ing] reconciliation and public interests demand[ing] it," as the country was "interested in . . . reform and finance and administration," public works and developing national resources.[63]

Though support for federal intervention was wavering, other pro-Reconstruction newspapers stood their ground. In publishing the Pierrepont letter, the *National Republican* provided a sentence-by-sentence interpretation, finding it to be "shrewdly calculated . . . to set the public to thinking." According to its staff, the communication supported the newspaper's charge that "misrepresenting or . . . withholding facts regarding the condition of the South" by Opposition journalists made them "responsible for this readiness to condemn needed interference by the Government," and thereby guilty of "crimes . . . hardly less heinous than those of the White League murderers themselves."[64]

Ten days later, the paper published special correspondence from Mississippi, and it wasn't pretty. Mocking Grant, "Tupelo" noted that "However tired the whole public may be with the 'annual autumnal outbreaks in the South,' the innocent victims thereof are much more so." He found it mind-boggling that the injured parties, not their tormentors, were the ones being condemned, but understood how daunting it was to convince a disbelieving citizenry: "It will be the duty of history to do justice to both the evil-doer and his victim. The public has no standard in the previous history of our country by which to judge of passing events in the South. It falls to comprehend what is meant by race antagonism." The reporter concluded with a dire prediction: "I take it for granted that the violence inaugurated by the Bourbon Democrats in Mississippi will have the desired effect, and that they will carry the State, . . . and then the peace of the graveyard will reign within her borders."[65]

"Tupelo" was tragically prophetic. Ames, essentially on his own without appreciable federal troop support, had to make a deal with the white leadership, who promised to lay down their arms in exchange for the governor inactivating his limited state forces. The agreement was a charade, with the "rifle-club campaign" ensuing as described by the *New York Daily Tribune*, which reported that Republican public meetings had been abandoned and county organizations decimated by "Numerous assassinations of local colored leaders," leaving them "at the mercy of their opponents."

The paper further reported that a subsequent Senate investigation "showed that over 400 political murders were committed . . . , the victims being all Republicans," and by Election Day the Republican party was disseminated. While Democratic ballot-box stuffing or "fraudulent counts in the counties where the negroes turned out and voted" took place, neither was necessary "in most places . . . , for the terrified and disorganized colored men did not make any attempt to poll their full vote. The Republican majority of 20,000 in 1873 was wiped out as with a sponge, and a Democratic majority of 30,000 substituted for it."[66]

Having achieved their goals of gaining control of Mississippi's House, Senate, and county governments, the Democrats moved against the remaining statewide Republican leaders in January 1876, when the new legislature convened. Laying the groundwork for Ames's removal, in February the black lieutenant governor, Alexander K. Davis, was impeached by the House on charges of receiving a bribe to grant an executive pardon in a murder case. The following month he was convicted after trial in the Senate (NB: six Republicans [five white, one black] voted for his conviction), and resigned.

With any chance of African American gubernatorial ascension eliminated, Ames was immediately impeached on charges generally acknowledged to be trumped-up. On advice of counsel, who saw no chance of acquittal given the circumstances (and compounded by having to pay all costs of defending himself, including witnesses' travel), Ames offered to resign on March 29 if the articles of impeachment were dismissed. The Senate agreed, and he stepped down; that evening the Democratic president of the Senate was sworn in as governor. The *New York Daily Tribune* provided the epitaph: "This was the end of the Republican party in Mississippi. In 1876 its Central Committee formally disbanded it, on the ground that a contest would be useless."[67]

On March 27, 1876, two days before Ames resigned, the Supreme Court handed down its unanimous decision in *US v. Cruikshank*. The Court upheld Bradley's District Court ruling overturning the convictions, employing much of their colleague's reasoning. They even extended his argument with a clear demarcation of the federal government's perceived responsibility toward its citizens: "Its authority is defined and limited by the Constitution. All powers not granted to it by that instrument are reserved to the States or the people. No rights can be acquired under the constitution or laws of the United States, except such as the government of the United States has the authority to grant or secure. All that cannot be so granted or secured are left under the protection of the States."[68]

The decision ignored what was happening in Louisiana and other parts of the South, and never even mentioned the appalling events that occurred in Colfax. The highest court in the land had gutted federal authority to protect its most vulnerable citizens from state and local authorities who not only denied them equal treatment under the law but tacitly sanctioned the use of deadly force against those who sought to use rights guaranteed under the US Constitution.[69]

HAYES AND THE END OF RECONSTRUCTION

A new president was going to be elected that fall, but the concatenation of events that led up to the 1876 campaign spelled the end of Reconstruction. Using the "rifle-club" strategy that had been so successful in Louisiana and Mississippi, gubernatorial candidate Wade Hampton and his followers sought to topple the Republican government of South Carolina.[70] One of the US deputy marshals monitoring the state's polls was a former USCT and Freedmen's Bureau officer, Captain James O. Ladd of the Left-Armed Corps, now a Columbia resident.

In a sworn statement given two weeks after Election Day on November 7, 1876, Ladd provided a devastating account of the tactics employed to deny voting rights to certain American citizens. En route to his assignment at the Laurens County Courthouse, he saw *"squads of men mounted and ready to mount* [the railroad] *who were part of a general organization whose avowed purpose was to overawe and intimidate republicans."* Hearing *"their remarks,"* Ladd understood that their intended *"threats and violent conduct"* would be employed to *"influence them to remain away from the polls or 'vote with us,' meaning the democrats."*[71]

When Ladd arrived at the Courthouse, within one hour *"yells of a turbulent and frightful character* [began], *coming from all quarters and lasting continually during the night, accompanied by frightful oaths, jeers, and discharging of fire-arms,"* the *"evident purpose"* of the *"constantly moving"* groups of riders through the county *"in furtherance of the . . . plan of intimidation . . .* [to] *drive off the large number of colored republicans who had congregated at and in the vicinity of the court-house from a large adjacent territory, there being four polling-places at and near the court-house. As a result, many colored voters did not even approach the court-house for fear of violence or bodily harm, and many returned to their homes before the opening of the polls the following morning, and did not attend the polls during the election."*[72]

Ladd backed up his deposition with detailed testimony on December 23 under a US Senate resolution. Asked why African Americans told him they had not voted, he replied that *"it was because of their fear, because of the intimidation practiced, that they might lose their homes, or that their lives were in danger. As an evidence of that, I returned to Laurens Court-House—I think it was two days after the election—with a view of getting the affidavits of individuals, with the intention of contesting the election in that county. I obtained several affidavits."*[73]

The Connecticut native, who had served his country so admirably in war, was doing the same in supposed peacetime. Uncompensated for acting as a Marshal, he paid his own expenses for work undertaken "*In the interest of the public good.*"[74] In his deposition, Captain Ladd ended on an anguished note: "*A positive assurance of ample protection, not only on that day, but in the future, when the excitement of campaign and election might be over, was what seemed essential, as these republicans do assert that the real danger they fear is in the future, when the protection of the United States marshals and United States troops are withdrawn from them.*"[75]

That petrifying prospect wasn't long in coming. In his incisive study of the 1876 presidential election, Roy Morris Jr. called it "the last battle of the Civil War." The Republicans, reeling from Grant's scandal-ridden second term and a major economic downturn, were fortunate to have solid support from Union veterans. As Morris observed, Northern ex-servicemen were concerned "that the benefits they had won on the battlefield— not least of which was the right of 700,000 former slaves to vote freely and openly in political elections—were about to be lost at the polling booth."[76]

Their apprehension was completely justified. Successful use of terror had made a mockery of the election process in many Southern states, and the patience of non-veteran Northerners had generally been worn thin by Reconstruction's toll. The Democrat Samuel Tilden won the overall popular vote and each Southern state that had undergone removal of federal forces, but the Republican Rutherford B. Hayes carried South Carolina, Florida, Louisiana, and Oregon, and was declared the winner of the Electoral College by one vote. After the Democrats contested these results, a fifteen-member Electoral Commission was established in January 1877 to decide the presidency.[77]

A Mississippi Republican later insisted that if voter intimidation "'had been suppressed at the beginning'" before 1876, none of the controversy surrounding the election and subsequent actions would have occurred.[78] Foner agreed with that assessment, seeing "the abandonment of Reconstruction . . . [being] as much a cause of the crisis of 1876–77 as a consequence"—had Republicans maintained their willingness "to intervene in defense of black rights, Tilden would never had come close to carrying the entire South."[79] Notwithstanding, the decision to certify Hayes as the nineteenth president remains highly controversial as to whether a deal was struck for the removal of federal troops.

Louisiana's Republican claimant for governor, Stephen B. Packard, was barricaded into the statehouse after Democratic candidate Francis T. Nicholls, a former Confederate general, staged a White League–supported coup in January to take over the government.[80] In his last days as president, Grant had Packard notified of his concurrence that "public opinion will [no] longer support the maintenance of State Government in Louisiana by the use of the military"; thus federal troops as before would "protect life and property from mob violence when the State authorities fail," but would not be employed "to establish or pull down either claimant for control of the State."[81] However, a detachment of infantry remained stationed near the Mechanic's Institute, the statehouse in New Orleans being used by Packard and his supporters.[82]

After taking office, Hayes sent a commission to Louisiana with the ostensible purpose of determining whether the federal troops could be safely withdrawn, delaying a decision "until I could determine whether the condition of affairs is . . . such as to either require or justify continued military intervention" in the state. On April 20, accepting the commission's recommendation and with Cabinet support, the president ordered the garrison's removal from their position to "such regular barracks in the vicinity as may be selected for their occupation." Hayes stated that his decision was based on the lack of constitutional authority for continuing federal military intervention, and "the assurance that no resort to violence is contemplated, but that, on the contrary, the disputes in question are to be settled by peaceful methods." Left unsaid was that Packard's position was now untenable, and Louisiana would come under Democratic rule.[83]

Five days later, Packard and all but one of his supporters left the statehouse; reluctantly, the governor announced that due to "superior forces," he was "abstain[ing] for the present from all active assertion of my government." Packard did not spare Grant or Hayes from criticism, asserting that had his "legal government been recognized, it could have sustained itself without the intervention of troops."[84]

A parallel situation existed in South Carolina, where Wade Hampton and Republican Daniel H. Chamberlain each claimed the governorship. Chamberlain and his allies had been sequestered in rooms at the statehouse under the protection of federal troops for months when, on March 23, both men were invited to Washington to confer with Hayes. After initially refusing on the grounds that he had been legally elected, Hampton traveled to Washington and met with the president.

While Chamberlain requested that a commission be appointed to adjudicate his state's election results for governor and lieutenant governor, Hampton was primarily concerned with removal of the federal garrison in Columbia. The former Confederate general got his wish—in accordance with his Cabinet's decision, Hayes on April 3 ordered the troops to be withdrawn the following week. Exactly at high noon on April 10, the personification of federal authority marched out of the statehouse; Chamberlain vacated the premises the following day to Hampton.[85]

In his accompanying announcement to South Carolina's Republicans, Chamberlain stated that he would "no longer actively assert my rights to the office of Governor." Just as Packard would do two weeks later, Chamberlain castigated the Hayes administration for "evad[ing] the duty of ascertaining which of two rival state governments is the lawful one." He further stated that "by the withdrawal of the troops now protecting the state from domestic violence, [the Executive branch] abandons the lawful state government to a struggle with an insurrectionary force too powerful to be resisted."[86]

Technically, Hayes had not pulled all federal troops from Louisiana and South Carolina. However, ordering their withdrawal from protecting two governors with legitimate claims to their offices despite organized violence and intimidation of black and white Republicans had the equivalent effect. According to Lane, "The Compromise of 1877 was less formal than the Missouri Compromise or the Compromise of 1850, but its basic logic was similar. The Union was to be preserved at the risk of the rights of four million Americans of African descent." Similarly, Foner stated that "1877 marked a decisive retreat from the idea, born during the Civil War, of a powerful national state protecting the fundamental rights of American citizens."[87]

The signs had been ominous and unmistakable for years. Having lost congressional control in the disastrous midterm elections, in late 1874 Republicans attempted to salvage what remained of Reconstruction in their last session as a majority. Despite three months of acrimonious debate, strong Democratic opposition and less than unanimous support within their own party, the Civil Rights Bill was enacted on March 1, 1875.

Meant to protect blacks' full and equal "enjoyment of the accommodations, advantages, facilities and privileges of inns, public conveyances on land and water, theatres, and other places of public amusement" from Jim Crow discrimination chiefly in the South, the law also criminalized the prevention of qualified citizens from serving as either a grand or petit juror in any federal or state court. However, sections specifying mixed-race schools and cemeteries had been eliminated, and there was legitimate concern that the act would not survive Supreme Court review. As Foner reported, it "represented an unprecedented exercise of national authority, and breached traditional federalist principles more fully than any previous Reconstruction legislation."[88]

Despite all attempts, there was no saving "the unprecedented experiment in social engineering."[89] In Reconstruction's troubled wake, the nation faced an all-important question—what now?

First Sergeant Robert A. Pinn, Fifth USCT. NATIONAL PARK SERVICE.

The Fight Against Jim Crow and the Grand Army of the Republic

In Loyalty, to maintain true allegiance to the United States of America, based upon a paramount respect for, and fidelity to its constitution and laws, to discountenance whatever . . . in any manner impairs the efficiency and permanency of our free institutions, and to encourage the spread of universal liberty, equal rights and justice to all men.

—COMMANDER JOSEPH W. O'NEALL, TWENTY-THIRD ANNUAL ENCAMPMENT OF DEPARTMENT OF OHIO, GAR, APRIL 24, 1889[1]

For twelve years, the former Confederate states were its focus, yet Reconstruction had a parallel impact on the struggle for equality in the North. The Fourteenth and Fifteenth Amendments ensured that black men could now exercise political power through the ballot, with African Americans entitled to the same protections under the law as Caucasians. But the North was not monolithic, its states differing on the extent to which blacks enjoyed rights (e.g., serving on juries) matching those of whites, or had equal economic or educational opportunities.

In the ongoing fight for freedom for all Americans, Union veterans individually and collectively needed to maintain their interconnected roles as potent moral and political forces. There is considerable evidence that white and black ex-servicemen throughout the remaining years of the nineteenth century did just that, with the representative Left-Armed Corps providing further confirmation in both respects.

Wm. Augustus MacNulty embodied the peacetime commitment of Union veterans to what they had strived to attain through war. On May 30, 1868, still working for the Freedmen's Bureau but now as a civilian, he and his family (wife, son, and mother) joined "the loyal colored people" of Culpeper, Virginia, to observe Memorial Day at the National Cemetery.

Abbie MacNulty's one hundred pupils marched in laden with flowers and wreaths, then Reverend Blair offered a prayer for the honored Union dead. After Abbie read a Browning poem, her husband delivered the holiday oration in which he celebrated "*your tender care and devotion for those whose heroic deeds have resulted in your liberation from bondage and cruel oppression*," reminded everyone that half of those interred were unknown, and spoke of the incalculable loss suffered "*to battle for the right*." The graves were then festooned, a hymn and the "Star-Spangled Banner" sung, and all then reassembled to return home.[2]

Three years later, MacNulty took part in the Republican nominating convention for the Virginia House of Delegates, at which he expressed high gratification "*at seeing so much harmony and good feeling prevailing in the ranks of our party in the county and State*," and another colleague appealed for all "to stand by the principles of the party of freedom and equal rights, . . . defended [Grant's] administration . . . and said . . . he would again be triumphantly elected." MacNulty helped to ensure that as a vice president for the Pittsburgh Convention of Union Soldiers and Sailors in September 1872, and chairman of the Culpeper County Republican committee.[3]

Other white members of the Left-Armed Corps stood by African Americans in one of the central elements of equality. As Daviess County School superintendent, William M. Bostaph reported frankly to the Missouri General Assembly in 1869 that due to "*little interest . . . manifested in . . . behalf*" of the "*one colored school in this county, . . . the school is not as prosperous as it might be, although it is doing much better than was at first expected*." He attributed this to the great interest of African Americans, who "*are doing all they can, and are accomplishing a great deal*" despite "*the opposition the education of the colored people had to contend with for a long time, and now, the stolid indifference, on the part of many of our citizens,"* which limited what could be achieved.[4]

As a disabled veteran who had transcended physical limitations through brain power, Bostaph pleaded on behalf of those who hoped to raise themselves through intellectual opportunity, and the nation itself: *"we hope the time may not be far distant, when popular education will be recognized in its true form, and regarded as it should be—necessary for the preservation of our political institutions."*[5]

Besides such individual efforts, Union veteran groups had been critical to both maintaining Republican control of the White House and Senate during Reconstruction, and its implementation. In addition to the political activities already described, high profile events, including many involving remembrance, emphasized biracial fellowship. In June 1869, the GAR, "various colored organizations, and a number of colored citizens" together attended commemorative services at the National Cemetery in Nashville.[6]

Yet, when Geo. T. Downing, a leading black restaurateur in Washington, attended similar ceremonies at Arlington National Cemetery at the same time and again the following year to place flowers on the graves of white and black soldiers, he was mortified to find separate exercises by race, and distinct differences in presentation, facilities, and monuments. The *National Republican* prominently featured his account in its June 9, 1870, edition.[7]

That same issue carried an angry response from Frederick Douglass's son Lewis, former sergeant-major of the famed Fifty-Fourth Massachusetts. Douglass accused Downing of "do[ing] injustice to the Grand Army of the Republic. There is not the slightest ground for the implication that there was any 'odious discrimination' in the matter of the decoration of soldiers' graves, colored or white, on the 30th day of May last." Citing his own service on three GAR planning committees for the ceremonies along with two other black veterans, Douglass denied there was any basis for accusation of prejudice regarding the ceremonies, as they were assigned to different posts without respect to race.[8]

The GAR National Encampment had convened in Washington a few weeks before the 1870 Memorial Day activities at Arlington.

During the meeting, the Committee on Resolutions unanimously adopted a measure asking that all Grand Army departments, posts, and members advocate for "the establishment and maintenance of homes and schools for the support and education of the orphans of Union soldiers and marines, without distinction of birthplace or of race," when their fathers' deaths were in battle or otherwise related to military service.

In another resolution, "while . . . recogniz[ing] the equality of all soldiers who were mustered in," the organization asked that a separate branch of the National Asylum for Disabled Soldiers be established in the South for "the colored veterans entitled to a home,"[9] presumably in addition to the Southern Branch already at Hampton, Virginia.

These endeavors and others to follow over the next few decades were unique in post–Civil War America. Donald R. Shaffer, a leading historian on black veterans, has reported on their conspicuous success in being accepted into the GAR due to its official "color-blind membership policy." This made the Grand Army exceptional in ignoring the standard custom of nineteenth century associations established by whites in the United States, namely to keep out African Americans.[10]

In a more recent book that focused on the GAR, Barbara A. Gannon stated that its "interracial nature" had not been stressed in earlier works: "Instead, while acknowledging black membership, scholars have argued that this organization treated African American poorly and that this treatment was somehow connected to the national retreat from black civil rights in the late nineteenth century."[11]

Yet the open bigotry of numerous Northern newspapers vividly illustrates just how atypical the Grand Army's racial inclusiveness was in its time. When controversy arose in mid-1869 over Lewis Douglass working at the Government Printing Office without being in the printer's union, the *Ottawa Free Trader* in Illinois reported: "The fuss about the nigger Douglas [*sic*] is still raging. The city typographical society, over the question of receiving him to membership, had a discussion so fiery that it ended in a quarrel, row and knock down. Meantime, women . . . are giving up their situations rather than work under the same roof with the nigger."[12]

Neither superb military service nor his father's prominence could earn Lewis Douglass general tolerance at his job, or elevate his status with some fellow citizens that was exemplified by a despicable racial epithet.

In February 1870, the nation's first black senator, Hiram R. Revels of Mississippi, took his oath of office,[13] the historic occasion marked by some Pennsylvania newspapers in the most degrading manner their staffs could muster. Philadelphia's *Evening Telegraph* reported the "mud-colored Mississippi parson" having been seated in the Senate, "There is at last a 'nigger in the national wood-pile.'"[14] Not to be outdone, the *Cambria Freeman* ridiculed the gratification Mrs. Revels felt by ascribing comments to her in ludicrous dialect.[15]

Two weeks later, the ironically named *Freeman* illustrated that the link between battlefield valor and postwar advancement in civil rights was repugnant to those who opposed equality for African Americans. The newspaper reported that former secretary of war and Pennsylvania Senator Simon Cameron had supported Revels by stating his belief that "'the tide of war would have gone against us had not 200,000 negroes come to the rescue.'"

While "rescue" was rather belittling to white soldiers ("joined the fight" would have been more apt), Cameron's basic premise was hardly an "atrocious calumny" as the *Freeman* claimed. Nonetheless, a familiar party, W. W. H. Davis, was cited to denigrate African American troops: "'*Mr. Cameron's statement would be highly creditable to the South if correct; but it is false, false in every particular, and Cameron knows it.*'"[16] Not only did Cameron not know this, neither did General Davis's fellow veterans—in November 1870 Senator Revels gave a "special lecture" in Buffalo that was sponsored by Chapin Post No. 2 of the GAR's Department of New York.[17]

As Shaffer observed, African American veterans were in the most favorable position for "mitigat[ion of] the indignities of black life during the last decades of the nineteenth century and the first decades of the twentieth" due to "the legacy of their service, and other advantages they enjoyed."[18] Black GAR membership, and the organization's singular interracial nature, were rooted in white veterans' appreciation for what

African Americans had done while wearing the same Union blue.[19] In the ongoing struggle for equality, acceptance of black veterans by their white comrades on both individual and group bases, grounded in a shared warrior identity, would be crucial.

THE LEFT-ARMED CORPS AND THE GAR

According to Gannon, approximately one-third of former Union soldiers were GAR members at the organization's zenith.[20] That percentage was eclipsed by the Left-Armed Corps, with 57 percent (153/268) confirmed as belonging to the organization at some point. Ardent participants, 46 percent (71/153) were charter, original or early members of the GAR/ local posts ranging from 1866 to 1889. Thirty men were members of two or more posts, and 20 percent (31/153) overall belonged to posts known to be integrated, and there was broad representation among the states of membership.[21]

The Left-Armed Corps enjoyed high ranks at all levels. A remarkable 35 percent (54/153) achieved post command, another ten topped out as senior vice commanders, and twenty-one others became post officers. Ten men became commanders in eleven departments: two in Connecticut, and one each in Florida; Georgia and South Carolina; Idaho; Michigan; New York; Utah; California and Nevada; Virginia; and Virginia and North Carolina. The Corps also supplied nine department senior vice commanders coast-to-coast (California; Connecticut; Georgia; Illinois; Maine; New York; Utah; Virginia and Wisconsin), and four junior vice commanders (Connecticut, New York, Ohio, and Virginia); five men sat on state councils of administration.

As for countrywide achievement, William M. Bostaph was elected senior vice commander in chief in 1909,[22] while three of his comrades served on national councils of administration, and five others as aides-de-camp to the commander in chief.

One of the Left-Armed Corps' few sailors rose to the highest echelon of maritime veterans, and also held positions of honor in the GAR. William G. McEwan, whose bravery during the battle of Mobile Bay so impressed Admiral David Farragut that he was transferred to the regular navy, retired as a lieutenant and assistant engineer in 1875.[23] In

1910 he was elected both fleet captain and commanding commodore of the National Association of Naval Veterans.[24] Four years earlier he had commanded the George G. Meade Post No.1 in Philadelphia, and later served two separate terms on the Department of Pennsylvania Council of Administration.[25]

Stuart McConnell has stated that from its "partisan origins in 1866 . . . the GAR soon foundered and by 1872 was virtually moribund. It revived in the late 1870s as a fraternal order, and by 1890 it had become a powerful lobby for pensions, 'correct' history, and a particular brand of American nationalism."[26]

The Left-Armed Corps reflects this pattern—of those whose general date of initial membership is ascertainable, 25 percent (31/126) joined the GAR between 1866 and 1872, while the remaining 75 percent (95/126) became members starting in 1875. Within the latter group, one-half had mustered in by December 1889.

Among the twenty-three who joined in the 1860s was Brevet Major R. Watson Seage, who would movingly recite his poem of war at Gettysburg more than twenty years later. In early 1868, he was junior vice commander of Post No. 1 in Detroit, with his brother Henry post adjutant and their reverend father John serving as post chaplain.[27] However, by 1872 the Department of Michigan was defunct, and a new state department would not be established until 1879.[28]

Harrison O. Thomas was in New Bedford, Massachusetts, on grocery business when he joined its City Guards (Third Massachusetts) for three months' service in April 1861. Discharged toward the end of July, the twenty-one-year-old promptly re-enlisted in the Eighteenth Massachusetts, this time for three years. After being shot in the right forearm at Fredericksburg on December 13, 1862, five inches of his shattered radius were removed by excision, leaving a "*distorted, powerless and useless*" extremity. Discharged on total disability in March 1863, he received permission to return to his regiment "*not as a soldier, but as a free and volunteer nurse.*" Following the Army of the Potomac at his own expense, "*during the year of my free labor I was at the side of over four hundred dieing soldiers, and by the aid of the Sanitary and Christian Commission's was enabled I trust to do very much good, in word work and deed.*" Appreciative of his efforts in their behalf, comrades called the maimed veteran "Citizen Thomas," a nickname he always used with deep personal satisfaction.[29]

After returning to Massachusetts, Thomas made two lifelong commitments. The first member mustered into Brockton's Fletcher Webster Post No. 13 in July 1867, he married Hattie Greenleaf Morton eight months later. Earning a living as custodian of the safe and deposit vaults at the Plymouth County Trust Company, he served Brockton and the Commonwealth of Massachusetts in its House of Representatives in the early 1890s. In 1910, Thomas's brethren paid formal tribute to his outstanding achievement as post historian, the compilation of war sketches for all six hundred members, past or present, over sixteen years in "a labor of love." His half-century membership in the Fletcher Webster Post was uninterrupted, the Department of Massachusetts having remained intact and active once it was permanently established in 1867.[30]

Like other Union veterans, those in the Left-Armed Corps mostly became GAR members in the wake of Reconstruction. Prospect, New York, native and newlywed George R. Farley was instrumental in founding John T. Thomas Post No. 39, which was chartered in May 1875, and commanded it for fifteen of its first twenty-one years. The bright, multi-talented ex-teamster who left Virginia minus the use of his right hand, would help to muster over two thousand comrades, an impressive number for such a small town, and never missed a Memorial Day celebration.[31]

Similarly, the first GAR post established in Auburn, Maine having lost its charter in 1876, former infantry sergeant S. Frank Haskell found time apart from his expanding clothing business and family in 1881 to become an original part of Burnside Post No. 47, which would flourish in both members and influence.[32]

In Ohio, the number of posts had diminished from three hundred in 1868 to just eight by 1875. However, by the mid-1880s the Buckeye State had hundreds of new active posts.[33] It was then that one of the department's most iconic members began his second Grand Army tenure by enrolling in Hart Post No. 134 in Massillon, the original Hart Post No. 2, he'd joined in 1868 having surrendered its charter ten years later.[34] Already a trailblazer as Stark County's first black attorney, Robert A. Pinn would break down barriers within America's foremost veterans' group.

Besides the GAR, many in the cohort pursued regimental, brigade, corps, and army-specific activities, along with local ex-servicemen and national disabled veteran association work. Ten were companions of the Military Order of the Loyal Legion of the United States (MOLLUS), a non-partisan organization of active duty and former Union officers which included five Republican presidents (Grant, Hayes, Arthur, Harrison, and McKinley), along with such Democratic stalwarts as George McClellan and Winfield Scott Hancock.[35] Left-Armed Corps MOLLUS companions included W. A. MacNulty and W. W. H. Davis, and it is hard to imagine two former Northern soldiers holding more conflicting political or racial views.

However, scholarly examinations of predominantly white Northern veterans after the Civil War have generally taken little notice of their involvement in politics. In his pioneering book on the GAR, McConnell devoted slight attention to its "obvious Republican partisanship" beyond limited discussion of previous studies.[36] After analyzing memoirs of former Union soldiers for changing attitudes about their war experience, Earl J. Hess noted that while Ambrose Bierce and some others were disillusioned by what took place in the South, "most Northern veterans did not pay much attention to the outcome of Reconstruction."[37] Studying both Union and Confederate ex-servicemen, Eric T. Dean Jr. similarly reported that "Civil War historians have long understood that for the first twenty years after the end of the war, the veterans were a largely dormant force."[38]

Regarding those who specifically looked at political activities, pension-related issues were Brian M. Jordan's major emphasis in his book on Union veterans. Having delved deeply into black ex-servicemen's postwar endeavors, those pursued by their Caucasian comrades in support of Reconstruction and associated civil rights legislation were barely mentioned by Shaffer. The same holds for David Blight despite his concentrated study of that period, soldiers' remembrance, and other factors, North and South.[39]

As for other noted historians, Foner did not explore the role of Union veterans, black or white, in his ground-breaking Reconstruction book, and there was no discussion of former Northern soldiers or sailors in Henry Louis Gates Jr.'s more recent work on Reconstruction.[40]

Yet, white Union veterans' political activism during Reconstruction and their related, generally enlightened views on such vital issues as emancipation, black male suffrage, and equal rights under the law have already been extensively shown in this book, and there will be more to follow. Attitudes toward African Americans were a crucial component of party membership after the Civil War, and as an influential, predominantly Republican voting bloc, Northern ex-servicemen supported landmark initiatives on behalf of their fellow black citizens.

In political affiliation, the Left-Armed Corps mirrored Union veterans overall, and Grand Army members in specific. Among 149 in the cohort for whom party membership could be determined, 94 percent (140) were Republicans and 5 percent (8) were Democrats. The Republicans overwhelmingly maintained a lifelong party affiliation from the time of the Civil War; five switched to the Prohibition (3) or People's/Populist (2) parties between 1889 and 1895, three to the Bull Moose/Progressive parties over 1908 through 1915, and a ninth had become a Democrat by the time of his death in 1922. Of 106 GAR members with known party affiliations, all but five were Republicans, with three Democrats, one Democrat-Populist, and one Prohibitionist.

Just what did it mean to be a Republican after Reconstruction ended? According to Foner, while "1877 confirmed the growing conservatism of the Republican party and portended a new role for the national state in the post-Reconstruction years . . . neither the humanitarian impulse that had helped create the Republican party nor the commitment to equal citizenship that evolved during the war and Reconstruction, entirely disappeared." However, what took place in the South would lessen in importance to Northern Republicans over time, along with diminishing support for enforcement of the Fourteenth and Fifteenth Amendments through federal means.[41]

The Struggle for Equality Above the Mason-Dixon Line

But in the North there were battles to be fought for equality, with the GAR and other Union veterans in ideal positions to provide leadership with respect to civil rights.

Emma Lou Thornbrough ably assessed the situation: "[I]n the nineteenth century the [Fourteenth Amendment] guarantees of 'due process' and 'equal protection of the laws' were ideals that fell short of attainment by Indiana Negroes. Removal of racial distinctions in the state Constitution and laws did not insure equality of treatment, and even the enactment of positive guarantees did not put an end to discrimination."[42]

In the supposedly more tolerant North, southern Indiana might as well have been below the Mason-Dixon line, given a prevailing "double standard of justice" under which "white men committed crimes against Negroes with impunity or only nominal penalties, while Negroes were severely punished for crimes against white persons." Particularly after the Civil War, antipathy toward black immigration led to commitment of violent crimes that included murder, with those responsible rarely held to legal account.

As a result, Thornbrough reported that African Americans in the Hoosier State made a conscious decision to focus their attention on attaining equality in education and voting rights rather than threaten whites (and hurt chances for black advancement in schools and at polling places) by seeking anything suggestive of "'social equality.'"[43]

The drive to secure equal educational opportunity was replicated in other Northern states, including Indiana's eastern neighbor. David O. Mull, who was shot in both arms at Kennesaw Mountain, Georgia on June 27, 1864, and lost his right forearm and *"headers of third and fourth fingers of left hand"* to amputation, returned home to Columbus, Ohio, five months later. Suffering from chronic diarrhea in addition to his upper extremity woes, he opened a grocery and married Harriet Poole in 1873. Unable to keep the store, he became a flagman at a railroad crossing, then "held a position in a city department which he had to resign because he was [physically] unable . . . to do the work."[44]

That elected post was Franklinton School janitor, which Mull fulfilled so effectively the Board of Education's Visiting Committee formally commended him in 1884. When his health failed in 1890, the board elected him truant officer for the Columbus schools (with a raise) in response to "enforcement of the compulsory school law." Mull died in office on December 20, 1890, finally succumbing to tuberculosis in both lungs three months shy of his forty-seventh birthday; his attending physician also attributed his *"persistent and profuse diarrhea"* to probable *"tubercular changes and desquamation of bowel."*[45]

With respect to integration of its African American pupils, the school system served by the former sergeant until his death had an admirable history. As described by James U. Barnhill, the process began in 1874 with the application of a class of black students "for admission to the High School, and all . . . who passed the examination were received." Next came admission of "colored pupils to the schools for white children, which was done without difficulty and with only one protest," followed by "distribution of the two higher Grammar grades of the separate colored school to the buildings occupied by white children."

Then, in 1881 the school board instructed the superintendent "to place all pupils in buildings in the districts where they dwelt," and when schools opened in September, "the colored people availed themselves of this privilege." The final step occurred in February 1882 when the building that had been reserved for African American children was sold, and "all the colored youth of school age" were distributed "to the other buildings."[46]

There would be no such integration, seamless or otherwise, in Illinois's southernmost city. Situated where the Mississippi and Ohio Rivers meet, Cairo was a natural crossing into freedom for persons escaping slavery and contrabands during the Civil War. Keen to become educated, they started classes in basic literacy for all ages that were expanded with the assistance of the Freedmen's Bureau and charitable organizations after the war. However, Cairo's black citizens realized that fulfillment of their educational aspirations would require the establishment of an organized school with qualified teachers.[47]

Their dreams seemed closer to realization when the third Illinois state constitution, ratified in 1870, directed the general assembly to "provide a thorough and efficient system of free schools, whereby all children of this State may receive a good common school education." As a consequence, the first general assembly to convene under the new constitution passed "An act to establish and maintain a system of free schools" in April 1872, which mandated "that all children in any district over the age of six and under twenty-one years shall have secured to them the right and opportunity to an equal education in the public schools."[48]

However, when McLean County built a separate school for African American children, the case was brought to court, which ruled that the county had no right under either the state constitution or Act of 1872 to do so. After an appeal made its way to the Illinois State Supreme Court, the McLean County Court's decision was affirmed. In their ruling, the justices clearly stated district school directors "have no power to make class distinctions, neither can they discriminate between scholars on account of their color, race or social condition." In keeping with the Supreme Court's ruling, the state legislature passed another free school law designed to protect the right of black children to attend public schools. Both the Supreme Court and the legislature mandated that African American students be afforded facilities and educations entirely equal to those of white students, but neither directed schools to be integrated in fulfilling that requirement.[49]

In Cairo, black children being afforded a free public education was bad enough for many residents. Seeing that coming, the city's *Evening Bulletin* published a series of lacerating editorials throughout 1869 and 1870.[50] A leading arguments was financial—white citizens would be paying the lion's share of the costs of educating African American children through taxes, while their parents, who for the most part owned no property, would contribute relatively little. But there was much more to the story, and it was ugly—insisting white children needed to "become debased in thought and action" in order to "lose sight of all [their] superior attributes," "The *natural, inborn* aversion the white child feels for the black cannot even be educated out of his bosom. It is part of his nature. The consequence of this state of feeling would develop itself in 'a divided house'—an 'irrepressible conflict' that would go on until the school became all black or all white—'all one thing or all the other.'"[51]

As a boy, Abraham Lincoln received little formal education. Entombed 200 miles to the north, he would never know that his memorable 1858 speech could be so corrupted in a malicious attempt to deny children what he had so desperately wanted.

But the law was the law, and Cairo was under state authority that included Illinois governor John M. Palmer, who emphasized that African Americans had the same right to public school education as whites.[52] In April 1870, Cairo's black police magistrate and civil rights activist, John J. Bird, spoke at a celebration of the Fifteenth Amendment. He took the opportunity to flatly state that African Americans neither wanted nor expected their children to attend white schools and could form, sustain, and staff their own schools. However, they had every expectation that black students would receive their fair share of public school funding and the same protection of their education as white pupils under the state laws, just as in another Midwestern state: "He pointed to the colored schools in Ohio—among the best disciplined and most nourishing of the land—as evidence of the ability of colored citizens to educate their own children, (separate and apart from the white, and without even the assistance of white teachers) when placed on an equal footing with other citizens."[53]

In the fall of 1871, Cairo's first colored school opened under the leadership of B. C. Talford and other teachers, all of them white. The city's black citizens resented the lack of input into the school's establishment and refusal to hire teachers of color, and it didn't take long for a polarizing episode to occur. A female white teacher became incensed while physically disciplining a young male pupil, and was clearly heard to express her wish that "'negro children were back in slavery with their masters'" by Alice Jackson. Off school grounds, the nineteen-year-old student told others what was said, only to be confronted by Talford, who demanded her denial of having heard any such thing. When she refused, the schoolmaster took a rawhide to the young black woman.

Cairo's African American community met twice to discuss the incident and express their outrage. The city's leading Democratic newspaper fully supported their point of view, condemning the use of corporal punishment, deeming the female teacher unfit for her profession, and advocating for Talford's firing: "The negroes, or a great majority of them, prefer to have their children taught by teachers of their own race, knowing full well that an intelligent colored man would take more interest in the moral and intellectual welfare of their children, than an ignorant white bummer, such as Talford, could." But even in backing blacks against whites, the *Daily Bulletin* staff was apparently unable to fully rein in their racism: "The white man who accepts a position in a colored school has no respect for himself, and cannot hope to command the respect of the negroes."[54]

Talford remained, and Cairo's black students attended a facility markedly inferior to those for white children that initially stopped at fifth grade.[55] Despite ongoing dissatisfaction with the schoolmaster, physical plant inequality, and the lack of possible advancement to higher education, the school was heavily utilized by the city's African Americans. By 1874 there were eight grades, and a second country school with a four-month session had been added. In July, Judge Bird spoke on "'The Education of the African Race'" during dedication ceremonies in Carbondale as requested by the president of Southern Illinois Normal College. He pointedly cited results of an evaluation of black schools, in which "The schools of Ohio, Indiana, Pennsylvania, Illinois and a number of other states were reported by their superintendents to be equal in advancement and average attendance, to the whites."[56]

Then in September 1876, "an intelligent colored man" from Ohio arrived to begin his work in teaching. College-educated, Robert A. Pinn made an immediate impression on Cairo's black and white residents alike. Whether they were aware of his war record is uncertain, but there was no mistaking his presence. Talford was gone, and by March 1877 Pinn was the colored school superintendent responsible for 220 students. He was one of four black teachers (one woman and two other men) lauded by the *Cairo Bulletin* for the colored schools' "flourishing condition" and having "made them much better than they ever were before." During an official visit of both the school board of directors and taxpayers' committee, the latter's spokesman indicated his satisfaction with how the schools were being managed.[57]

When the Grammar Department in which Pinn taught was publicly examined by the same groups the following week, its members were quite impressed by the students' "great progress" and their alacrity and accuracy of response to questions on various topics. The board of Directors and Tax-Payers' Committee deemed the school to be "one of the most orderly and attentive we have ever had the pleasure of visiting, and the scholars all seem to be imbued with a single purpose—that of making the most of their time, and learning all they can while the opportunity is open to them." Praising Pinn as "a well educated and thorough gentleman . . . [who] . . . takes great pride in his school," the Committee ascribed its "high state of perfection" to "his skill and energy as a teacher."[58]

The colored schools' progress under Pinn's leadership hadn't come easily. In fact, the situation was so difficult that he enlisted the help of his academic mentor and former commanding officer Giles W. Shurtleff in finding another position. Writing to the American Missionary Society on Pinn's behalf in June 1877, the Oberlin professor noted his friend's "brilliant success in the face of bitter opposition." However, Pinn agreed to return to Cairo when its Board of Education acceded to his terms, including a monthly salary of $65.[59]

What a dignified black man born free in another state was up against, along with his colleagues, students, and their parents, was typified in the August 9 edition of the *Cairo Bulletin*: "Circuit Clerk John Reeve has gone to St. Louis. It is said he will bring a whole 'nigger show' back with him. He has gone on the hunt of minstrel talent."[60]

By stunning contrast, Republican Governor Shelby M. Cullom and William K. Ackerman, president of the Illinois Central Railroad, along with other dignitaries, toured the city's public schools in December. Pinn and the colored school were among those cited by Cullom and Ackerman "for having brought the Cairo schools to so high a standard and placing them on a level with the best in the state."[61]

In March 1878, a white resident sent a letter to the *Bulletin* advocating for the re-election of two public school directors, particularly based on his belief that a change in the board "would result in no good to our public schools generally but more particularly to the colored schools." He was sure that Cairo's black population ("'niggers' if it suits better") was "satisfied, even well pleased, with the educational advantages afforded them under our present public school system."[62]

Sadly, this observation was far from the truth. Despite the advances that had been made in less than a decade, Cairo's colored schools were not only separate, but significantly unequal to the facilities attended by Caucasian students. As shown by the letter-writer, even some sympathetic whites seemed to think racial epithets were necessary lest other whites be offended by statements of support for African Americans.

After two years in Cairo fighting for black children's access to quality education, Robert Pinn apparently had enough. He left for another teaching position in Newberry, South Carolina, but within a year returned to northern Ohio to pursue legal studies.[63]

The ongoing lack of national consensus as to government's role in public education, and ever-present racial issues, were epitomized by an 1875 court case in Brooklyn. With merger into New York City twenty-three years away,[64] the independent city's board of education exercised complete control of its public schools under an 1850 legislative act. When an African American minister, Reverend William F. Johnson, tried to force the local white school principal to admit his son rather than the boy's attending the school for black children, the civil rights case came before Supreme Court Judge Gilbert.

His honor's decision was flabbergasting. As reported by the *National Republican*, "The court held that common schools are public charity; that benefits conferred by them are a free gift from the State, and like every other donor the State may prescribe in what manner and upon what terms and conditions the gift may be enjoyed." Washington's *Evening Star* then explained what ensued from his amazing premise—according to Gilbert, the school board's governing legislation meant "participation in the privileges and benefits of common schools forms no part of that body of political and civil rights which are protected and secured by the fundamental law [Civil Rights Act]. Therefore, Judge Gilbert says, the 14th amendment has no application to the case."[65]

In New York, the *Sun* provided a lengthy excerpt from the decision further showing the basis for Gilbert's findings, with his thinking and subsequent conclusions all too familiar in the view that existing law was not violated, "unless such schools are inferior or at an inconvenient distance, or are obnoxious to some other objection from which it can be legally inferred that the accommodations, advantages, facilities, and privileges afforded by them are not equal to those furnished in schools of the other class. The statute, by granting equal privileges, does not confer the right to enjoy them in common with any class of persons or in any particular school house."[66]

TURMOIL OVER EDUCATION FOR AFRICAN AMERICANS

Nine years after Pinn departed from Cairo, another member of the Left-Armed Corps found himself in the middle of a national debate over segregation and the education of African Americans. The First Congregational Church of Atlanta, originating from Georgia's first school for blacks, was founded in 1867 by its white teachers and personnel from the American Missionary Association. Most of the funding for the church's physical plant came from the association, with the African American community providing both labor and additional financial support. Its buildings stood in a white neighborhood near Atlanta University, a black institution created by the association whose students had erected the parsonage.

Originally integrated, by 1883 the First Congregational's only non-black parishioners were teachers from Atlanta University, with Reverend Evarts Kent the latest in a series of white pastors from New England. But the bonds among the church, school, and organization were still strong. The American Missionary Association continued to provide most of the university's funding through its donors; Georgia's only financial contribution was $8,000, half of the yearly interest generated from public lands apportioned to the states by the federal government for educational objectives.

Atlanta University's pupils from Georgia had always been exclusively black, but five white students from out of state who were the children of faculty members and one of Reverend Kent's sons attended school along with the African Americans. This seemingly innocent convention, rooted in both pragmatic and idealistic motives and done without fanfare, suddenly turned explosive in 1887.[67]

Under Georgia's constitution, "a thorough system of common schools" was maintained that was "free to all citizens of the State, but separate schools shall be provided for the white and colored races." As pointed out by the *New York Evening Post*, the same situation prevailed across the South, and in "many Northern States until recent years."[68] But did the constitutional stipulation apply to Georgia educational institutions that were not common schools? When the state university board of visitors made an official report to Governor John B. Gordon of interracial education at Atlanta University, the issue became one of great public attention.[69]

In response to the board's notification and resulting furor, State Representative William Glenn, in July 1887, introduced a bill that would criminalize the teaching of black and white children together at any institution of learning. A teacher, principal, president, secretary, or trustee at such a school would face a fine of $1,000, six months in jail, or a year in one of Georgia's dreaded chain gangs. The measure's originator clearly stated his desire to ensure that "laws necessary to forever separate the white and black races" be enacted, as "Race prejudice is a natural prejudice, and it is foolish to try to overcome by legislation anything that is repugnant to human nature." Glenn continued: "'There can be no estimate of the evils that will arise from a commingling of races at young and impressible ages in unrestricted intercourse, each imbibing the worst ideas of the other. Miscegenation of ideas may be as fatal as physical miscegenation, and the mental hybrid resulting from the coeducation of the races, as much a monstrosity as the physical hybrid could be.'" In a joint session of the Georgia House and Senate, the legislature's educational committee made a favorable report on Glenn's bill.[70]

Reaction from the state's African American community and Northern newspapers was swift and fierce. Throughout Georgia, black "indignation meetings" drew large crowds that crafted resolutions expressing their fury and denunciation of the bill. Representatives Wilson and Crawford, the House's only African Americans, submitted a minority report condemning the Glenn bill as an abridgement of both the US Constitution and the Bill of Rights within Georgia's constitution, and a needless interference "with the rights and privileges of citizens, whether white or colored, in the matter of educating their children"—they recommended against the measure's passage.[71]

In the New York State capital, the *Albany Evening Journal* was livid, finding it hard to imagine a "more brutal and barbarous law," with "the chain-gangs . . . composed of the most filthy and degraded criminals of the South," and it being "proposed to put among these hardened characters a school teacher whose only offense has been the recognition of the truth of human equality, affirmed in the Bible and the Declaration of Independence." The *Journal* insisted that "It is time that the voice of protest was raised against the treatment of the colored race in the South. That race has been deprived for years of its political and civil rights, and this Glenn bill caps the infamous climax."[72] On August 2, the House approved the bill by a 124–2 vote, Crawford and Wilson the lone dissenters.[73]

Overall, the coverage outside Georgia was notable for its precision, scope, and depth of understanding. The *New York Evening Post*, pinpointing Atlanta University as the bill's target, addressed its implications for any Georgia school not supported through public funds, and termed the measure "simply an outburst of race prejudice in its most offensive form."[74]

Two weeks later, the paper examined the "bitter comment[s]" of several African American newspapers, including a critical excerpt from the *Atlanta Defiance* on the very issue of school integration. It flatly stated "'intelligent negroes'" across the United States wanted "'mixed schools, . . . and sooner or later are going to have them,'" "'not for the sake of mixing with the whites, but [as] . . . the only door through which we can get equal and exact justice. It is the only thing that will wipe out this color question. It is the only thing that will make the negroes feel that they are true Americans. It is the only thing that will teach the whites of this country that the negro is his equal.'"[75]

The *Albany Evening Journal* reported that since the Fourteenth Amendment's adoption blacks in the South had made "remarkable progress," and similarly focused on education. It cited the *Chicago Advance*'s recent survey of 286 "representative" Southern African American men, in which 229 stated that black parents generally were interested in their children's education, "even mak[ing] sacrifices to secure instruction for them," and 195 seeing improvement in the quality of colored schools.

Further noting that black ownership of property in Georgia had almost doubled between 1880 and 1885, the *Journal* concluded: "Material prosperity, however, follows inevitably upon education and if the children of colored parents in the South are being educated, as the Chicago *Advance* shows, increase in wealth, position and political influence must be theirs in time."[76]

No one could have predicted the firestorm unleashed by an obscure state legislator with a proposed bill, but there it was. While Northern Republican and African American newspapers had led the charge, a number of Southern papers and Democratic journals in the North also voiced their objections.[77] On August 9, the Republican *Lowell Daily Courier* discussed the concerns of Northern Democrats, and their reported pressure on fellow party members to suppress the bill in the Georgia Senate. Three weeks later the newspaper noted that due to "outburst public sentiment," the state legislature "seem[s] to be taking the back track on the Glenn bill."[78]

The Massachusetts daily's perspicacity was shown on September 1, when newspapers nationwide reported that the Glenn bill had likely been scuttled by a House resolution in which the Senate concurred, stating that "[I]n the future the governor be directed not to draw his warrant for the annual appropriation of $8,000 to the Atlanta university under the act of March 3, 1874, until such a plan of expenditure . . . will secure [its] exclusive use . . . for the education of colored children only, in accordance with the declared and settled policy of this state on the subject of co-education of the races." The *Troy* (NY) *Daily Times* saw the resolution as fulfilling two aims of Georgia's governor and his Democratic allies: eliminating the white faculty members of Atlanta University, and "escaping from the necessity of action upon the Glenn bill."[79]

If Governor Gordon, a former Army of Northern Virginia lieutenant general, was an newspaper reader, he might have had second thoughts about whether white teachers from the North would simply leave Georgia. Before Evarts Kent became a man of the cloth, he proudly wore a soldier's uniform; battling Gordon and his men in the Wilderness, the Sixth Vermont private lost the use of his right hand.[80] Twenty-three years later, he again opposed the Governor in a critical fight, as had been made clear by the Savannah *Morning News* on August 20.

In its story, the *News* reported that Kent, "the white leader of the Houston Street Colored Congregational church," stated publicly that "he sends one son to the Atlanta University (colored) and two sons [actually, another son and his daughter] to Storr's school, a colored institution on Houston street, supported by the American Missionary Society." It further reported that Kent "patronizes the schools because the training is superior, and . . . he believes that the co-education of the races is right," and that he "denounces the Glenn bill as wrong, unchristian and unconstitutional, and thinks that notwithstanding its passage he will continue to send his children to colored schools, because he believes that the bill will be declared unconstitutional." Kent was then directly quoted: "'*The Bostonese are a law-abiding people, who believe in the co-education of the races and know its beneficial results from practice.*'"[81]

Round two came September 2 when the *Burlington* (VT) *Weekly Free Press* reported that "A rumor assigning a puerile reason for the sending of the son of Mr. Kent to the University having appeared in the Atlanta Constitution, Mr. Kent sent that paper the following ringing note:

> '*Editors Constitution:—I learn through your columns this morning that my son attends Atlanta University "because he is a playmate of the other white children who attend." I know of no responsible authority for such a statement.*
>
> '*My son attends Atlanta University because in the judgment of his parents, it affords a technical and intellectual training more thorough and varied than that of any other school in the city; because in practice it accords with the most enlightened nubile sentiment of the country; and because under existing circumstances his presence there bears plain witness to a faith in the divine doctrine of a universal brotherhood.*'"[82]

What the *Weekly Free Press* added would have been enlightening for Gordon:

[T]he good old mother and spirited sister of Mr. Kent, residing in New Haven, almost exult in the possibility that the beloved son and brother may be considered worthy to suffer persecution ["working in a chain gang"] in such a case; and if it comes we cannot doubt that he will prove true to his Vermont blood and lineage.[83]

To make matters worse, the Georgia legislature's face-saving resolution was not fooling anyone who truly understood the situation. When the *Lockport Daily Journal* in New York printed Frederick Douglass's letter of August 17 in which he scorned the Democrats as "the party of the Glenn bill," the paper added a knowing analysis: "We are aware that popular indignation has compelled or may compel the same Assembly to yet consider new resolutions which have been offered but the bottom effect even of the new ones is to drive white teachers from the South."[84]

As anticipated, the Georgia Senate rejected the Glenn bill by a 25–13 margin, then approved its replacement on September 22 in a 24–14 vote. In line with the earlier resolution, the bill mandated separation of the races in any Georgia educational institution, with none to accept both black and white pupils. Should any school violate the law, it would receive no appropriation of public funds designated for educational use, nor would their graduates be eligible for teaching positions.[85] Just as expected was the House's refusal to accept the new measure and insistence on its original bill, followed by the Senate's approving a resolution reiterating its own position. The impasse continued until the legislature adjourned in late October, which effectively killed the Glenn bill.[86]

The reactions of two Northern newspapers, one Democratic and the other Republican, were illuminating. The *New York Evening Post* made the dubious claim that the Georgia legislature had resolved the situation "in a manner which goes far to redeem the reputation of the State." This was based on the paper's assertion that the Senate had resisted calls for passage of the Glenn bill based on a desire to avoid caving to Northern pressure, while finding a way of "carrying out the policy of the State regarding public education, which requires separate common schools" through its own measure.[87]

In Vermont, the *Free Press* saw things differently. Its staff attributed the Senate's rejection of the Glenn bill to "public sentiment in the North, fear of the political consequences, and a good deal of sharp criticism from the South itself." Accurately predicting the impasse that followed, the *Free Press* considered "This is good as far as it goes. It is not to be expected that the Southern whites will give up their ideas on the color question at once."[88]

While the newspapers were far apart in these views, both condemned the ongoing enforcement of the "color line" in many Northern states. Each described recent events in Ohio and Fort Scott, Kansas, in which the admission of black students to formerly all-white schools had engendered bitter opposition. With evident relish, the *Evening Post* blamed Republicans in two of the cases.

Given its legislative history, the circumstances in Ohio were complicated. The state's infamous "Black Laws" had begun with its admission to the Union as a free state, and included denial of public school education for black children. Yet, both Ohio University and Oberlin College were among the nation's first institutions of higher learning to admit African Americans, and in 1849 some of the "Black Laws" were repealed. Unfortunately, while African American children could now legally receive an education, new legislation in 1853 mandated separate schools for the races, with Ohioans of color totally responsible for funding their institutions.[89]

The major civil rights initiatives and achievements during Reconstruction had their effect in Northern states, including Ohio. While its prohibition against integrated schools remained on the books, individual towns and cities began opening their educational doors to African American pupils, such as Columbus did. Reacting to increasing pressure for integrated schools statewide, the legislature finally repealed the 1853 law and mandated mixed-race institutions in 1887, along with striking down the remaining "Black Laws."[90]

Response to the new order varied from peaceful compliance to outright defiance. In early June, the *Marietta Semi-Weekly Register* published its summary of a report by the superintendent of schools in Cincinnati. With the board lacking "legal authority for maintaining . . . separate schools, . . . colored pupils hav[ing] a right to attend the same public schools as the whites [and] the authorities . . . liable to prosecution for excluding them," it had become imperative to act.

Education could continue "in the colored school buildings, provided both whites and colored pupils are received. The board is not justified in maintaining these colored schools at the expense of $30,000 per year, when pupils can be taught in mixed schools at $10,000." As a result, "Supt. White . . . recommended . . . closing of the colored schools and . . . admission of [their] pupils to the other schools of the city. He would be run out of town for such recommendation in a city of the 'New South.'"[91]

The *Register*'s staff must have been saddened when such resistance arose within their own state. In the southern Ohio town of Oxford, there was significant opposition to applications of black students to enter schools that had been exclusively white. After the board of education, acting on a request from the town's white community, ordered African American pupils back to the colored school, their parents filed suit. The district court ruled in favor of the black citizens, holding that local school boards had to comply with the state's laws on education. An almost identical situation arose in Ripley, with an Ohio court again ordering a town's school board to desegregate its public schools; even more extreme was the action taken by the school board in Yellow Springs, which closed all educational institutions rather than comply with the new law.[92]

What took place in Kansas closely paralleled the events in Ohio. When admission of black children to previously segregated schools was actively resisted in Fort Scott, a suit was filed on behalf of Buford Crawford, who wanted to attend an all-white school nearer to home rather than walk a much greater distance to the all-black school. The suit, undertaken by Crawford's father Robert, was based on rights guaranteed under the Kansas State Constitution and Fourteenth Amendment, and would determine whether the state legislature's declaration that public schools be free to all Kansas children between ages five and twenty-one took legal precedence over the dictates of local school boards.

The Kansas Supreme Court ruled in Crawford's favor, causing the *Iola Register* to declare on November 18, 1887, that the question had been settled: "No child can be excluded from the public schools of Kansas on account of his color." That proved unduly optimistic, as the plaintiff was unable to enter his desired school. Robert Crawford obtained a writ of mandamus from the Supreme Court that compelled both the Fort Scott Board of Education and superintendent of public schools to admit his son as ruled. However, Fort Scott was able to circumvent the court's decision and resist integration of its schools through use of a decades-old statewide classification system based on town size.[93]

The *Burlington Weekly Free Press* conclusion was apt and disheartening, but in echoing William M. Decamp's words from 1865, the paper also expressed some hope: "When we see evidences of such narrow prejudice in States like Ohio and Kansas we certainly should be somewhat lenient in our judgment of such a sentiment in Georgia. In time the New England freedom from prejudice of color is bound to prevail throughout the land, and men will be judged by their merits and not by the color of their skins."[94]

The final outcome of the Glenn bill controversy offered the same duality. In January 1888, the $8,000 appropriation offered by the state contingent on accepting scholastic segregation was declined by Atlanta University, which told the Georgia government that it had no intention of stopping the practice of educating students without regard to color. As reported by the *Albany Evening Journal*, the university issued an appeal to "Northern philanthropists who founded the college to sustain it."[95]

Through its act of moral courage, Atlanta University supported African Americans' right to non-separate, equal education for its children, but there were other ramifications. In late March, black Georgians convened in Macon, and compiled a roster of grievances about their current status that were classified into "social, educational, political, judicial and moral" by the *Atlanta Constitution*. As reported by the *Boston Journal* and reprinted in Vermont's *Bennington Banner*, there were disturbing signs among the list of complaints. That the leading social concern was being charged first-class fare for railroad tickets, only to be often forced into second-class or smoking cars,[96] was indicative of the 1875 Civil Rights Bill's ineffectiveness toward this type of discrimination.

As expected, the Glenn bill was a major aspect in discussions about education. The convention supported the white Atlanta University faculty's steadfast opposition, but did not insist on mixed-race schools and accused the state of unfairly keeping the declined appropriation, rather than finding another way to use it for black education. However, the convention's leading topic was administration of the laws, with inadequate jury representation, lynching and cruel administration of the penal system specified.[97]

The apprehensions of black Georgians were not restricted to one side of the Mason-Dixon line. At their root were the inequality and bigotry faced by African Americans throughout the nation, but of greater intensity and outright danger in the South. However, the considerable overlap among the categories of concern allowed for some optimism. With educational and social challenges directly related to political and judicial circumstances, potential solutions might be pursued through these avenues.

Black parents' availing themselves of the courts, backed by applicable state and federal law, to force recalcitrant school boards in the North to open their institutions to students of color would have been virtually impossible before Reconstruction. The situation was grimmer in the South, mainly due to the lack of comparable legislation in the former Confederate states and still-potent legacy of slavery, but the Fourteenth Amendment was the law for the entire nation.

Fighting Jim Crow

The Left-Armed Corps' ongoing identification as predominantly Republicans was indicative of Union veterans' belief that political activism was critical to maintaining what had been achieved through war. With another presidential election looming, a group of ex-soldiers and sailors in New York, including party stalwart Anselm F. Smith of the Left-Armed Corps, appealed to their comrades in arms in July 1880. After a reminder that "your work was not done" in 1865, but continued through three successful campaigns "crowned with the affirmative suffrage of the Nation," they came right to the point: "A thousand Generals of the Union Army . . . could not palliate nor annul the terrors and blood-shed with which the Democratic party has unitized and again sets in the field a Solid South against the patriotic Volunteers of the peace-loving North. The struggle is again upon us. It is our country that calls."[98]

Later that summer in Lansing, a featured speaker at the annual reunion of Ingham County's Union veterans was Alexander Cameron, late of the Sixteenth Michigan and VRC. As eloquent as he had been fifteen years earlier with a pen, the longtime Republican in the midst of a distinguished career in public service spoke with charity for defeated foes, but not their cause. He reminded his fellow "*60,000 ex-soldiers of Michigan, their wives, sons, daughters, immediate relatives and friends*" of their "*sacred trust of guarding constitutional liberty, the cause for which you fought, and for which many brave ones gave up their lives. Never lend a deaf ear or be silent when the rights of any comrade or any portion of our people are being trampled upon. Never be silent when truth and justice demand that your voice shall be heard in their defense.*"[99]

When Grover Cleveland's election in 1884 broke the string of Republican presidents, there was trepidation among African Americans about its impact on civil rights. Frederick Douglass blamed the South for its role in Cleveland's victory, stating it was "'made solid not by discussion and deliberate choice but by bullet and bludgeon, by midnight assault and assassin'" that prevented an honest polling.

However, he still had "'hope even of the Democratic Party. Though it is by history and antecedents bitterly opposed to every measure of justice and equality urged in our favor, it is still composed of men . . . with heads and hearts like other men. The world moves and the Democratic Party moves with it. The Democratic Party may not be a good party, but it may be a wise party, and wisdom in statesmanship is sometimes safer than simple goodness.'"[100]

Black citizens had ample reason to be worried about the ongoing fight for equality in changing political times. It was encouraging in August 1883 when the first case tried in Washington (and only the second countrywide) for criminal violation of the Civil Rights Act was decided in favor of an African American minister from Connecticut denied service at a restaurant there.

In his decision, Judge Samuel C. Mills emphatically stated: "'All guests must be given equal privileges in the places designated for them. They must be accessible to all respectable persons at a uniform rate. The defendant in discriminating against the complainant on account of race and color was guilty of a misdemeanor.'" The stalwart GAR member's ruling was rendered doubly unique by the District of Columbia's status as a territory, thus directly subject to Congressional jurisdiction.[101]

But there were disquieting signs even with this positive result. It was uncertain whether the decision would be upheld by the US Supreme Court, and in its coverage that supported both the ruling and courts "lend[ing] their assistance in stamping . . . out . . . blind prejudice," the *Buffalo Evening News* nonetheless observed: "To treat a negro well does not imply that he shall be placed on a social equality with his white neighbor, by any means. The intelligent negroes do not ask that, do not expect it, and probably would not accept it if offered to them."[102]

The veracity of this stunning viewpoint, not uncommonly held in the North, would be tested by the Supreme Court's long-awaited ruling on five cases of discrimination bundled together for review of the Civil Rights Act's legality. Spanning the country (Kansas, California, Missouri, New York, and Tennessee), they were "prosecutions under that act for not admitting certain colored persons to equal accommodations and privileges in inns or hotels, in railroad cars or in theaters," with each defended on the basis of the Act's "alleged unconstitutionality."[103]

On October 15, 1883, a crushing blow was dealt to the cause of equality. With only Justice John M. Harlan dissenting, the Supreme Court found that the first two sections of the Civil Rights Act were unconstitutional due to Congress lacking authority for their enactment under either the Thirteenth or Fourteenth Amendments. The eight justices held that "the thirteenth amendment gives no power to congress to pass the sections referred to, because that amendment relates only to slavery and involuntary servitude, which it abolished and gives congress power to pass laws for its enforcement."

Given its guarantee of equal protection under the law, the Fourteenth Amendment was not so easily dismissed. However, with tortuous logic, the court managed to do so by holding that the amendment's prohibition against states' "depriv[ing] any person of their liberty or property without due process of law" and concomitant granting of power to enforce the prohibition "was not intended to give congress power to provide due process of law for protection of life and property, which would embrace almost all subjects of legislation, but to provide modes of redress for counteracting the operation and effect of state laws obnoxious to the prohibition."

In other words, African Americans could not rely on the federal government and its courts for justice and compensation from discrimination, but rather upon the very same states that had passed legislation instituting Jim Crow restrictions on their access to "accommodations and privileges" that the Civil Rights Act sought to protect.[104]

Richard T. Greener, Harvard's first black graduate and the dean of Howard University's law department called it "the most startling decision of the Supreme Court, so far as the colored people are concerned, since the infamous obiter dictum of Chief Justice Taney." Then he made a stunning statement that echoed the concerns of African Americans in Georgia, and was deeply rooted in the degrading nature of Jim Crow. Noting that "In other countries oppressed races have enjoyed civil or social rights long before they were admitted to political ones," Greener said he "would much rather be deprived of my political rights than my social ones. I can live without suffrage; I can exist without office; but I want to have the privilege of travelling from New York to California without fear of being put off a car or denied food and shelter solely because I have a trace of negro blood in my veins."

After emphasizing the Civil Rights Act was not only constitutional, but based "on the common law of the Anglo-Saxon race brought over to America," he offered a cautionary insight reflective of the bigotry and racism infecting the country in the late 1800s: "The non-enforcement of the civil-rights law which permitted a pious and venerable negro bishop a short time ago to be thrust from a railway car to Georgia although he had paid his fare, may cause Archbishop McCloskey to be thrust from a car in some Roman Catholic hating community. It may deny Mr. Adler or Mr. Weiss, distinguished Hebrews, the comforts of some third-rate hotel by some anti-Semitic community."[105]

The decision was predictably hailed across the South, both for its negative impact on equality and obliteration of a vestige of despised Reconstruction. The *Memphis Daily Appeal* saw it as "another proof that we are gradually returning to the safeguards of the constitution and are freeing ourselves of the barnacles fastened by fanaticism, which found its opportunity during civil war and the reconstruction period."[106] Likewise, the *Easley Messenger* of South Carolina reported that "A strong undercurrent of public opinion would have forever prevented the social equality, contemplated by this infamous bill, conceived in hatred and passed by a dominant party to humiliate the citizens of one section of our common country."[107]

However, the extent to which many Northern newspapers appeared to agree with the *Daily Appeal*'s assessment that "The negro has not lost his civil rights by the decision of the court, but is only prevented from asserting in hotels and places of amusement a social equality repugnant to the whites"[108] was demoralizing for African Americans and their white supporters in the movement for equal rights of citizenship.

Deeming the Civil Rights Act as essentially "a dead letter" since its passage, the *New York Daily Tribune* felt it was more harmful than beneficial for blacks, as their "occasional demands . . . under the authority of the law, have tended to irritate public feeling, to keep alive antagonism between the races, and to postpone that gradual obliteration of unreasonable race distinctions which the march of events since emancipation has tended to bring about."[109] The *Sun* blamed the Republicans, reporting that the Act's authors "knew it was impotent and worthless from the start. Instead of being a benefit to the negro, it has proved to be an aggravating injury, by stimulating prejudices and by exciting discontent."[110] Similarly, the *Daily Los Angeles Herald* scorned the legislative bestowing of "a social equality with the whites upon the black man" that "multitudes of the people of the United States . . . regard . . . as neither judicious nor constitutional" in its lauding of the Supreme Court decision.[111]

On the other hand, numerous newspapers across the country criticized the ruling, and remained steadfast on civil rights. In Kansas, the *Emporia Weekly News* published the Supreme Court decision while stressing "it yet comes within scope of the United States courts to declare void any law passed by a state making discriminations against the citizen on account of color."

But neither the paper's staff nor the government of Kansas stopped there. Informing its readers that "So far as the colored people of this state are concerned their rights are not affected by this decision, being amply protected by the following law," the *News* then provided the full text of "An act to provide for the protection of citizens in their civil and public right." This was accompanied by Secretary of State W. H. Smallwood's certification "that the foregoing is a true and correct copy of the original enrolled bill, now on file in my office."[112]

On October 22, two thousand people packed Washington's Lincoln Hall to its rafters for a mass rally. The elite among black (including Frederick Douglass, Blanche Bruce, and Richard T. Greener) and white leaders from political and religious realms renowned for working "in behalf of equal rights and justice" led unanimous voting on resolutions protesting the Supreme Court decision and affirming commitment to the cause.

Ever leonine, Douglass then told the crowd, "We have been grievously wounded in the house of our friends," and stated that "this decision has inflicted a heavy calamity upon the seven millions of the colored people of this country, and left them naked and defenseless against the action of a malignant, vulgar, and pitiless prejudice . . . In humiliating the colored people of this country, this decision humbles the nation."[113]

Yet this would be the rare occasion when the most famous African American was surpassed in eloquence. After Robert G. Ingersoll assumed the lectern, he lived up to his reputation as one of the nation's finest orators. "The Great Agnostic," who before becoming the Illinois attorney general in 1866 had commanded a state cavalry regiment, delivered a superb legal dissection of the ruling ("unworthy of the august tribunal by which it was delivered") and appealed for equality under the law:

The supreme court has failed to comprehend the spirit of our age. It has undervalued the accomplishments of the war.

The old issues are again upon us: Is this a nation? Have all citizens of the United States equal rights without regard to race or color?

If this is not now a free government, if citizens cannot now be protected, if the three amendments have been undermined by the supreme court, we must have another; and if that fails, then another . . . until the constitution shall become a perfect shield for every right of every human being beneath our flag.[114]

Both agitation against the decision and fervent support continued to extensive newspaper coverage nationwide. Then Justice Harlan's dissenting opinion was filed and released to the public on November 17, and it was electrifying. He began by calling the grounds upon which the Court's opinions rested "'entirely too narrow and artificial,'" the "'substance and spirit of the recent amendments of the Constitution hav[ing] been sacrificed by a subtle and ingenious verbal criticism.'" Ensuring that no one missed the point, Harlan sought to "'express an earnest conviction that the court has departed from the familiar rule requiring in the interpretation of constitutional provisions, that full effect be given to the intent with which they were adopted.'"[115]

On that basis, Harlan focused on the realities of discrimination Congress sought to remove under the 1875 Act:

"They are burdens which lay at the very foundation of the institution of slavery as it once existed. They are not to be sustained, except upon the assumption that there is still in this land of liberty a class which may yet be discriminated against . . . a free man is not only branded as one inferior and infected, but, in the competitions of life, is robbed of some of the most essential means of existence; and all this solely because they belong to a particular race which the nation has liberated. The same general observations are applicable to Jews."

As to the opinion's concept of Congressional power, "'It has been the established doctrine of this court during all its history, accepted as vital to the national supremacy, that Congress, in the absence of a positive delegation of power to the State legislatures, may by legislation enforce and protect any right derived from or created by the national Constitution."

Justice Harlan concluded: "'I venture, with all respect for the opinion of others, to insist that the national legislature may, without transcending the limits of the constitution, do for human liberty and the fundamental rights of American citizenship, what it did, with the sanction of this court, for the protection of slavery and the rights of the masters of fugitive slaves.'"[116]

Brilliantly, the judge had invoked the despicable *Dred Scott* decision and past injustices in a fervent plea that the Supreme Court, as part of judicial review for constitutionality, take into account what laws and amendments were intended to accomplish.

For all his scathing arguments, the Supreme Court's ruling stood, and its potential impact continued to be debated in the wake of Harlan's dissent. The *Vermont Phoenix* found his opinion "learned, candid and able," yet in deeming the court's decision consistent with postwar "public sentiment" regarding Congressional power, predicted that "no ill is likely to result from it."[117]

The *Albany Law Journal* singled out the published remarks of Reverend William W. Patton, DD, LLD, as the "most succinct and sensible . . . which we have seen." Howard University's highly respected president stated that the ruling was hardly unexpected, had not "'set forth any political doctrine contrary to the rights of the colored people'" and left African Americans "'as to legal protection just where it leaves white people,'" enumerating the intact Congressional and state civil rights protections the Court had affirmed. He then pointed out that the likely unfavorable verdict on a black individual's suit for damages relating to Jim Crow discrimination in the South "'would be and has been true under the civil rights bill, which has largely been a dead letter in many of the states.'"

As to what African Americans should do, Patton advised them to "Refrain from an unwise railing at the Supreme Court, acquaint themselves with the facts and principles of the case, and stand up hopefully and courageously for their legal rights, all over the Union.'"[118] When all was said and done, Jerrold M. Packard's observation is most fitting: "Utterly unsurprisingly, this 1883 decision opened the floodgates to a sharp increase in the growth of Jim Crow."[119]

Five months later, the same justices adjudicated another major civil rights legal action to a different outcome. Known as the Ku-Klux cases, the convictions of five Klan members doing time in a Georgia penitentiary for "threatening, beating and otherwise intimidating colored voters" during a congressional election were under appeal to the Supreme Court. Their lawyers maintained that the conspirators had acted as individuals and jurisdiction thus belonged solely to the state courts, not to the federal court in which they had been tried. The US Circuit Court for the Northern District of Georgia countered that argument, holding that "while the right to vote is given by the state, the law giving rights in a federal election is the law of the United States, and to maltreat a citizen for exercising this right is to violate the law of the national government."[120]

On March 3, 1884, the Supreme Court ruled in "Ex parte in the matter of Jasper Yarborough and others." Justice Samuel F. Miller, whose opinion represented the court, said of the Fifteenth Amendment: "This new constitutional right was mainly designed for citizens of African descent. The principle, however, that the protection of the exercise of this right is within the power of Congress is as necessary to the right of other citizens to vote as to the colored citizen, and to the right to vote in general as to the right to be protected against discrimination." In furtherance of this point, the Justice stated that

> The Government must have the power to protect the elections, on which its existence depends, from violence and corruption. . . . It is only because the Congress of the United States through long habit and years of forbearance has, in deference and respect to the States, refrained from exercising these powers they are now doubted.

> The rule to show cause in this case is discharged and the writs of habeas corpus [for the prisoners' release] denied.[121]

The decision received considerably less attention and press coverage than the Civil Rights Act ruling, and though favorable, apparently did little to encourage federal intervention on behalf of blacks who were being intimidated, assaulted, murdered, and lynched for simply exercising their voting rights as American citizens.

The struggle for equal opportunity intensified throughout the 1880s into the century's last decade, with progress in education in some regions offset by ongoing segregation and inferior facilities elsewhere, especially in the South, as we have seen. With respect to race, historian John D. Smith has classified the 1890s as America's worst period: "Separate and unequal—backed by the constant threat of racial violence—characterized the Jim Crow South and set a discordant tone for race relations throughout the United States. North and South, the nation was obsessed with race and racial distinctions."[122]

EQUALITY IN THE GRAND ARMY

The nation's largest and most conspicuously biracial organization now found itself under intense scrutiny regarding social equality. Would men who had faced death together continue to affiliate in the GAR decades after the war? If not, what were the implications for African American advancement as the country moved toward a new century? Was integration a desired goal, or should whites and blacks stay within their own communities, schools, places of worship, and associations?

For Robert Pinn, these questions were easily answered. In January 1886, he was installed as the elected commander of Massillon's GAR Post, of which he was one of two African Americans within a large membership. A major black newspaper, the *Cleveland Gazette*, proudly reported Pinn's ascension to leadership among his white comrades as "not only a tribute of respect to him, but a just recognition of the colored soldiers, all who helped to fight the battles of the war of the rebellion."[123]

The maimed veteran was certainly admired in his hometown and county. Even the *Stark County Democrat*, which wrote of "coons" and deliberately ascribed demeaning dialect to African Americans with accompanying "Uncle Remus" and "Auntie Chloe" cartoons, treated Pinn with considerable respect.[124] There is little doubt that his status as an attorney and Medal of Honor recipient influenced the *Democrat*'s reporting, just as Pinn was acutely aware of the racism that continued to plague the country.

Raised in a state with "Black Laws" that he had worked to repeal,[125] the Ohioan saw first-hand what "separate but equal" really meant while in Cairo. Yet he had obtained an excellent education at an integrated college, had both white friends and clients, and was esteemed for valorous service to a country that had initially spurned his efforts to enlist. Pinn's life experience was well-rounded and quite unique for a man of color in his time, so when he read in the *Cleveland Gazette* of plans for an all-black GAR post, he responded almost immediately:

MASSILLON, O., Nov. 29 [1886].—*Editor GAZETTE.— Sir.—I saw in your last week's issue that there is a desire on the part of the colored ex-soldiers of your city to organize a GAR Post exclusively for colored soldiers. Why is this? Sir, the Grand Army of the Republic is indeed what its name implies, a grand institution. It knows no creed, race, color nor politics; it invites all honorably discharged soldiers who served in the Union army during the war of the Rebellion to enter its ranks, and it is ready to receive them in "Fraternity, Charity and Loyalty."*

There are more than a half dozen GAR Posts now in your city, and there are colored soldiers members of some of them, and I believe that any colored soldier who is worthy will be received.

Then why set up a "side show?" O how long will my people persist in drawing a color line for themselves! I am ashamed of them. As soldiers we are all working for the same great object, "Fraternity, Charity and Loyalty," then why not work together?

We fought side by side with our white comrades; our blood mingled and drenched the Southern soil; our united efforts saved our common country for the abode of freemen, and now in this sublime time of peace we should not be the first to say we will have no part with our white comrades in perpetuating and enjoying that which is our common heritage. It is an insult to our comrades and a slander upon our Grand Army. Some one will say that certain colored men have been refused admission, which, I have no doubt, is true; white men have also been rejected. Some men of both races, though they have an honorable discharge, are not fit to belong to the GAR: but, sir let a colored man in good standing in society apply and he will not be refused.

I hope I will hear no more about colored posts.[126]

That his view was not an idealistic pipedream is strongly supported by Gannon's research findings. Despite instances of black veterans being rejected for admission by their white comrades just as Pinn noted, she reported that "hundreds of GAR posts" throughout the nation actively sought members of both races: "Although white veterans made up the majority and dominated these organizations, African Americans, while in the minority, fully participated in post life."

Given prevailing racial attitudes in nineteenth century America, such activities were striking in their steadfast defiance of contemporary mores. Further, Pinn's concept matches Gannon's observation that "an inter-racial post represented GAR members' greatest aspirations, to create an organization where veterans of every race, creed, or ethnicity could come together as comrades."[127]

Yet within the GAR, there was geographic variation in acceptance of integration. Gannon detected that among Northern states, black veterans were less likely to be members of mixed race posts in New York, New Jersey, and Pennsylvania than in the Midwest. She then proposed that a major factor in the state-by-state differences was whether white members served in the Eastern or Western theaters. As a higher proportion of African American soldiers fought in the West, and war experiences in common create strong ties, this is an intriguing and plausible argument buttressed by examples of posts in which black and white members participated in the same battles. However, Gannon also noted that decisions to integrate were predominantly made locally amid general encouragement by the state departments,[128] and thus likely to be multi-factorial.

Analysis of the Left-Armed Corps Grand Army data reinforces Gannon's overall observations. Of the thirty-eight New York posts of membership only one was integrated, with the same among Pennsylvania's ten posts; conversely, 42 percent (8/19) of Massachusetts, 41 percent (7/17) of Ohio, 67 percent (4/6) of Connecticut and 67 percent (4/6) of Kansas posts were integrated. Illinois and Indiana provided three more integrated posts (out of seventeen total), while Minnesota, Missouri and Iowa each had an integrated post out of an aggregate of nine.

Whatever the Grand Army's shortcomings, the organization clearly offered its African American members definite advantages in terms of pride and public involvement. As Shaffer explained, "because equality for black veterans was at the heart of how they judged their progress as men, they valued the idea of racial equality espoused by the GAR, even if the reality did not always measure up. . . . In the GAR, [the concept] was respected and, to a surprising extent for the time, actually implemented." Similarly, Gannon reported that "most white veterans accepted black Americans, and these men participated in the GAR's political life at the state level."[129]

However, both historians aptly noted that few GAR members of color attained high-ranking positions at departmental levels despite active post involvement and dedicated service to the organization. Gannon found their ceiling was inevitably junior vice commander, reporting that blacks filled this third-ranking slot in three Midwestern departments (Illinois, Ohio, and Indiana) and one mid-Atlantic (Pennsylvania) at some point.[130] In addition to her list, two African Americans served as junior vice commander of the Department of Delaware, with William H. Jones, born into slavery, elected to the position in 1886.[131] While impressive, these were almost all one-shot achievements without re-election; still, Gannon perceived them as "an important validation of the interracial nature of the GAR."[132]

Ohio's only black junior vice commander certainly substantiates this viewpoint. After five straight years as president of the state encampment and a current member of the department staff, Robert Pinn was elected by his peers to their third highest office in April 1888. He returned to a joyous reception—as reported by the Massillon *Daily Independent* and reprinted by the *Cleveland Gazette*, an "enthusiastic crowd" welcomed a "surprised" Robert Pinn back home. After "stepp[ing] off the train . . . to . . . hearty cheers . . . [and having] his one good arm nearly shaken off," he graciously accepted the honors, and the "Hart Post, the Sons of Veterans, and a great number of friends fell in and marched to the post headquarters" while a band played along the way. There, Pinn thanked everyone "not only for the hearty reception, but for the efforts put forth, which had undoubtedly secured his election, [which] . . . was by a greater majority than that of any other officer."[133]

As was his way, Junior Vice Commander Pinn carried out his responsibilities with commitment and thoroughness, submitting an excellent final report to the department commander.[134] While he never again served in a position of command, in June 1889, GAR national headquarters appointed him an aide-de-camp reporting to the adjutant general; Pinn was joined by another Buckeye, former president Rutherford B. Hayes.[135]

The proliferation of integrated posts did not stop the creation of all-black units, nor did their establishment automatically mean that prejudice was the reason. Demographic factors played a role (such as a post being located in an African American neighborhood), as did the desire of veterans of color to maintain strong shared connections and take advantage of help from the greater local black community. On the other hand, many all-black posts were founded in Northern cities in which gaining admission to all-white posts had been difficult and where a significant number of African American veterans lived.[136]

Even in an organization that valued their collective military service, African American GAR members periodically were forced to take public positions reiterating their soldiers' pride and concomitant claims to manhood equal to that of white veterans. One such instance arose in 1885 surrounding Ulysses S. Grant's death. While it did not originate from the GAR or anyone in authority, men in New York's all-black posts were offended by a request that they serve as grooms in his funeral parade.

One member stated that black troops were "comrades of the dead general, not servants" and had been placed by Grant "at the front" of battles, where they acquitted themselves with courage. As a group, the black veterans made it evident they would "appear in the procession as a post of the grand army, which has never blushed for the conduct of its colored troops." That is precisely what happened; in addition, three black companies of the veteran guards marched in the Great Procession to honor the general and ex-president.[137]

GAR matters involving race were extensively covered by newspapers across the political spectrum, in addition to the independently owned, unaffiliated *National Tribune*. Established in 1877 for former Union servicemen and their families, its Grand Army and overall veteran-related reporting were first rate.[138]

Two illustrative examples of race-related incidents occurred in 1889, the first addressed by the *National Tribune* in August. When Henry Johnson, a black member of Zook Post No. 11, in Norristown, Pennsylvania, died in the Montgomery Almshouse, his comrades took responsibility for the body. Having made arrangements for Johnson's burial in the cemetery associated with the Almshouse, his post was outraged when graveyard officials refused to allow their friend to be interred as planned. Place was found for him in another cemetery, but Johnson's Grand Army brothers (and the *Tribune*) made it abundantly clear how they felt about Montgomery's actions: "The refusal to permit the burial of the body on account of the color of the man is bad enough; but, just think, the pet dog of a family named Steinmitz was buried in the cemetery with great pomp. A daily newspaper last week very appropriately headed an article in reference to the matter, 'Dead Dogs Preferred—A Cemetery Draws the Line at the Negro Veteran.'"[139]

On the other hand, the *Troy Daily Times* of November 7 published a story that reflected negatively on the GAR. The sizable Pratt Post No. 127 of Kingston, New York, one of the region's "most influential organizations," admitted several members of a black post that had disbanded, including George F. Kierstad, "an intelligent colored man" who held a position of responsibility at the city's West Shore railroad station. However, when his wife, "a prepossessing and cultured colored woman" was proposed for membership in the women's relief corps organized by the post wives and daughters, "The members of that body thought matters were going too far. It was well enough for the veterans to associate together, but as to having a colored woman in their ranks that was out of the question, and when the ballot-box was opened it was found that there were sufficient black-balls within it to reject her." The *Daily Times* duly noted that "The colored residents of this city and vicinity are at present highly indignant over the rejection" due to what the paper termed "the color-line" in the GAR relief corps.[140]

While in this case it was a Republican newspaper decrying bigotry in a GAR affiliate organization, such incidents were manna from heaven for Northern Democratic and Southern publications with a different agenda. In January 1890, the *Fair Play* of Ste. Genevieve, Missouri, reprinted an item from New Hampshire's *Latonia Democrat* that specified denied admission of "a black veteran to a Connecticut Grand Army post," "seven out of eight Republicans in Topeka, Kan., scratch[ing] the name of a colored candidate," and offices denied to "negroes in Ohio cities who have passed the highest examination for places on the police force and elsewhere" in favor of "their white competitors," and concluded, "it is every way proper for Northern Republicans to go slow in their criticisms of the way the Southern people handle the race issue."[141]

Fair or not, the foremost national organization that officially had no color line was being judged by a higher standard than any other group by both its allies and detractors. The marked attention paid to an integrated Grand Army was also reflective of the times. In full view of their fellow citizens, an avowed apolitical body of Union veterans would undergo its greatest crisis over the country's most inflammatory and polarizing issue.

MAJOR WILLIAM WARNER, COMMANDER-IN-CHIEF G. A. R

Major William Warner, Forty-Fourth Wisconsin. THE NEW YORK PUBLIC LIBRARY DIGITAL COL-
LECTIONS.

The Grand Army of The Republic Keeps the Faith

Buffalo Express: If the southern departments wish to divide on the color line, let them. The order would be better off without men who try to introduce so un-American a principle into the Grand Army of the Republic.

—*IOLA* (KS) *REGISTER*, AUGUST 21, 1891[1]

There had long been racial problems in the Department of Louisiana and Mississippi. Throughout the 1880s, African American ex-servicemen had been unable to gain admission to posts in either state due to opposition from white members, obstruction from department commanders, and inaction from GAR national leadership.[2] It did not go unnoticed—in 1887, black veterans reuniting in Boston censured the department for refusing to charter an African American post.[3] Yet when the situation finally exploded in 1890 the igniting spark was, of all things, the funeral of Jefferson Davis.

After the former CSA president died on December 6, 1889, a Committee of Arrangements convening the next day included Captain Jacob Gray, who commanded the Department of Louisiana and Mississippi. Plans were made for a religious service, bishop's eulogy, concluding ceremonies, and procession to the cemetery in New Orleans; his suggestion of a military funeral also readily agreed upon, Gray's reflections on Davis went national.

Stating "that he would be proud as a soldier of the United States to honor the memory of the illustrious patriot, soldier and statesman of the South" who "had been also a soldier of the United States . . . who . . . rendered distinguished service," Gray would not "fail to recognize that he was a great and pure man." The Commander continued, "'If it is agreed that the body of the dead chieftain shall be borne into the cemetery upon the shoulders of the old veterans, I, as a representative of the Grand Army of the Republic, shall certainly demand to have the right to assist in the performance of that sad and honorable duty.'"[4]

While Confederate ex-servicemen were delighted by his remarks' "fraternal spirit," they were icily received by other Union veterans. Grand Army members in Pittsburgh were furious in their denunciation, with two of their leaders wondering if Gray's actions warranted expulsion; all agreed he had no right to drag the GAR into the event.[5]

Former General Morris Schaff, a prominent citizen of Pittsfield, Massachusetts, infuriated comrades in his city and then countrywide when his December 9 telegram to Gray, signed as a GAR member, was published: "Participate with the South in the funeral of great chief. Your record on the field will stand it now, and time will explain it hereafter." Numerous veterans disavowed the West Pointer's sentiments, emphasizing that they did not appreciate Jefferson Davis being "recognized by one of their number as a great chief."[6]

On the original program, the GAR was to march as a body directly behind former Rebel servicemen. But as the funeral approached, Commander Gray was feeling the heat. The *New York Herald* reported that "outside pressure was brought to bear to prevent the Grand Army men from participating as an organization," and a meeting was held the night before "to prevent dissension in their own ranks." The Department as a whole decided that it would not join the procession as an organization, but members were welcome to participate as individuals.[7]

Not everyone in the North agreed. Pennsylvania's *Lancaster Daily Intelligencer*, a Democratic newspaper in a Republican district, taunted those in the GAR for their "paroxysm of frenzy" over the compromise terms of participation: "The fashion of the town is to attend the funeral, and the members of the GAR want to be in the fashion . . . Jefferson

Davis and the Southern people whom he led, committed a political offense against the nation which they tried but failed to disrupt. They were brought back to it by force. Their states are again in the Union. They govern their states; they are citizens of the United States in full feather; and no account is kept against them of their transgressions."[8]

On December 11, Davis was interred in Metairie Cemetery "with the most imposing ceremonies the South has ever witnessed. The funeral . . . was a far grander demonstration on the part of the South than any one had expected." Among his pallbearers were the current (Gray) and former (General A. S. Badger) Department Commanders, joined in the funeral procession by around fifty of their comrades, all wearing Union veterans' badges, but no GAR insignia.[9]

In its funeral coverage, the *New York Herald* seemed incredulous that besides the GAR en masse, something else differed from the original procession planning: "Several days ago Colonel James Lewis, a leader of the negroes in this city, called upon the Committee of Arrangements . . . to know what steps had been taken [regarding] . . . colored organizations. . . . The committee replied that they would be given a good place, and made good its pledge by constituting an eighth division, of which Colonel Lewis was selected as marshal."

But no black organization claimed a spot, and not one African American marched, other than "various colored bands." The paper reported an additional "notable feature"—"the absence of negroes from the route of the procession. As a rule, they crowd the streets on such occasions, but today there was only a sprinkling here and there. Whether this fact was due to design or to accident or was a mere coincidence has not been ascertained."[10]

Why Lewis, one of the first black Union officers,[11] would make such an astonishing request is lost to history; as for the *Herald*, was its staff truly unable to grasp why African Americans wanted no part of ceremonies lauding the leader of the *Confederacy*?

Amid the funeral-related tumult, the *National Tribune* took a low-key approach, reporting on December 19 that the forty Union veterans who joined the procession "will surely be disciplined, if not expelled from the Grand Army."[12] Little did the organization or anyone else know that the Davis Affair would embroil the GAR in a high-profile controversy that would be debated across America for more than two years.

By early January 1890, Jacob Gray was reeling from criticism inside his department and out, particularly in the North. In a move generally seen as payback for the lack of support from his comrades, their leader suddenly decided to approach African Americans with an offer to organize a separate post, which he would support for admission to the department. He had obtained GAR Commander in Chief Russell A. Alger's approval, and black veterans immediately established the Cailloux Post of New Orleans; the news broke nationwide on January 5 in such papers as New York's *Sun*.

There is little reason not to doubt that the motivation for Gray's actions was a sudden case of racial enlightenment. As the *Pittsburg Dispatch* reported on January 6, when elected department commander, he had "solemnly declared that his right hand would wither before he would sign the charter of a negro post." Outraged at what had now taken place, white members "charge openly that his action was intended to revenge himself on them because they would not turn out at the Jefferson Davis funeral, and they even accuse him of saying: 'Well, if they will not turn out with the whites, I will give them a chance to turn out with the negroes.'"

White Union veterans in Louisiana and Mississippi were not alone in their views. On the same day as the *Dispatch*'s report, the *Omaha Daily Bee* published an interview with Colonel Lewis, who for ten years had unsuccessfully fought for GAR admission of black veterans in the Gulf. Their formal petition had been submitted to "several department commanders here, each of whom rejected it on some frivolous ground, one of them being 'expediency,'" which as defined by Lewis "meant color and nothing else." The former captain of the First Louisiana National Guards, who held several important federal and municipal positions in the decades following the war and was among the country's most respected and powerful African Americans, clearly intended to take advantage of Gray's actions, no matter what their basis: "'[A]s I understand it, by way of retaliation as much as in justice to the colored ex-soldiers, . . . he has granted our people the right to organize a post, which we have done. In the states of Louisiana and Mississippi there are about thirty thousand colored soldiers, all of whom will become members of the posts as soon as possible.'"[13]

Within days the department's djutant general, Captain H. C. Bartlett, resigned rather than authorize the new black post's charter. Feeling Gray "'has made a very serious mistake . . . by introduc[ing] something that will be of no real benefit to the colored men, and will do much to annoy and perhaps disintegrate the organization as it now exists,'" Barlett expected other resignations would follow his;[14] what actually ensued was much worse.

In February, a sad, nonviolent reenactment of the Civil War took place in New Orleans, as the Department of Louisiana and Mississippi split apart. The deepest fears of its white membership had been realized when nine all-black posts totaling 840 veterans were admitted, versus the original eight posts and 325 ex-servicemen. Despite being vastly outnumbered, the white members refused to allow any African Americans to participate in department proceedings, including election of officers. After an all-Caucasian leadership headed by George T. Hodges was voted in, dissident whites joined the black delegates and selected a mixed slate, including Jacob Gray as commander. With both sides claiming sole legitimacy, the GAR adjutant general supported the right of the black posts to vote for department officers, but the final decision would supposedly be made at that year's national encampment—in the meantime, the two organizations would stand.[15]

While the GAR color line in the Department of Louisiana and Mississippi was the major ongoing story, newspapers also closely followed the organization's racial circumstances in other parts of the country. At the end of January, the *Gazette and Farmers' Journal* of Baldwinsville, New York, reported that the seating of delegates from black posts at the Georgia State Encampment led many officers to withdraw from the event.[16] On the other hand, the *Syracuse Weekly Express*, attending the New York State Encampment the following month, found "no distinction of race or color in the Grand Army of the Republic," and no problems with hotel accommodations. The newspaper also stressed the presence of such delegates of color as department chaplain, Reverend

John Little, and two post commanders (one current, the other past), Brooklynites all.[17]

Back in the Gulf, a two-man committee appointed by Commander in Chief Alger arrived to investigate the department. Deciding that formation of the black posts was not legal under GAR rules and regulations, they recommended a new muster be performed with in-depth examination of all the African American applicants for membership eligibility. Based on their findings, in July Alger ordered Gray to be tried by court-martial for his actions.

When the national encampment met in Boston the following month, the department was represented solely by the eight white posts and commanded by Hodges. There was no formal discussion of the situation among the delegates, but Alger regretted "some disagreements in the Department of Louisiana and Mississippi, drawn upon the color line." The departing national leader hoped that soon "all may share the rights granted by our laws, and that harmony will prevail everywhere," and stated his "determination to recognize as a comrade the equal rights of every man, no matter what his color or nationality," if qualified by service and honorable discharge.[18]

The *National Tribune* reported black veterans in Boston "enjoyed themselves immensely at the Encampment. They did not conceal the fact that they were gratified with the reception the people gave them all along the line of march."[19]

Then, two months later, the newspaper carried a stunning announcement. In an effort to solve "many of the problems which are disturbing the white comrades in the Departments of Alabama, Arkansas, Delaware, Florida, Georgia, Kentucky, Louisiana and Mississippi, Maryland, Missouri, Texas, Virginia and West Virginia," its members were seriously considering the formation of a separate "Colored Department" that would admit black veterans from all the South, if not the entire nation.

According to the report, they believed this would result in a large increased African American membership with the ability to productively work among their own race rather than "the limited numbers belonging to the white Departments in that territory." Realizing there might be objection to a new department geographically cutting across other departments, the plan's advocates brought up the war's USCT precedent of a national organization rather than separate state units. While claiming full recognition of blacks having rights in the GAR equal to theirs, "whatever they may think of the justice of drawing the color line, the condition of public opinion in the South must be taken into account." The *Tribune* concluded, "The matter is well worthy of the most serious attention."[20]

Whether the GAR would formally establish a color line was indeed of "the most serious attention." As the Twenty-Fifth Annual National Encampment approached, the nation's eyes turned toward Detroit for the long-anticipated showdown on the most volatile issue of the day. The leading spokesmen for the Department of Louisiana and Mississippi were past commander and now judge advocate A. S. Graham and current Commander Hodges, both of whom gave interviews before the encampment's start.

Anticipating significant opposition from Northern members, they insisted the department fully intended to leave the organization if their demands weren't met. Graham stated that the conflict originated from Gray's breach of long-standing department policy: "The Grand Army posts of Louisiana and Mississippi have always refused to grant charters for negro posts on the ground that the GAR is a social organization and has power to restrict its membership to those who are agreeable, in a social sense, to its members." If black veterans in the new posts were deemed eligible, they would constitute "a separate and independent department" in the best interests of all concerned.

Hodges made a similar argument: "'Unless the thing is straightened out during this encampment, there won't be a white member of the GAR south of the Ohio or Potomac a year hence. They are outnumbering us in the posts, thus putting us directly under them. That we will not stand. Now we want to rule ourselves, and have the colored people go by themselves. . . . All we ask is a provisional department, embracing Florida, Louisiana, Mississippi and Texas.'"[21]

The African American cause was led by Colonel Lewis, who when asked about problems in the Pelican State sarcastically replied, "'Did you ever know when there was not trouble in Louisiana?'" He pointed out that "there are 24,800 colored men enlisted in the army from Louisiana, more than from all other states together," which gave them an equal right to establish GAR posts. After Alger's recognition they did so, but even with more than one thousand members, "'we are not recognized by the commander of our department. We get no representation in the convention and are ordered to report to the commander-in-chief. We have prepared a strong case on the matter and all I ask is twenty-five minutes in which to present it to a committee or to the convention itself. I claim the order is not a social one, but a historic and fraternal one.'"[22]

The GAR silver anniversary encampment opened on August 4 in spectacular fashion. Two hundred thousand people watched as it took five hours for all 25,000 members of the grand procession, including past commander in chief Alger and ex-president Hayes, to pass the reviewing stand. But as the *New York Herald* noted, once the parade was over, "political questions are expected to develop fast," with one topic in particular hanging over the gathering: "The color line is talked of with more or less reserve by most Northern white veterans, General Alger and other prominent men refusing to discuss it, until it comes up before the encampment. It is claimed that there will be no bitterness shown in the convention."[23]

No bitterness? On the eve of the debate, the *New York Evening Post* told its readers that "The controversy over the color line in the Grand Army is full of interest." After reviewing where things stood, the paper made a dire prediction about what Northerners would learn about the race problem in the United States: "When they see that white men who fought to save the Union will not consent to have their Grand Army posts controlled by black men who fought for the same cause, they will understand better than before the implacable nature of the hostility of Southern whites to negro rule in government."[24]

Another New York newspaper saw the situation in a different light. The *Statesman* of Yonkers recognized a golden opportunity, and captured the essence of why a veterans' organization decision on an internal matter meant so much: "It is anomalous and discreditable that there should still exist 'a color question' in the ranks of the Grand Army of the

Republic. If there was any society in which all comrades in arms should meet as equals, without regard to color or previous condition of slavery, one would suppose it would be in a convention of the survivors of those who fought for the Union. Yet this band of comrades still discriminates against the colored veterans of the war."[25]

Seconding Lewis's points about lack of recognition and represen- tation, the *Statesman*'s staff concluded: "The time has come when the GAR will do away with this grotesque anomaly. The society to-day is an historic association, and it is unworthy of its essential dignity to regard it merely as a social club."[26]

When outgoing Commander in Chief Wheelock G. Veazey addressed the delegates, it appeared that the GAR would not meet the *Statesman*'s expectations. The Vermont Republican, who had served in his state's Senate and on its Supreme Court, was clearly distressed by what had taken place. But based on the information gathered through investiga- tions and other sources, he had come to believe "that a large majority of both white and colored Comrades in the Department of Louisiana and Mississippi are strong in the conviction that it would be for the best interests of all individually and of their Posts and of the Order to have a separate Department in Louisiana and some of the other Gulf States."[27] As a result, Veazey had some thoughts for the incoming commander in chief: "My best judgment, after a year of painstaking investigation, is that it would be wise to confer the authority upon my successor to create such a department. . . . I am sure he will see objections to it, but he may also find it the best and perhaps the only shield for the full protection of the colored Comrades."[28]

It is conceivable that the *National Tribune*'s October 1890 report had been a trial balloon from GAR management, preparing the membership for support of a separate black department. But the commander in chief's was not the final word; the question would go before a select delegates' group for formal discussion and decision the following day.

That evening, the proposed new Department dominated conversa- tions. As reported by the *Brooklyn Daily Eagle*, "scores of delegates" had received "dispatches, the majority from the East and West, urging that the encampment should declare itself in no uncertain way on the right of the black men to meet the Southern whites on an equal basis under the shadow of their posts." Veazey personally received numerous notes of protest from members, among them Department of Ohio Auditor E. W. Poe: "'Our colored comrade fought for the same cause and flag that you and I did. Then why not allow him all the rights guaranteed him under our ritual? You cannot rightfully, justly or manfully do him less.'"[29]

In addition, the men who comprised the delegates' special committee found themselves besieged throughout the night by other delegates and comrades from the rank and file, all of whom were against a proposed separate department.[30]

The five-man committee on the commander in chief's address made their reports the next evening. In a stunning development, three former national commanders and a past commander of the Department of Connecticut[31] came to a decision in dispute with Veazey. Fully supporting their black brethren, the four pointed out that since its inception, the GAR "has never turned from its Post door any deserving comrade, however humble, on account of his nationality, creed or color." In a powerful and moving statement, they adamantly refused to accept a racial divide within the organization:

> During that fierce struggle for the life of the nation, we stood shoulder to shoulder as comrades tried. It is too late to divide now on the color line. A man who is good enough to stand between the flag and those who would destroy it when the fate of the nation was trembling in the balance is good enough to be a comrade in any Department of the Grand Army of the Republic. No different rule has been or ever will be recognized by the survivors of the Union army and navy. No Department should be established for any color or nationality.[32]

A major basis for Veazey's recommendations had been petitioning of seven of the African American posts for a separate department. However, when representatives for some of the posts came before the committee, they claimed that their petition had not sought a separate department, but rather the creation of an integrated department in Louisiana as in other states. Further, they expressed opposition to a separate department on behalf of themselves and those they represented. As a result, the committee concluded that "Had this information been before the Commander-in-Chief, as it was before the committee, we believe that he would not have made the recommendation he did."[33]

The fifth committee member, W. S. Decker of Colorado, concurred with Veazey and issued a minority report resolving that the commander in chief be given the authority to organize new departments in existing departments provided there would be no detriment to GAR goals or the departments. When discussion was opened with the other delegates, Decker insisted that he endorsed the majority report, and noted his service in a black regiment. However, he did not think his resolution would establish a color line, and cautioned the other delegates "not [to] judge the condition of affairs down there to be such as you see in the State of Michigan and other northern States. . . . Colored men belong to the Post in the city in which I live, and they are welcome there. But a different condition of affairs exists down in the southern States."[34]

At one point hissing from members in the audience, in particular African Americans, interrupted his presentation but subsided when the presiding officer threatened to clear the packed galleries.[35] After Decker was finished, the dialogue that ensued among delegates was distinguished by its honesty, solemnity, and high emotion, as veterans from the West and former Border States explained why they stood with the majority report.

One of its authors, past commander in chief William Warner, spoke of black and white solidarity in the Department of Missouri that grew despite his being warned against mustering in African American posts. He then reminded everyone that during the war, the sight of a black face meant a friend: "He went to the field and fought for the flag of the country, a flag that never up to that time had protected him in anything but bondage."

Directly confronting his Southern comrades' fears of how whites in their home states would react to a department "composed of niggers, in the parlance of the country," he admonished them to remember that it was they "who held in bondage, and the men who restrained from liberty, the men that are now raising their hands and pleading with you not to desert them in this hour of their agony." Warner ended with a warning for all GAR members, "as our heads are silvering o'er with the frost of years," not "to go back upon the principles for which we fought and for which we bled."[36] His remarks drew repeated applause, and "the convention yelled for a full minute" after he finished.[37]

The views of two African American delegates were critical to the discussion. Robert Johnson of the Department of the Potomac wanted to know "why it is that you want to shove us off now in a separate Department, when we always have been in one Department, and of all of the institutions that we belong to no other institution has brought us so near together as the Grand Army of the Republic." As white and black soldiers had been "friends and brothers together" in the field, Johnson insisted that staying one department was imperative even if separate posts were needed in the South. Pointing out the nation's worsening race problem, he asked, "If you turn your back upon us, whom shall we look to, where shall we go?" Seeing honesty, "principle," "charity," and "loyalty" among his comrades, he did not think such a thing would happen.[38]

Edward A. Richey of Kentucky spoke proudly of the successful incorporation of colored posts (15 percent of overall) into a department that had initially been hostile to black membership. Emphatically stating that African American veterans wanted no part of a separate department, he conveyed their belief that such a move would result in exclusion from state encampments, ostracism, and eventual removal from the GAR altogether.

Linking the stormy racial climate and a collective African American warrior identity, Richey said, "We know something of hard times and we know just what it is to be Grand Army men." Seeing the proposal as a sign that some Southern white members "want to turn their backs on us in this our time of trouble," he expressed the hope he would "be able to return to Kentucky and say to my comrades that the National Encampment will stand by the colored comrades all over this land."[39]

The tension in the air fairly crackled when Decker interrupted Richey on one occasion, and he shot back: "'You are one of the ducks that hide their badges down our way while you are flirting with the Democrats.'"

According to Washington's *Evening Star*, "This brought down the house and the uproar was terrific."[40] The incident illustrates just how unique the GAR was in 1891 America—where else could a black man display such open hostility to a white man in front of hundreds of people and be celebrated for it?

Department of West Virginia delegate H. S. Northcott was pleased to see African American members at the encampment, but he was also surprised "to hear that he should become a subject of controversy now at this late day when he had been recognized as a citizen." He was "willing to recognize him as a comrade and take him into my Post notwithstanding I am a southern man," and thought "there should be no color line drawn."[41]

By the time A. S. Graham had his chance to speak, the high degree of antipathy for the proposed department was palpable. He began by observing "that this matter has not appeared before you in the sense in which we wish to have it," and then denied that the department of Louisiana and Mississippi was driving out black veterans because "They have never been in." Graham echoed Decker's argument: "Those of you who have never lived any length of time in the South, can have no conception of the state of society there." He then insisted that he and his comrades "will be among the first to maintain the rights of the colored man before the laws and tribunals of this country; give him free protection in his wife, his family, his children and property, and equality before the law. [But] There the matter ends."

Having chosen to live, raise families, and have their children marry in Louisiana and Mississippi, Graham said "It is right that we should conform to the social laws and rules that surround us." He then took a progressively more belligerent tone, criticizing black veterans for being ungrateful to white ex-servicemen for what they had done for them, and was adamant that the commission did not grasp the "true situation, [otherwise] you would look at the matter in a very different light from what you do now." Not only were the black posts "organized in fraud, and . . . supported in corruption ever since," but if legitimized, "there would be eight or ten or fifteen white men, perhaps, in a Post, perhaps twenty-five and there would be two or three hundred colored men, and it would be a case of the tail wagging the dog. The dog would be nowhere anymore."[42]

At that touchy point, James T. Johnston of Indiana asked: "Don't you think if you will open your doors and take the colored soldier in and take him by the hand and say to the rebels of the South, he is better than the man who fought against his flag, that you would kill this thing out down there?"[43]

Graham dismissed the concept as "impossible." Earlier he had characterized integrated posts in the North as a "very different thing," as they included "three or four colored men, nice men, respectable men, whom you all know and speak to every day on the street. They come into your Post and you treat them well," although not allowed leadership roles, with their membership essentially passive. According to Graham, what he and his comrades wanted was to muster into a new separate Department "ten thousand colored men, good men, respectable men, good men and not the dregs of the street, not the offscourings and the convicts out of the penitentiary. Not that kind of people." In that way, he claimed, the "honorable colored men who stand on this floor" who had "elevated themselves" could now "aid in elevating the others who are way down" as "a credit" to the GAR. After reconfirming his position that the disputed colored posts contained men who did not meet the criteria for GAR membership, Graham was done.[44]

Like Decker, Graham's comments had elicited hisses, along with cries of "No!" at one point, and he was "stung by the demonstration." In a manner the *Evening Star* later characterized as menacing, he told the encampment, "'The quicker you fix this matter up the better.'" The newspaper reported on the astounding events that followed: "A score of delegates rose as he sat down, but hundreds of voices clamored for a vote. The scene was a bedlam. In the midst of the uproar Gen. Veazey put the question of adopting the minority report. There were a good many ayes, but an avalanche of noes [*sic*], the veterans in the gallery making as much noise as the delegates on the floor. Then the majority report was put and carried in the same way, while white and colored men jumped upon chairs, waving hats, canes and handkerchiefs and creating pandemonium."[45] But not all GAR members were jubilant: "The southern delegates took their defeat very much to heart, and one of them shouted above the din, 'That's good-bye for us.'"[46]

Once he could again be heard, Commander Veazey told the delegates, "I have an application here, comrades, that the official reporter be authorized to give to the press the full debate upon this question upon which action has just been taken. There is danger otherwise that it will be misreported." The encampment fully agreed, and discussion of separate departments in the GAR was now in its annals, available to all who wished to read about it.[47]

THE GAR REJECTS A COLOR LINE: THE NATION REACTS

In its August 7 coverage of the previous evening's astounding events, the *World* concluded, "By the order of the Encampment the question is settled for the time being, but of course the trouble is not."[48] The newspaper then reported in its evening edition that the Department of Louisiana and Mississippi's white members "had hoped that the scheme would go through, particularly after its substantial endorsement by Commander-in-Chief Veasey. They now renew their threats of leaving the order." Not surprisingly, "Discussions of the question waxed warm in the hotel corridors and elsewhere last night. The point is more bitterly discussed than any that has previously come up in the Grand Army."[49]

The *New York Herald* showed how deeply the men of the Gulf resented the encampment's refusal to sanction a color line. On August 8, the paper reported that they believed the decision "will prove the death blow instead of the salvation of the colored veterans south of Mason and Dixon's line." Commander Hodges continued to claim they had sought African American representation in the GAR through provisional department establishment, but were thwarted by the encampment. Now, the men of color faced a Kafkaesque situation: "'As the matter stands they can't get any charters from our department, and our department is the only body with authority to grant charters in our jurisdiction. We don't want the colored men in our posts and we won't have them; so they get into the GAR. The charters granted by any one but our department are invalid and will not be recognized.'"[50]

Act Two of the drama remained to be played, but the impact of what took place in Detroit was immediate and unmistakable. Newspapers from coast to coast praised the Grand Army's decision, and recognized its significance in tumultuous times.

The *Omaha Daily Bee*, noting the GAR had faced "few questions of greater importance, as a test of the character and spirit of the organization," said it should be "heartily commended for the stand it has taken regarding the race issue." In Minnesota, the *Worthington Advance* told its readers that the Grand Army had "honored itself by its manly and heroic refusal to draw any color line, or make any class distinctions in its membership." Likewise applauding the failed attempt at segregation, the *St. Johnsbury Caledonian* of Vermont stated: "The men with dark skins did some valiant fighting during the rebellion, and their lighter-hued comrades at Detroit evidently believed that valor tells, by whomsoever exhibited." Another New England newspaper, the *Hartford Post*, well articulated the larger issue: "The black, in peace, shall be our brother still. It is not a social, but a patriotic, a humanitarian question; question of gratitude, of manliness."[51]

Recognizing the exceptional nature of the veterans' stand on race, some papers seized the opportunity to criticize other organizations for not showing similar fortitude. The *Evening Herald* of Shenandoah, Pennsylvania, published its second editorial about the decision on August 22, declaring that "The Grand Army of the Republic has done what a great many so-called Christian people are afraid to do or are too full of worldly prejudice to do." Its staff further pressed the point by quoting the *New York Independent*, which had taken a matching stand in a striking piece:

"Whose business is it to set an example of righteousness? Is it the business of the Church of Christ Jesus, or of a humane organization of the Lord's army, or of the relics of any army of physical warfare! Yet here we have a body of men of all faiths and no faith, men of the world, gamblers and profane, irreligious and infidels, as well as Christians, voting in overwhelming numbers to do right by their humble and despised comrades while a Christian church, and more than one of them, stumbles and falls prostrate before the temptation to pass their colored brother by on the other side.'"[52]

Just days later, what the newspapers reported was sadly demonstrated by a secular body. In Philadelphia, the Patriotic Order Sons of America, organized in 1847 "to preserve the Public School System, The Constitution of the United States and our American way of life,"[53] was having its national encampment. In a situation so closely paralleling what had occurred in Detroit that it was eerie, the Order was debating its own color line in the meeting hall of George G. Meade Post No. 1, GAR. The constitutional committee presented a majority report that recommended the word "white" be removed from the association's membership qualifications, under which African American camps had been barred from its ranks. A minority report was then put before the encampment urging "that the proposed amendment was not for the good of the order at the present time," its advocate insisting "that to retain the word did not mean that the order was violating or aiming against the rights of any colored citizen."[54]

As the *Pittsburg Dispatch* further reported, the black president of the city's Washington Camp No. 579, Stephen B. Gipson, was then "introduced and made an impassioned speech, in which he pleaded earnestly for the recognition of the colored man as a brother in the order. His remarks were received with rounds of applause." Discussion of the proposed amendment ensued, which the paper characterized as "turbulent and fiery" and involving "many members."

Despite Pennsylvania's entire sixty-four-man delegation voting yea in multiple balloting, the amendment failed due to thirty-two opposing votes from Western and Southern members, including Illinois and Ohio acting as a solid bloc, and a four-fifths majority being necessary to change the Order's constitution. The *Fort Worth Gazette* noted that a telegram from New Orleans arrived during the debate—drafted by the Louisiana State Encampment, it read: "'We wish that the national encampment at least postpone action on the color question another year. Further discussion will bring more light and a better understanding on the real conditions of the South to our brethren of the North who can then act more advisedly.'"[55]

On the heels of the Patriotic Order Sons of America decision, yet another national organization directly addressed the issue of race. The Union Veterans' Union, seventy-five thousand members strong, held its sixth annual encampment in Cleveland at the end of August.[56] In his address, outgoing Commander Clark came out strongly against any color lines in the Union: "The black soldier, on the battle field, fought and won his way to membership in any and all organizations where patriotism was the test and bravery and endurance the requirements and any organization of this character that would deny him was unworthy [of] the name patriotic order."[57]

The great concern African Americans had felt over the GAR controversy, and their collective relief at its outcome, was confirmed by the response of both the mainstream and black presses. On August 8, the *Sacramento Daily Record-Union* reported on the proceedings of the African Methodist Episcopal (AME) Church Conference in California's capital, during which members "severely criticised the action of the Grand Army Encampment in drawing the color line at the instigation of a few Southern members." When the result turned out to be the opposite, "a special committee prepared and reported [a] . . . telegram" signed by Presiding Bishop Abraham Grant and five other AME ministers that had been sent to William Warner in Detroit: "DEAR Sir: The California annual Conference of the African Methodist Episcopal Church, now in session, desires to express its appreciation and thanks for the effectual defense made in behalf of the negro veterans of the GAR."[58]

According to *The Appeal*, an African American newspaper in Minnesota, at an August 14 post-lecture reception among the Twin Cities' black elite, "three cheers [were proposed] for the GAR, in its decision on the color line; they were given with a will."[59]

In another large Midwestern city five days later, prominent African American citizens paid a personal visit of thanks for one man's contribution to the veterans' verdict. At his Kansas City home, William Warner welcomed the delegation, whose spokesman read group resolutions attesting to his "prompt action and eloquent appeal to justice

[that] succeeded in turning a wavering sentiment into an overwhelming victory for the equality of man." Warner assured his guests that the gratifying plaudits were undeserved, but took their demonstration "to reflect the sentiments of the colored race throughout the country." He felt most fortunate to be a member of an organization that "never had had and never will have a color line," and "praised the devotion of the African race to the Union cause"; his impromptu speech was gratefully accepted.[60] When the former congressman visited Washington in early September, a similar reception from leading members of the city's black community awaited him at his hotel.[61]

On August 22, the *Washington Bee*, an African American newspaper in the nation's capital, "congratulate[d] the Grand Army of the Republic upon the decided manner in which it sat down on the 'color line' business of a few Negro-hating Yankees in the South."[62] Further showing how closely blacks followed the actions of predominantly white organizations with respect to integration, a month later the *Bee* published a letter from a former member of the Seventh Michigan cavalry, who "in speaking of the 'Patriotic Sons' expressed his surprise at their vote to prevent colored men from membership, said: 'In that which gives the Grand Army and Union Veterans Union its nobility the colored soldier had his share.'" The letter continued: "'The Negro soldier earned his right to a place where the white soldier earned his, with his life upon the hazard. Their blood mingled on many a battle field, shed in the same cause, as freely and bravely by the one as by the other. The tie that binds us together is neither black nor white. It is red, and those who have given of their veins to it in the comradeship of war are not to be denied the comradeship of peace.'"[63] On September 12, the *Appeal* made the same point as the *Evening Herald* and *New York Independent*: "The Grand Army of the Republic, by its refusal to recognize the color line, set an example which we hope our churches may find grace enough to follow."[64]

Not all Northern press coverage of the GAR's decision was favorable. Ohio's *Stark County Democrat*, reporting on the quick disbanding of Vicksburg, Mississippi's GAR post in reaction to the encampment's ruling, nastily added, "If these old soldiers were Democrats the g.o.p. organs, from California to Maine, would proceed to abuse them like pickpockets." The *Iron County Register* in William Warner's home state of Missouri contrasted the commander in chief's "calm and judicial" discussion of separate departments with that of the committee Warner chaired, "composed chiefly of Republican politicians" who "united in a report . . . full of sounding rhetoric, condemning Gen. Veazey's recommendations." Comparing the delegates' open discussion to "a Republican convention" and scorning Richey's riposte to Decker, the *Register* claimed that the "large majority" voted "against what was stigmatized as a Democratic policy," although it had actually been "advocated by a life-long Republican who comes from the strongest Republican State in the Union."[65]

In New York City the *World* objected to the decision and accused the GAR membership of hypocrisy: "The Northern veterans who undertake to legislate for their white comrades in the south must first put themselves in their place. If they can even truthfully say that they would willingly join a lodge, a club, or a church conducted and governed by colored men, their support of Mr. Warner's recommendation may be justified, but not otherwise."[66]

While the *World's* staff's logic is questionable in specific relation to the encampment's principled stand, they certainly had a point, given the extent of racism in the North and nationally. On August 10, the *Sun* published an article that began, "The rubbing out of the color line in the Grand Army has caused expressions of wonder in some quarters that any such line should exist." The paper then detailed the total segregation of Union armies, and how little had changed since the Civil War, including the appalling lack of African American officers or opportunities for promotion: "So, too, in the regular army to this day colored soldiers are never enlisted for the white regiment. There are two distinct regiments for colored men in the cavalry and two in the infantry, and they are found nowhere else. These colored regiments also have always had white officers almost exclusively."

Regarding black officers, a handful of "colored lads have been educated at West Point and . . . been assigned as subalterns to the colored regiments" in "a rare exception to the rule of white commissioned officers" for such units, "while in the appointments to Second Lieutenancies from civil life there are no colored men."[67]

In September, an episode of Jim Crow discrimination in the North received national exposure. John P. Green, an attorney, two-time Republican member of the Ohio House, and author of the legislation to make Labor Day a holiday, had traveled from his Cleveland home to make an invited address at the Amalgamated Council of Trades meeting in Cincinnati. On arrival he checked into a suite at the Gibson House. However, when Green entered the dining room for dinner, the hotel manager informed the African American that he could not eat there, but would be served in a private room per "the usual custom . . . [to which] other distinguished colored men who had stopped at the hotel had never objected." Offended, the attorney told the manager that if he was not seated in the dining room like all the other guests, he would leave the hotel. Getting no satisfaction, Green retrieved his luggage and went to the Burnet House, where he registered and ate his dinner in its dining room without incident, "the color line . . . not drawn so closely" at his new hotel.[68]

Word soon got out, and the council's indignant labor committee reported the incident to several Republicans, who immediately cancelled all the rooms reserved for William McKinley at the Gibson House. When the gubernatorial candidate arrived in Cincinnati, he was taken to his new accommodations at the Burnet House. Of further note is that Green had suffered even worse treatment in the Queen City during the previous year's Labor Day festivities, when no hotel would allow him to stay; he eventually lodged with a member of the celebration committee.[69]

As was usually the case when ill treatment of black citizens in a Union state became known, Southern newspapers took advantage of the situation. Within a week the *Brenham Weekly Banner* in Texas informed its readers that "The drawing of the color line in Ohio, and that by Republicans" in the Green affair "'should be made a note of by the colored people of the South for future reference when the Ohio papers commence their tirade of abuse against the South for the way they treat the negro, and then send the chicken home to roost.'"[70]

Concerning the GAR, for all its decision's deserved status as a litmus test for racial tolerance, the Department of Louisiana and Mississippi's color partition did not automatically end. As the new commander in chief, John Palmer of New York, would later say, "I had hoped that the action of the twenty-fifth national encampment at Detroit would have settled all existing differences in this department, and I would be relieved from the unpleasant disturbances encountered by my predecessors."[71] Unfortunately for Palmer this was not the case, and how he handled the situation would reflect significantly on the Grand Army and its membership of half a million veterans, white and black.

Things hardly got off to an auspicious start in 1892. Around New Year's Day, a meeting of the department's white associates was held in response to the commander's being "called on to recognize the full equality and fellowship of the colored ones" in follow-up to the encampment's ruling. Rather than agree to accept black comrades as directed, the white posts overwhelmingly voted to give up their charters at the following month's encampment.[72] By stark contrast, Civil War veterans in Brooklyn were strongly considering disbanding Kings County's black posts and incorporating their members into the existing white posts, a move that "would tend to do away with the color line in the Grand Army of the Republic."[73]

As expected, when the new African American posts came to New Orleans in February for the Department of Louisiana and Mississippi Encampment they "were refused admission or representation, although their dues were tendered and declined" and "entirely ignored." After sending their reports and dues to GAR national headquarters, Commander Frederick Speed was again told to recognize the eight black posts, which he refused. On March 3, Speed issued the following general order: "'The commander-in-chief has ordered that these posts be recognized. This order the council of administration, under a full sense of the gravity of the act, and aware of the possible consequences of their refusal to comply, decided that they could not conscientiously obey—and the department confirmed and ratified their action.'" The *National Tribune* reported this "will probably lead to some complication and may be deemed insubordination, for which they would be liable to have their charters withdrawn. The whites are determined to have no 'nigger in theirs,' and are indifferent as to the outcome."[74]

Palmer, perceiving that he had no discretion to act otherwise given his designated authority as commander in chief and the national encampment's decision, directly confronted the department's "open defiance and revenge." As he later explained in his address to the 1892 national encampment in Washington, DC, "If the officers of this department were unwilling to abide by the rules of the national encampment it was their privilege to resign and permit others to be chosen who would, but they had no right to attempt to thwart the action of the national encampment by an effort to bring about a dissolution of the department by an illegal act."[75]

On April 25, Palmer suspended Speed and placed Senior Vice-Commander D. M. Durkee in command, instructing him to recognize the black posts and report to headquarters by May 15. Four days before the deadline, Durkee reported that no application had been made by the posts, and on May 19 presided over a special session of the department in which, by a 32–2 vote, it decided to disband and surrender its charter. As reported by the *Rochester Democrat and Chronicle*, the department adopted resolutions that recited "the division's grievances, allege the disagreeable circumstances that would arise from the admission of colored men to a fraternal and social organization, and gave the legal technicalities upon which the colored posts were refused recognition." In addition, the eight white posts were advised "to follow the example of the encampment and surrender their post charters—a course of procedure to which all the posts have already pledged themselves."

Palmer literally read the news in the paper that evening, an indication of how closely America was following events as they unfolded. An exasperated commander in chief said he would suspend Durkee the next day for not complying with his orders, and place the junior vice commander in charge: "If he declines to obey orders then I shall be required to place some one else in command of that department."[76]

The promotion of George W. Miller did not augur well, the *Elmira Gazette and Free Press* reporting that he "is said to be as firmly opposed to the negroes as the two deposed officers." Almost on cue, the department's assistant adjutant general, Charles W. Keeting, telegraphed headquarters "that Comrade Miller considered himself no longer a member of the order, as the department in special encampment had voted to surrender the department charter." The fait accompli was the May 26 receipt at national headquarters of the department's charter, "Surrendered May 19, 1892" written across it in red.[77]

In response, on June 2 Palmer declared, in accordance with Grand Army rules and regulations, that all actions taken at the special meeting were null and void; appointed "Past Department Commander A. S. Badger pro tempore"; and returned the charter to him. The commander in chief told Badger the charter remained in force and ordered him to recognize the black posts; Badger took department command the next day.[78]

One of the cleverest barbed comments on the incredible happenings came from the *Lowell Daily Courier* on June 4: "The Southern GAR white men must be near-sighted if they can't recognize a colored post. Timber of that hue was pretty conspicuous in the Union breastworks in the sixties and it was fast-black."[79]

The Massachusetts newspaper's point was spot on given charges leveled by Speed before his suspension. According to the *Wichita Daily Eagle*, he had complained that the African American posts were "comprised of a motley crew, mainly of teamsters, cooks, officers' servants and camp followers, some of whom served in the Confederate army, and no effort was made when the posts were organized to determine whether they had been honorably discharged from the Federal army, and they should not have been recognized by the grand encampment."

In answer, after Palmer reorganized the department he ordered a complete, thorough inspection of all the new posts. Speed's highly insulting allegations turned out to be baseless; as the commander in chief told the 1892 national encampment, "the reports of the inspecting officers as filed at national headquarters show that each comrade produced either his discharge, pension certificate or satisfactory evidence of service."[80]

The restructured Department of Louisiana and Mississippi held its encampment in New Orleans on August 6, with delegates from thirteen posts (the nine new black posts and four others) in attendance as full participants. According to Palmer, he had been "advised that this was the most harmonious in the history of that department." Further gratification came next month in Washington, when he reported that the department was represented at the national encampment by its highest number of attendees ever.

Concerning the entire ordeal, Palmer frankly acknowledged the financial and emotional price he and the Grand Army paid to do what the organization believed was right concerning Louisiana and Mississippi: "It had cost the national encampment more money, time and energy . . . than all other departments combined, from the inception of the order to the present time."[81]

The national encampment that met in Washington beginning September 20 was the largest to date. In his fine published account, Charles E. Benton of the Department of Massachusetts put the number of Grand Procession participants at 65,000, and another 30,000 veterans not marching due to physical or other considerations. Proudly stating that the GAR "is believed to be the only organization that has effectually wiped out the color line," he noted many posts' "black and white comrades [were] marching side by side," along with numerous African American posts "from some departments, especially those of Virginia and Maryland."[82]

Reluctantly or not, the GAR had become the center of a raging controversy. With the entire country watching, the organization's refusal to accept a color line, indeed choosing to stand by its African American comrades at the expense of other veterans in the South, was admirable and historic. As Shaffer stated in his examination of the Grand Army's actions, "Palmer's willingness to sacrifice large numbers of white veterans in order to integrate the black posts in the department was extraordinary, as was the fortitude of the Grand Army rank and file at the Detroit encampment. That the GAR accepted black members was unusual enough in the Gilded Age. However, the fact that many white members, even in the Upper South, opposed separate departments for white and black Union veterans in the Lower South was even more remarkable."[83]

This appraisal notwithstanding, Shaffer still reported that to a degree, the hullabaloo over the Department of Louisiana and Mississippi was "merely pretense." The historian's point of view was supported by lack of newspaper coverage of similar problems in other parts of the deep South, including Alabama and Texas, and overall segregation within the GAR at the local level.[84]

This was substantially in agreement with McConnell's earlier assessment: "In its last, major public debate on the subject . . . the Grand Army stood its ground against segregation. While the color line was officially repudiated, it remained in force nonetheless." Citing "informal blackballing" of African American applicants to white posts, separation of posts by race, and additional southern departments disregarding the encampment's decision, he concluded that "Black veterans, in short, were admitted to the GAR on terms of formal equality accompanied by informal discrimination."[85]

As noted, Gannon's later scholarship led to a different conclusion about the integration of black members in the Grand Army. While Shaffer's and McConnell's points about departments in the lower south other than Louisiana and Mississippi are well-taken, additional pertinent information bears reviewing.

In April 1890, the *National Tribune* reported about a new white Woman's Relief Corps (WRC, the GAR female auxiliary) organizing in Florida. The Corps' past national president, well received by black "sisters" and "comrades," hoped they would "do something nice Memorial Day. The color line is drawn so closely, there is but little chance for improvement, and even now it costs something to be loyal to the old flag."[86] This provides a critical racial perspective for what appeared six months later in the same newspaper.

When Fred S. Goodrich read the *National Tribune*'s October 23 article about the possible formation of a separate, multi-state colored department in the South,[87] he was dumbfounded, and so informed his Grand Army comrades in a letter published by the *Tribune* on November 6. Noting that the proposed black department would include Florida, its current commander had "no knowledge of such a fact existing in that State. We charter colored Posts, and meet the colored comrades in the same spirit of fraternity that we do white comrades," and had "never heard a complaint from any, or the color line broached in any Post or out of it."

Goodrich then got more personal:

It has always seemed to me that a man who voluntarily offered his life in defence of a country that had signally failed in its protection to him, was good enough to belong to any Post of the GAR, provided he held an honorable discharge from the service of the United States, was a decent man and complied with the Rules and Regulations of the Order. I do not recollect that any of the boys complained about them getting in front of them at Fort Wagner, Baton Rouge, or Petersburg . . . So let us push on to a higher citizenship by inculcating the doctrines of the GAR.[88]

Articulately and passionately, Commander Goodrich presented the exact argument against a color line that would be made at the national encampment nine months later. His department's advocacy for its black comrades as not only full and equal members, but Americans entitled to the same rights and protections as all other citizens consistent with GAR principles, is significant in its own right. That it came from a state in which Jim Crow was actively in force makes Goodrich's declaration even more noteworthy.

As it had with Florida, the *National Tribune* provided a sense of the Texas color line in May 1892. George Smith did not protest being condemned to die at the end of a Lone Star State rope, but "object[s] most strenuously to the fact that he is to be hanged on the same day and gallows that a negro is to render satisfaction to the law." Sardonically, the *Tribune* felt "Mr. Smith should take consolation from the fact that the next day he won't know the difference."[89]

Six months later, a black post in Texas contacted national headquarters to lodge a complaint that neither the state's department nor Louisiana's would grant their charter. Commander in Chief A. G. Weissert, who gave immediate orders for its issuance, was quoted by the *St. Paul Daily Globe*:

"The race war in the Grand Army circles of the South . . . is assuming a graver aspect than ever before . . . I have been collecting statistics from Florida to Texas. It is my intention to make a tour of the South and make a searching inquiry . . . [and] propose to see that the colored soldiers are recognized by the state departments and posts of the Grand Army. I will lay down the laws to the offending posts, and if they refuse to recognize the colored soldier they will be dismissed from the Grand Army without ceremony."[90]

Weissert's expedition took him to two sensitive sites in April 1893, with decidedly mixed results that were reported in the *National Tribune*. The reorganized Department of Louisiana and Mississippi was flourishing—while five posts had given up their charters, eleven newly formed posts helped boost membership by a staggering 100 percent to almost thirteen hundred.[91]

The week before, Weissert had been praised for being the first commander in chief to visit the Department of Texas, but there were ominous signs. Its encampment enacted a resolution that struck from GAR records "an order passed at El Paso last year, recommending applicants for the organization of negro or colored Posts to apply to the Department of Louisiana and Mississippi." However, as the *Tribune* noted, "The matter is now in the same condition as before the El Paso meeting," meaning that black posts remained unchartered in Texas.[92]

Weissert's pronouncement about African American posts would ultimately go unfulfilled as far as Texas was concerned. When a black post was subsequently formed in Austin despite department objections, the national Council of Administration's Executive Committee reviewed the documentation and ordered its commander to charter the post. When he insisted that the applicants were not eligible for GAR membership, the new commander in chief, General Ivan N. Walker, who had "inherited . . . the unsettled question" from his predecessor, "deemed it advisable to send a trusted and impartial comrade to visit Austin and ascertain the true condition of affairs."[93]

Former Department of Indiana Commander Gilbert R. Stormont traveled to Austin, where he met both the black candidates and white Grand Army members; after assessing the situation, he was satisfied there were grounds for some of the department's concerns. After speaking with the aspirants, they decided to withdraw their charter application. When Walker explained all this to the Thirtieth Annual National Encampment at St. Paul, Minnesota, on September 3, 1896, he was clearly troubled: "If this action had not been taken, and the report of Comrade Stormont had shown the applicants worthy of membership in our Order, the Post would have been mustered. I never shall forget that the only men who aided and shielded me in my escape from a rebel prison had black faces. This is a serious problem in Southern Departments, but no honorably-discharged veteran should be discriminated against on account of the color of his skin. There must be other and valid reasons for his rejection."[94]

Beyond the color line itself, the Grand Army and Union veterans in general were intimately involved in other race-related concerns as the years since the Civil War grew into decades. The 1892 national encampment's opening procession (with Old Abe still leading the Department of Wisconsin) had followed the same route as the 1865 Grand Review, as Comrade Benton related: "The former parade marked the successful issue of a long and desperate struggle to maintain the authority of the government, and it ended by accomplishing more than was intended at the start—it accomplished the liberation of five millions of human slaves."

He then addressed aging, meaning and remembrance of an increasingly distant war:

> The veterans are far past middle life, only the youngsters and boys of the war that have not passed fifty. As the column moved past for eight long hours in one unceasing tramp . . . it seemed as if a page of the nation's history was illumined that the newer generation might for one brief day see, and realize, a vivid past. The spectators were most of them younger, and many of them foreign-born, and far more than half of them had no recollection whatever of those exciting times.
>
> The old issues are dead, but new issues have arisen and always will arise.[95]

Those "new issues" stemmed from the nation's oldest and most divisive issue, and its resolution remained as elusive as ever. Reconciliation between North and South, and how the Civil War was to be remembered, were not only interrelated with black Americans' fight for equality amidst Jim Crow's degradation and violence, but critical elements in themselves that became more contentious as time went on.

JUDGE JOSEPH W. O'NEALL

First Lieutenant (promoted but not mustered) Joseph W. O'Neall, Thirty-Fifth Ohio.

CHAPTER 7

Reconciliation, Resistance to the Lost Cause, and Lynching

Gauged by this standard, we cannot say that a law which authorizes or even requires the separation of the two races in public conveyances [163 U.S. 537, 551] is unreasonable, or more obnoxious to the fourteenth amendment than the acts of congress requiring separate schools for colored children in the District of Columbia, the constitutionality of which does not seem to have been questioned, or the corresponding acts of state legislatures.

—*PLESSY V. FERGUSON*, 1896[1]

When the Society of the Army of the Potomac held its annual reunion at Saratoga Springs, New York, in June 1887, Chauncey M. Depew spoke to the "thinking bayonets" of the Union's largest army and others in the sizable audience. The president of the New York Central freely acknowledged that Yank and Reb alike "believed he was fighting for the right, and maintained his faith with a valor which fully sustained the reputation of Americans for courage and constancy." However, "one side or the other was wrong. It was slavery and disunion or freedom and union, and one must not only yield, but die."[2]

Depew then stated: "The God of battles decided for liberty and nationality, and no surviving soldier who fought in either army to-day doubts the righteousness of that verdict. The best and bravest thinkers of the South gladly proclaim that the superb development which has been the outgrowth of their defeat has been worth all its losses, its sacrifices and humiliations."[3]

It is unknown upon what information Depew based his absurd assertions. After their steadfastly opposing Reconstruction, and with Jim Crow discrimination flourishing, a prominent longtime Republican was somehow declaring that the former Confederate states had fully accepted the Union's victory, the moral superiority of the causes for which it fought, and the shame of their own defeat. What his comments epitomized was a growing desire for reconciliation between North and South, with historical accuracy or the reality of current conditions not necessarily part of the mix.

That same year, Army of the Potomac veterans expressed very different sentiments about their former Army of Northern Virginia adversaries. As detailed by Carol Reardon, a planned reunion of the two legendary forces at Gettysburg met significant resistance. Possible return of captured Confederate battle flags was vehemently opposed by surviving members of the Fourteenth Vermont, including Captain W. C. Dutton. In speaking for his comrades, Dutton denied any hostility toward their old foes, but drew a clear demarcation between their respective tenets: "While we were loyal, they were traitors; and the leaders of this most causeless and wicked rebellion, ought to repent in sackcloth and ashes and thank God that a long-suffering, and forgiving nation, permitted them to live; for the penalty of treason is death."[4]

In June, a monument was dedicated to the Fifteenth Massachusetts at Gettysburg, with regimental commander, Brevet Major General Charles Devens Jr., the primary speaker. On his second term as an associate justice of the Massachusetts Supreme Judicial Court after serving in the Hayes administration as attorney general, Devens delivered a powerful message about the Civil War's meaning. Like Dutton, he avowed no animosity toward the Confederates, but "stand[ing] by these glorious graves," he insisted upon a precise, dispassionate understanding as to who had fought for what:

[W]e cannot confound the heroes and martyrs of a noble cause with those whom the twin furies of treason and slavery lead forth to battle. . . . It is the cause which sets our brethren apart among the myriads who people the silent cities of the dead. We should not be true to their just and lasting fame if in any sickly sentimental gush of reconciliation we should hesitate to assert that the principles for which they died were right, and those against which they fought were deeply wrong.[5]

Despite these criticisms, a reunion of Pickett's Division and the Philadelphia Brigade took place in July 1887. In an appraisal reflecting a rising national viewpoint that entailed grave implications, the *Lancaster Daily Intelligencer* reported that the successful fraternization between "the Blue and the Gray . . . clearly indicates that the war and its passions is now only a memoir . . . as the years roll on, the bitterness is being forgotten and the sweetness, in the recollection of brave deeds on both sides, is constantly increasing."[6]

The *Troy Daily Times* had a much different view of the same event. The Republican publication was disturbed by the "simply astounding . . . readiness with which the Democratic newspapers of the North, with a few honorable exceptions, have taken to glorifying the 'lost cause' and magnifying the heroism and devotion of the confederate soldiers." While recognizing the Rebels' valor in war and the positive aspects of old foes getting together and honoring each others' dead, the newspaper's staff issued a dire warning about the threat posed by revisionism: "But among all these greetings and fraternizations the fact should never for a moment be lost . . . that the cause of the Union was the cause of justice and right . . . [and] the stern lessons that the war taught . . . the people of this country can afford neither to forget nor to belittle."[7]

This was only a prelude to what took place at Gettysburg the following summer. Twenty-five years after squaring off in battle, thousands of Union veterans joined two hundred of their Confederate counterparts in a three-day commemoration arranged and dominated by the Society of the Army of the Potomac. Some found it poorly managed and New York–centric, former Rebels stayed away in droves, President Cleveland avoided attending, and unlike the Society's predominantly Democratic leadership, the Grand Army had essentially no role in its planning or execution.[8] Of greater significance was that on the heels of the previous reunion, the 1888 gathering led to more controversy and a deepening rift over reconciliation and memory.

Two speeches stood out in both respects. The remarks of General Lucius Fairchild, whose left arm was amputated due to wounds received on that very field while leading the Iron Brigade's Second Wisconsin,[9] were quoted by the *Salt Lake Herald*: "Men of the north did not love men of the south less, but they loved the old flag more and men of the south did not love the old flag less, but they loved State sovereignty. This, Mr. President, I think tells the whole story. The old flag still remains. (Cries of Amen.) And they all say Amen from the Gulf to the lakes."[10]

A three-time Republican governor of Wisconsin who spent ten years as a high-level diplomat under two Republican presidents before becoming GAR commander in chief in 1886[11] must have known that his declaration regarding the war's causation was utterly preposterous. In light of the principled stand Fairchild would take three years later against a Grand Army color line, it is likely his comments stemmed from the gathering's spirit of reconciliation, rather than what he truly believed about the rebellion.

The reunion's featured orator, famed author and journalist George William Curtis, was an early Republican with impeccable anti-slavery credentials who later served as chairman of the commission to reform the civil service during the first Grant administration. However, he crossed party lines in 1884 to endorse the Democratic presidential candidate, Grover Cleveland.[12] His speech, more complex and nuanced than Fairchild's, presented a corresponding challenge in interpreting its intent and underlying precepts.

Curtis began by saying that along with "'the brave soldiers of the blue and grey,'" "'the bitter of all our national differences—human slavery'" was buried at Gettysburg. Staying on that theme, he declared that if the United States was to stay the world's standard for "'free government,'" "'our first duty is to remember that Constitutional liberty has its own laws, and that by respecting and enforcing them, can liberty for ourselves and for all men be preserved.'"[13]

So far so good, but when he raised the dilemma of "'suffrage subject to the Constitutional guarantee of a Republican form of government, and of no discrimination against race or color,'" things got dicey. Calling the vote "'the mainspring of the heart of our common life,'" Curtis insisted that the "'practical remedy for its coercion or its repression, . . . is local, not national. The citizens of this magnificent commonwealth [Pennsylvania] cannot reach across the Potomac and impose their will respecting the suffrage upon the mother of States [Virginia], nor can the States of New England dictate legislation to the States of the northwest.'"[14]

He then offered his solution to this contentious, critical issue by invoking "'Washington, Jefferson and Madison [taking] counsel with Alexander Hamilton and Dr. Franklin and Rufus King and Roger Sherman, bent upon a common purpose, but with regard to every local condition,'" with their descendants "'confer[ing], fraternally forbearing until the real problem of the suffrage and all other problems are solved . . . This is the auspicious result . . . if the spirit of this day and of this field should become the spirit of our politic and then . . . as the essential reason of sectionalism disappeared with the war, its disappearance in fact, in feeling and in political action, would be the crowning glory of Gettysburg.'"[15]

In publishing Curtis's speech, the *Salt Lake Herald* said his "masterly effort" contained "grand sentiments."[16] True, but if one looked under the fluent veneer, its darker connotations were unmistakable. Curtis surely was aware that his claim of suffrage protection being a state matter was legally and morally fallacious. The Thirteenth, Fourteenth, and Fifteenth Amendments were federal, as were the Civil Rights Acts, and the Supreme Court's decision in *Yarborough et al.* had reiterated the federal government's primacy in defending the rights of all eligible voters. It was a tragic matter of public record that blacks by the thousands and supportive whites had been terrorized and murdered during and after Reconstruction to prevent American citizens from exercising their elective franchise, and lynchings were on the increase.

Given what had taken place since 1865, Curtis's statements concerning voting rights were highly offensive. To further suggest that brotherly restraint modeled on a contrived gathering without blacks (in July 1863, no soldiers of color were serving in or alongside the Army of the Potomac) would solve the nation's racial problems, or that sectional-ism had vanished with slavery's destruction, was an affront to living and dead Union veterans (white and black), non-veteran African Americans, and their civilian white advocates.

That the event had been agenda-driven was not an uncommon per-ception. The *Burlington Weekly Free Press* saw it as an attempt for former generals like Dan Sickles "[as] sharp democratic politicians . . . to make some thing for their party." Yet, except for Benjamin Butler, "No Union soldier of any prominence, . . . threw cold water on the project: and many labored earnestly to make the reunion a success. But as a fraternization of the blue and gray, and as a piece of political machinery, it was a failure; and it is not likely that it will be repeated very soon."[17]

That thought was shared by others, including Major General Henry W. Slocum, former XII Corps commander and two-term Democratic representative from New York,[18] who told the press, "'It went off all right, I suppose, but it was a very delicate affair to handle. I hope they will not have it again. Once is enough for such reunions.'" Two other officers were much more critical when they spoke at a morning campfire for delegates from the numerous GAR posts in Gettysburg, with Army of the Potomac veterans also in attendance.[19]

John P. S. Gobin was an attorney who rose from lieutenant to brevet brigadier general while fighting in all three theaters (including two terms with the Army of the Potomac, though not at Gettysburg), and became commander of the Department of Pennsylvania in 1886.[20] As reported by his home state's *Butler Citizen*, Gobin "was tired of hearing so much gush about Pickett's charge, as though they were the only heroes of the day. He said they simply charged across the field and were met and repulsed by men as brave and reckless as they. . . . He thought more dis-tinguished deeds of valor had been performed by divisions of the Union army," and gave specific cases.

As to fraternizing, Gobin stated that Grand Army members were willing to be friendly with their old adversaries but were also getting fed up with "the glorification of a veteran simply because he wore a gray uni-form with a Southern flag printed on his badge. That badge meant trea-son and rebellion in 1861, and what it meant then it meant now." Having scorned the overuse of reunion as a means to "hoist certain individuals into notoriety at the expense of the principles for which the North had fought and to the elevation of the principles of disloyalty," he then concluded to unrestrained cheering: "'I want it to be distinctly understood, now and for all time, that the men who wore the blue and fought on this field were everlastingly and eternally right and that the men who wore the gray were everlastingly and eternally wrong.'"[21]

When the applause subsided, another prominent Union veteran rose to address his comrades. In early 1861 John Taylor had enlisted as a private in the Pennsylvania Reserves, which was a battle-hardened unit by the time they engaged at Gettysburg on Day Two. Now a lieutenant, he led his men in a harassing pursuit of the enemy through the "Valley of Death" below Little Round Top. After promotion to the staff of Brigade Commander McCandless, he was captured at the Wilderness, and despite three escape attempts remained a prisoner of war until being exchanged in March 1865.

When Taylor spoke at Gettysburg, he was a successful insurance executive and so highly esteemed by the Grand Army that, after serving as commander of the Department of Pennsylvania, he was appointed national quartermaster general in 1881, a position to which each successive commander in chief re-appointed him for over a decade.[22]

He was even less interested in Blue and Gray get-togethers than Gobin. Noting his ten months of Rebel imprisonment, the related "indignities heaped upon him and his comrades and the spirit he had since seen continually manifested," Taylor "'wanted no part or lot in this intolerable slobber and gush, and if I did take part in these reunions . . . with men who are wearing rebel badges, I would be untrue to the comrades of my old company who fell on this field and some of whom are now resting in this beautiful cemetery.'" The reception to his remarks matched that accorded to his Keystone State associate.[23]

It is further revealing that those in the GAR who attended the reunion had good things to say about one old adversary in particular. CSA Lieutenant General James Longstreet, who commanded the Army of Northern Virginia's First Corps at Gettysburg as Lee's most trusted subordinate, told an enormous crowd at the national cemetery:

"'I changed my suit of gray for a suit of blue so many years ago that I have grown myself in my reconstructed suit of blue,'" a transition that had left him persona non grata among Confederate veterans. Longstreet later made even more of a positive impression when he attended the dedication of a monument for Gosline's Zouaves, where he wept over and kissed the regiment's bullet-riddled American flag.[24]

After the reunion, vocal Union veteran backlash continued against the tone reconciliation was taking, and the serious repercussions. In April 1889, Department of Ohio commander Joseph W. O'Neall delivered a stunning address to the state encampment on how memory should coincide with history: "Comrades, let no sickly sentimentality that would make the blue and the gray equal, they are equals never, turn us aside or swerve us from duty. Let us not forget the war, let us rather remember it . . . Let it ever be more honorable to have worn the blue than to have worn the gray. Let treason be made dishonorable, and the flaunting of the rebel flag under any pretense be an insult; loyalty be rewarded and made honorable."[25]

O'Neall then told the Encampment, with whom he had earlier sworn to "encourage the spread of universal liberty, equal rights and justice to all men," of an "address [made] before the Southern Historical Society" by South Carolina Senator Wade Hampton, in which the former Confederate General said, "'Let our children be taught the history of the war which began with the settlement of Jamestown, and for the time being ended at Appomattox Court House.'" O'Neall said in response, "'Let our children be taught the history of the war which began with the settlement of Jamestown and Plymouth Rock and forever and ever, thank God, ended at Appomattox Court House.' For say what you will that war is ended. You, my comrades, with your muskets shot to death in this country the hellish doctrine of secession and human slavery."[26]

On June 12, yet another group of veterans gathered on the Gettysburg battlefield. This time, former soldiers from Michigan came to dedicate monuments to their state's valorous service during the epic three-day clash. Twenty-six years had elapsed, but those who put their lives on the line had hardly forgotten why.

Captain L. H. Salisbury of the Fourth Michigan told his comrades: "This was God's fight, and you were His chosen instruments to turn back the tide of rebel invasion and place the seal of doom upon the efforts of those in rebellion to plant a government in this land with human slavery as its corner stone."[27]

Unlike Salisbury, Captain Charles R. Miller had not fought at the Pennsylvania crossroads town, but was made an honorary member of the Fourth Michigan for the occasion. After invoking John Brown's invasion of Harper's Ferry, Gettysburg and Lee's surrender at Appomattox as the three pivotal scenes of the "great tragedy of our history," the Western theater veteran sought to explain that the war had produced a "nation, better, purer, stronger and nobler, free in fact as well as free in name."

Miller also saw beyond America's progression, as "the whole human race made a long leap onward and upward during these four glorious, terrible, mournful years." Through this great effort "two great truths were so proven" they would never again be questioned: "One is, that no man has any right to hold any other man in bondage; the other is, that no State nor any number of States has the right to secede from the Union."[28]

R. Watson Seage of the Fourth Michigan, whose mutilation during the battle's second day rendered him a permanent Left-Armed Corps member, linked worthwhile sacrifice and reconciliation (but not of respective cause) in his commemorative poem's conclusion:

If then these sufferings made us free,
And gave our bond men Liberty,
We'll say: Thrice blessed the chastening be,
   And thank the Lord for Gettysburg.

Let us in unity to-day,
Lift up the prostrate foe and say
The Northern Blue and Southern Gray
   Brothers shall be since Gettysburg.[29]

In speech after speech, year after year, Union veterans placed slavery's destruction alongside maintenance of the Republic as the underlying roots and great achievements of the Civil War, and strongly resisted (indeed, bitterly resented) any attempt to portray Northern and Southern service-men as equivalent in the righteousness of their causes. When Washington's birthday was celebrated in 1890, another Left-Armed Corps officer seized the opportunity to differentiate Blue and Gray for a new generation.

A highly respected citizen of Rochester, New York, Captain Alonzo Mabbett had served as the Monroe County superintendent of schools from 1879 to 1880.[30] Given the honor of addressing 1,500 public school students and their families and friends at city hall, he made a memorable speech in which the young scholars were asked

> *to consider the flag an emblem of the national government in which they would soon take part. . . . He believed that if right principles were instilled in the minds of the school children to-day, if danger should in the future threaten the country, as young men they would rally to the defense of the government.*

> *He was sorry that in some sections of the country such principles were not taught. The lost cause, states' rights and a brood of pernicious teachings took the place of love for the national government.*[31]

Understanding why the Civil War was fought, what it attained in the 1860s and following decades, and what it had cost were hardly exclusive to the Union's aging veterans. On Memorial Day 1891, in WaKeeney, where John W. Reynolds of the Left-Armed Corps was a leading member of Post No. 197,[32] the *Western Kansas World* published a superb essay on the holiday's meaning and the need for its observance by "every loyal citizen of the great Republic": "[To] show respect and reverence for the memory of the men, who, for more than four years, subjected themselves to the wind, snow, rain and heat, and the privations, hardships, dangers and sufferings incident to cruel war, in order to preserve and purify with their life blood, the constitution founded by the fathers of our country—the fathers of universal liberty and equal rights to all."[33]

RECONCILIATION AND THE RISE OF THE LOST CAUSE
North-South reconciliation and how the Civil War was remembered in following decades remain issues of controversy and significance well

over a century later. David Blight has made a compelling case for "three overall visions of Civil War [that] collided and combined over time": "reconciliationist," "white supremacist," and "emancipationist." He categorized his study as ultimately "a story of how the forces of reconciliation overwhelmed the emancipationist vision in the national culture, how the inexorable drive for reunion both used and trumped race." Blight saw this process as having been facilitated by "a resurgent cult of manliness and soldierly virtues recycled in thousands of veterans' papers, speeches, and reminiscences. But such a moral equivalent of war came increasingly to exalt the soldier and his sacrifice, disembodied from the causes and consequences of the war." For Blight, this fostered "popular forgetting" that eventually led to a Northern Democratic and Southern slant to reconciliation.[34]

This general perspective has been shared by other historians. Foner reported that "The road to reunion was paved with the broken dreams of black Americans, and the betrayal of those dreams was indispensable to the process of reunion."[35] Despite their military accomplishments, African American veterans were hardly spared—as Shaffer noted, they "were forced to fight against the defamation and trivialization of their service in the collective national memory. Not only did white Americans grow more forgetful of black service as the years passed, but also the national interpretation of the war became increasingly dominated by white Southerners."[36]

In this regard, Andre Fleche has stated that "The dominant interpretation posits that the increasing need for sectional reconciliation between white Union and Confederate veterans forced northern ex-soldiers to forget and abandon their black comrades."[37]

But the actual extent to which white Union veterans contributed to these developments is definitely open to question. As has been shown, time and again they furiously denied any assertion that their motivations for fighting were indistinguishable from and morally comparable to those of the Confederates. Just as consequential were white veterans' associated staunch support and open appreciation for the dedicated service of their black comrades, exemplified by the Grand Army's adamant refusal to draw a color line.

In using some different methods and a high proportion of new primary material, the findings about the biracial relationship of Northern veterans in this book coincide with those of Fleche, who observed that through their sustained recognition of black soldiers' Civil War efforts rather than reuniting with former Confederates, the majority of white Northern veterans provided no support for the "increasing discrimination, disfranchisement, segregation, and racial violence" against African Americans.

Unlike Blight, Fleche found that "In their memoirs, publications, and memorial celebrations, black and white Union veterans formulated a joint vision of the war at odds with the more reconciliationist, segregationist, and racist trends found in postwar society as a whole."[38] The political activism, writings, public statements, and commemorative efforts of Union veterans presented in *One More War to Fight* are in full agreement with this statement.

M. Keith Harris has also challenged the popular historical standpoint: "Emphasizing exceptional events and implying extensive rejection of the causes and consequences of the war conceals important features of Northern Civil War memory." Characterizing suggestion of a Southern predominance in war remembrance as "gross misstatement," Harris reported Union veterans "articulated and fought to preserve memories of a war that pitted a Northern vision of Union against the institution of slavery—efforts that ultimately undermined the movement toward reconciliation."[39]

More recently, Caroline E. Janney expressed similar arguments in reporting that Union and Confederate veterans' ongoing remembrance and defense of their causes "ensured that Reconciliation would not come to dominate the landscape of Civil War memory—at least during their lifetimes." Another critical point made by Janney is that "Union veterans could embrace both reconciliation and emancipation. One did not preclude the other."[40]

This observation is consistent with Hess's earlier study of Northern servicemen. He ascribed the 1890s "deluge" of Union "memoirs, reminiscences, and diaries by everyone from cooks, privates, and chaplains to colonels, generals, and political leaders" to increasing trepidation that growing sectional closeness and distance from the war would nullify the meaning of their triumph. With the Lost Cause mentality gaining public acceptance, alarmed Union veterans "sought to remind people that one should support the reconciliation of North and South. . . . Confederate soldier[s] deserved respect for [their] sacrifices . . . but that there was just no way to compare the Southern and Northern causes."[41]

It is sadly and undeniably true that a national deficit in memory about African American military service grew into near-total amnesia, with grave ramifications. However, assigning appreciable blame for this development to their white comrades is groundless. We have seen abundant evidence that Union veterans, black and white, generally maintained a strong bond based on soldiers' pride and a shared warrior identity, in which forgetting the contributions of fellow ex-servicemen would be unthinkable.

Similarly, an evolving appreciation for the courage of men against whom thousands of battles had been waged is hardly unexpected, particularly as the combatants aged and their exploits became part of history. But honoring enemy valor certainly does not automatically entail validation of the cause(s) for which they fought, and the likelihood of that occurring with a conflict so deeply ideological as the Civil War was essentially nil.

Despite attempts to downplay the profound disparities between Union and Confederate war aims, Northern veterans kept slavery at the heart of the conflict, just as Southern ex-servicemen strove mightily to remove any vestige of the peculiar institution from the vaunted Lost Cause. Others might portray the underlying reasons as indistinguishable from one another and celebrate sacrifice and commitment alone, but not those who had risked everything.

As for race, both slavery and white supremacy defined the Confederacy and underlay the Civil War, while Reconstruction was a noble failed attempt to establish a biracial society. Although nineteenth-century America exhibited anti-Semitism, anti-Catholicism, and other bigotry to extents shocking to current-day sensibilities, Jim Crow discrimination directed against its black citizens occurred on another scale. Across the country, African Americans faced major challenges to voting and other civil rights, access to quality public and private education, occupational advancement, social equality, and, particularly in the South, their very lives.

No matter what an individual of color achieved, blackness defined their place in American society, and often tainted whites who treated them with respect. In 1892, the *National Tribune* reported that "the Medical Society of Washington [DC] draws the color line very closely" by banning from membership all African American physicians who graduated from Howard University, along with any white doctor who taught there. As for white physician graduates from the institution, they could join the Society only after pursuing a course of study at a university which did not admit blacks.[42]

Educated African Americans in the North were hardly immune to racism. One month before the *Tribune*'s story was published, the *Wichita Daily Eagle* reported on a nasty situation at Yale Law School. After two men were selected by the school's dean to give a presentation for a prize, a white senior from Missouri refused to participate due to his competitor's being black.[43]

Even when superb performance in combat was lauded, there could be denigration based on skin color. In 1894, *The Morning Call* in San Francisco published three articles about courageous actions during the Civil War, the last devoted to Sergeant William H. Carney of the Fifty-Fourth Massachusetts. The way M. S. Littlefield began the story showed awareness of prevailing racial attitudes among his readers: "The best evidence of valor men can give on the battlefield, or any place else, is their readiness to die for a principle, or at the command of a superior. I am about to bring a negro forward as a hero, and in doing so I am aware that it may be called bad taste, but truth is truth, and justice justice, without regard to color."[44] Having called the sergeant "an unusually intelligent negro," Littlefield provided an excellent description of the battle for Fort Wagner and Carney's extraordinary efforts to rally his comrades by snatching the flag from the mortally wounded regimental bearer and planting it at the parapet under galling fire, then carrying the colors despite receiving two serious wounds (one each in his leg and head) on his way back to Union lines.

With "his face . . . so covered with blood that it was impossible to tell if he was white or black, for the blood of all heroes has the same hue," his surviving Fifty-Fourth comrades recognized both he and the flag, which they had presumed was captured by the Rebels, and "bore back the sergeant." As for the colors, "not till an officer appeared [would] he could be made to loose his hold on the flag. Then, weak from torture and loss of blood, he handed the colors to his captain. "[45]

Up to that point, Littlefield's account is quite accurate given what is known about the battle and Carney, and relatively respectful of the soldier's being African American. Then, in one sentence, he falls prey to the era's racism by writing that the sergeant "gasped" to his superior, "'Before de Lor,' sah, I nebber let dat flag tetch de ground!'" instead of what Carney actually said, "'Boys, the old flag never touched the ground.'" To compound the insult, the article included a drawing of Carney, captioned with Littlefield's invented quote, that depicted the valiant soldier on his knees before a white officer, handing him the flag.[46]

How pervasive the acceptance of Jim Crow and belief in black inferiority had become by the late 1890s is further shown by both the Supreme Court ruling that would set back civil rights for more than half a century, and how most of the country reacted at the time.

African Americans' wishes for equal treatment on railroads such as Greener had expressed were cruelly dashed by the intolerable situation prevailing throughout the South. In July 1895, Northern blacks who traveled to Chattanooga for a religious organization's meeting were livid at being subject to Tennessee's "Separate Car Law," which meant upon arrival being ejected from their assigned seats and forced to ride in "Jim Crow cars." On the basis of alleged violation of the 1887 Interstate Commerce Act, Dr. Ernest Lyons of New York filed suit against the Baltimore and Ohio Railroad,[47] soon followed by an associated watershed case.

As detailed by Harvey Fireside, Homer Plessy, a New Orleans leather craftsman with one black great-grandparent (thus classifying him as an "octoroon"), agreed to challenge Louisiana's own Jim Crow "Separate Car Law" mandating African Americans be seated apart from whites on trains within the state. The defendant represented pro bono by

Union veteran and longtime civil rights advocate Albion Tourgée, *Plessy v. Ferguson* made its way to the nation's highest court.

In an 1896 decision that Fireside justifiably ranked second only to *Dred Scott* as the most disgraceful ever handed down by the US Supreme Court, seven justices (one justice recused himself and Justice John Harlan masterfully dissented, just as he had done thirteen years earlier in the related civil rights cases), ruled against African Americans' right to integrated train travel. That was bad enough, but the court extended the odious "separate but equal" concept to education, which the case did not explicitly involve.[48]

Despite the decision's great import, its May 18 announcement received relatively little press coverage compared to the 1883 civil rights ruling or generated much outrage like *Dred Scott*. The *New York Evening Post*'s story was typical of Northern newspapers in devoting one paragraph to the decision,[49] while more attention tended to be paid in Southern newspapers. When the *Weekly Messenger* of St. Martinville, Louisiana, whose masthead included the motto, "Justice to All," informed readers of the decision on May 23, it fairly boasted of Harlan's "one dissenting voice," and its implications: "The supreme tribunal of the United States having rendered this decision, the principle of the 'Jim Crow' car is now finally established in this State; and much discomfort and irritation will be saved to white people as they travel in Louisiana—Times-Democrat."

On the other hand, the *Roanoke Daily Times* recognized the decision's significance, and provided both the majority and dissenting views in its balanced report of May 19:

Justice Brown dismissed the case with a very brief opinion, merely saying that the State legislation in this case was analogous with legislation providing separate schools for colored and white children.

Justice Harlan, in his dissenting opinion, said that it would be just as reasonable to require separate coaches for Americans and foreigners, . . . men of Latin race and . . . Teutonic, or . . . men of differing views on political or religious questions, or to require

. . . one side of the street . . . be set aside for whites and the other for blacks. He contended that the law was repugnant to the thirteenth amendment. Railroads were, he said, public highways to the use of which citizens are entitled.[50]

Northern newspapers that did address the decision, particularly those that leaned Republican, were generally negative. On May 19, the *New York Tribune* said the ruling "must be accepted as the law of the land," but there would be "widespread sympathy with the strong dissenting opinion of Justice Harlan." The paper concluded that "it is unfortunate, to say the least, that our highest court has declared itself in opposition to the effort to expunge race lines in state legislation." Two days later, Minnesota's *Princeton Union* was fiercely more contemptuous of the decision: "Think of this in a land where all men are created free and equal. What a travesty on justice."[51]

As would be expected, the most vociferous denunciation came from African Americans and the black press. In June, the Philadelphia and Baltimore conference of the AME Zion Church unanimously approved a resolution that "heartily indorses and gratefully accepts" Justice Harlan's dissenting opinion, with accompanying explicit criticism of the nation's highest tribunal: "'We are led again to affirm that in the questions in which we have been and are particularly interested, we have, in the trying hours of our history, found on the Supreme Bench the justice named seemingly our only friend.'"

In August, the African American *Iowa State Bystander* reported that among the resolutions of the newly merged National Association of Colored Women were commendation of Justice Harlan's dissent, along with separate condemnations of blacks who "patronize the railway companies maintaining 'Jim Crow' cars" and "the lynching of Afro-Americans in the south, as well as mob violence and the convict lease system." The committee report was delivered by Ida B. Wells-Barnett, who was terribly experienced about such issues.[52]

As Packard stated, "The *Plessy* decision did not create Jim Crow . . . But it legitimized Jim Crow in law. For another six decades the vast majority of the nation's blacks would be forced to endure this

American nightmare."[53] Indeed, the Supreme Court's ruling was so devastating that the cause of equality would need every champion in the years to come.

JIM CROW IN THE SOUTH AND NORTH

Born into slavery but emancipated while still a child, Ida B. Wells was orphaned at sixteen, then used her Holly Springs, Mississippi, academy schooling to become a teacher and support her younger siblings. After moving to Tennessee in 1883, she continued to work as an educator and attended Fisk University, but conditions in the Volunteer State changed the course of her life. When ordered to give up her first-class seat and move to the crowded smoking car while in transit to Memphis, Wells refused and was removed from the train. She promptly sued the railroad, with her suit initially successful but subsequently lost on appeal to the state Supreme Court. Wells began to write about racial issues and became an owner and editor of *Free Speech*, in addition to her teaching. After being fired from her job for an 1891 editorial criticizing the Memphis school board, she turned to journalism as a full-time profession.

The following year, a black-owned grocery opened outside Memphis proper and immediately did well. A white merchant whose business suffered as a result tried to intimidate the three proprietors into abandoning their store, but when they stood firm, he gathered a mob and incited a clash that led to violence. After the black grocers were arrested and jailed, their store was destroyed, its inventory pillaged and the remnants left for their tormenter to buy at public auction. Within days, the three African Americans were removed from the jail, put on a train, and murdered in cold blood.

When Wells supported the men in a furious editorial, she became the whites' next target. Fortuitously out of town when they stormed the newspaper's office, the *Free Speech* premises were demolished, and her business manager informed that Wells would be lynched if she ever returned to Memphis. Financially ruined but alive, she fled north and began her rise into one of America's greatest civil rights activists.[54]

Although not the issue of contention, lack of African American access to equivalent educational opportunities was incorporated into the misery of post-*Plessy* Jim Crow. Besides substantiating "separate but equal" in the South, the court's decision threatened to stop or even reverse the painstaking progress in Northern school integration. In 1899, when a judge in Queens, New York, denied a black woman's motion to force her granddaughter's admission to a white school by the borough superintendent, the justice stated that his ruling was constrained by the *Plessy* decision.[55]

The sweeping impact of America's fin-de-siècle obsession with race included a potent political effect that incorporated national remembrance. Patrick J. Kelly explained how Republican concern over the populist allure of Democratic presidential candidate William Jennings Bryan led to a distressing swing in party strategy for the 1896 election. Both "indifferent to the intensified attacks on the social and political rights of African Americans and eager to promote a patriotic nationalism based on the reconciliation of whites in the North and South," the GOP "distanced [itself] . . . from its historical role in revolutionizing U.S. race relations during the Civil War and Reconstruction." Indicative of the new direction, Kelly pinpoints the first postwar absence from the Republican platform of any insistence that black voting rights in the South be secured through federal intervention.[56]

It is a sad paradox that the successful campaign of America's last president who fought for the Union was based on a deracinated view of the Civil War that did not emphasize emancipation. According to Kelly, "the nationalist rhetoric of the powerful and well-financed McKinley campaign played an important role in solidifying the reconciliationist vision within American culture."[57]

In a further irony, another military action would provide added impetus for sectional rapprochement at the expense of African Americans. As Blight explained, the four-months-long Spanish-American War, officially waged to liberate Cuba and establish its independence, was also "infused with imperial language, nationalism, and racial supremacy." In the spirit of reconciliation and rewarding Southern support for the war, President McKinley appointed high-ranking former Union and Confederate officers to important army slots, despite their rather advanced ages.

The circumstances of the ex-Rebels who became generals of US Volunteers varied significantly. At the time that the Senate confirmed their commissions as major generals, Fitzhugh Lee was consul-general at Havana and Joseph Wheeler a congressman from Alabama. When the old cavalrymen took their oaths together on May 6, they were the first of the newly appointed officers at their rank to be sworn into US service. While Lee's commission was expected due to his position in Cuba, Wheeler actively sought his new rank, writing the president on February 17: "In case of any trouble with Spain, remember that my tender of services is on file at the War Department."[58]

The third former Confederate general to receive a similar appointment made no such overture; in fact, he had done the opposite. On May 4, the *Lexington Gazette* in Virginia reported that "Gen. Thomas L. Rosser has not offered his services to the government for the Cuban war and does not propose to do so." His reasoning was basic: "'If we really have war with Spain, young men for officers, soldiers and seamen are who we shall need and not rheumatic, deaf and blind major-generals who know nothing of modern tactics or modern weapons, who cannot drill a squad without a prompter or mount a horse without a ladder.'"

Indisputable logic, but he was nevertheless confirmed as a Brigadier General of US Volunteers on June 15. In considering Rosser's part in the war effort, the *National Tribune* was hardly swept away by the tide of reconciliation: "the noisy, unreconstructed, never-surrendered rebel Brigadier, is to command the Third Brigade of the Second Division of the First Corps, consisting of the 2d Ohio, 1st Pa. and 14th Minn. That will be a pretty unpropitious crowd for any rebel ebullition."[59]

At sixty-two, only Wheeler would take the field. Commanding a cavalry unit that included Colonel Theodore Roosevelt and his Rough Riders, whom Wheeler praised in his action report of the June 25 Battle of Siboney, he famously led a charge while roaring, "'Give the Yanks hell, boys. There they go!'" While this might have seemed incongruous, the prevailing opinion was expressed by the *Washington Times* in the general's obituary of January 26, 1906: "It was the fighting blood of the sixties that spoke, but it was driving Joe Wheeler to fight for the Yankees as hard as he ever fought against them."[60]

For African Americans, the war was a polarizing issue. Many prominent civil rights leaders were opposed to participation in a military campaign against other people of color, particularly when their own freedom remained to be fully won, lynching of African Americans was a national disgrace, the army was segregated, and few black officers were in service.

However, the desire to again prove themselves as citizens and fighting men overrode such considerations, as demonstrated by the May 1898 meeting of former Louisiana governor P. B. S. Pinchback, Colonel James Lewis, and Captain J. W. Lyons with Secretary of War (and former GAR commander in chief) Russell A. Alger. The delegation advocated for an all-black composition to the "immune" (predominantly to yellow fever) regiments due to "the especial service the colored troops, bred in the southern climate, and most of them used to conditions similar to those to be confronted in Cuba, would have in the campaign." While Alger would not commit to that, his promise that several units would be African American was fulfilled, with the War Department responding to pressure for officers of color by commissioning black company lieutenants among the enlistees.[61]

In the war's early days, the regular army's four black regiments comprised its full complement of African American soldiers. Having spent the last two decades stationed in the West, their gradual acceptance by the civilian populations of those states for their "sobriety, manliness and courage in defending life and property from Indian depredations" led to full equality with their white comrades. As the *Sun* further noted in its lead story on May 1, they had "rightfully, come to believe that they are entitled to the same privileges and immunities in public places and accommodation and the like as white soldiers." But when ordered south in preparation for war-related service, the "Buffalo Soldiers" discovered they had entered a different country.

The Twenty-Fifth Infantry's arrival in Chattanooga began the process of "inconvenience and the degradation of their manhood and self-respect" despite wearing United States uniforms. Subject to Jim Crow restrictions on lodging, "amusement and entertainment," their camp at Chickamauga Park, Georgia, became sole refuge from verbal abuse and arrest on trumped-up charges. But the last straw was Tennessee's

Separate Car Law to which they were subject on the train between Chattanooga and the camp. Ordered to separate from their white colleagues for the "Jim Crow car," the enraged black soldiers refused to exit the common coach, whereupon the conductor stopped the train and would not move unless he was obeyed. Only when an adjutant from the post commanded them to heed the conductor did they move, but humiliated and bitter, the men agreed henceforth to use the cars only in dire necessity.

As bad as conditions were in Tennessee and Georgia, even worse awaited the Twenty-Fifth's detachment, which traveled through to Key West, Florida. The white residents wasted no time in expressing resentment at their very presence, which led to a confrontation between a policeman and two of the troops. After a sergeant was arrested, several of his comrades secured his timely release at their demand. Despite the circumstances, all the soldiers concerned were disciplined by the army.

The *Sun* noted racial animosity was the rule in Key West, a riot having earlier been incited by a white citizen who interrupted a trial to ask for recruits to assist him in lynching the black defendant. Unsurprisingly, those African Americans who took part in the melee were either prosecuted, financially and socially ruined, or escaped, while the white man who instigated the entire sordid episode "was made the hero of the hour and is to-day regarded as 'one of the best citizens'" in "such a community that the brave black solders were forced by the orders of the government."[62]

Yet the New York daily, which had presented the entire story in full defense of the Buffalo Soldiers while denouncing Jim Crow legislation, concluded bathetically: "But the wave of patriotism in the Southern states is widespread and genuine, and comprehends all the races of the nation. The war will undoubtedly draw all the people closer together. The old flag will float over the black troops and the white troops, and if General Fitzhugh Lee gets a command and goes to Cuba he will have no braver soldiers than the black ones in his brigade, and he will recognize and appreciate the fact."[63] This view fulfills Kelly's observation that the election of 1896 "intensified a bellicose conception of a nation-state united along sectional and class lines just at the moment the United States stood ready to enter as an aggressive player on the world stage."[64]

Black army regulars were joined by several thousand African American enlistees to the war effort. However, like their white counterparts, the majority of black troops did not experience battle or even leave the United States, although a few units performed postwar garrison duty in Cuba. Volunteers of color stationed in the South were subjected to the same civilian hostility and Jim Crow discrimination as the Twenty-Fifth Infantry, with little support from the army or most of their white officers when they reacted with understandable resistance or fury.

Those Buffalo Soldiers, predominantly regulars, who did see combat acquitted themselves admirably and were praised in both army reports and US newspapers. The Ninth and Tenth Cavalry regiments, renowned as frontier Indian fighters, made a similar mark in Cuba. In the US Army's first battle, the Tenth played a significant role in bolstering Colonel Theodore Roosevelt and his Rough Riders. Both cavalry units and the Twenty-Fourth Infantry performed splendidly in the later battle of San Juan Hill, while the Twenty-Fifth Infantry delivered the coup de grâce at the battle of El Caney with their stunning assault on the fortified Spanish position.

However, with scant improvement in civil rights or even basic respect for African Americans resulting from their Spanish-American War service, most volunteers were relieved to be discharged. The regulars fared little better, as non-commissioned officers who received commissions in volunteer units were reinstated to their prewar units at prior ranks and, along with enlisted men, found Jim Crow unchanged when they returned to a not so grateful nation.[65]

To its credit, the *National Tribune* exposed white soldiers' racism. In September 1898, the Second Texas regiment, led by its colonel, refused to be paid by a black paymaster. Deeming this "the color line drunk, crazy, idiotic," the newspaper reported that paymaster-General Stanton backed his man, telling the Texans that "They would take it from him or not at all." Apparently green overrode black, as they agreed to receive their payments from the African American after due reconsideration.[66]

On the other hand, an anonymous Texas trooper served as narrator in a poetic effort to recognize the courage of black soldiers. When reprinting "The Rough Rider 'Remarks,'" based on the battle of Las Guasimas and subsequent actions in which the African American Tenth US Cavalry distinguished itself, the *World* of New York City made comparison to "Banty Tim." Readers then and now could judge for themselves whether the new work was "the kind that exults and ennobles" as the newspaper claimed:

"I never had no use for a nigger,
      A yellow mulatto I didn't admire;
But I lay that day with finger on trigger
      And watched the colored cavalry fire,
And thought out loud, as we waited for orders,
      'If them there darkies should break on our right
'Twould be good-by to the first Rough Riders!'
      And I wished to God them niggers was white,"
            Said the Rough Rider.

"There was bullets from front, and rear, and flank.
      And nary other support in sight
Save them nigs of the Tenth, in single rank;
      And them there darkies they acted white!"
            Said the Rough Rider.

And there's them niggers, a fighting still,
Right in the nastiest part of the mess;
      I swear, when it comes to a stand-up fight,
Or to stay by a comrade in distress,
      You bet your sweet life them darkies is white!"
            Said the Rough Rider.

"There is plenty of sand in troops that stand
      Such a rain of bullets as comes this way;
In this kind of a game I'll fill my hand
      With them black devils that fight for play.

For beauty they don't show up very much;
    For color, they're off a little bit,
But the way they git there beats the Dutch;
    They may lack beauty but they don't lack grit,"
        Said the Rough Rider.

"Here's a darky now with an artery cut;
    Say, doc, can't you put a compress on?
There ain't no time to be fooling about,
    If you do the cuss will surely be gone.
I've seen such before; I'll grip that hole
    And stop the blood as long as I can,
A nigger? Who says it? Blast my soul
    If that there darky ain't a MAN!"
        Said the Rough Rider.

"The cowboys always pay their debts;
    Them darkies saved us at Hell Caney;
When we go back on the colored vets,
    Count Texas Bill as out of the play,"
        Said the Rough Rider.

W. A. B., Washington, D.C.[67]

In his book on black soldiers, James N. Leiker noted that the African American press published this work and others after the Spanish-American War in an effort by "racial uplift proponents" to utilize "a growing discourse of patriotic songs, stories, and veterans' memoirs to link their goals with those of the white majority and thus reduce the color line."[68]

A similar desire may have motivated the African American lead authors of a history of black military service that spanned the Revolutionary War period to what took place in Cuba. Published in 1899 by Herschel V. Cashin, receiver of the U.S. Land Office at Huntsville, Alabama, and journalist Charles Alexander, it included "The Rough Rider 'Remarks'" along with personal accounts of soldiers of color. The volume's introduction was written by none other than Major General Joe Wheeler, who was generous in his praise of the "unfaltering courage and devotion" shown by the Tenth in the engagements upon which the poem was based.[69]

The proposed analogy between "The Rough Rider 'Remarks'" and "Banty Tim," which had remained popular among Union veterans,[70] fits up to a point. Both Banty Tim and the black horse soldiers prove themselves to a previously dubious white observer through battlefield valor. Tilmon Joy's life is saved by the African American, while the Rough Riders are not only rescued by the Tenth US Cavalry, but the narrator returns the favor by serving as a human tourniquet for a black trooper. Both Tilmon Joy and the Rough Rider vow to stand by their African American comrade in peacetime (presuming the latter from the reference to "colored vets"), but the circumstances are quite different.

Joy risked his status among racist whites by supporting Tim's rights as a human being rather than property in 1865, while the Rough Rider clearly states he previously "had no use for a nigger" thirty years after the Civil War. In the latter case, the excellent service record of black Union soldiers, three milestone amendments and Reconstruction had no impact on the white cavalryman's deeply negative views of African Americans, and he only recognizes them as men after witnessing their fortitude in combat. It is sobering that the black press would seize upon this work as a vehicle to lessen prejudice when it is steeped in racist language and content, and ignorant about civil rights efforts and African Americans' military history, but their reaction is quite understandable given the status of blacks in the United States at the turn of the century.

Indicative of the racial hatred that festered in the South was the issue of black postmasters. In July 1897, the McKinley administration reportedly abandoned its plan to appoint African Americans to fill vacancies in many localities where whites had previously held the office. According to the Clinton, North Carolina, *Caucasian*, Postmaster General James A. Gary not only assured two Georgia Republicans that his original selection for the Augusta post would be withdrawn, but no black man would be made postmaster "at places like Atlanta, Savannah and Charleston. The Postmaster General said this was a social as well as a political matter, and that he would not inflict on any community a colored postmaster, provided it never had one before."[71]

Subsequent events graphically displayed why such a stance may have been considered. In September, Isaac Loftin, the black postmaster at Hogansville, Georgia, was shot multiple times at his home. For weeks newspapers across the country reported him murdered, and that an African American delegation had come to see the president about Loftin's death. When the postmaster finally surfaced after three weeks, alive but with a disabled arm, the black-owned *Richmond Planet* in Virginia reported that "The attempted assassination . . . has aroused the entire country and has had an opposite effect from that anticipated by his would be murderers." That was apparent; not only would he stay at his post but "President McKinley has stated that this treatment of Mr. Loftin will not in anywise effect his determination to appoint colored men in the South to office."[72]

In late February 1898, that resolution was tragically tested by what the *Salt Lake Herald* called "One of the most horrible crimes ever perpetrated in the United States." Frazer B. Baker had been named postmaster at Lake City in Williamsburg County, South Carolina, three months earlier to some protest, and the situation rapidly deteriorated. After three attempts had been made on Baker's life and he moved his family, house, and office to town outskirts, the county's state senator pleaded with his constituents not to kill the black postmaster. He then joined another state senator and the county's congressman in asking the postmaster general to remove Baker on account of his color, but Gary refused. One week later, Baker's building was riddled with shots from concealed riflemen that were aimed deliberately high to send an unmistakable warning.

According to the *Wichita Daily Eagle*, "Baker did not move his family, and gave no evidence of being frightened. He felt confident of protection from Washington." At 1:00 a.m. on February 22, Baker's home and office were put to the torch, and laying in wait were more than one hundred armed white men. When the flames awakened the postmaster and his wife, four daughters including a ten-month-old infant, and his son, the mob opened up on the building with pistols and shotguns. Baker reached the door first and was quickly shot dead. Mrs. Baker, cradling their baby in her arms, attempted to open the door over her husband's corpse. The first bullet that struck not only fractured her arm, but continued on a fatal path into the infant's brain; a second wound in her leg was so incapacitating that she would have been burned alive if neighbors had not dragged her out of the building. The oldest daughter's leg and arm were both fractured, another girl suffered a broken arm and serious abdominal wound, and a third received a bullet through her right hand. To complete the horror, the bodies of Baker and his baby daughter were incinerated in the inferno.[73]

Denunciation and revulsion for the unspeakable crime were instant and universal. According to the *Sun*, "The affair is publicly condemned all over the State, and people are calling on the Governor to have the murderers punished." The *State* of Columbia, South Carolina, was especially appalled at such actions occurring "'where people read and vote and sit on juries; . . . Christianity is professed; . . . the church and the schoolhouse send out their teachings, and the supremacy of law, the enforcement of justice are the conditions of the social compact! Great God, could Apache savages be more cruel, more ruthless, more lustful of mood than those civilized white men of Williamsburg county?'" That same evening a coroner's jury was formed and performed the grisly task of viewing what was left of Baker and the infant.

While Mrs. Baker and her two daughters remained critically wounded, the federal post office department immediately announced separate rewards for arrests and convictions of those who had burned the office and the murderers of Baker and his child. Gary and his men were "prepared to press the matter to the limit," and as further reported by the *Sun*, the postmaster general "decided to suspend the office temporarily, and it will very likely be abolished entirely, as will every other office where similar outrages occur."

The *Salt Lake Herald* spoke for many in the North when it specified Baker's "offense" as "being a black man and holding the position of postmaster," and drew upon the sad history of such terrible events: "When a crime like this is committed in the south, the country is usually treated to a nauseating dose of sophistry about negroes . . . being murdered or lynched for the 'usual crime,' when the fact is that they are murdered and lynched on any or on no pretext. Could anything be more revolting, more inhuman than to fire upon a woman with a babe in her arms?"

Having no faith in state authorities, the *Herald* put the onus elsewhere to ensure justice for a US official "murdered in cold blood, . . . if it takes years of time and thousands and thousands of dollars. If the government does not do this it will bring disgrace and reproach upon itself."[74]

LYNCHING: JIM CROW'S ULTIMATE HORROR

On March 4, a mass protest meeting drew 2,000 people to Chicago's Bethel Church. The African Americans adopted several resolutions on lynching in general and the Baker case in particular, which they said "mark[ed] a culminating point in the era of lynching and outlawry against the negro." They thanked Representative William Lorimer for swiftly notifying his House colleagues about what had taken place in Lake City and getting an investigation started.

Then, in an unprecedented move, the president and Congress were directly addressed about the violence that had taken so many black lives: "This is no new story. It is a record written in blood during the past thirteen years. . . . How many American citizens have been butchered in these years no mortal tongue can tell, but statistics of reported cases of lynchings shows that the number of mob murders has been as follows":

1885: 184	1888: 142	1891: 192	1894: 190	1897: 156
1886 :136	1889: 176	1892: 235	1895: 171	
1887: 122	1890: 176	1893: 200	1896: 131	

A total of 2,174 American citizens, put to death in thirteen years without the semblance of law.

Your petitioners plead for no favor they ask only for justice. Lynching has become a national crime, and the Nation must act or stand disgraced in the eyes of the civilized world. Hence this petition to the chief magistrate of the Nation. Not for words, but for action. Henceforth apology is insult and indifference a crime.[75]

Two weeks later, Ida B. Wells-Barnett personally presented the resolutions to McKinley at the White House, accompanied by Illinois Senator William E. Mason and several members of the state's congressional delegation, including Lorimer. According to the *Alexandria Gazette*, the president gave assurances to Ms. Wells-Barnett of the post office department's and Department of Justice's determined efforts to bring those responsible to justice, "and that the Attorney General was now considering what further steps the government could take within the limits of federal jurisdiction."[76]

While attempts were being made to secure widow's benefits for Mrs. Baker, she remained destitute and recuperating with her three wounded children in a segregated Charleston hospital. One daughter was permanently crippled, and Mrs. Baker was herself months away from returning to independent living. In the meantime, the family was being totally supported by the city's African American community.[77]

At McKinley's insistence, the government pursued Baker's killers with uncommon zeal. Lead post office inspector Buella and his undercover operatives proved to be effective investigators, and arrests of white Lake City residents on federal murder charges began in June 1898. The following month, both Mrs. Baker and an involved party who turned state's evidence testified at a hearing for the first five defendants and the case was remanded to district federal court. More white citizens were arrested and held without bail, but as Washington's *Evening Star* reported on August 1, the prosecution began to run into all sorts of roadblocks. Despite being charged with murder, all the defendants were released on bail, and their defense team was hard at work at discrediting the testimony of the government's primary witness. According to the *Star*, he had been quickly arrested and convicted on a spurious larceny charge and was in county lock-up; in addition, there were reports of intimidation and threats made to other witnesses.[78]

With the situation seeming to languish, many African Americans doubted the murderers would ever be called to account.[79] Then in January 1899, a leading Lake City citizen became its thirteenth white resident indicted for the Baker lynchings, and by April the case came before the grand jury and the trial began in the Charleston federal court. The government had left little to chance, with two men indicted for the killings agreeing to testify against the remaining eleven defendants and more than one hundred witnesses expected to appear. When Presiding Judge W. H. Brawley, a former Confederate soldier who lost an arm in the war, stated that "'a more heinous crime has rarely darkened the state's history,'" it appeared all was in place for Postmaster Baker and his daughter to finally get justice. The remains of his family would be there, fervently hoping that would occur.[80]

The lead prosecutor was W. A. Barber, former attorney general of South Carolina, who presented a strong case. The two men who were directly involved provided detailed testimony against their friends, including the murders' planning, the search for oil to be poured on Baker's house, the oil's firing, and the ghastly results. Three witnesses (a member of the coroner's jury; an older black man; a witness at the original inquest) all testified to threats against their lives if they told the truth about defendant identification or presented other relevant evidence. Post office inspector Moye stated that the residents of Lake City gave no assistance to his investigation and actively blocked his efforts, and that those individuals who came forward and testified had to move away as soon as their neighbors became aware of their cooperation with the government.[81]

Having received an exceptional and emotional charge from Judge Brawley, the jury deliberated for twenty-five hours. Despite the overwhelming case against the defendants, on April 22 the jurors reported being unable to reach a verdict. The presiding judge, clearly stunned, cried when he made reference to the terrible crime in his brief dismissal of the jury and the case, which would be assigned for retrial by the next court. Although he was not surprised by the mistrial, Barber spoke of lynchings: "'I feel sorry for the south that this blot is upon us. It affects us all over the world. It robs us of material prosperity and of the high moral and social position to which we are entitled. It ruins the worth of our investments. If it is not stopped, then shut the school house, burn the books, tear down the churches and admit to the world that Anglo-Saxon civilization is a failure.'"[82]

Unfortunately, that was not all Barber had to say on the subject. Despite having worked so hard to convict the Bakers' murderers and expressed his belief that lynchings were calamitous for the South, the ex-attorney general offered this astounding opinion: "'I believe in the lynching of negroes confessedly guilty of criminal assault. It is the only protection of the women of the south, especially of the rural districts. Otherwise I am opposed to lynchings.'"[83]

Despite the national attention and heinous crimes committed in the case, and usual federal court procedure, the Justice Department decided against retrying the defendants.[84] An understandable yet gut-wrenching decision given the scant likelihood of obtaining convictions in another trial, it meant no forthcoming justice for the Bakers, living or dead, and black citizens reacted with disgust. Within two weeks of the mistrial, the New England Conference of African Methodists issued an irate resolution from New Haven expressing its abhorrence of "'the fiendish and lawless course permitted by the State and Federal governments of our land against one portion of her citizens . . . The farcical trial in the late Postmaster Baker's case miscarried because prejudice prevails to such an extent that conviction and punishment seem impossible in certain parts of our country.'"[85]

African Americans were not alone, as outrage at the Baker case and lynching itself was expressed throughout the North. On May 20, three hundred whites, most of them women, met in Boston for an anti-lynching meeting featuring speakers of both races. Julia Ward Howe was among those on the platform, and the eighty-year-old author of "The Battle Hymn of the Republic" had not lost her way with words: "'I hold to it that the federal government is bound to see to it that the Afro-American vote in the South is properly counted, and that military protection be afforded the Afro-Americans in dangerous sections. If the central government cannot do this, Americans might as well take down their flag and raise the black flag of piracy.'"[86]

The Baker murders hardly had the same effect in the South. Censure of McKinley's policy of appointing black postmasters only increased after the despicable events, like the Norfolk *Virginian-Pilot*'s summer 1898 declaration that their "selection . . . for a Southern white constituency is offensive," and other such denunciations summarized by the *Tazewell* (Virginia) *Republican* in late October. The latter also discussed the resignation of P. A. Twyman, the African American postmaster at Junta, Franklin County due to white citizens boycotting the post office, and the newspaper's conjecture that Twyman feared sharing Baker's fate.[87]

For callousness and utter indifference, perhaps nothing surpasses the *Atlanta Constitution*'s anger at the postmaster general's May 1899 discontinuation of the Lake City post office due to the Baker lynchings. When the *Appeal* reported this to readers, its staff blamed the town's white residents for protecting murderers and scoffed at their meager punishment of temporary loss of mail service. The African American newspaper also made a savage point about prevalent racial double standards, asking what would have taken place if the inhabitants of Lake City had been black and "the postmaster and his family who would then be white, had met the fate Baker and his family did." There was no doubt as to the bitter truth of the answer: "[T]hat town would not have had a place on the map in twenty-four hours afterward, but would have been merely a pile of ashes and rubbish, and the perpetrators of the crime, as well as quite a number of innocent Afro-Americans, would have been food for the flames, if there was any of their bodies left after the usual pruning process was indulged in."[88]

When the good citizens of Florence, South Carolina, a community nearby Lake City, vigorously objected to the July appointment of the black minister J. E. Wilson as postmaster, it came as no surprise. Neither did the *Memphis Commercial Appeal*'s comment as reported by the *Washington Sentinel* on August 26. Furious at the Baker family being used as part of an "anti-lynching crusade," the *Commercial Appeal* accused "the hystericals of Boston" of "eulogizing fiendish criminals" rather than "urg[ing] upon the negroes the necessity of removing the main cause of offense." If they would "show that their sympathies are not with the criminals who are lynched, but for the whites who feel compelled to join with the mob, then they may be able to accomplish something." In sum, "No right thinking person can blame the Southern people for resenting the attempt of certain Northern agitators to add fuel to the flames of the race trouble."[89]

The post office and Justice Department had strived to convict the Lake City murderers but just could not overcome deep-rooted bigotry. However, the government's lack of provision for Baker's family, despite his having been a federal officer when slain, was unforgivable. Luckily for his survivors, "the hystericals of Boston" saw to their solvency and comfort, purchasing a home for them in Chelsea, Massachusetts, and William Lloyd Garrison Jr. spearheaded an effort to raise funds for its furnishing.[90]

Reconciliation between the country's two sections over the racially turbulent 1890s was both indicative of the deteriorating conditions for African Americans in the South and a contributing factor. Two aspects of the process are enlightening—commemoration via war monuments, and joint activities involving Union and Confederate veterans.

In September 1891, Troy, New York, celebrated the dedication of its Rensselaer County Soldiers' and Sailors' Monument with a huge procession of local military and GAR post members, Sons of Veterans, and numerous county and city officials reviewed by such celebrated ex-servicemen as Generals Dan Sickles and Stewart L. Woodford.[91]

Woodford was a good choice to deliver the day's featured oration. A highly educated New Yorker, he was an assistant US attorney when the war broke out and joined his home state's 127th Regiment as a lieutenant colonel in September 1862. He became chief of staff for Major General Quincy A. Gillmore of the Department of the South, and in association with promotion to colonel in March 1865, assumed command of the newly formed 103rd USCT and Charleston, South Carolina. In June, Woodford and his men were transferred to Savannah, Georgia, where they performed garrison and guard duty until mustering out in April 1866. A Republican, he became New York's lieutenant governor soon after his return to civilian life, and, as recounted in chapter 2, had memorably endorsed congressional Reconstruction at the September 1866 Soldiers' and Sailors' Convention in Pittsburgh.[92]

Twenty-five years later, Woodford first paid "'reverent tribute to the great army of the rank and file—that army of loyal hearts and clear brains, that army of thinking bayonets, the citizen soldier of the great republic.'" He then addressed remembrance in both parts of the reunited nation, noting that while in the North monuments are built "to the soldiers of the Union," in the South they are raised "to the soldiers of the lost cause."[93]

Woodford concluded in a manner befitting an individual who had led troops of both races, and in the war's last months refused a Charleston resident's request to order separate days for blacks and whites to receive rice because "he did not intend to use the words white, black or colored in any official order": "'We were right, forever right, because we fought against slavery and for freedom; because we fought against secession and for Union; because we fought for the future, for progress and for the rights of man.'"[94]

It is illuminating to compare this speech to the May 1898 ceremonies dedicating the statue of an admired Left-Armed Corps member. More than ten years after Brevet Major George Q. White's retirement from the Army in late 1870, he and his family moved from Philadelphia to Saint Paul, Minnesota, where he joined the Northern Pacific as a supply agent. His new colleagues included the company's general manager, General Herman Haupt, with whom White traveled to Boston on business in 1881. They made quite a pair, the former Mississippi River Ram Fleet officer and the renowned engineer who had brilliantly served as chief of construction and transportation on the Union's military railroads during the war.[95] In light of what each had done, their discussions during the long train trip can only be imagined.

The move to Saint Paul was quite happy for White, his wife Caroline, and their two daughters, as all enjoyed living there and taking part in the city's cultural and charitable activities; in 1885 he left Northern Pacific to join St. Paul Fire and Marine Insurance as an agent. That same year, White was instrumental in founding the MOLLUS Commandery of the State of Minnesota and was honored with election to the pivotal office of Recorder from the organization's inception. A dedicated family man, he was devastated by Caroline's death in 1891, and thereafter devoted himself to veteran endeavors. These included membership in the GAR Acker Post and commanding the Association of Survivors of the Mississippi Marine Brigade and Ram Fleet in 1896. But the Commandery was his first love, as he continued to serve as Recorder and the association's acknowledged heart and soul.

In the early spring of 1897, White got off a trolley and hurried to board a connecting cable car when he fell. Although the tumble was initially not considered serious, he suffered from a long-standing liver ailment that had defied diagnosis, and over the next several days his condition worsened. Five days later he lapsed into a coma and died on March 28, with autopsy revealing that the fall appeared to have exacerbated his underlying condition. He was buried in Oakland Cemetery after a simple, private funeral with "no flowers, and an entire absence of display or ostentation," per his wishes, and delegations from his veteran organizations in attendance.[96]

In August, White's Loyal Legion comrades decided to honor their friend by a monument in his memory. A committee was appointed and fundraising plans agreed upon;[97] in less than a year the memorial was ready for dedication.

On May 10, 1898, a crowd of several hundred that included Loyal Legion and Acker Post members, along with many other friends of White's, gathered at the cemetery to pay tribute to his life and accomplishments. All agreed on the beauty of the monument, twenty-four feet of "perfectly white Vermont granite" topped by "a large granite ball" upon which a spread-winged American eagle of bronze rested. Its inscription noted the edifice's creation by the Commandery in White's "Loving Memory," his army rank, Commandery founding, position, and years of service, and dates of his birth and death.

Beyond honoring the final resting place of their comrade and glorifying God, General R. N. Adams delineated two more reasons for his friend's monument: "To teach the living, in silent and impressive eloquence the lessons of patriotism; To inspire in the hearts of the present and the coming generations the spirit of heroic devotion to country."

Archbishop and MOLLUS companion John Ireland gave the formal address of dedication, eulogizing White's Civil War service and overall military tenure, his many fine qualities and abiding love for and dedication to the Loyal Legion, and its role and that of the Grand Army in "spreading patriotism among our fellow citizens."

Ireland surely knew that American troops were sailing from Tampa for Cuba and others mobilizing at Chickamauga for transport to Tampa that very day: "How precious was our victory we see today, when Federal and Confederate, Northern and Southern, sing together praise to the Stars and Stripes and press together in serried mass around the banner to wreathe it in the glory of new victories . . . never a war there will be so holy, so just, so precious in gifts to America and to the world as that which was waged to preserve the Union."[98]

Acclaiming the perceived unity of purpose and love of country shared by North and South, Ireland used the words "patriot" or "patriotism" no less than twenty-five times, but two words were glaringly absent from his speech: slavery and emancipation.[99] Not only were the primary cause and one of two major results of the Civil War utterly avoided by both Adams and the archbishop, neither man made any mention of White's forty-two months of excellent service in the Freedmen's Bureau.

Reconciliation was overcoming historical truth, with an ill-defined, pervasive patriotism exalted as the greatest of virtues and the incendiary racial situation ignored. The nation's leading voice on lynching and "mob violence" bristled at the state of affairs. At year's end, when Ida B. Wells-Barnett spoke to the Afro-American Conference, she contended that the "'greatest menace to the negro is the indifference of the press to our wrongs. The white people have no quarrel with the negro who is content to stay in his place and be a servant. But we who are agitating are not content and will never be until we get our rights.'" She also expected no appreciable federal help: "'The President who once had our respect is too busy looking after the Confederates to bother about the negro. We have heretofore made our indignation meetings ridiculous by our efforts to show off, but in future we must control ourselves and command respect.'"[100]

Her acerbic words and another Civil War dedication ceremony captured the country's mood as the nineteenth century was ending. On May 30, 1900, a monument from the State of Maryland recognizing the men of North and South who fought at Antietam was presented to the National Government. It was a dazzling occasion, with President McKinley (who had served in the battle), numerous Cabinet members, more than twenty senators, sixty congressmen, hosting governor, hundreds of Confederate veterans, and thousands of their former adversaries in blue assembled on the battlefield at Sharpsburg. The Maryland National Guard, GAR, Southern veteran organizations, Sons of Veterans from both sides and Brockenbrough's Maryland Artillery survivors were all represented.

In his featured address, McKinley reflected on "'the difference between this scene and that of thirty-eight years ago. Then the men who wore the Blue, and the men who wore the Gray, greeted each other with shot and shell, and visited death upon their respective ranks." Now, they shared a "'loyalty to the government of the States, love for our flag and our free institutions.'" Lauding the event as a "'tribute to valor and hero-ism, and the sacrifices of the Confederate and Union armies,'" the presi-dent claimed "'the valor of both is the common heritage of us all,'" and the war's "'achievements, every one of them, are just as much the inheri-tance of those who failed as of those who prevailed, and when we went to war two years ago, the men of the South, and the men of the North, vied with each other to show their devotion to the United States.'"[101]

Such thoughts were anathema for African Americans. Fifteen months after the Antietam dedication, the *National Tribune* published a letter from a black Union veteran in Midland, Virginia, who wanted to know if he could be forced to vote for his state's $3 levy tax for Confederate soldiers under threat of disenfranchisement. Fearing loss of his right to vote, Alexander Robertson nonetheless stated, "I am not going to get money from the Government to pay to Confederate soldiers What little money I get I want myself."

The *Tribune*'s editor replied that it was difficult to predict "in what shape the suffrage clause will finally pass the Virginia Constitutional Convention. The plan . . . has been proposed merely, but it has met with much favor. It certainly does seem hard that Union veterans should be taxed to pay pensions to rebels, but that is what is being done now all over the South."[102]

After Virginia's Constitution replacing the one written in 1870 during Reconstruction became law in July 1902, impoverished whites and almost all of the state's black citizens were disenfranchised due to newly imposed voting requirements that included a poll tax and rigorous literacy test.[103]

Major General of Volunteers John W. Geary. LIBRARY OF CONGRESS PRINTS AND PHOTOGRAPHS DIVISION. BRADY-HANDY PHOTOGRAPH COLLECTION.

CHAPTER 8

Commemoration and Controversy

How to Honor the Civil War Dead

We are ready to forgive—we hold no malice—but we will never consent by public national tribute to obliterate the wide gulf which lies between the objects, motives and principles for which we fought and our comrades died, and those for which the Rebel armies banded together, and for which their dead now lie in numerous graves.

—JOHN A. LOGAN, COMMANDER IN CHIEF, GRAND
ARMY OF THE REPUBLIC, JUNE 2, 1869[1]

After leaving the army and then the Freedmen's Bureau, by 1871 James O. Ladd had advanced to chief clerk in the South Carolina State Treasury Office when he resigned to enter the private sector. Married to Priscilla C. U. Thouron in 1866, and with three small children to support, his motivation may well have been financial.

Spending almost two years with the Chronicle Publishing Co. as superintendent and treasurer and the Washington-based *Daily Chronicle*'s business manager, he took over authority of the Bank of the State of South Carolina's assets under its Receiver at Charleston in 1874. Several months later, he returned to newspaper business management with the Republican *Union Herald* of Columbia.

In 1876 Ladd permanently resumed governmental work in multiple roles. He was South Carolina's special deputy collector of internal revenue through March 1882, then spent more than two years as postmaster at Cheraw, Chesterfield County, until being replaced by a Democrat after Cleveland's election. Appointed the state's commissioner of the US Circuit Courts in late 1876, Ladd served continuously through 1890 with the exception of a nine-month stint as US attorney from 1879 to 1880. Commissioned as postmaster at Summerville, Berkeley County, by Benjamin Harrison during a senatorial recess in April 1891, then formally nominated in December. Ladd remained in the position for more than two decades before retiring from government service.[2]

James O. Ladd was a Northern native who spent most of his adult life in the South, compiled a fine public service dossier and pursued veteran-related work that included high-ranking Grand Army positions and major efforts on behalf of former soldiers and sailors in need. However, reconciliation was bedeviling many Union veterans as their time in uniform and immediate years following grew more remote, and Ladd would ultimately act at lamentable variance with his admirable record in war and during Reconstruction with respect to African Americans.

On August 9, 1889, he and thirty other Union veterans joined in a ceremony that was unforgettable in content and setting. Escorted by ex-Rebel soldiers who had manned Fort Sumter throughout the Civil War, Ladd and his comrades were mustered into the GAR within the structure that had received the Confederacy's opening shots. Appropriately, the new post was named for Major Robert Anderson, who had been in command until the fort's capitulation. Presiding over the ritual was Albert E. Sholes, senior vice commander of the Department of Georgia, under which jurisdiction the Charleston post fell. When more accurately renamed the Department of Georgia and South Carolina in 1893, Ladd would be its first elected senior vice commander.[3]

The *Evening Times* in Washington called the new organization "South Carolina's First GAR Post," then contradicted that designation: "There was a post of the GAR in this city in 1870, but it was composed mostly of colored men and politicians. The present post is composed of Union soldiers who have settled there since the war, all whites, and none of them politicians."

More accurately, Pennsylvania's *Somerset Herald* cited the New York *Mail and Express* in calling it South Carolina's "first white post of the Grand Army of the Republic." To the *Newberry Herald and News*, "This is the first post of the Grand Army, of any respectability, that has been organized in Charleston, the cradle of secession." To assure South Carolinians about any hint of Reconstruction, the newspaper added, "Naturally there are some officeholders in the post, but none of that class which overran the prostrate State from 1868 to 1876."[4]

Just what had happened to the original GAR post in Charleston, "respectable" or not? Grand Army historian Beath noted that the Department of South Carolina paid its dues "for the term ending December 31, 1868," but by 1871 was among those departments deemed "'disorganized and dormant'" and which "showed no signs of life."[5] On June 25, 1868, the *Charleston Daily News* reported the GAR "has a local habitation and a name in South Carolina, and that Charleston is the headquarters thereof,"[6] consistent with the dues payment record.

Further review of available South Carolina newspapers uncovered no additional information from 1868, or any relevant articles in 1869. However, on May 17, 1870, the *Daily Phoenix* of Columbia reported Quartermaster General Montgomery C. Meigs had directed national cemetery superintendents to make all necessary preparations for decoration of Union soldier graves on May 30. In providing the GAR with a copy of the Meigs order, the federal government officially recognized the association's existence for the first time.

In turn, Grand Army headquarters likewise instructed all posts; per the May 25 edition of the *Charleston Daily News*, "annual decoration of the graves of the Union dead, buried at Magnolia Cemetery, will take place on May 30th. Shaw Post No. 1, of this city, will conduct the ceremonies, . . . assisted by a number of ladies and friends."[7] Thus, the truly first GAR post in South Carolina, presumably named after the martyred commander of the famed Fifty-Fourth Massachusetts, has now been identified.

One week later, the *Charleston Daily News* published a lead story on the Memorial Day ceremonies and grave decorations carried out under Shaw Post sponsorship. Its members and friends arrived at Magnolia Cemetery by special train and then marched into the burial grounds led by a cornet band. They were joined by the all-black first battalion of the Charleston light infantry and a sizable group of African Americans who had walked from the city. By 4:00 p.m. there were 2,500 spectators, three-fourths black, and the reviewing stand packed with numerous women, white and African American city officials, and three speakers.

The Shaw Post veterans, carrying "drooping banners," slowly proceeded to the stand in time with the band's dirge, receiving salutes from the infantrymen as they passed. Commander Reed began with brief remarks, then Reverend Dr. Webster's opening prayer, followed by the speakers, all prominent men and Northerners.

Major David T. Corbin was a captain in the Third Vermont when his serious wounding at Savage's Station, Virginia, and ensuing miserable treatment in Libby Prison led to his discharge in September 1862. Nine months later, he joined the VRC at the same rank and served in the Freedmen's Bureau at Charleston as a brevet major until early 1867, when named US attorney for South Carolina. Also elected to the state Senate in 1868, Corbin would soon be instrumental in prosecuting hundreds of Ku Klux Klan members.

General William Gurney, a Quaker born in Flushing, Long Island, received a severe arm wound near Charleston in December 1864 while leading a brigade. During his recuperation, Gurney was appointed the city's commandant and came to be regarded by Charleston's citizenry as a just and non-punitive administrator. He returned in late 1865, and after establishing a successful business in cotton and rice, would agree to serve as county treasurer in October 1870.

William J. Whipper was an attorney and free man of color from Pennsylvania who served in the Thirty-First USCT (and court-martialed after an altercation with a white officer), and within two years of coming to Charleston in 1866, was elected to the state general assembly from Beaufort County.[8]

In May 1870, each speaker paid tribute to those whose graves were to be festooned, while stressing that celebrating the bravery and sacrifice of Union soldiers should not lead to bitterness between former adversaries. However, their discussions of the war's underlying causes differed in significant ways. Corbin never mentioned slavery and cautioned against "say[ing] or do[ing] anything that would wound or humiliate those with whom they contested." Gurney flatly stated that the honored dead lost their lives "that right might triumph over injustice, and that freedom might be given to those who had been kept in bondage . . . Those who had fought against us . . . fought for an 'effete idea,' upon which the world had set the seal of condemnation, but they fought with a zeal, devotion and bravery which were worthy of a better cause."

Whipper, speaking last, said of the Confederates that "while he consigned to infamy the cause for which they fought, yet he could not forget their zeal and bravery in fighting." He then drew a sharp contrast between North and South:

> The contending parties fought for two different ideas. One for liberty, which was brought over in the ship which landed its living freight on Plymouth Rock; the other for the maintenance of an oppression which was brought to this country in a low black schooner which sailed up the James River in 1620 . . . Not until it could be borne no longer, was the dread . . . sword resorted to, which resulted in oppression being overthrown and a Union, in which all could think and act alike, was restored.

After Dr. Webster read a poem for the dead, the living decorated their graves with flowers and floral arrangements, and the solemn rites were concluded.[9]

It is striking just how well these speeches delivered by ex-soldiers decades earlier would have fit into the reconciliation-centric 1890s. All cited Rebel valor, with one white veteran advocating for sectional fraternity to produce national unity, while another's declaration that the eradication of slavery was a righteous aim distinct from the detested Southern cause is consistent with Union veterans throughout the postwar decades. As for Whipper, his review of slavery's history, pervasiveness, and destructiveness reflected African American insistence, veteran or not, on equality as the ultimate goal.

On Memorial Day 1871, the Shaw Post again took the lead in paying tribute to their comrades interred at Magnolia Cemetery but was not mentioned in the *Charleston Daily News* description of the May 30, 1872, ceremonies for decorating the graves of the cemetery's Union dead. Just as Beath had reported, the landmark organization was gone; while the proceedings included no speakers, a prayer was said, odes sung, flowers placed by children, and "military companies and civic societies" were invited to attend.[10]

There would be no more Memorial Day ceremonies at Magnolia Cemetery, as all remains of the Union dead were disinterred and transported to the National Cemetery at Florence in February 1873.[11] But on May 31, there was a noteworthy gathering in Beaufort at South Carolina's other National Cemetery, founded in 1863 for burial of federal troops from the city's occupation and re-interment of others "from various battle fields in Florida, Southern Georgia, and the Sea Islands, from Charleston harbor to Braddock's point, the extreme southern limit of the State boundary." By modern count, they number 14,000 Union soldiers and veterans. Of these, 4,400 are unknown (including almost 3,000 prisoners of war from Millen, Georgia), while 1,700 of the dead are known to be black; 117 Confederates are also buried here.[12]

On Memorial Day 1873, the cemetery's thirty lovely acres dotted with 2,600 newly planted trees were visited by approximately two thousand African Americans and seventeen whites. Postponed to 5:00 p.m. due to excessive heat, the proceedings took place in a torrential rain that no one appeared to mind. A small formation of soldiers marched onto the cemetery grounds and formed "a hollow square" for the speakers, the state's black lieutenant governor Richard H. Gleaves and William J. Whipper. After their presentations, formal exercises concluded with the reading of a poem by white US commissioner and Beaufort clerk of Court of Common Pleas, H. G. Judd. At that point, flowers were laid upon the Union graves by the women in attendance.[13]

These early postwar Memorial Day ceremonies demonstrate the great importance placed on commemoration and associated opportunities for African Americans to celebrate the sacrifice and tangible attainments of Union soldiers, black and white. Biracial attendance at such proceedings was also critical in showing the commitment to achieving equality for all citizens during the heady but stormy days of Reconstruction.

However, the tensions and antagonism between North and South were deeply rooted and bitter. While remembrance could bring people together, it could also divide, as was starkly revealed by heated debates regarding the location and decoration of graves decades before reunification took hold in the late nineteenth century.

In September 1867, a new Civil War cemetery was being dedicated, but unlike its model predecessor at Gettysburg, there was controversy. As Susan Trail has detailed, the Maryland state legislation that authorized the Antietam burial ground's formation included language providing for Confederate dead to be interred, but in an area separated from the Union dead. The dedication ceremony itself was criticized for decided lack of mention of why the war had been fought, with the notable exception of impromptu remarks by Pennsylvania governor John Geary, a Republican and former Union general. However, the possibility of Northern and Southern soldiers being buried in the same national cemetery created the real firestorm.[14]

When he withheld Pennsylvania's appropriation due to the planned inclusion of Confederate dead, Geary powerfully explained his decision to the state legislature: "'it is proposed that the loyal states construct cemeteries for their heroic dead and then desecrate them by the burial therein of those who [made war] . . . against the country . . . and even to erect monuments to their memory. Carry out this purpose and what inducement can be hereafter offered to the loyal citizen to fight against treason, when he feels assured that should he fall in battle, the traitor's grave will be honored equally with his own?'" While not objecting "'to giving decent sepulture even to the Rebel dead, those who consider them deserving of honorable testimonial may give them. It is our duty to render honor only to whom we believe honor is due.'"[15]

Another Republican governor, Reuben E. Fenton of New York, took a different tack when he wrote to the trustees. Accepting that the legislation and their subsequent actions sanctioned burial of Confederate dead within cemetery grounds, he clearly saw it as an opportunity for reconciliation between North and South, when "'our countrymen are now engaged in the work of reconstructing the Union on the basis of universal freedom . . . and restor[ing] to the Southern States a prosperity infinitely greater than that which slavery and rebellion conspired to destroy, it is impossible to believe that they would desire to make an invidious distinction against the moldering remains of the Confederate dead, or that they would disapprove of their being carefully gathered from the spots where they fell, and laid to rest in the National Cemetery on the battle-field of Antietam.'"[16]

On January 17, 1868, a third Republican offered his opinion by writing directly to Governor Fenton and quoting Governor Geary at length. John Covode was a highly respected sixty-year-old congressman from Pennsylvania who had been a committed abolitionist before the war, an active member of the Joint Committee on the Conduct of the War during it, and a dedicated supporter of Reconstruction and African American equality in its aftermath, having been a leader in the House of Andrew Johnson's impeachment.

Beyond these credentials was a highly personal qualification. Having watched three sons go off to war, he spoke of them in his letter. His eldest, George H. Covode, rose to a colonelcy and command of the Fourth Pennsylvania Cavalry, only to be shot by partially hidden Rebels whom he had mistaken for his own soldiers outside of Trevilian Station, Virginia, in June 1864. Seriously wounded, he ordered his men to leave him to await capture along with their other incapacitated comrades: "The Rebels soon came up, and, as I have been told, shot him again when he lay helpless on the ground, stripped him of his sword, money, watch, boots and clothing, and left him naked to die. An old colored woman, living in the neighborhood, brought him water to drink while he was dying. The next day he was buried in her garden."

His youngest son joined the Fourth at just fifteen, and after being captured at White Sulphur Springs, Virginia, in October 1863, was eventually sent to Andersonville. He was one of the regiment's few members to survive imprisonment but came home more dead than alive, his health wrecked: "the energetic, intelligent, hopeful, self-reliant, brave boy, who left my house to fight the enemies of his country, has not returned to me, and he never will return." His third son served out his full enlistment, apparently unharmed.

While there were inaccuracies (Covode repeatedly and unfairly said Fenton recommended "national honors to the Rebels" whom had died at Antietam, when the New Yorker actually supported their burial in the National Cemetery with no specification of ceremony), Covode's unrelenting censure and his having admittedly written the letter "with grief," the representative's take on the governor's viewpoint was by and large correct in its expression of what Covode believed was a widely shared "shocked and outraged" reaction of "hundreds of thousands of loyal men, whose hearts yet bleed with wounds received in the . . . war" to the thought of "do[ing] honor to the authors of their sorrows and the workers of their country's woes." Pointingly, invoking Fenton's lack of personal military service or that of a son (which were true), Covode deeply "wish[ed] you had imitated the manly and sympathetic behavior of Governor Geary, of Pennsylvania, a soldier and a statesman, who . . . repelled the proposition to mingle the Rebel with the Union dead under the Antietam monument."[17]

Covode's letter provoked a furious rebuttal from John Jay II, Fenton's appointee as New York's representative on the Antietam National Cemetery Board of Trustees. He roundly criticized Covode and Geary for ignoring the restrictions imposed on the trustees by the authorizing legislation. While acknowledging that "the abettors of slavery . . . treated with contumely the dead bodies of the blacks . . . and . . . after the battle of Bull Run, desecrated the bones of Union soldiers," Jay accused both men of manifest injustice and insensitivity when it came to the burial of slain Confederates: "For myself, I recognize no such national demoralization—no such bankruptcy of honor in the American people. I have confidence enough in their manly virtue to believe . . . [they would endorse the sentiments] of Charles the fifth, when urged by the monks to inflict vengeance on the remains of Luther, 'Gentleman, we war not with the dead.'"[18]

Here were four Northern Republicans intensely disagreeing as to whose honor, and what purpose, was involved in the burial of Union and Confederate dead. Given the emotional, symbolic, and political repercussions, it is hardly surprising that the issues of interment and festooning of veterans' graves would fester then and for decades to come. A perfect example arose months later when the *Hudson* (New York) *Daily Star* sarcastically noted that "Bangor, Me., gave a May-day breakfast for the freed men, while in the South the graves of the Confederate dead were decorated with flowers. A slight difference."[19]

On June 4, 1869, the views of two more prominent Northerners were published, and could not have been more dissimilar. The chief justice of the US Supreme Court, Salmon P. Chase, was invited to decorate the graves of Union soldiers buried at Charleston's Magnolia Cemetery on Memorial Day but had to decline due to late notice. In his letter of May 29, Justice Chase expressed his regrets and related optimism that *"may we not indulge the hope that ere long we who adhered to the National cause will be prompt also to join in commemorating the heroism of our countrymen who fell on the other side,* and that those who now specially mourn their loss, . . . and resuming all their old love for their country and our country, one and indivisible, will join with us in like commemoration of the fallen brave of the Army of the Union" (italics his).[20]

In the same edition of the *New York Daily Tribune*, a June 2 order by the Grand Army's commander in chief would not only establish its policy on the decoration of Rebel graves but also crystallize the association's view of the Northern and Southern causes that would be maintained throughout the rest of the century and beyond.

"Black Jack" Logan, considered one of the finest volunteer generals produced by the Civil War, was officially responding to questions as to why Confederate graves at Arlington National Cemetery had not been decorated, like those of Union soldiers, on Memorial Day. He reported that the Marine Guard followed their instructions and had "discharged their duty in a proper manner and spirit." Logan then further explained that this was rooted in the Grand Army's desire "to honor and serve the principles and institutions for which its members and their dead comrades fought." Placing flowers on Union graves and preventing the same act "in the national cemeteries . . . on the graves of such Rebel dead as may be buried therein . . . [is] not because we cherish any feelings of hate or desire to triumph over individual foes, but because we seek to mark in this distinction and manner the feelings with which the nation regards freedom and slavery, loyalty and treason, Republican principles and slaveholding oligarchy."[21]

Within one week, the chief justice articulated his strong feelings about the GAR standpoint, as did John E. Williams, president of the

National Metropolitan Bank in New York, regarding Chase's views. However, neither letter (Williams to Chase and Chase's reply) was printed at the time, but days after the chief justice's death on May 7, 1873, the *New York Tribune* published his response. At Williams's request "in justice to the living and the dead," the *Tribune* printed his letter the next day so that readers had the complete "correspondence on conciliation."

On June 4, 1869, Williams informed Chase that while he "read with painful dissatisfaction" of the chief justice's hope Northerners would soon formally honor dead Confederate soldiers for their courage, he also perused "with lively satisfaction, the noble sentiments" of Logan, quoted in their entirety. The bank president concluded: "Look on this picture and then 'on that,' and then say which is most worthy and most becoming the position of the Chief-Justice of the free United States of America—aye, of a true, unambitious American citizen."

Six days later, Chase answered a man he knew from his days as Lincoln's treasury secretary, and did not recall fondly: "Doubtless you remember occasions upon which your active hostility to measures of finance which . . . I thought indispensable to the success of the National arms and to the permanent welfare of the country, caused painful dissatisfaction to me." After these pleasantries, Chase got right to the point: "I have no sympathy with the spirit which refuses to strew flowers upon the graves of the dead soldiers who fought against the side I took; and I am glad to know there was no such spirit among those who joined in decorating the graves of the soldiers of the Union who lie buried at Magnolia Cemetery."[22] The story went national, including the *Daily Phoenix*.[23]

JIM CROW CASTS ITS SHADOW OVER HONORING GRAVES IN THE SOUTH

Within ten years of war's end, Americans were honoring the remains and resting places of their dead and, to some small degree, those of former enemies. However, joint decorating of graves rarely occurred, with no evidence of black participation or endorsing groundswell among Union veterans in general, nor were Southerners festooning the graves of African American soldiers with flowers or showing any other sign of respect. None of this was surprising, given the situation in the former Confederacy.

Reconstruction's collapse and the worsening encroachments of Jim Crow were exacting a terrible toll on African Americans, and those individuals, white and black, who had been foremost in the fight against both outcomes struggled to maintain their optimism and sense of accomplishment. One such person served as featured orator for the 1880 Decoration Day ceremonies at the National Cemetery at Beaufort, and his words were revelatory when compared to what he had previously said in an identical setting.

By the time David T. Corbin spoke on May 31, he and Daniel H. Chamberlain, years earlier, had shouldered the major responsibility for prosecuting the Ku Klux Klan in South Carolina under considerable constraints. As respectively US attorney for the state and its attorney general, in 1871 and 1872 they diligently attempted to convict, under federal law, the Klan's most dangerous members for violent crimes committed in South Carolina. The results were neatly summarized by J. Michael Martinez: "In one sense the Klan was broken and never again would it rule a community or a state with as much power as it had in the South Carolina Upcountry during 1870–1871. In another sense, few Klansmen were punished to a degree commensurate with their crimes."[24]

As he stood before the cemetery gathering, Corbin surely thought of his partner, forced out of the governorship after Hayes became president, and his own post-Reconstruction political career derailed by machinations and partisanship. In 1870 he was concerned about the feelings of defeated Confederates, but ten years later he had a profoundly different message to convey to the largely African American audience: "'You have at great cost of blood and treasure been made free, and clothed with all the rights of citizens. As such you participate, on equal terms, with your white fellow-citizens in all the functions of government [which] are high and important trusts.'" With that in mind, he "'would have you learn . . . to be right in all your political faith and doctrine . . . owe[d] . . . as a debt of gratitude to those choice spirits, who for forty years . . . pioneered your cause and struggled on in your behalf while you knew them not, till your cause was won and you were free.'"[25]

Apologetically unable to attend, former governor Chamberlain spoke through a letter read by another famous South Carolina Republican. Robert Smalls, who in 1862 piloted the Confederate steamship *Planter* out of Charleston Harbor under the cover of darkness to the Union fleet and freedom for himself, his wife and two children, and thirteen other African Americans, was now in between two stints as a United States congressman. Smalls relayed Chamberlain's message: "'[The day's] lesson and voice is political freedom under the Constitution and Union for all men. Till the day shall arrive when every man in our country shall enjoy the ballot without molestation or fear, the heroes of our great wars should be our monitors and guides in the battles of our day.'"[26]

As anti-black violence, discrimination, and Supreme Court–sanctioned Jim Crow continued into the new century, biracial efforts involving another Left-Armed Corps officer demonstrated that Union veterans could act compassionately toward their Confederate counterparts without forgetting why they fought, or for whom.

After thirty-two months working conscientiously for the Freedmen's Bureau as assistant sub-assistant commissioner at Richmond, Brevet Captain Benjamin C. Cook was discharged from the army in December 1868. Having married Nettie E. Hess on New Year's Day 1867, and become a new father, he stayed in Virginia and was appointed an assistant revenue assessor in December 1869. Promoted to inspector of tobacco at Richmond, he remained in that office throughout the 1870s, upholding his reputation for quality government service.[27] He also found time to invent an "Improvement in Broom-Heads" designed to provide farmers with a long-lasting and easily replaceable head for their corn brooms; his patent was approved in 1873.[28]

In 1872, Cook began his lifelong participation in a combination of political and veteran activities by serving as secretary to the Convention of Union Soldiers and Sailors at Pittsburgh and a Republican Supervisor of Elections, while also founding the GAR Department of Virginia US Grant Post No. 1 and being elected its first commander.[29]

In 1881, Cook was rewarded for his able federal work by President Rutherford B. Hayes's nomination as collector of customs for the District of Richmond.[30] This coincided with his rise within the Grand Army—in 1882 he began two years as Virginia representative to the National Council of Administration and was both elected department commander and selected for the national Committee on Resolutions in 1884.[31]

With the GAR doing its best for impoverished and debilitated Union ex-servicemen, its new Virginia leader met several times with Richmond's Mayor Carrington, a former Confederate colonel, about his comrades in similar desperate straits. There being no Grand Army equivalent to provide relief, Cook and another ex-Rebel officer, Colonel Peyton Wise, planned a month-long fundraising fair to be held in Richmond for the creation of a soldiers' home for "disabled and needy Confederate soldiers."

A nationwide appeal was made to GAR posts, and numerous high-ranking former officers from both sides were invited to attend the May 14, 1884, opening of the "R. E. Lee Camp Fair." After explaining that he regretfully could not attend due to being on crutches from a non-war injury and unable to travel, one Union general in New York sent his hope for the Fair's success—US Grant then stated former adversaries "can well afford to be the best of friends now, and only strive for rivalry in seeing which can be the best citizens of the grandest country on earth." The Richmond *Daily Dispatch* would go on to note that the enthusiastic response and generosity of the Grand Army and non-affiliated Northerners "elicited the warmest gratitude of our people."

Three years later, the project's success was captured by the *Wichita Eagle*, which reported that, with the particular support of GAR posts, monetary and article donations to the Fair garnered sufficient funding "to build the confederate soldiers' home at Richmond, and the 'R. E. Lee, camp No. 1, confederate veterans' was organized." Every camp that was subsequently founded derived its charter from the original.[32]

Notwithstanding his many accomplishments, multi-faceted prominence, and good salary, Cook's time in Richmond was nearing its end. With his term as collector of customs set to expire on February 5, 1885, he declined any opportunity to be considered for reappointment in light of the upcoming presidential inauguration of Democrat Grover Cleveland.[33]

The Cook family relocated to Attica, Harper County, Kansas, where the one-armed veteran soon became a leading member of their new community. In October 1886, he received the county Republican convention's unanimous nomination for a seat in the state House of Representatives, to which he was easily elected the following month.[34]

Just as in Virginia, Cook devoted considerable time to politics and veterans' affairs and stayed faithful to his Republican and Union roots. When he spoke with the *Wichita Eagle* in July 1887 about his work on behalf of Southern ex-servicemen, Cook made it clear that "*he has no fight to make now against confederate soldiers but he is opposed to surrendering the battle flags which he and his comrades captured on a hundred battle fields to southern politicians.*"[35] Appointed to the Department of Kansas's legislative committee in 1888, he played an active role in instituting a state soldiers' home, including the committee's 1889 report to both elected chambers at Topeka.[36]

Having maintained friendships and contacts in Richmond that enabled Cook to pursue business opportunities back east,[37] by 1897 the family returned to the city, where he was under consideration for reappointment to the Customs Service now that a Republican again occupied the White House. While waiting, in February 1898 Cook was among distinguished Union and Confederate veterans who met to form an association for establishing a national park preserving the Fredericksburg, Chancellorsville, Wilderness and Spotsylvania Court House battlefields.[38]

Cook's patience was rewarded in May 1898 by special temporary appointment as deputy clerk in the US Internal Revenue Department, a popular decision that led to permanent assignment as deputy collector.[39] Ever active in the GAR, he was elected commander of Phil Kearney Post No. 10, and hosted commander in chief Albert D. Shaw during a March 1900 visit, including escorting the general on a call to a former commander of the R. E. Lee Camp, Confederate veterans.[40]

As for Cook's political activities, the September 1900 Republican City Convention to which he was a delegate was notable with respect to race. In an assignment received with praise, Cook was chosen by the African

American chair to serve on the city committee—regarding the gathering itself, the *Richmond Times* reported that a "striking feature . . . was the prominent part the negroes played in the proceedings and the share of honors they got. There was a negro chairman, both temporary and permanent; negro sergeant-at-arms, negro secretary of the new City Committee; negroes in large numbers on the delegation to Manchester, and negro orators galore . . . Sometimes as many as half a dozen negro orators held the floor at once."[41]

Elected commander of the Department of Virginia and North Carolina and its representative to the National Council of Administration in 1902, Cook took the initiative on a project reported country-wide. The Kearney Post's jurisdiction included the graves of more than thirty thousand Union soldiers, and for years its members had honored them on Memorial Day by placing "a small emblem of the stars and stripes . . . wound within a wreath of flowers" on each man's final resting place. In 1902 the tradition was expanded to include the graves of Northern soldiers throughout the state, with Seven Pines, Fort Harrison, Cold Harbor, and Glendale (where Cook would preside) chosen as sites for commemoration by a service, memorial address, and decoration.[42]

On March 4, 1906, Captain Benjamin C. Cook died suddenly of heart failure, with pulmonary congestion and probable kidney involvement contributory factors. While this was unexpected, physical problems over the past twenty years made his accomplishments even more impressive. According to Cook's longtime physician, he had suffered terribly from *"necrosis of the stump of an amputated arm . . .* [that] *produced violent neuralgia, which was so great that it attacked his health, and resulted in his death,* [in addition to] *. . . dyspepsia which produced violent vertigo and rendered him unfit for business of any kind. The necrosis produced violent pain that . . . undermined his general health.*[43]

At almost sixty-seven, Cook left his wife of thirty-nine years and daughter Kate to mourn, along with numerous friends and colleagues. After burial in the National Cemetery at Richmond, his Kearny comrades adopted "eloquent resolutions" on his post's "deep sense of loss" and that to the GAR, and he was memorialized by the *National Tribune*.[44]

Overall, Cook had lived in Richmond about thirty years. During that time, residents of the former Confederate capital held him in high regard for his honesty and integrity, and he greatly aided Southern veterans *in extremis*. Yet he never suggested Union and Confederate servicemen fought for equivalent reasons, gave less than his full attention to the needs of Northern ex-soldiers and sailors, nor turned his back on African Americans when they most desperately needed support.

As reconciliation took hold, these were the tensions faced individually and collectively by Union veterans, mainly (but not exclusively) those who lived in the South. Blue and Gray associations began to form, like in 1890 at the initiative of GAR Post No. 7 at Vicksburg, Mississippi, and the Confederate Veterans' Vicksburg Camp in order to hold a week-long reunion that May. The concept went national the following year, with one of the organization's first lodges formed at Mobile, Alabama.[45]

In an era of sectional rapprochement, the actions of America's foremost veterans' organization, while mindful of political realities, reflected its biracial composition and longstanding, emphatic positions on Northern versus Southern causes. In preparation for the September 1895 GAR National Encampment at Louisville, its first to be held in the South, Confederate Association constituents were "cordially and earnestly invite[d]" to attend all three evening Campfires: "So come and let us shake your hands and, as far as possible, introduce you to our Northern brethren, who will join us in bidding you a hearty welcome." By the same token, the *National Tribune* took pains to note that "colored veterans were treated with special consideration, in contradiction of the report about the color line being drawn in Louisville."[46]

Lest there be any doubt, the Grand Army would go just so far in service of reconciliation. At the 1896 National Encampment in St. Paul, Commander in Chief Walker told his comrades about correspondence exchanged with Charles Dana of New York regarding a proposed parade in which Union and Confederate veterans would march together under the American flag but in their own blue and gray uniforms. On December 30, 1895, General Walker informed Dana that though the courage of those "who bore arms against us" was fully recognized, and they would be "gladly receive[d] and welcome[d] . . . as citizens to all the privileges and honors of a common country we both now love," that did not alter the GAR's "conviction . . . that those who . . . fought for their country and were in the right, while those . . . who . . . fought against their country . . . were wrong, and no sentimental nor commercial efforts to efface these radical distinctions should be encouraged by any true patriot."

On January 13, 1896, he followed up with Dana: "The sooner those who wore the gray cease trying to symbolize the 'lost cause' by flag or uniform, and representing themselves as a distinct part of the people of our common country, the sooner will a fuller realization of the 'festival of patriotism and fraternal cooperation,' which you suggest, be brought about." Citing the "innumerable letters and resolutions that came to Headquarters" in "overwhelming" support of Walker's stated position, "the project of the proposed parade was abandoned."[47]

While the organization as a whole was standing by its membership and principles, individual associates, posts, and departments were proving less steadfast, particularly when it came to their black comrades.

In July 1898, the *Syracuse Daily* reported about "a love feast [at Richmond, VA] between members of the Pickett camp of Confederate Veterans and a GAR committee from Philadelphia" at which the latter invited the former to attend its August reunion. When making the offer, the committee head said, "'Since Fitzhugh Lee, Joe Wheeler and Thomas L. Rosser have donned the blue uniform and been appointed to high positions, we feel that Mason and Dixon's line has been wiped out.'"[48]

The invitation was enthusiastically accepted by the Pickett Camp, but as time for departure drew near, it became apparent that not all GAR men in the City of Brotherly Love welcomed the Confederates' attendance. On July 29 the Grand Army Association of Philadelphia passed resolutions in opposition to the visit that included disclaiming any direct or indirect participation in the planned encampment, charging it was a profit-making venture for the park's owner, and that the organization wanted no part of placing their "former enemies on exhibition even at the low price of 15 cents for admission to see a 'real, live Johnny Reb.'" Letters (signed and not) and copies of the resolutions were made available to the Southerners, who decided to attend nonetheless.[49]

After arriving in Philadelphia on August 7, matters did not improve. The Pickett Camp was furious to discover an African American post had been appointed to the welcoming committee by the GAR, and that the reception committee included another veteran of color, who joined everyone at the head dinner table. When it further learned that black posts would serve as procession escorts the following day, the camp's executive committee threatened to not participate in the parade if the African Americans marched. Three of the Confederate Veterans were so offended they left for Richmond before receiving the host committee's answer.

Incredibly, the Grand Army men agreed to remove their African American comrades from any further activities. To the Pickett Camp's dismay, four black units still joined the following morning's parade to Independence Hall, where Mayor Warwick greeted the visitors, and speeches were delivered by dignitaries from North and South. There would be no further racial imposition upon the Southerners; as the *Richmond Dispatch* stated, "In deference to the emphatic expression of nearly every member of the Richmond delegation, this element was to-day excluded from the banquet hall, and it has been promised that it shall not reappear upon any future occasion."

The Virginia newspaper concluded: "However sincere may have been the desire to obliterate the divisions between the North and South, this reunion has demonstrated that there is another line far more clearly defined than the line of Mason and Dixon: **THE COLOR LINE**."[50]

Four days later the *Richmond Planet* assessed the Pickett Camp's behavior as "sickening, and did not reflect any credit upon the 'soreheads' who were growling." It then offered an explanation of how African Americans should be treated that was stomach-turning in its own right. The *Planet* reported that "we always have colored men in parades, . . . even if they do nothing else but carry a bucket of ice-water," which "gives tone to the occasion and indicates that some old Virginia aristocrats are somewhere in the procession." It further explained that "In all first class receptions, the colored brother is invited, even if he be required to wear a white jacket, apron, and sit down to a repast after the white folks have passed into the other room for other refreshments."[51]

The *Staunton Spectator and Vindicator* chimed in: "the mingling of the Blue and the Gray was not according to the show bills, the Blue was too *dark* a blue, and was so strongly scented with African musk, that the old Rebs had to move camp or go to the hospital, so they moved back to Pickett camp, Richmond, Va., in rather quick time."[52]

On August 19, a letter from Iowa Grand Army member Fitzroy Sessions was published that captured the revulsion felt by Union veterans over the events in Philadelphia (done "to the shame and eternal disgrace" of that city's GAR). Insisting that "[the] colored post had every right to be there that any white post had," Sessions "would be willing to sacrifice the friendship of all ex-Confederates holding such narrow prejudice and that they should go to hades or where they choose, before I would do such injustice." As to abandoning "the colored man who was our only friend South during the war, who aided the captured, the sick, and the wounded at the risk of his life, who fought bravely under greater risks and hardships than ours," that "would render us contemptible."[53]

He ended with pertinent commentary on the ongoing Jim Crow treatment of African American soldiers in parts of the North, including his own: "I wish also to say it seems to me illogical, wrong and damnable, that a colored company in the enlightened state of Iowa, and its capital Des Moines, should not have the same rights and privileges as a white company. The blacks both as volunteers and regulars have ever excelled. It is a pitiful lesson of narrow prejudice and injustice. It is shameful."[54]

CONFLICT RAGES OVER THE CITIES OF THE DEAD

Given his stellar work in three different military units during the Civil War and Reconstruction, coupled with the various federal and GAR positions of authority he held, James O. Ladd appeared to ideally fulfill Robert Small's expressed wishes. When he was elected commander of the Department of Georgia and South Carolina at its annual encampment in March 1898,[55] Ladd had lived in the Palmetto State for over thirty years, and no Union veteran could have been more conscious of all that had occurred in South Carolina since 1865 and the present conditions.

His political acumen and high standing in the region were signified by his leading role, along with Vanderbilt Benevolent Association of Charleston President, Colonel A. C. Kaufman and other prominent citizens, in garnering gubernatorial and national senatorial support for the conversion of Castle Pinckney in Charleston Harbor into a sanitarium for disabled enlisted and commissioned veterans of the US Army and Navy. The effort began in 1897 and continued for several years, receiving the endorsement of both the GAR and United Confederate Veterans. That the venture never came to pass was no reflection on Ladd and his colleagues but, rather, the structure's dilapidation.[56]

But something Ladd did successfully establish would tarnish his well-earned reputation for racial enlightenment. As Bruce E. Baker reported, African Americans began celebrating Decoration Day at the Florence National Cemetery in 1889, with increasing attendance and speakers over the following years until 1899. For this first ceremony after the Spanish-American War there was (inexplicably) no black participation, and former department commander Ladd officiated at the proceedings. According to Baker, this was just the opportunity the state GAR had been awaiting—to make Decoration Day an exclusively white affair.[57]

Three weeks later the *Evening Times* reported that the Florence Grey and Blue Memorial Association, an all-white group "consisting chiefly of Confederate veterans and the[ir] sons and daughters" had been formed at Ladd's suggestion. Their mission was decoration of Union and Confederate graves, with the hundred-member association to seek "permission to co-operate with the sons and daughters of the Confederacy and the Union Veterans on occasions of memorial exercises. Next year a prominent Confederate veteran will be invited to make an address at the national cemetery."[58]

The May 30, 1900, Decoration Day ceremonies in Florence followed this to the letter, as the Grey and Blue Memorial Association and two GAR post commanders assisted Ladd, who again presided at the National Cemetery. After an oration was delivered by Florence attorney W. F. Clayton, a former Confederate naval officer, the Grand Army's "regular decoration service . . . was then observed." The *Richmond Dispatch* added: "At Beaufort, this State, there was the usual Decoration-Day celebration, but only colored people participated. A few of the colored Grand Army of the Republic and young uniformed militia and large crowds of negro excursionists from Savannah and Charleston repaired to the National Cemetery, preceded by a brass band."[59]

Jim Crow now extended to decoration of Union graves, thanks in large part to a Freedmen's Bureau official who had once commanded black troops with distinction, and was contemptuously kept captive with them by soldiers who wore the same uniform as those welcomed as honored guests in preference to African American veterans and their supporters. Consistent with his actions, Ladd's report on South Carolina to the national encampment that August was reconciliation rhetoric of the highest order: "events of national character occurring in connection with our recently acquired outlying possessions have stimulated impetus to the formation of a general patriotic sentiment before which all sentiment of sectionalism gradually recedes."[60]

Three years later, when the Department of Georgia and South Carolina Junior Vice-Commander James P. Averill reported to the 1903 national encampment on "'The Federal Dead who rest in the National Cemeteries in the South,'" he said that "At Florence, S. C, eighty miles distant from the nearest G. A. R. post, a society has been formed known as the 'Florence Blue and Gray Memorial Association,' composed of citizens, ladies and school children of the town, and a small contingent of Grand Army Comrades. This Association has assumed the trust of conducting the services and decorating the graves ['on Memorial Day with a miniature flag and fragrant blossom'], and is fulfilling it in the most satisfactory manner."[61]

While factual statements, they did not tell the whole story. Averill chose not to mention that African Americans, including veterans, were excluded from the Florence ceremonies by the association and department leaders. Why? It is likely he was concerned about how the encampment would react to such a betrayal of Grand Army principles and its comrades of color.

Tragically, it would hardly be the last, as we shall see how acts of unfaithfulness to black equality and advancement, and the causes for which Union servicemen had risked their lives, would arise from quarters running the gamut from expected to shocking, including an African American member of the Left-Armed Corps.

Brevet Captain Joseph B. Foraker, Eighty-Ninth Ohio. BIOGRAPHICAL DIRECTORY OF THE UNITED STATES CONGRESS.

CHAPTER 9

Betrayal, Remembrance, and Standing Fast

This book, written in the hope that all members of the race still
fettered by ignorance or spiritual blindness may by its teachings be
inspired to noble thoughts and deeds, is dedicated to all American
men and women of Negroid ancestry who have grown to the full
stature of manhood and womanhood.

—WILLIAM HANNIBAL THOMAS, 1901[1]

Fifth USCT sergeant William Hannibal Thomas seemed to have much professional success, including service in the South Carolina House and on the bench in Reconstruction's wake.[2] However, as shown by his biographer John D. Smith, Thomas's "rank opportunism, his craving for recognition, and his propensity for dishonest and unethical, if not illegal, behavior" in multiple aspects of his life included desertion of his wife and children, and sexual misconduct.[3]

Yet for decades his character flaws were not widely known. In 1884, Thomas was so highly regarded by African Americans that his opinion on Cleveland's election was sought along with those of Frederick Douglass and other "leading colored men." The veteran's response was noteworthy for his calling the president-elect "*particeps criminis*, and the chief beneficiary of the disfranchisement of a large body of his fellow citizens by his own party," use of ornate language, and a fair degree of incomprehensibility as to viewpoint.[4]

275

By the turn of the century Thomas was living in relative obscurity in Massachusetts, but that would soon change. In January 1901, the Macmillan Company published *The American Negro: What He Was, What He Is and What He May Become*, in which, as summarized by Smith, Thomas "denounced blacks in the harshest and crudest of terms as physiologically, intellectually, morally and culturally inferior to whites and identified blacks, not whites, as the cause of the contemporary Negro 'problem,'" while distinguishing "between mulattoes like himself, whom he considered superior, and Negroes, whom he judged to be hopelessly depraved."[5]

Promoted by his publisher as an authoritative study of African Americans, the *New York Times* praised Thomas for avoiding the "sentimentality" that marred previous books on the subject, while claiming he demonstrated empathy toward fellow people of color. Regarding the latter, the newspaper noted that while Thomas faced condemnation by other blacks, "on the other hand he proves to the satisfaction of most candid minds that the white man's scheme for the regeneration of the negro contains several grave faults."[6]

This was a charitable way of putting it; when the *Saint Paul Globe* reviewed *The American Negro* in early March its staff delivered a spot-on, devastating assessment of "a view of the negro character as disparaging as any negro-hater has ever expressed." They found Thomas considered African Americans to be "incapable of involved or consecutive thought," their "language and conduct . . . purely imitative . . . actions without reason or moral purpose" underpinned by "a very primitive state of passion and impulse." He believed Reconstruction was "folly, and injurious" to blacks and whites alike and "does not think political rights essential to . . . uplifting of the negro."

Thomas's lack of adequate statistical study or evaluation of black education were criticized, his "fervid declamations" characterized as chiefly rooted in "inadequate data or upon personal impressions of certain classes." Yet, while slamming his incessant "antipathy often seen in those of mixed blood to negro characteristics," the newspaper somehow deemed the work "valuable for inciting a keen interest in the subject."[7]

The *Globe* also addressed the pernicious effect Thomas's book was having on African Americans just two months after its publication: "The Southern newspapers have welcomed . . . 'The American Negro' for as strong an argument for the repeal of the fifteenth amendment as has yet appeared." In fact, backlash from the black press and national leaders had started in February, a *Colored American* headline from Washington, DC, dubbing Thomas with the sobriquet that would haunt him: "A Modern Judas Iscariot."[8]

The overall repulsion African Americans felt for *The American Negro* was in marked contrast to positive reviews that Thomas initially received from some mainstream Northern newspapers. However, by mid-April, the *New York Tribune* noted the author was attracting "extremely sharp criticism, some of it personal in character." It cited Macmillan in reporting that "the most violent attacks upon him have been made by the New York religious press, while the Boston religious press seem to agree that Mr. Thomas's book is one greatly needed to shake the North out of its easy optimism in regard to the future of the negro."[9]

That same day, the *Colored American* published a damaging exposé of Thomas's record, including expulsion from the Western Theological Seminary in his last year (1868) due to "criminal intercourse" with the woman who later became his first wife; an 1877 indictment in Newberry, South Carolina, "for 'corruptly and fraudulently' seizing and selling property," followed by his skipping out on bond and failing to appear in court to answer the charges one year later; and ongoing non-payment of an outstanding debt for rent in Newberry. The newspaper concluded: "These disclosures will explain more fully than any words of ours who this man is who has presumed to set himself up as a critic and censor of the Negro race."[10]

Within one week, the *Washington Times* reported that Reverend C. T. Walker, pastor of New York City's Mount Olivet Baptist Church, deprecated Thomas from the pulpit as "unreliable and incompetent as a witness against his race." Walker brought up his checkered past and added Benedict Arnold and Aaron Burr to Judas in the list of historical comparators for Thomas.[11]

Paradoxically, Thomas may have contributed (albeit briefly) to civil rights as a common object of black scorn. As Smith observed, the detested book brought together African Americans "when [their] status . . . was at a low ebb" and "accomplished the apparently impossible—it temporarily united the warring Booker T. Washington and W. E. B. Du Bois factions."[12]

Washington, whose classic autobiography *Up from Slavery* came out two months after *The American Negro*, was himself a controversial figure among African Americans. Unlike Thomas, this was not due to personal or professional improprieties, or outrageous claims against the morality of black women or African American clergy. Rather, it was Washington's accommodationist stance on black-white relations, non-confrontational style, and promotion of pursuing trades and technical education instead of professions that increasingly came under fire as conditions worsened for Southerners of color.

In April 1898, the *Washington Bee*, while lauding Washington as "one of our great men" and "a great leader," questioned "his right to the exalted place of sole [black] leadership given him by a section of the southern white press." In an eerie portent of accusations Thomas would face, the newspaper called Washington "an apologist" who followed "a steady practice of thundering against many evils of the negro, but he seldom thunders against the evils practiced by the whites if he thinks it would be unpopular." Censuring Washington for consistently avoiding public discussion of atrocities committed by Southern whites against blacks, the *Bee* did not hold back: "He has not written or spoken a word about the assassination of Postmaster Baker, nor of any of the other outrages that have sent death into the ranks of the colored people of the south."[13]

Up from Slavery appearing on the heels of *The American Negro* was seized upon by the national press. In March 1901, the *St. Louis Republic* said of Washington's inspirational autobiography, "it seems almost in answer to [Thomas's] . . . harsh criticism of the negro race," and compared his gloomy view of African American progress to Washington's optimism when writing about his own struggles.

The *Republic* also found similarities, as "Mr. Thomas admits . . . Mr. Washington's work at Tuskegee [Institute] is admirable, but agrees with [Washington] . . . in condemning [most] . . . negro clergymen and teachers. . . . Both are of the opinion that a mistake was made in granting the franchise to the negro. They unite in thinking that it is in the knowledge and practice of agriculture and a country life that the negro's best hope lies."[14]

From the South came further affirmation of Washington's views. On March 29, the *Florida Star* discussed his character and methods, saying he "knows the race limitations but unlike some others of his color does not excuse them nor throw up his hands at the forbidding prospect." In a patronizing, unnerving assessment, the *Star* reported that "The primary idea of this American Moses is to open the eyes of his people to their exact status among the whites, to teach them what to expect and what not to expect, what they may achieve and what for them is impossible. It is a hard doctrine, but simply another case of 'must be cruel only to be kind.'"[15]

Just one month after Washington's book was released, yet another work from a prominent African American emerged, and was instantly compared to *The American Negro*. On April 6, the *Buffalo Courier* declared *The College-Bred Negro* "A wholesome antidote for the pessimistic and perplexing utterances of William Hannibal Thomas," and cited the distinction its editor, Dr. W. E. Burghardt Du Bois, had won as "'the best-educated Negro in America.'"[16]

The descendant of several generations of free blacks, Du Bois's background differed greatly from those of Washington and Thomas. Born three years after the Civil War in the integrated Massachusetts town of Great Barrington, he was raised there and pursued a preparatory college curriculum at the local high school. Du Bois received a bachelor's degree from Fisk University in Nashville in 1888, then entered Harvard, from which he obtained another BA in 1890, a master's degree the following year, and the school's first doctorate by an African American in 1895 after a two-year fellowship in Germany. A professor at Wilberforce University in Ohio from 1894 to 1896, he took a position as an assistant instructor at the University of Pennsylvania before joining the faculty at Atlanta University as Professor of Economics and History in 1898.[17]

Du Bois led his institution's investigation into "College-bred Negroes" like himself. The inquiry was incorporated with proceedings from the "Fifth Conference for the Study of the Negro Problems" held at the University in 1900 and published together. Its conclusions, accurately summarized by the *Courier* in a highly favorable review, dramatically bridge the past (represented by Washington and Thomas), present, and future (personified by Du Bois and Ida B. Wells-Barnett) of black achievement, progress, and demands for equality.

Along with the vast majority of African Americans needing "common school and manual training," "industrial and technical training and trade schools" were in great demand. At the same time, there was a separate and growing necessity for "higher training of persons selected for talent and character to be leaders of thought and missionaries of culture among the masses." To accommodate this, maintaining a number of black Southern colleges were recommended in order "to supply thoroughly trained teachers, preachers, professional men, and captains of industry."[18]

Du Bois ended the study by paying tribute to Washington's work ("I yield to no one in advocacy of the recently popularized notion of Negro industrial education, nor in admiration for the earnest men who emphasize it"), and "fail[ed] to see anything contradictory or antagonistic" in his own framework for "providing the rudiments of an education for all, industrial training for the many, and a college course for the talented few."

But clearly seeing beyond the circumscribed scope of the Tuskegee Institute founder's vision, Du Bois contended "that its widest realization will but increase the demand for college-bred men—for thinkers to guide the workers," and that all those striving for African American progress would not disagree "if they but remember this fundamental and unchangeable truth: *the object of all true education is not to make men carpenters—it is to make carpenters men.*"[19]

In the twentieth century's first year, the newly issued publications of three African Americans had generated much nationwide interest and debate. The most flawed of the trio, on both a personal level and in the validity, clarity, and constructiveness of his ideas, spent the shortest time in the limelight.

By June, the *Appeal* was invoking his professional obituary with understandable schadenfreude: "The 'Spectator' pays its compliments to 'Judas Iscariot Hannibal Thomas' in these words: 'Let the wretch live on, execrated by his own, condemned by the white race, and cursed by all things animate.'" His biographer confirmed Thomas's fate, noting that "After 1901, white supremacists continued to cite *The American Negro*, but it rarely entered mainstream conversations about race." Smith further stated that "Black intellectuals, for their part, wisely allowed the sensation caused by Thomas' book to fizzle out while they focused on more pressing issues, notably . . . crushing poverty . . . , disfranchisement, segregation, and the frightful upsurge in racial violence."[20]

They had little choice; as the *Washington Bee* noted in 1898, Booker T. Washington was hardly inclined to address such concerns. More than three years later, the African American *Broad Ax* of Chicago pointed out conflicting facets of his having become the most famous black person in the United States. It first stated that Washington had "assumed the mantle of leadership laid down by the late, lamented Frederick Douglas [*sic*]."[21]

He had indeed ascended to that role, but it was in substantial part bestowed upon him by whites rather than solely by blacks, as the *Washington Bee* had alluded to. By contrast, the fiery Douglass had transitioned from abolitionist to uncompromising advocate for racial, social, and political equality without missing a beat; though backed by prominent white allies, his prestige clearly derived from African Americans.

The *Broad Ax* then observed that Washington "has made for himself an enviable reputation as an educator. Will his political leadership be as successful? Not if the present policy is kept up." This tied in with his having "dined with President and Mrs. Roosevelt at the White House Wednesday. Prof. Washington is the first Negro to be honored in such a manner."[22]

It indeed was a groundbreaking occasion, but the choice of Washington was telling. His considerable accomplishments on behalf of African Americans, and lifelong dedication to their welfare, were certainly worthy of respect and praise. Yet Washington was a safe black leader whom powerful whites could depend upon to not give offense or take controversial stands, and they could demonstrate an ostensible acceptance of African Americans by utilizing him as their designated national representative for the race.

It could fairly be argued that Washington's methods were calculated to ensure ongoing financial and political support for the Tuskegee Institute and other avenues for black industrial education and training, which was quite laudable. However, these career paths and his overarching concept for racial uplift were increasingly anachronistic for ambitious young adults of color, particularly Northerners like W. E. B. Du Bois. Yet, Washington would continue to enjoy great overall popularity with African Americans, and his clout had to be reckoned with by blacks who believed in a more aggressive and uncompromising approach to civil rights.

Twelve years younger than Washington, and appalled when confronted by Jim Crow in Tennessee, Du Bois was also painfully aware of Northern racism. In his landmark 1899 examination of a black urban community, *The Philadelphia Negro: A Social Study*, he asked: "How long can a city say to a part of its citizens, 'It is useless to work; it is fruitless to deserve well of men; education will gain you nothing but disappointment and humiliation?' How long can a city teach its black children that the road to success is to have a white face?"

Du Bois offered a searing example of the bigotry faced by African Americans within the professions that surely hit close to home, as he described how a University of Pennsylvania graduate with a degree in mechanical engineering and good recommendations "obtained work in the city, through an advertisement, on account of his excellent record. He worked a few hours and then was discharged because he was found to be colored. He is now a waiter in the University Club, where his white fellow graduates dine."

Du Bois added a scathing footnote: "And is, of course, pointed out by some as typifying the educated Negro's success in life." The account was so disturbing that the *McCook Tribune* in Nebraska repeated it in detail as one of "many individual cases in support of his somewhat bitter deduction" in its story on *The Philadelphia Negro.*[23]

Unlike Thomas and Washington, in 1901 Du Bois was just getting started on his amazing career. In the future lay such major achievements as co-founding the National Association for the Advancement of Colored People (NAACP) along with Wells-Barnett, other eminent African Americans, and distinguished white supporters of racial justice and equality; a virtual library of important works including his essay, "The Talented Tenth" and the classic book, *The Souls of Black Folk*; and his longtime editorship of *The Crisis*, the NAACP's main publication.[24]

RACISM TAINTS MEMORIES OF THE WAR

The detailed discussion of Thomas, Washington, and Du Bois illustrates how race-obsessed the United States was forty years after the Civil War began, the schisms that existed among blacks trying to combat Jim Crow and its influence, and how these impacted those Americans whose great military and postwar societal triumphs occurred in an ever distant past. While a good proportion of surviving Left-Armed Corps members and fellow Union veterans continued to manifest racial tolerance, remembrance and fidelity to service, often in relation to Grand Army activities and through the *National Tribune*, some others did not.

On Memorial Day 1897, a special event took place at Boston's Music Hall, "Ceremonies Incident to the Unveiling of the Colonel Robert G. Shaw Monument." As part of the celebration for Augustus Saint-Gaudens's magnificent bronze bas-relief sculpture of the Fifty-Fourth Massachusetts, then as now on display in Boston Common opposite the State House, over two hundred officers and enlisted men from the Fifty-Fourth and Fifty-Fifth Infantries and Fifth Massachusetts Cavalry marched and Booker T. Washington spoke. The featured oration was aptly delivered by famed Harvard psychologist and philosopher William James, whose brother "Wilkie" was the Fifty-Fourth's Adjutant and among those wounded during its furious attack on Fort Wagner. Just as fitting, one of the honored guests seated upon the platform was fifty-nine-year-old Colonel Joseph Wiley Gelray.[25]

Five months later, a letter appeared in the *National Tribune* from another veteran, C. B. Hutchings of San Francisco, who had been reminded of a life-changing experience by an item the paper had run about "the negroes from Louisiana at the Encampment at Buffalo."

He was among Union forces at Port Hudson, Louisiana on July 9, 1863, when they took possession after the Confederates' surrender. The initial assault began on May 27 with the all-black First and Third Louisiana Native Guards "on the extreme right," and their losses had been terrible.

As Hutchings explained, the "flag of truce to bring in the wounded did not cover the dead and the colored regiments," so that "all of the dead [black soldiers] remained where they had fallen" when he rode over to the Native Guards' position six weeks later. He called the exclusion of African American troops from the truce "one of the most detestable acts of the whole war . . . As this was their first opportunity to show the white troops their desire to help us, it seemed as if every black soldier wanted to lay down his life then and there. When it is my privilege to march in a Grand Army procession I am only too happy to march by the side of my black comrade."[26]

Yet, even cohort members who had shown fairness toward citizens of color could be insensitive in action and attitude reflective of the times. When attorney Mosley Hall published his 1895 history of Vergennes, Vermont, "'Nigger Hill'" was included among "names of several localities smack[ing] of the early settlers' habit [of] sacrificing euphony to terse description."[27]

Four years later, a benefit for the Elks was headlined by the full US Marine Band. The *Washington Times* reported that among its "most attractive features . . . was the singing of Miss Nelly MacNulty . . . who makes a specialty of singing that class of compositions known as 'coon songs,' and is probably one of the best amateurs in that line in the city."[28]

That the daughter of Wm. Augustus MacNulty, whose outstanding work in the Freedmen's Bureau and decades-long advocacy for black equality as a staunch Republican have been shown throughout this book, would become locally renowned for her talent in such a genre is sadly telling about racial obliviousness during this era.

How else to characterize the wildly enthusiastic reception accorded Consul General Fitzhugh Lee when he arrived in the nation's capital on April 12, 1898? Greeted by a large crowd, many of whom wore buttons with his likeness and shouted "'Our next President!,'" he was taken to the State Department, where Union and Confederate veterans were waiting, along with a large crowd of government workers.

As reported by the *Evening Star*, officers from the Confederate Veterans Association and Union Veteran Legion elected to the reception committee included Ira Broshears (another Left-Armed Corps member) and Corporal James Tanner. The latter was chosen to give the welcoming speech at "a monster serenade," complete with the Marine and Seventy-First Regiments Bands, at the Pennsylvania Railroad depot that evening.[29] The adoring press coverage did not include opinions of African Americans and other Union veterans regarding the presidential candidacy of a man who couldn't vote in the 1868 national elections due to his high-ranking participation in armed rebellion against the United States.

Broshears had taken a leadership role in such Union Veteran Legion activities before. As its chaplain, he offered "a fervent prayer" at the organization's 1897 memorial services before Rev. Dr. L. T. Townsend of Boston delivered the evening's address, "'Story of the Citizen Soldier of America.'" In true reconciliatory fashion, Townsend insisted the two armies "at Gettysburg were not personal enemies, but were contending as a result of conflicting principles; and each was conscientious in the beliefs and theories." Broshears was not responsible for his fellow minister's presentation, but as a Legion officer he was likely involved in arrangements for the event, and Townsend spoke in line with its stated objectives.[30]

Such episodes notwithstanding, it was apparent that as the hard-earned respect for black Union veterans was fading in memory and attitudes among white Americans, their brothers in blue generally remained an exception. It was also clear that service in the nation's latest military action had not appreciably improved African Americans' overall status or race relations.

In 1900, a Spanish-American War veteran from the Twenty-Fourth Infantry was seated on a murder case jury in Salt Lake City, only to be removed at the insistence of fellow jurors solely due to his being black. The *Colored American*, in reporting the incident, thought the judge should have summoned the courage to dismiss the eleven white jurors: "What we need in high places are men who are conscious of their integrity and insist upon it that in the eye of the law all men of all races are absolutely equal."[31]

Neither amity nor equality within the military was ensured by wearing the same uniform. In September 1904, the *Minneapolis Journal* reported a dismal story from Gainesville, Virginia, about the bitterness between white Southern troops and black soldiers on maneuvers.

A Maryland officer said "'It's all right as long as they keep the negroes on their own side of the field. I don't see what they wanted to bring them here for anyway. The niggers were not any great shakes in the war except as a casus belli, and now they rub them under our noses in the army maneuvers and give them the camp next to ours.'"

Another white officer brazenly refused to salute or even acknowledge a black superior, but the animosity went much deeper. An officer from Texas stated flatly that if his unit found themselves near the African American regiment, "'I'll tell my men to load with ball and cartridge and go at them. We had a ruction with them at Fort Riley last year at bayonet points, and it will be the same here if the generals do not look out.'"[32]

The sight of black men in US Army attire appeared as hateful to Southern soldiers as it had been in 1864, but at least reconciliation was working out: "Outside the southern militia the feeling among the residents of this section of Virginia is extremely friendly. The stars and stripes are flying from many of the farmhouses where once the stars and bars waved, and groups of northern officers are the guests of many southern families."[33]

However, in the GAR, what African American veterans thought about joint Union/Confederate activities still mattered. In a contretemps extensively covered by the *Brooklyn Daily Eagle* during May 1905, black comrades in the borough were asked in writing by the Ladies Auxiliary of Grant Post No. 327 to avoid attending a fair at an armory and marching in the upcoming Memorial Day parade "in order to save themselves any undue humiliation."

When the post general membership was informed of the letter, they unanimously voted for "strong resolutions" that included "an emphatic disclaimer by the post of any responsibility for the letter of withdrawal of the invitations and voiced the loyalty of the post to all comrades of whatever color, creed or nationality."

What had taken place? According to Commander Pierre Zeno of the all-black William Lloyd Garrison Post No. 207, "'I understand that ex-Confederate soldiers are to participate in the parade and have been assigned to places ahead of all but two posts. I want to serve notice . . . that no negro veterans of the Civil War will march behind any Confederate rebels. White men may be comrades enough to do so, but black men never, never will.'"

But even more was at stake, as Zeno stated in his letter to the Grant Post: "'If there are white comrades who do not want to treat us as comrades here in Brooklyn, we want the comrades of the state and nation to know it. If we were good enough to die for this country we certainly ought to be good enough to be treated as men.'" He then scored the "proscription and ostracism in the South [that] is carried to such an extent as to successfully defy the laws of the nation, [and the] Northern social ostracism, un-Christian and un-American hemming in all colored people as by a cordon of fire. It is the duty of our whole people to morally aid in carrying on the natural work of true emancipation."

Henry Ward Beecher Post No. 620, another African American post commanded by department chaplain James A. Tappan, had also been asked to stay away, and they protested just as the Garrison Post. When he heard about the controversy, former Brevet Lieutenant Colonel William Hemstreet of the Eighteenth Missouri wrote Zeno to "congratulate you on your manly stand. It is a bright spot with your race."[34]

Within two weeks, the Confederate veterans decided to withdraw from participating in the parade, and the Grand Army of Kings County's memorial and executive committee announced that all its posts would march on Memorial Day. This declaration came at a meeting with six thousand of its members, who "voted to hear all the colored delegates had to say." The issues were discussed in detail, with Grant Post Commander Butt personally apologizing for the "error" of "excluding the colored comrades and taking the entire blame upon himself." According to the

Daily Eagle, "This statement was so flattering to the indignant colored men that they hastened to shake hands with all concerned directly in their inclusion, and for several minutes the gathering resembled a camp meeting love feast."[35]

The question remained as to why anyone associated with a Grand Army post in Brooklyn thought it appropriate to deliberately exclude African American comrades from activities in favor of Southern ex-servicemen. Yet, black veterans were given full opportunity to voice their opposition to an injustice and achieved a satisfactory resolution. Further positive outcome was announced the next month by the *New York Press*, which reported that the Garrison and Beecher Posts "are about to consolidate," a "result . . . brought about by the strong unity of feeling which was recently cemented by the firm stand . . . taken by them in regard to the Grant Post incident."[36]

In 1906, another situation involving black soldiers was reported nationwide, staying in the headlines for years as either the "Brownsville Raid" or "Brownsville Affray." President Roosevelt's professed enlightened views on race would come under question, further unraveling the decades-long affiliation between African Americans and the Republican party. Due process, constitutional guarantees and legal equality took center stage throughout the shocking affair, during which a Union veteran in the twilight of his political career would come to embody moral courage.

The Twenty-Fifth Infantry, experienced soldiers who had earned a reputation as well-disciplined and efficient troops, including some who had fought in Cuba and the Philippines, was ordered to Fort Brown, Texas, in July 1906. With the white citizens of Brownsville openly opposing the stationing of African American troops, it was no surprise that their commander said his men had been "'subjected to indignities since their arrival.'" In an incident, which he connected to the violence that subsequently erupted, Major C. W. Penrose described how after two uniformed blacks passed "some women . . . standing on a sidewalk talking with a [white] man," he "knocked one of the soldiers down with the butt of a revolver and was reported to have said: 'I'll teach you to get off the sidewalk when there is a party of ladies on the walk.'" Once the

African American arose, "the white man [reportedly] . . . covered him with his revolver, saying: 'Leave, or I will blow your brains out.'"

Around midnight on August 13, shots were allegedly heard in the fort's vicinity, and according to townspeople, up to twenty soldiers of the Twenty-Fifth then came into Brownsville and indiscriminately fired hundreds of rifle shots into homes, bars, and a hotel. Frank Natus, a white saloon employee, was killed, and popular police lieutenant M. Y. Dominguez lost his right arm. Twelve black troopers were subsequently arrested along with a recently discharged regimental member and held for grand jury investigation.

The inquiry was quite thorough, and no charges were filed due to lack of probable cause. The men were released and joined their comrades in Fort Reno, Oklahoma, where the War Department had ordered their removal from the Brownsville area. Given the reports of white men becoming armed, four hundred rifles being sold in the town, and threats made against the African Americans, their transfer seemed to be prudent.[37]

What followed was not. The army's investigation involved sworn statements but no hearings, and held suspected and unsuspected alike to the same judgment due to no one coming forward or admitting guilt. The resultant report preferred no formal charges (shots fired into civilians' homes being the main accusation), but the president, believing "a conspiracy of silence" also existed, found it sufficient for a draconian decision. On November 5, Roosevelt followed the inspector general's recommendation by summarily ordering all 167 black enlisted men, who had been in service at Fort Brown that night, to be dishonorably discharged from the army and banned from military or civilian federal employment for the rest of their lives.

The national midterm elections took place the very next day, but the president's decision was not announced until the day after. African Americans across the country were outraged at both his action and when it was made public, and there was little doubt that had they been aware before the election, Republicans would have lost a significant proportion of their votes.[38]

THE BROWNSVILLE AFFRAY AND ONGOING
STRUGGLE FOR JUSTICE

Denunciation for Roosevelt's order swiftly came, led by African Americans nationwide. He was vilified during a Thanksgiving service for four AME churches in New York, with almost every parishioner contributing to a relief fund for the cashiered soldiers. Concluding his sermon, Rev. W. H. Brooks outlined why his flock should give thanks: "again we have disappointed the world, for the soldiers in disgrace have acted as brave men, not resentful children; thankful that the press of the country with few exceptions has condemned such drastic measures; that the conservative people north and south do not countenance such impulsive actions."[39]

As reported by *The Commoner* of Lincoln, Nebraska, on December 7, "Negro citizens throughout the north and west have held mass meetings to protest against the dismissal by President Roosevelt . . . Thousands of petitions have been forwarded to the White House urging the president to withdraw his order of dismissal."[40]

In Washington, after first thinking the Twenty-Fifth had committed the crime as revenge for "prejudice throughout the South against colored soldiers," a distinguished white citizen also doubted their collective guilt.

Ohio Senator Joseph B. Foraker had served three years in his state's Eighty-Ninth infantry and Signal Corps, leaving the army as a brevet captain days short of his nineteenth birthday. Following graduation from Cornell University, Foraker practiced law and later became a judge. Entering Republican politics, he served as Ohio governor from 1885 to 1889, and in 1896 began the first of two consecutive terms in the Senate.

In examining the testimony upon which Roosevelt had based his decision, Foraker immediately "saw . . . it was flimsy, unreliable and insufficient and untruthful," and thought it his responsibility to bring about an investigation to determine "whether . . . any of the men did participate, either by actually engaging in the shooting, or by making themselves accessory, either before or afterward"; then, should any be guilty, "ascertain[ing] who they were and [restricting] the punishment . . . to them, . . . in that way [establishing] the innocence of the others," who would then be acquitted. Foraker thus made "a resolution directing the Secretary of War to send to the Senate all information in his possession on the subject" upon Congress's reconvening in December."[41]

A furious Roosevelt complied with the Senate request for case documents and testimony, and vigorously defended his decision by insisting that the "evidence proves conclusively that a number of the soldiers engaged in a deliberate and concerted attack, cold blooded as it was cowardly . . . to terrorize the community and to kill or injure men, women and children in their homes and beds or on the streets . . . at an hour of the night when concerted or effective resistance or defense was out of the question and when detection by identification of the criminals in the United States uniform was well nigh impossible."

The president went on: "A blacker [crime] never stained the annals of our army. It has been supplemented by another, only less black, in the shape of a successful conspiracy of silence for the purpose of shielding those who took part in the original conspiracy of murder." He concluded by stating that "men, in the uniform of the United States army, armed with deadly weapons, sworn to uphold the laws of the United States," had "committed or connived at . . . murder. They perverted the power put into their hands to sustain the law into the most deadly violation of the law."[42]

It is hard to imagine more incendiary allegations, particularly in light of the times. An American president, fully aware that countless African Americans had been lynched and otherwise terrorized by night riders since the Civil War, was accusing black soldiers of the same unspeakable crimes committed under the cover of darkness. In answer, Foraker offered a resolution empowering the Committee on Military Affairs to conduct its own independent investigation if deemed necessary upon reviewing the information Roosevelt had submitted; after much debate, it was adopted on January 22, 1907.[43]

Four days later, the already tense relationship between the two Republicans became an irreparable rift. On Saturday evening, the president unexpectedly launched a public personal attack on Foraker over the Brownsville affair at a Gridiron Club dinner. When Roosevelt finished his speech, the Ohio senator rose and responded with identical contempt regarding the chief executive's conduct toward the dismissed black troops. One observer likened the episode to a boxing match, and news of it spread like wildfire.[44]

The *National Tribune* closely followed the Brownsville matter, including publishing a letter in February from a white veteran calling for justice for the dishonorably discharged soldiers. Highly skeptical of their guilt, Captain Peter Shippman of the 113th USCT advocated for an impartial inquiry, thinking "a . . . Dreyfuss [*sic*] conspiracy to rid the Army of the 'despised niggers'" was likely to be found. Through the newspaper, he urged fellow veterans who had been officers in black regiments and witnessed African American soldiers' "courage and valor in battle" to draw upon their military service and associated racial enlightenment in "counteract[ing] the baneful prejudice of low-grade politicians . . . I do not deny but that I am a radical on many issues, the same as I was in 1861 when I shouldered my musket at the call of our sainted Lincoln as a Black Republican Abolitionist, but I had the satisfaction of seeing most of my comrades coming my way of thinking before we got thru with our job. By the way I have never yet seen cause to change my principles."[45]

After a time-consuming investigation, the Committee on Military Affairs in March 1908 decided by a 9–4 vote that black enlisted men were responsible, but those involved could not be identified. The four dissenting Republican senators, including Foraker, issued their own minority report concluding "that the testimony failed to prove anybody in the battalion had participated in the shooting, or was guilty of having entered into a conspiracy of silence to suppress the truth." On April 14, Foraker addressed the senate, masterfully reviewing the case and all related findings, then discussed two bills (one of which he sponsored) that would provide for re-enlistment of the troops.

He ended with a memorable appeal for justice and equality arising from a career in the law, a white Union veteran's remembrance of black comrades' heroism, and the impact of both on what was now taking place:

Who are these men that it should be even suggested that they should be treated worse than common criminals?

They are the direct and worthy successors of the brave men who so heroically died at Petersburg, at Wagner, and on scores of bloody fields that this nation might live.

Faithfully, uncomplainingly, with pride and devotion, they have performed all their duties and kept all their obligations.

They ask no favors because they are Negroes, but only for justice because they are men.[46]

On December 14, the president sent the Senate an unanticipated special message. Roosevelt reported that a detective hired by the War Department had obtained a confession from a former soldier in the Twenty-Fifth Infantry implicating several of its members in the shooting, and "the raid was part of a conspiracy which was formed before the negro troops were sent to Brownsville." The president maintained his rock-solid belief in their collective guilt: "The investigation has not gone far enough to enable us to determine all the facts, and we will proceed with it; but it has gone far enough to determine with sufficient accuracy certain facts of enough importance to make it advisable that I place the report before you."

A livid Foraker delivered a stinging retort excoriating Roosevelt for conducting a "secret" investigation of innocent men while the Senate had not yet finished its own inquest. He made a statement that would prove all too true: "'I am of the opinion that when this thing has been gone to the bottom of, all honest men will be ashamed of it.'"[47]

Two days later, the *Broad Ax* reprinted an editorial from the *Boston Herald* on the president's message that superbly summarized all the investigations conducted to date. As the *Herald* pointed out, if Roosevelt's statement about establishment of the blacks' guilt were true, "'corroborative evidence on that point would now be unnecessary. But the proof has never been produced.'" Copious sworn testimony had been given by the Twenty-Fifth's officers and particular enlisted men before "four different tribunals," with no "warrant for conviction or . . . specific indictment" forthcoming. The local county grand jury "heard the evidence directed against suspected members of the Negro companies," with no bill reported against any man, and two army court-martials "failed to find proof of guilt." After both soldiers and civilians testified under oath before the Senate Committee on Military Affairs, it could not "identify any member of the three companies with the disturbance in Brownsville."

The *Herald* concluded: "Repeated accusation and assertion of the guilt of these soldiers by the President is not equivalent to proof. The dismissal of the Negro troops was an arbitrary act, for which the civil, military and congressional tribunals have failed to find justification."[48]

It hardly went unnoticed in the president's message that he suddenly recommended that Congress pass a law enabling the secretary of war within a year "to reinstate any of these soldiers whom he, after careful examination, finds to have been innocent and . . . to have done all in his power to help bring to justice the guilty." The *Herald* saw this as Roosevelt's apparent recognition of how weak his position had become—why else leave open the possibility of returning to army service men upon whom he "'had already pronounced wholesale condemnation'"?

The newspaper staff called the president's special message "'an extraordinary climax'" to an ongoing miscarriage of justice, with a new whiff of "'manufactured evidence [that] discredits the case of the administration.'" They realized the general public had little concern about justice for the accused black soldiers from the start, "'and influenced by prejudice which has been incited against the senatorial champion of these soldiers, may not be inclined to consider the case on its merits.'" But the *Herald* held out hope that these latest developments might prove helpful to the African Americans' case.[49]

The *Broad Ax* also ran a death notice amplified by the enmity between Roosevelt and African Americans. Having never fully recovered from his wounding at Fort Wagner, Sergeant William H. Carney was discharged from the Fifty-Fourth Massachusetts in June 1864. Marrying the following year, in 1869, he began thirty-two years as a mail carrier in his hometown of New Bedford. Although his actions under fire in South Carolina were the first by an African American soldier deemed worthy of the Medal of Honor, Carney did not receive his country's highest military award until 1900. At sixty-eight, he was working as a messenger at the Massachusetts State House when he died from injuries suffered in an elevator accident, across the street from the marvelous monument that depicts his beloved regiment resolutely marching off to war behind their mounted colonel.

Carney's home state and fellow citizens did not forget what he had done and what he had meant to them. Hundreds paid their respects as he lay in-state, wrapped in an American flag, and Massachusetts lowered flags at all state buildings to half-mast in his honor. Many dignitaries attended Carney's funeral, including his supervisor, Secretary of State William M. Olin, whose office remained closed for the day.

The implications of Carney's life for present events were unmistakable. As the *New York Evening Post* noted, "[the] question of pay for colored troops became as much an issue for Congress as the Brownsville affair is to-day . . . finally, by a special act of Congress, the government abandoned its attempt at discrimination and the men of the Fifty-fourth and all other colored regiments received the full army pay for the full period of their service."[50] Would this scenario of delayed evenhandedness hold for the Twenty-Fifth Infantry?

The year of 1909 was critical in the Brownsville Affray. President-elect William Howard Taft would enter the White House in March, but Roosevelt was not the only renowned Republican leaving office. Four years before direct popular election of senators was established by the Seventeenth Amendment, the Ohio legislature selected Theodore E. Burton over Foraker, effectively ending his political career.[51] But he had two remaining months to officially work in support of the African American soldiers.

Wasting no time, the outgoing senator carefully reviewed information that Secretary of War Wright had submitted concerning the detectives' employment in the ongoing probe, including evidence that his predecessor, Taft, had approved their use and payment. Addressing the Senate on January 12, Foraker accused the president and president-elect of having illegally diverted $15,000 in public funds to pay the private detectives. He characterized both the manner of their compensation and utilization as "'atrocious, revolting and shocking to every sense of fairness, justice and even common decency.'"[52]

Within a month Foraker's unrelenting pressure paid off when Rhode Island Senator Nelson W. Aldrich, a Republican leader and yet another Union veteran, brokered a deal. In exchange for Roosevelt's not having to formally admit being wrong, the Senate would enact a compromise bill enabling most of the dismissed black troops to not only apply for re-enlistment, but receive both accrued back pay and applicable allowances in full. A victory for Foraker and the soldiers, it was reported as such nationwide; after the bill passed the Senate on February 24 and the House three days later, Roosevelt signed it on March 2 in one of his last actions as president.

As finally approved, the bill authorized the secretary of war to appoint a Court of Inquiry consisting of five army officers of at least colonel rank "to hear and report upon all charges and testimony" relating to the Brownville Affray and dismissal of the Twenty-Fifth Infantry's noncommissioned officers and other enlisted men. The court would submit a final report to the secretary within one year regarding "any non-commissioned officer or private" found qualified for re-enlistment, who would then "be considered to have re-enlisted immediately after his discharge," and thus "be entitled, from the date of his discharge . . . to the pay allowances, . . . other rights and benefits that he would have been entitled to receive according to his rank from said date of discharge as if he had been honorably discharged . . . and had re-enlisted immediately."[53]

For Foraker, his triumphant swan song was tinged with melancholy: "I would not have been content with the bill as it passed had it not been that I knew that with my retirement from the Senate no one would remain in either that body or in the House of Representatives who would champion the cause in which I had so long labored."

He realized that anyone without his great knowledge of the case would be unable to master the huge amount of accumulated material, even if they had "time, ability or willingness to undertake" such an endeavor in order to craft a better bill. With respect to the law enacted, Foraker objected that the standard for re-enlistment eligibility was not specified as lack of proven guilt as either perpetrators or accessories after the fact. This left open the possibility that the court would use proof of innocence as its determining criterion; unfortunately, he was prescient in his concern.[54]

African Americans were nonetheless highly relieved at the turn of events, and equally grateful for the Ohioan's struggles against the Roosevelt administration on behalf of the dishonorably discharged battalion. In a splendid article of tribute, the black-owned *Nashville Globe* pinpointed the Affray's deeper meaning, and what they perceived Foraker had accomplished: "He . . . won a fight for the greatest principle underlying American liberty—that of the right of trial before an impartial court by an impartial jury before conviction can be had and punishment inflicted. He waged a struggle for the preservation of the most sacred principle of American jurisprudence which rightly entitles him to the lasting gratitude of every citizen of this country, regardless of race, color or condition."[55]

On March 6, two days after his retirement, Washington's African American community held an evening reception for Foraker. The Metropolitan AME Church was packed, with hundreds more turned away at the door. Presented with a beautiful silver loving cup that a moved Foraker said "'will be cherished in my family forever,'" he told the cheering assemblage of his absolute conviction that not one soldier was guilty, and that his proof of the detectives' testimony having been "deliberately fabricated" motivated the newly ex-president to sign the bill. Of the Affray itself, Foraker said, "'When I sum up my twelve years in the Senate, I find that everything holds a subordinate place in my heart to Brownsville. I waged that fight without stopping to consider the consequences.'"

Engraved inside the two-foot, six-pound loving cup was the last sentence of his April 14, 1908, call for justice in the Senate.[56] Months later he received another treasured memento of appreciation, a "gold watch fob, with a raised inscription depicting the life of Alaskan miners" from black citizens of that American territory.[57]

With Foraker out of the picture, the cashiered soldiers' fates now rested with the court of inquiry investigating the Brownsville Raid for the final time. Not only reinstatement but also the question of guilt for the shootings and alleged cover-up would be determined by the five retired generals (one lieutenant, one major and three brigadiers) selected by Taft's secretary of war, Confederate veteran Jacob M. Dickinson.[58]

Their huge task began in May 1909 and promised to take several months to complete, as 325 people had given sworn statements, and the record included almost nine thousand pages of documents that needed to be reviewed.

In the meantime, the battalion's dismissed soldiers faced a difficult situation. Any applicant for re-enlistment had to testify before the court, and as astutely reported by the *Evening Star* on July 28, would expect to be "closely questioned as to his whereabouts and movements on the night of the raid and his knowledge or lack of knowledge as to the raid and the participants." While financial factors and military status under the bill were certainly inducements, seeking reinstatement was not without risk: "if the pending investigation shows that any one of the soldiers was connected with the midnight raid he will be turned over to the proper authorities for prosecution and punishment."

How many ex-soldiers would come forward was unknown—as the *Star* explained: "It is accepted as an assured fact that no man who actually took part in the raid will jeopardize his safety by voluntarily appearing before the court for examination . . . all the discharged soldiers are beyond the jurisdiction of the court, being no longer in the army." As no inquiry to date had found the battalion innocent of either the shooting or subsequent willful silence, could the court be trusted to render impartial judgment?[59]

By November, Secretary Dickinson had received four partial reports and submitted a progress report of his own to Congress. He informed the House that the court had been able to contact eighty-two of the 167 men who had been discharged, seventy-six of whom wanted to testify and six who didn't. As the court had deemed "it necessary to visit the scene of the shooting affray," Dickinson "directed it to proceed to Brownsville, Tex.," after which its sessions in Washington would recommence, and those men who so wished could "appear before the court."[60]

The *Brownsville Daily Herald* called this a "new exhibition of congressional lenience towards the uniformed criminals who committed the grossest outrage that ever blackened the annals of the United States army." While such a reaction from within the affair's epicenter was hardly unexpected, other whites in the South were just as angry.

The *Herald* quoted extensively from the *San Antonio Light*, which blamed the entire investigation on Foraker and unnamed congressional supporters and expressed concern the inquiry might "restore to the United States army some of the red-handed murderers who assassinated Frank Natus and attempted to massacre women and children in Brownsville," further enhancing the Twenty-Fifth's "blot of infamy."[61] The court convened in Texas at the end of November and began to take testimony.[62]

On April 6, 1910, based on the previous record and an additional several thousand pages of testimony gathered as part of the new inquiry, the court released its findings. In a unanimous opinion, it reported the totality of evidence sustained the black soldiers' guilt on charges by Brownsville's mayor and other citizens of having shot into occupied homes in their town, killing one man, maiming another, and fatally wounding his horse.

In addition, the court found (with one dissent) the regiment's officers negligent "in not performing their duties properly, immediately prior to the affray, and in not ordering an inspection of the regiment immediately after the raid on the town, instead of at daylight, several hours later." The generals asserted that if an immediate inspection had been carried out, "several of the culprits would have been discovered. In addition, if the officers had performed their duty properly before the raid, the affray could not have occurred," in the opinion of the court.

In light of the verdict, an additional court finding was astounding. In a 3–2 opinion, the generals recommended fourteen of the battalion's dishonorably discharged enlisted men for re-enlistment under the terms set out by Congress, although no explanation was given as to why these men, and no others, were selected. As specified by the act creating the court of inquiry, its findings were final, with the secretary of war responsible for carrying out its recommendations.[63]

On February 21, 1911, the War Department reported that all of the soldiers singled out by the court of inquiry had been reenlisted, the Senate passing an accompanying resolution later that day. Three days later, acting secretary of war Robert Shaw Oliver submitted their names to the Senate, officially ending the Brownsville Affray.[64]

A few years later, the *Sun* would somehow declare the disgraceful affair "a blessing in disguise" for the fourteen reinstated soldiers, each of whom "must regard himself as a Croesus, if he has not already dissipated the bounty bestowed upon him by a just Government." Reporting their accumulated back pay ranged from $1,289.75 to $2,419.65, the New York newspaper saw enlisted men as spendthrifts in general, but singled out African American soldiers as "the most impecunious" due to being "born gamblers."

Presuming that relatively few of the battalion's dismissed men were "actually guilty of the atrocity," the *Sun*'s staff gave the court of inquiry credit for "listen[ing] to the pleas of the applicants" and becoming convinced that those reinstated had no complicity, "either as principals or as accessories." As for their comrades, "Some of the innocent are dead; others, no doubt, are still recorded as discharged without honor, being too ignorant to avail themselves of the chance of vindication. We trust that none of the guilty is in the honor and back pay list."[65]

Not surprisingly, Joseph B. Foraker saw it differently, characterizing the court of inquiry's work as "shameful." Nine years removed from the night of violence that ended in death and debility, and ruined scores of lives, his fury had not abated: "I [don't] doubt if the Government had spent the one-tenth part to discover the men who shot up Brownsville that it did spend to convict its innocent soldiers of a crime they never committed, the truth would have been easily and long ago established."[66]

But the final curtain had not rung down just yet on the Brownsville Affair. There were two more scenes to be acted out, one of retribution at the time, and another of vindication more than half a century later, long after the controversy had been forgotten.[67]

As we have seen, the gulf between Booker T. Washington and W. E. B. Du Bois was already ample, but Roosevelt's actions throughout the Affray had rendered it even wider. Du Bois was outspokenly critical of the president, and in September 1908, cited Brownsville as a major reason why African Americans should not vote Republican in the upcoming elections. Washington anticipated such trouble—as reported by John D. Weaver, in 1906 he initiated steps to prevent 500,000 black voters in the North from abandoning the Republican party due to revulsion over the soldiers' cashiering. These measures involved Washington's use of his status with Roosevelt and other prominent whites as the nation's foremost African American leader as leverage "to pressure a great many black editors into soft-pedaling the Brownsville issue."

In reality, there wasn't much choice between the white supremacist Democrats (who nominated William Jennings Bryan) and the increasingly racially neglectful Republicans. While there was more black opposition to Taft than any prior GOP presidential candidate, likely due in significant part to the Affray, the African American vote still swung Republican along with whites at the polls.[68]

But when the party split into progressive and conservative factions led respectively by Roosevelt and Taft during the latter's administration, the Affray became a major concern for Republicans. In November 1910, America's most controversial black individual spoke in New York for the United Colored Democracy on the topic, "'Roosevelt was not present to help the colored race at the Brownsville affair; now we ain't here to help Roosevelt.'"

The lecturer was World Heavyweight Champion Jack Johnson, the first man of color to hold that title. Refusing to accept any restrictions due to blackness, he flouted the era's racial mores by openly romancing and marrying white women, his flamboyance and utter lack of humbleness antithetical to what Americans expected of Negroes. The hatred Johnson aroused fueled the ongoing search for a "Great White Hope," Caucasian America's hostility mounting as he easily dispatched each one in turn. He also made many African Americans uncomfortable—Booker T. Washington was proud that the world's greatest heavyweight was black but dismayed it was someone like Johnson.[69]

New Yorkers of color immediately tried to counteract the Champ's support for Democrats by holding a rally of their own in Brooklyn, praising Roosevelt's civil rights record, but most African Americans were not buying it. When Taft's black supporters later attempted to use the Affray against Roosevelt to gain votes in the 1912 primaries, citation of the president's statements about Brownsville while secretary of war were devastating. Believing each to be equally culpable in cashiering innocent African American soldiers, blacks turned away from Taft and Roosevelt (running as an independent Bull Moose) in an unprecedented bloc vote for Democrats, including presidential candidate and eventual winner, Woodrow Wilson.

As the *Broad Ax* observed, "The independent and progressive Afro-American voters without any doubt about it remembered Theodore Roosevelt and President William Howard Taft and their connection with the 'Brownsville affair,'. . . [and] dealt them a body and a knockout blow in their necks on the day of the election."[70] An episode that would fade into oblivion had changed the political landscape of the United States.

The inexorable passage of time was transforming the country in other ways. The men who had provided vital support for African Americans since the 1860s, and their principal fraternal association, were diminishing in political power and sheer numbers. However, Union veterans of both races still possessed individual and collective influence, and strove to sustain their relevance and the country's memory in the new century. In that effort, the man who had risen the highest in the GAR among all his maimed brothers was afforded the perfect venue and opportunity.

A LEFT-ARMED LUMINARY SPEAKS OUT
FOR FREEDOM AND EQUALITY

Amid the Left-Armed Corps' outstanding participation, service, and achievement in the Grand Army, no one ranked William M. Bostaph. In August 1909, he was elected senior vice commander in chief of the nearly quarter million member organization at its national encampment in Salt Lake City. Of his special welcome home, the *Ogden Standard* reported that the Chamber of Commerce's honor reception was a smashing success, "and it seemed as though the entire population of Ogden turned out to greet the distinguished man."

Bostaph was unable to address the crowd until its long and loud cheering subsided. Then the former Pennsylvania farmer who went to war at sixteen and lost the use of his right arm before his eighteenth birthday, only to become one of the nation's finest hydraulic engineers, seized the moment with an extraordinary speech.

He traced the country's history of slavery ("*various compromises were proposed, all of which served to postpone rather than settle the controversy between the slave and free states*"), including its misconstruing the Declaration of Independence "'*to mean white men only,*'" the detested *Dred Scott* decision, *Uncle Tom's Cabin,* and Lincoln's election. Bostaph then spoke of the war, stalemated until the twin victories at Gettysburg and Vicksburg "'*turned the tide,*'" leading to Appomattox "'*and the total destruction of organized resistance to the authority of the United States government.*'"

But the work of Northern veterans was far from finished, as anyone who joined the Grand Army had to not only have served honorably in the US military, but also done

> "*all in his power to crush secession, restore the Union of the United States and strike the shackles from three million men and women then held in bondage, and restore to them their God-given right to life and liberty, and write a new legend on the glorious Star and Stripes— that of liberty and union forever, and absolute equality before the law to all men, black as well as white.*"

> "*No man can occupy a position so high as to admit him into the Grand Army of the Republic without these qualifications, and none is so humble that, possessing them, can or will be excluded.*"

The men of the Union, white and black, had both a legacy and admonition to impart:

> "*Those who form the membership of the Grand Army of the Republic . . . deliver* [the flag] *to you as the emblem of equal rights wherever its folds are unfurled, but, in doing so, admonish you that eternal vigilance is the price of liberty, and warn you that vigilance once relaxed will soon lead to where liberty is but a name.*"

At age sixty-four, Bostaph felt the pangs of collective mortality ("'*one by one our comrades are passing behind the veil that separates time from eternity"*), but also pride of accomplishment and *"'confidence into the future and see this great nation still greater, . . . and when the heat of passion engendered in that great struggle of '61–5 shall have passed away, then and not till then, let the epitaph of the Grand Army . . . be written, and we feel assured . . . it will be a just one.'"*[71]

In troubled times, the GAR's second in command not only depicted the causes for which more than two million men had fought but also emphasized both the profound meaning of Union victory and the responsibility of Americans living and not yet born to ensure that what war and decades of peace had accomplished would be sustained and built upon.

Bostaph's unwavering commitment to freedom and equality for all the country's citizens and protection of their waning legacy was matched by the Grand Army's rank and file, as would be shown in a controversy that raged throughout 1910. The firestorm centered on the Confederacy's shining paladin and had enduring ramifications that have recently taken center stage, but the details and full story have essentially been lost to history

THE LEE CONUNDRUM

Of all the myths about the Civil War and its aftermath, perhaps the most problematic involve Robert E. Lee, general in chief of the armies of the Confederate states. The saint-like veneration in which he continues to be held in many quarters, and his place among American icons,[72] directly affects how the men who served the Union are regarded, as the following account illustrates:

> I felt coming in on me a strange sense of some presence invisible but powerful—like those unearthly visitants told of in ancient story, charged with supernal message. Disquieted, I turned about, and there behind me, riding in between my two lines, appeared a commanding form, superbly mounted, richly accoutred, of imposing bearing, noble countenance, with expression of deep sadness overmastered by deeper strength. It is no other than Robert E. Lee! And seen by me for the first time within my own lines. I sat immovable, with a certain awe and admiration.[73]

Its author was not a Lost Cause zealot, slavery advocate or Southerner. Portraying Lee on his way to surrender to Grant was Major General Joshua Lawrence Chamberlain, the young Bowdoin College professor of rhetoric and modern languages who went to war while on sabbatical,[74] and became one of the Army of the Potomac's finest officers. Chamberlain was awarded the Medal of Honor for his leadership of the Twentieth Maine's resolute defense of Little Round Top at Gettysburg, and prematurely given last rites when terribly wounded at Petersburg, Virginia. By April 1865, he had become so esteemed that he was chosen to receive the Army of Northern Virginia's formal surrender.[75]

Lee was indeed an impressive figure, and his personal magnetism was undeniable. However, here is a highly decorated Union general officer who almost died in a war to defeat the Confederacy, invoking the supernatural in describing the commander of the army whom he had so courageously opposed. This was not unlike Grant's recounting of the surrender at Appomattox, in which he called Lee a "man of much dignity" who "was dressed in a full uniform which was entirely new," while the general in chief of all US Armies was in his "rough traveling suit, the uniform of a private with the straps of a lieutenant-general, I must have contrasted very strangely with a man so handsomely dressed, six feet high and of faultless form. But this was not a matter that I thought of until afterwards."[76]

What is missing from these glowing depictions is the stark reality that Lee, son of a Revolutionary War hero and governor of Virginia, nephew of a signer of the Declaration of Independence, and husband of a great-granddaughter of Martha Washington, was ultimately defeated by a tanner's son in muddy boots leading an army of soldiers held in contempt by Lee's own men.

Alan T. Nolan examined the symbiotic relationship between the celebrated general and his government, and why both were doomed: "In sum, Lee entered and fought the war with sectional partisanship, a Southern aristocrat's feeling about the inferiority of Northern people, a zealous commitment to the Southern cause as truly just, anger over the North's conduct of the war, and a belief in slavery."[77]

What of Lee and the Union serviceman? Fresh off their greatest victory at Chancellorsville, Lee wrote of his Army of Northern Virginia in May 1863: "There never were such men—in any army before, & there never can be better in any army again. If properly led, they will go anywhere & never falter at the work before them."[78]

Lee's uncanny ability to take the measure of opposing generals apparently led him to underestimate the Army of the Potomac, mistaking poor command leadership for deficiencies in the men themselves. As his army marched toward Pennsylvania for a fateful encounter with its nemesis, Lee's misappraisal of the Northern soldier would prove disastrous for the Confederacy. At Gettysburg one army was indeed "properly led" to victory, but its men wore blue. It is quite possible, indeed likely, that Lee neither understood the Union citizen soldier, who differed from his men in many ways, nor what they had come to represent.

Conversely, how did Northern veterans regard him at war's end? A newly unearthed document published in the March 1866 edition of *The Soldier's Friend* provides an intriguing insight. In Washington the month before, the Soldiers' and Sailors' National Union League "unanimously adopted, with great applause," a preamble and four resolutions about Lee. Believing they spoke for their comrades, the veteran organization expressed their views on the man who personified the Confederacy. They wanted Lee tried for treason, flatly denouncing him as a traitor to the United States and its flag, and an enemy of African Americans; vehemently objected to the idea of returning to Lee any portion of Arlington, which had become the nation's military cemetery; and held him in part responsible for the treatment of Union prisoners.[79]

Just or not in all its claims, the contemporary opinions of a large group of Union veterans on the Army of Northern Virginia commander and Confederate general in chief could not be plainer. Unlike some of their officers, men who had fought the Rebels on thousands of battlefields over four years were not inclined to be professionally forgiving when it came to Robert E. Lee. Moreover, their national organization's statement of February 1866 is strikingly discordant with prevalent modern concepts about him.

Further contrary to popular belief, Lieutenant General Robert E. Lee did not automatically transform into the Lost Cause's incarnation immediately after his death in 1870. As Thomas L. Connelly observed, prior to 1890, Marse Robert "was not yet what he would become, the almost godlike hero of the South. Nor was he yet considered a national symbol of the nobility of the Southern experience." However, over the next two decades that would change dramatically: "By 1910 he was a national hero."[80]

However, many Northerners tended to tread lightly over the Lee legend even before then. In 1889 the *National Tribune* strongly opposed Southern states (including Georgia, whose House had just passed a bill) making his birthday a legal holiday. The newspaper noted that both Lee's education and antebellum life as "a sworn officer of the United States Army" had been supported "at the public expense." However, "unlike [George H.] Thomas, [David] Farragut and many other Southern men, he violated his oath and became the chief leader of the insurgent forces in the most stupendous fratricidal war of modern times."[81]

At the same time, the *Tribune* celebrated "The purity of Gen. Lee's private character and the nobility of his personality [which] will never be questioned. His bravery and soldierly qualities will go down in history unblemished."[82]

In January 1903, a bill was proposed in the Pennsylvania House to create a state commission for a Lee equestrian statue that would be permanently placed at Gettysburg. However, the deal would be negated unless an appropriation of $20,000 from the Keystone State was similarly approved by Virginia and a matching commission established by its legislature.

Opposition quickly arose within and outside of the Pennsylvania government. Numerous Grand Army posts across the state reviled the bill and its possible (if highly unlikely) passage. The legislation's champion, Alexander K. McClure, who was representing Gettysburg in the state Senate when war broke out and later became a noted author and journalist, was not surprised by the extent of negative veteran reaction. He attributed their disapproval to having "erroneously accepted the measure as an intended honor to General Lee and his cause," rather than what he claimed was the bill's true purpose: "[T]he proposed monument is intended to give historic value to the most memorable battlefield of the country, and to present General Lee as one of the many heroic chieftains of both sides who are illustrious representatives of American valor."

After asserting three-fourths of letters "from Pennsylvania soldiers of distinction" favored the bill, McClure oddly chose to quote former GAR commander in chief Robert B. Beath, who "doubtless expresses the views of the great majority of our veterans": "'General Lee is certainly entitled to honor among his own people as their great war leader; he is entitled to great honor, in my opinion, for his stand against guerrilla warfare when the battling was over, and for the highly dignified course he pursued after the war until the day of his death—still, I think a statue at Gettysburg out of place.'"[83]

Another ex-Union general from Pennsylvania strongly disputed those who adamantly opposed the monument. As quoted in the South Carolina *Anderson Intelligencer*, W. W. H. Davis wholeheartedly supported the project: "'*Why, of course, build a monument to Lee. He was a great soldier and the country will be proud of him. The time will come when there will be no distinction between the soldiers of the North and South who fought in the civil war.*'"[84]

This opinion was consistent with Davis's open disdain for racial advances associated with the war, his minimizing differences between North and South, and an action he took that Union veterans overall had long resisted. At the Southern Industrial Convention of 1901 in Philadelphia, he returned to the Charleston delegation a Confederate naval flag captured in 1864 while he was commanding the federal troops on Morris Island.[85]

But just as they showed in 1866, former Northern servicemen were hardly in thrall to Lee or his growing mythical status. In 1902 the *National Tribune* published a nauseating, revelatory eye-witness account by Captain R. K. Beecham of the Iron Brigade's Second Wisconsin, in which he described events that followed his capture during the Army of Northern Virginia's 1863 campaign in Pennsylvania.

Over several days, around fifty African Americans were held under their own guard in close proximity to the white prisoners of war. Noting the lack of black soldiers in the Army of the Potomac or supporting units at the time, Beecham could not state with any certainty whether the captive men of color were associated with the Union military: "I only know that they were Lee's prisoners." He warned "that what I am about to relate is true, although it was so utterly devoid of humanity and so unnecessary and uncalled for that its truth may be doubted . . . [T]wo or three times beeves were killed by the guards, of which we received a portion of the meat, but to these black men they gave only the offal . . . on [which they had] . . . to subsist or starve. Was there any excuse for this? Oh yes; the same excuse that in the 'befo' the wah' days was an excuse for every act of inhumanity; a justification for every crime in the category against the black race—they were only 'niggahs.'"[86] Captain Beecham's report is consistent with recent scholarship verifying that African Americans (both those born free and former slaves) were taken captive by Lee's army during its Gettysburg campaign.[87]

Ironically, a law enacted during the Civil War would give Union veterans their last, best chances to individually and collectively express their feelings about Lee, in particular, and the Confederacy, in general. Under legislation passed on July 2, 1864, the National Statuary Hall was established, and the president empowered to ask every state to provide up to two statues, marble or bronze, "of deceased persons who have been citizens thereof, and illustrious for their historic renown or for distinguished civic or military services such as each State may deem to be worthy of this national commemoration." These would be placed in the House of Representatives' Old Hall in the Capitol.[88]

When Congress enacted the law, and Lincoln signed it, no one could have dreamed how one leading Southern state would ultimately choose to fulfill its sculpture allotment. In January 1903, Virginia state senator, Don P. Halsey, proposed a bill that would commission a new statue of Robert E. Lee for inclusion in Statuary Hall, joining the bust of George Washington already in place. In anticipation of the bill's passage, Virginia's House delegation and other Southern representatives planned to meet with Secretary of State Hay to ascertain whether the law allowed

Congress to reject a state's presented statue if the federal government objected to the individual portrayed.[89]

The bill, though well received by Virginians, was not uniformly praised statewide. An unenthusiastic *Richmond Times* reported a "diversion of opinion as to the expediency of such a step . . . at present" and expressed its concern that Northerners would think the Old Dominion was "trying to force General Lee upon them." The paper then added a rather peculiar reservation: "Our only fear is that some day the North will appropriate him, as it has appropriated George Washington. Robert E. Lee is Virginia's hero, and the South's hero, and we are unwilling even to divide honors with the North."[90]

Two days later, an aghast *National Tribune* dispelled any such apprehensions. Reporting work would begin on the Robert E. Lee sculpture once Virginia's legislature appropriated the funds, the newspaper's staff emphatically stated how they viewed the possibility that an individual whose fame derived from "efforts to destroy the Government" could have his statue "placed in the National Capitol alongside those of Washington, Jefferson, Webster, Grant, and Lincoln, who labored so hard and well to save the country and build it up to greatness. Lee . . . among those patriots would be a desecration which would ruin the value of the Nation's Hall of Fame."[91]

But the law was open to interpretation, and the nation's capital was soon abuzz in discussion. The *Richmond Dispatch*, *Alexandria Gazette*, and *National Tribune* all carried stories on the precedent involving Wisconsin's presentation of a statue of Father Jacques Marquette. While the famous missionary and explorer who discovered the Mississippi River along with his partner Louis Joliet was welcomed by the Senate and his sculpture accepted, neither occurred in the House due to Pere Marquette's depiction in clerical garb. The American Protestant Association (APA) objected and attempted to have the statue (which had remained under a cloth) removed from the Capitol. Heated discussions between Catholics and the APA ensued, with Marquette's statue remaining in Statuary Hall without ever being formally recognized by Congress.[92]

Two weeks after its first report, the *National Tribune*'s disgust had not lessened, as it flatly stated that to place Lee's likeness in Statuary

Hall "would give [it] a new character entirely, and . . . make it a shrine for those who worship the Lost Cause. The thought is intolerable."[93] Not surprisingly, reaction to the issue from Union veterans and their supporters was swift in coming.

At the first annual encampment held after Virginia's proposed action, the Department of the Potomac unanimously adopted a resolution of protest against "'one of the chief exemplars of treason [being] exalted in high places.'" During its simultaneous convention in mid-February, the Department's WRC endorsed several resolutions against "desecration of the National Capitol," asking "every Department in the United States [to] adopt similar ones and protest to the members in Congress."[94]

The women of the department were even more vehement in their denunciation than its men. Like the *National Tribune* in 1889, the WRC disparaged Lee for breaching his constitutional oath and more than three decades of receiving "sustenance and support" from the United States while wearing its uniform, and also accused him of setting an example of disloyalty for two hundred other West Point–educated officers to follow.

As for Lee's postwar record, they noted that he never "uttered a word that expressed regret or sorrow for his acts of desertion and treason." While bearing "no malice toward a single survivor of the men in rebellion" and having "the tenderest charity for all," the WRC would never "consent to have treason thus condoned, and disloyalty thus exalted and glorified, for the emulation of generations yet unborn."[95]

During an evening commemoration of Lincoln's birthday (February 12), a former congressman addressed his Logan Regiment comrades in the Union Veterans' Union. Colonel Henry G. Worthington reviled the Lee statue offer, feeling that "the ghost of countless thousands of Union soldiers would rise from their graves in silent protest if such a proposition were carried out," an opinion unanimously endorsed by all attendees.[96]

Despite such passionate objections, on February 14, the Virginia Senate passed Halsey's bill by a 32–2 vote, along with legislation to fund the Lee statue. Yet within a week the upsurge of stinging opposition from Union veterans across the Potomac and nationwide could not be ignored in the former Confederate capital. Richmond's own *Times Dispatch* reported "that Republican members of Congress from States of the North and West are being overwhelmed with protests. These come from Grand Army of the Republic organizations and from individuals. A member told me today he had no idea that sentiment against the proposition was so strong."[97]

On March 5, the bill was passed by the Virginia General Assembly on a 44–7 tally, with no debate. Noting how much resentment had already been provoked, the *Evening Star* accurately predicted, "While the act of placing the statue will be many months, possibly several years off, inasmuch as the statue must be determined upon, there is every prospect that [a revival of] vigorous opposition will be aroused."[98]

Two weeks later, critics of the Lee statue proposal received backing from an unlikely source. Although under state statute it would become law anyway within five days, Virginia governor A. J. Montague declined to sign the Halsey bill. Believing that if Lee were alive, "'he would be more opposed . . . than anyone else. General Lee did not need any such monument, and it ought not to be forced against any such considerable opposition as has developed. No man admires General Lee more than I, but I regard this effort to honor him as unnecessary, unwise and inexpedient.'"[99]

Before the congressional session ended in March, Midwestern House members had their say. Kansas Representative Charles Curtis called placement of Lee's statue in the Hall "'a disgrace . . . I will not sanction an official honor for a traitor,'" with his delegation colleague James M. Miller in full agreement. Representative Henry A. Cooper of Wisconsin thought it ill-advised to pay tribute to an individual "who had tried to destroy the government."[100]

Two other Republican congressmen from the heartland, both Civil War veterans, invoked the North's most iconic and controversial antislavery figure. Iowa representative John F. Lacey caustically suggested that "the next thing . . . the Virginia Legislature will be wanting to put in the Capitol [are] statues of the Captors of John Brown under the guise of their having performed a 'patriotic service.'" Going one step further, Representative Edgar Weeks of Michigan proposed a bill based on "'the

State of Virginia and other Southern States . . . [having been] . . . particularly benefited by [Brown's] disinterested and philanthropic career in behalf of the oppressed.'"

On that basis, Weeks resolved "'That a statue of John Brown of Osawatomie, Kan., in marble or bronze, with appropriate pedestal, be erected in or upon the United States Custom-House and Post-office Building or grounds in the city of Richmond, in the State of Virginia.'"[101]

According to the *National Tribune*, Democratic representative Harry L. Maynard of Virginia demonstrated "how the shoe fits when on the other foot" when he took umbrage to the proposed resolution of his colleague from across the aisle: "'The State and people of Virginia would resent and resist in every possible way the accomplishment of the plan outlined by the gentleman from Michigan and the men whom he doubtless represents.'"[102]

Maynard may have lacked a sense of the absurd, but this was a dead serious business. Union veteran John Q. Evans of the Fifth Wisconsin asked in the *National Tribune*, "'If the statue of Gen. Robert E. Lee is placed in the National Capitol, would it not be appropriate to place two others—one of Benedict Arnold, the other of Judas Iscariot?'"[103]

Work related to the Lee statue (sculptor Edward V. Valentine being contracted; establishing an oversight commission for it and a replica of Houdon's Washington; making appropriations for both) progressed in Virginia[104] while fierce opposition to its being on display in the Capitol continued unabated. Over the next several months Grand Army posts in various states adopted strong resolutions of dissent, as did the Departments of West Virginia and Kansas at their annual encampments, and the Kansas WRC at its yearly convention.[105]

Despite this, in May the *Washington Times* claimed that resistance to the Lee statue was waning, and supported its position by anonymously quoting a former GAR commander who "'fail[ed] to see why Virginia should not erect the statue'": "'Forty years have passed since the civil war, and the wounds have nearly all healed. The war with Spain solidified the country. Let it remain that way. If Virginia intends to honor her great son, the Grand Army should not try to oppose her . . . Scores of former Confederates have been sent to the Senate and House by their States.'"[106]

One month later, the *Guthrie Daily Leader* in Oklahoma perceived a completely different situation taking shape in Washington. According to the paper, it was a certainty that some action regarding the statue would take place at the annual encampment in San Francisco. This was due to "various state commanders of the loyal legion and different Grand Army posts . . . adopting resolutions of state condemning the proposition of Virginia and vigorously protesting against the Lee memorial," all "addressed to the commander in chief . . . and . . . intended to be brought up for consideration during the encampment."[107]

On July 9, the *Minneapolis Journal* ran a similar story about the upcoming August encampment. The paper reported as "practically settled" that the Grand Army would petition Congress to amend the 1864 law "by providing that no statue shall ever be installed there of a man who has borne arms against his country." The *Journal* forecast that the resolution to be adopted would "be couched in temperate language, but there will be no mistaking its purpose or the seriousness of the old soldiers in passing it."

According to leading GAR members in Minneapolis, "resolutions against the Lee statue have been passed by practically every post and commandery of the Loyal Legion." As all Grand Army delegates who would be in San Francisco had received copies, "The demand upon the encampment for action . . . will be so strong that it cannot be resisted."[108]

Yet it was, as no protesting resolution was adopted in San Francisco. As reported by the *Washington Times*, "a large number of the delegates to the encampment declared against interfering with Virginia's selection, and the question was not raised."[109] Despite all efforts by its own membership and the MOLLUS, the leading Union veteran organization somehow refused to take a stand on the Lee statue.

Unlike the Grand Army, another national association of Northern ex-servicemen had no such qualms. Two months after the GAR encampment, the Union Veteran Legion closed out its annual meeting in Dayton, Ohio, by adopting "a resolution bitterly protesting against and denouncing the plan of placing a statue of Gen. Robert E. Lee in the Hall of Fame." As the *Saint Paul Globe* further noted, "The resolutions assert that such an act would be an insult to the Union soldiers now living and to the memory of soldiers dead."[110]

The very next day, news came that led the *Washington Times* to expect that "opposition to the acceptance of the statue will become more pronounced than ever." As commission chairman, state Senator Halsey verified that a statue design with Lee clad in a Confederate general's uniform had been accepted. In a display of mind-boggling logic, Halsey justified the commission's decision on the basis of Lee having earned "favorite son" status with Virginians through Confederate military service, because without this, Lee's "one other claim to fame," serving Washington and Lee University president postwar, would have been inadequate for his selection for Statuary Hall placement.[111]

The year 1903 closed as it began, with Grand Army members voicing their hostility toward Lee being honored at the national Capitol. To a man, the Frank Reed Post of Tuscola, Illinois, adopted a resolution in protest, asking their congressman "to use his vote and influence against it."[112] That would be Vespasian Warner, who entered the Union Army as a private in June 1861 and left it as a brevet major five years later. In 1905, the Harvard-educated lawyer would become commissioner of pensions;[113] like his Republican colleagues Lacey and Weeks, Warner should possess a comrade's awareness of the depth of Union veteran opposition to the Lee statue.

With that the controversy went dormant in the North, only to re-emerge several years later with an accompanying ferocity that would dwarf what had previously occurred.

Fred C. Barger—1865 Cartes de Visite. CHAUTAUQUA COUNTY
HISTORICAL SOCIETY, WESTFIELD, NEW YORK.

CHAPTER 10

The Lee Statue

The Grand Army's Last Stand

I [mean] . . . *no unkindness, but to protest against blending in the minds of present and coming generations ideas of right, of wrong, loyalty, disloyalty, patriotism and treason, in an indistinguishable mass. Each of them has a distinct and totally different meaning, and they should never be confused. The men who saved the Union are in a class by themselves.*

—Brevet Major Fred C. Barger, Forty-
Ninth New York, June 30, 1915[1]

In August 1909, the *National Tribune* ran two stories that took months to fully sink in among Union veterans. The first announced the Lee statue's completion and that Virginia would request its formal acceptance for display along with the Washington figure; two weeks later the *Tribune* reported the placement of both inside Statuary Hall. Robert E. Lee in full Confederate dress uniform was now within a few yards of Generals James Shields (Illinois) and Phil Kearney (New Jersey) clad in Union blue, while the Washington statue replaced the "old plaster cast" that had held its place. The bronze Virginians were mounted on marble, Lee towering over the first president, despite their actual disparity in height.[2]

The *National Tribune* kept its readers apprised of new developments. On December 16, it reported that the John Brown Anniversary Celebration adopted a resolution for placing a statue of their namesake next to Lee's, as "'there should also be one of the liberator of the colored race.'" The paper also noted that Virginia, having "called off all her arrangements for the dedication and acceptance of the statue," was indicative that a Confederate-clad figure in the Hall of Heroes was unlikely to receive official consent.[3]

With the statue now ensconced in Washington, Grand Army headquarters and newspapers nationwide were inundated by denunciations from individual Union veterans and posts. In mid-January, the *Elmira Star-Gazette* reported an Illinois post scornfully adopted resolutions asking President Taft to place "a statue of Benedict Arnold, robed in British uniform" in Statuary Hall so "'that future generations may revere his name and enshrine in their hearts fond recollection of his patriotism and love of country.'"[4] When the *National Tribune* noted two weeks later that a reader wanted New York to force the issue by submitting an Arnold statue, the newspaper icily commented that, unlike Lee's figure, it was "unthinkable that Congress would permit . . . ['that traitor's effigy'] to stand one hour inside the Capitol walls."[5]

The *Tribune*'s staff had already made its position explicit by comparing Virginia's push for official acceptance of the Lee statue to the prewar South's insistence on "cramming [slavery] down the throats of those who did not like it and making all of the rest of the country virtually slave States."[6] Publishing correspondence and news from around the United States, the *National Tribune* was a prime outlet for Northern veterans' wrath.

Its January 27 edition contained typical examples of the fury Lee's statue unleashed. A former serviceman whose Illinois post was dead set against the figure wondered "why should we not also have Forrest, the murderer, and Wirz, the inhuman keeper of Andersonville, in the Capitol?" At the same time, an Oregon post formally protested to their senators and representatives that they vote against the statue being accepted.[7]

By mid-March, the *Tribune* reported that GAR posts throughout the Union had been protesting, as "condemnation of the comrades . . . swift and their action emphatic." The newspaper well summarized the resolutions so far adopted, and outlined its plans for keeping veterans informed by printing them as fast as they could.

While preferring to publish all of the resolutions "in full, because they are so filled with the old-time fire and vigor of the men who preserved the Nation," it was impossible due to their general length. With that in mind, the *Tribune*'s staff provided an enlightening characterization of the one aspect in which they were "all very much alike": "They consider that treason once is treason always, and that a man who would have destroyed the Flag and the Nation the Flag represented can never under any condition or circumstance have his name, character and reputation purged of that one treasonable fact."[8]

A typical series of such resolutions were adopted on March 18 by Lafayette Post No. 140 in New York City, commanded by Fred C. Barger of the Left-Armed Corps. While *"with a soldier's appreciation of the valor of our late opponents in arms, and with the earnest wish that we may all as brethren dwell together in unity,"* the membership strongly objected to an obliteration of *"the distinction between 'loyalty' and 'disloyalty' by placing on the same plane the service of those who fought to destroy and the service of those who fought to save the Nation."* To ensure their views were known, copies of the preamble and all resolutions under Barger's signature were to *"be forthwith sent"* to all of the following: *"the Commander-in-Chief of the G.A.R., the Department Commander of this and every other State, to each Post in this State, to the President and Vice President of the United States, to the Speaker of the House of Representatives and to each* [New York] *member of Congress,"* with additional copies provided *"to the daily press of this city and to such portion of the press of the country as the Commander may designate."*[9]

The enduring influence of Union veterans was demonstrated by the first formal federal government action taken in response to their outrage. On March 31, Massachusetts Senator Henry Cabot Lodge presented a petition from forty Grand Army posts in his state opposing congressional acceptance of the statue, with Lee characterized as "'a traitor whose name should not be mentioned save with contempt.'" Their opinion was shared by comrades throughout the nation, such as the Merriam Post in Connecticut that could not "find words to express its abhorrence of a man of his standing and education and fine character, who should so far forget himself as to turn traitor to the country that had made him what he was."[10]

Besides enabling Grand Army members to publicly express their opposition, the *National Tribune* was a trusted source for breaking news about the Lee statue. At the end of March, the newspaper quoted speeches by two past commanders in chief that signaled the rank and file's advocacy would face stiff resistance. Samuel S. Burdett was against the statue's removal, which he feared "'would light a flame that would set our whole firmament on fire.'" This was a legitimate concern, but his reconciliation-tinted and historically questionable comments, and expressed lack of understanding of objections to Lee, were galling for Union veterans: "'He was the second great figure in the greatest epoch this country or the world has ever seen. I have never believed that Lee's heart was in the fight on the side where he offered himself. He was the victim of a cult which had taught the Southern people that there was not and should not be a Nation, but that to the State the supreme allegiance belonged.'"[11]

At the same Boston meeting, Corporal Tanner defended the statue's remaining in the Hall for a different reason: "'It is the law, and we who imperiled our lives in defense of law will do nothing but talk in opposition to its enforcement, whether we agree to it or not. Lee's statue makes no motion; but as it stands there it is an eternal witness of the power, the magnanimity and glory of the great Nation which he tried to destroy and failed. And so I say let it stand.'"[12]

But Northern ex-servicemen were in no mood to allow others to act as if empowered to convey opinions on their behalf. In March, New York Central Railroad president Robert Brown told an Iowa Society of New York dinner audience that, on behalf of 78,000 Hawkeye veterans, "'I wish to say that not one of them would ever raise his voice to prevent the placing of the Lee statue in Statuary Hall.'" This statement drew an immediate response from the *National Tribune*, who wondered "where Mr. Brown gained the right to speak for the splendid Iowa soldiers who made such a magnificent record for the State during the war . . . his utterance was entirely gratuitous and uncalled for."[13]

When they read the *Tribune*'s report and editorial refutation of Brown's remarks, "loyal veterans, as well as the patriotic citizens of

Iowa" were outraged. On April 28, the newspaper reprinted an open letter to Brown from Robert Kissick of Phil Kearny Post No. 40 in Oskaloosa. Referring directly to the *National Tribune*'s article, the post's patriotic instructor and survivor of three years of war asked the railroad executive, "'who authorized you to make such an untruthful statement? Where did you get the information to base your statement on? Were you an Iowa soldier? If so, please give me your company and regiment?'"

Standing on his "nearly 30 years" of intimate identification with the Grand Army of Iowa, Kissick believed he could "'truthfully say that substantially all the veterans of the State are opposed to a statue of Lee being in the Hall of Fame at Washington. I do not know of one favoring it being there. My Post . . . the second largest in the State, is making an effort to have the Congress condemn and remove the statue from the National Capitol.'"[14]

As for Lee himself, Kissick ensured that Robert Brown and anyone else who read the letter knew exactly where he and his comrades stood: "'I am sending you some literature showing in what estimation Gen. Lee is held by the Grand Army of the Republic in Iowa. I can assure you that his reputation is that of "a traitor to freedom and his country," wholly unworthy of having his statue placed in the National Hall of Fame alongside of genuine American patriots.'"[15]

Union veterans in Illinois shared the views of their neighbors to the immediate west. As recounted by the *Tribune* on March 31, Grand Army men in Chicago erupted when a member (who cast the lone dissenting vote) spoke against a resolution condemning Lee's figure at the Capitol. Concerning statues, the thousand attendees in Memorial Hall cheered another comrade's assertion that the Daughters of the Confederacy's recently dedicated Wirz Monument at Andersonville was more than sufficient.[16]

As for surviving Left Armed Corps members, Barger was hardly alone in his vocal resistance. In late April, the *National Tribune* ran a protest against Lee's statue from the Pittsfield, Massachusetts W. W. Rockwell Post's entire membership, including signatory Adjutant James H. Anthony, and a vitriolic message from the Burnside Post of

Auburn, Maine, whose founders almost thirty years earlier included the still active S. Frank Haskell. In a unanimous vote of he and the other 159 men "'*who sacrificed their health and their material interests*'" in service of an imperiled Union, they protested against placing a statue of Lee, "'*whose treason in any other Nation but this would have cost his prompt execution at the order of a field court-martial upon capture, in . . . the Capitol . . . dressed in the Confederate uniform . . . it is an insult of the most flagrant nature, and so intended by the Virginians who caused it to be placed where it is.*'"[17]

Ongoing newspaper coverage gave a good indication of where the controversy was heading. At an April meeting held in Troy, New York to discuss the Lee statue, the Willard Post agreed that resolutions of protest needed to be adopted at the upcoming state encampment in June. The city's *Times* report also showed that the fight for equality remained important to Union veterans, as a former post commander spoke of the Maryland legislature attempting "to deprive the colored man of his electoral privilege, thus violating the fourteenth and fifteenth amendments of the Constitution, and stigmatized it as a disgrace to that state that could never be eradicated. . . . His remarks were heartily applauded."[18]

Noting nation-wide "strenuous opposition" to the statue, the *National Tribune*, on April 28, summarized its history and reported that "almost every Northern Senator and Representative" now shared Senator Lodge's experience of presenting petitions of protest from their states to Congress. As promised, the paper then printed resolutions from sixteen posts in the East (Maine, New Hampshire, Massachusetts, New York, and Pennsylvania), Midwest (Ohio, Iowa, and Illinois), and West (Oregon and Washington).[19]

Two months later came an omen of what would likely take place at the upcoming national encampment. Convening in Syracuse on June 22, the Department of New York Encampment was closely monitored by the influential New York City press due to the Lee statue imbroglio. The *New York Tribune*, in noting that the two frontrunners for Grand Army commander differed on the matter and Corporal Tanner, a member of the Resolutions Committee, was against any protest at all, expected that a resolution in that direction would be voted down.[20]

The prognostication proved to be wrong. De Witt C. Hurd, who opposed placing Lee statues in the Capitol, was elected department commander, and the Resolutions Committee clashed fiercely before Tanner obtained consensus on a "carefully worded resolution" unanimously endorsed by the encampment's two thousand delegates. Focusing on the "provisions of the act of July 2, 1864," the department resolved that the president ensure it would be legally "'construed . . . to the end that it shall be determined that no statue having thereon any badges or uniform which bears evidence of a disloyal action to the national government under the Constitution shall be accepted or permitted to remain in the Statuary Hall in the national Capitol.'"[21]

One day earlier the Department of Washington had adopted a resolution of opposition during its state encampment, as had the Department of Indiana the previous week.[22] GAR members on both coasts and in the Midwest had now officially taken a unified dissenting stand at the organization's second highest level.

Objection to the statue's placement incorporated disapproval of an associated custom. On July 7, the *National Tribune* noted that an Ohio veteran who adamantly opposed Lee's figure in the Hall also "earnestly and emphatically protests against the display of the rebel flag on public occasions, or in fact on any occasion." Why? B. W. Poole cautioned: "'Let us never forget ourselves or allow our offspring to forget that treason can be spelled in but one way, or mean anything else than what it spells.'"[23]

Two weeks later, the *Tribune* reported that many more posts had passed resolutions of protest against the statue, including the Department of West Virginia's Hoffman Post. Its membership additionally requested that Congress criminalize the use of "any other flag than Old Glory, the National Star Spangled Banner. . . . on public occasions or in public places."[24]

Individual and collective veteran activism continued over the summer, but at the end of July came a major setback that only intensified the animosity.

The snowballing hostility to Lee's presence in Statuary Hall, particularly the Department of New York's official stance, had begun to worry President Taft, who asked Attorney General George Wickersham to render an opinion on the law under which the statue had been submitted by Virginia. Wickersham's decision and Taft's approval without comments were announced on July 31 to extensive press coverage.

In his opinion, Wickersham noted having read the New York State Encampment resolutions and Tanner's associated communications. While acknowledging that, at the time of the act's passage in July 1864, it was highly unlikely Congress anticipated a state would choose anyone "then engaged in warlike rebellion against the government of the United States" for placement in the hall, "Nevertheless, perhaps in the hope that what Mr. Lincoln so fittingly described as 'this scourge of war' might soon pass away and that a re-united country might be realized, Congress placed no limitation in the act upon the exercise of the discretion of any state in selecting those persons whom it 'may deem to be worthy of this national commemoration.'"[25]

This was an equitable assessment of the situation, to which Union veterans could not reasonably object—but that was not all Wickersham had to say. The attorney general stated that, over the almost-half-century since the Civil War ended, "Robert E. Lee has come to be generally regarded as typifying not only all that was best in the cause to which at the behest of his native state he gave his services but also the most loyal and unmurmuring acceptance of the complete overthrow of that cause." He declared that Virginia's designation of him "as one illustrious for distinguished military service is therefore natural," Lee's being "in . . . Confederate uniform" an expressive testimony to the nation's "magnanimous" and full forgiveness of "any unsuccessful efforts to destroy the Union," and that acceptance of the statue would "symbol[ize] . . . acceptance without misgiving of a complete surrender and a renewed loyalty" and "provoke no opposition."

Wickersham, having found that "independently of the question of taste," Congress had not restricted states as to whom they chose "to honor in this way," nor "vest[ed] in any official any censorship concerning the costume in which a statue may be depicted," concluded: "Therefore, under the existing law, I am of the opinion that no objection can be lawfully made to the placing in Statuary Hall of the national Capitol of a statue of Robert E. Lee, clothed in the Confederate uniform."[26]

The attorney general's decision was not surprising given the act's limitations, but his totally unexpected comments on Lee were inflammatory, and the *National Tribune* immediately responded on August 4. Finding "fault . . . in the law itself" but not in his interpretation, the staff felt Wickersham went "into some quite unnecessary obiter dicta, which, like the same obiter dicta of the Supreme Court in the famous Dred Scott decision, will arouse sharp discussion. It is unfortunate that [he] did not confine himself to an explicit statement of the law."

After quoting Wickersham's section about Lee, the editorial stated that he "missed the vital point. War legislates and decides even more strongly than Congresses and courts. . . . Those who plotted to bring about [the Civil War] and attempted to destroy the Nation deserve in the interests of eternal justice oblivion, if nothing worse. The Confederate uniform on the leading General of that war can mean nothing less than a glorification of rebellion against the National authorities, and if it has any meaning it is to incite others to emulat[ion]."[27]

Not only had the newspaper disparaged Wickersham's thinking with respect to Lee, it denounced his overreaching by invoking the Supreme Court's most infamous decision, which involved slavery to boot. But this was hardly the last word on the attorney general's opinion from the *Tribune*, Grand Army, or individual Union veterans.

Just one week later, the newspaper published an excerpt from an interview Judge Loren W. Collins had given to the *Minneapolis Tribune*. The *National Tribune* reported that Collins, a former GAR judge advocate general and past commander of the Department of Minnesota, agreed not only with its view that Wickersham's interpretation of the law was correct but that Taft "should have admonished the Attorney General that he had gone outside of his proper lines in rendering his opinion." According to the judge, "[Wickersham] had absolutely no business to pass on the ethical question involved. You might as well put a Confederate flag in the Capitol and say that it stood for all that was best and ideal in the Confederate cause as to put Gen. Lee's statue there in a Confederate uniform and justify the act on those grounds. Gen. Lee stands for a cause that thousands of Union soldiers gave their lives to overthrow. Even more than the man the uniform typifies that cause."[28]

The August 11 edition contained an interview with another past high-level GAR officer who regarded Wickersham's position on Lee quite dissimilarly from Collins. Fully supporting the attorney general, former commander in chief Eli Torrance said that with the Civil War ended, "'the first duty of every patriot, North and South, was to forget as far as possible the bitterness of the strife, to "bind up the Nation's wounds," and to mutually treasure the heroism and self-sacrifice of the American soldier.'" Torrance claimed Lee was "one of the foremost in this patriotic duty" and that he would be given history's "high praise for his sincere and unqualified acceptance of the results of the war." As for his uniform, being "among the great Generals of his age, it seems altogether becoming that he should [so] appear . . . if not [in] blue, why then it must be the gray."[29]

Torrance notwithstanding, the overall reaction of Union veterans to the attorney general's opinion matched those of the *National Tribune* and Judge Collins. In the August 13 *New York Evening Post*, First Lieutenant Thomas Sturgis of the Fifty-Seventh Massachusetts drew upon having been under Rebel fire to eloquently explain why he and his comrades disputed Wickersham's decision and demanded Congress amend the 1864 Act. Sturgis felt that the attorney general and scores of others who did not fight in the war "and know it only as a matter of history," completely "misunderstand the feeling that existed between the soldiers of the two armies, and fails to grasp, in the slightest degree, the principle that animates the vast number of surviving Union soldiers and their sympathizers throughout the North, for whom I speak, in opposition to the Lee statue in the Capitol. He talks of magnanimity, forgiveness, complete surrender, etc., all of which are foreign to the question as we see it." By putting Lee in CSA garb and placing him in the Hall, "Virginia . . . does so, not to commemorate his noble character and civic services (else why the uniform?), but conspicuously his services and effort to destroy the nation. Against this we shall continue to protest as a degradation of our national ideals."[30]

Sturgis expressed a common concern of Union veterans, that other Southern states could follow Virginia's precedent and submit statues of such Confederate icons as Jefferson Davis, Raphael Semmes, or Nathan Bedford Forrest, "who permitted his soldiers to massacre two hundred colored soldier prisoners at Fort Pillow."[31] William Hemstreet, who had supported Kings County's two black posts years before, echoed Sturgis's apprehensions about celebrating the Lost Cause in a letter published four days later in the *Brooklyn Daily Standard Union*: "reassertion of a political heresy . . . should not be indulged at any time, but particularly if inspired by an unreconstructed element of secession, as malignant as ever, proved by the fact that within the last few months we have seen published or heard spoken such expressions as these: 'The Confederacy is not dead but sleeping;' 'The Confederacy is in the saddle again;' 'We shall have better luck next time;' 'Lee will be remembered when Grant is forgotten and the Capitol is dust;' 'We got a quarter of a million of 'em, by—' (The wanton murder of that many patriots for defending their country.)"[32]

Hemstreet pointed toward the September National Encampment for approval of a unanimous resolution insisting Congress act against such statues, as "seem[ingly] almost enough solid reasons have been already given to silence the weak apologies for this recrudescence of State sovereignty—this national stultification—this ridiculous anachronism. . . . The spirit that has placed the Lee statue there is disloyal, unrelenting and defiant at heart."[33]

Four days after Wickersham's opinion was released, the *National Tribune* told its readers that "Numerous and emphatic protests against the placing of the Lee statue in the Hall of Fame of our National Capitol continue to pour in." These included veterans' suggestions for how Lee's placement in Statuary Hall could be made palatable.

A resident of the National Soldiers' Home in Tennessee thought Congress should enact a law requiring a foot tablet for each statue "setting forth the principal characteristics or accomplishments upon which each one's fame is founded"; his choice for Lee was "'famous as an ingrate, perjurer and traitor.'" To a Kansas comrade, the optimal method was "for a half dozen old veterans around Washington to go with good sledge hammers and knock the statue into fragments and pitch it into the street," toward which he offered $5.00 for associated expenses.[34]

Such suggestions kept arriving from all over. The Department of Minnesota's Robson Post adopted a resolution that a Lee statue in the Hall of Fame was no more deserving than one of Benedict Arnold "and is no more appropriate there than . . . the rebel flag on the dome of our American Capitol beside Old Glory."

Similarly, N. D. Thompson of the Sixtieth Indiana, in solidarity with "thousands of the old boys," thought it "Just as well [to] place Benedict Arnold and a lot of other arch-traitors there." Along those same lines, J. E. Stannard of the Fourteenth Connecticut proposed that a section of Statuary Hall be "set off to be known as 'Traitors Corner'" and filled with all applicable statues, and "that they may be more conspicuous he suggests that they be painted red."[35]

Department of Utah commander Thomas Lundy was so furious about Lee statue's presence in the national Capitol that he proposed a novel resolution for passage at the upcoming national encampment. He wanted all sculptures submitted by the loyal states returned for display in their respective Capitols and replaced by statues of "rebel Generals and statesmen" sent from every former Confederate state. Once the "Hall of Horrors" was so filled, Lundy would have "over the entrance put this legend, 'Here are the men that tried to destroy this Union and to perpetuate human slavery,' that after generations would know where to place them historically."[36]

Underpinning the passion, pride, and defiance being mustered by aging Union veterans against Lee's place of honor was an undeniable despair, deepened by angst over both the causes for which they had fought so long ago and their legacy.

Commander Lundy stated, "'I never expected to live to see the day when rebels would be eulogized for accepting peace when they could do nothing else. As for rank and file, I am heartily with them in condemning the Lee statue.'"[37]

An Ohio veteran said the situation "makes us old Union soldiers almost feel that our work was in vain, but our patriotism is as strong as ever for Old Glory." Another Grand Army member wrote from

Tennessee, "'The South may eulogize Lee to the skies, but history will prove that what is written is written, and all that can be said in the way of apology for his acts cannot wipe out the stain.'"[38]

Orderly Sergeant W. B. Blanchard of the Sixteenth Vermont told the *National Tribune* that he attended a monthly meeting of twenty veterans from twelve different states at his post in Oregon. Among the questions that came up for discussion, he and his comrades wanted the newspaper to answer these: "First. Why is the Lee statue allowed in the Capitol? Second. Why is the Confederate flag allowed to be raised anywhere in the United States? Third. Why is any State allowed to disfranchise the colored people?"[39]

Their New York comrade, S. T. Putney of the Tenth Corps, plaintively wrote the *Tribune*: "'When we consider the treatment that Benedict Arnold received in the British Parliament and the action of the U.S. Senate on the statue of Lee, we wonder why Loyalty and Patriotism are esteemed so much.'"[40]

Using the *National Tribune* as his forum, R. Gunn of Philadelphia asked, "'By what manner of reasoning can "this Nation have a new birth of freedom?" as proclaimed by the immortal Lincoln. Is treason's uniform to accomplish this by entering the most sacred shrine of the Nation as a token of reconciliation? . . . If the Lee statue is to remain in the Hall of Fame, the answer must be reversed on the penalty of treason being death, . . . and the cripples who saved the Nation from destruction may struggle for bare recognition.'"[41]

It troubled Union veterans that Americans born after the Civil War did not understand their profound resentment toward the Lee statue, but when one of their own exhibited similar incapability, it was downright maddening. On September 1, the *National Tribune* printed several responses to the comments of past commander in chief Torrance, and the former soldiers and sailors of the North gave full vent to their derision.

Frank P. Eckert of the 124th Illinois was incredulous that Torrance "believe[d] for a minute that the simple act of surrendering his sword to Gen. Grant at Appomattox . . . changed [Lee] from a rank traitor . . . [to] a Union-loving patriot." To Eckert, placing Lee's statue in the Hall of Fame was a supreme "insult to the men who wore the blue now living and to the memory of those who gave their lives," and "Torrance's excuses and attempts to justify [actions of] the President, Attorney-General and the State of Virginia . . . only suffice to lower him in the estimation of his comrades thruout the United States."[42]

Torrance's remarks left H. H. Herring, commander of Post No. 108 in the Department of Minnesota, "deeply mortified and chagrined," and compelled to register his protest both personally and on behalf of numerous comrades in the state. Regarding Torrance's observations on Lee's loyalty to the United States, and that of the defeated CSA, Herring stated that "True, the war closed in the North, but how in the South? If the Commander does not know, I want to inform him that the Southern aristocracy, who was responsible for the late unpleasantness, are as disloyal today as they were in '61. They have never accepted the results of the war, and never will until the last vestige of that old oligarchy and their teachings are wiped from the face of the earth."[43]

The post commander then invoked the life-altering experience of combat he and his brothers in arms had survived, and how it continued to impact their views, political and otherwise: "Gen. Torrance perhaps never charged a battery and saw his comrades fall, one after another, by his side. I am not informed of this, however, but I do know that all who saw real active service and bore the heat and horrors of the struggle will not for a moment give way to such maudlin sentiment."[44]

Having served as rear-admiral of the National Association of Naval Veterans, J. F. R. Foss knew how influential a former GAR commander in chief's opinion could be, which spurred apprehension that "readers of this generation may feel justified in assuming that veterans of the Union army and navy approve the sentiments expressed" by Torrance, or have doubts about "offering their lives and services to help preserve the Nation that Robert E. Lee did his utmost to destroy."

To preclude any false impressions along these lines, Foss stated categorically that "If these Union defenders were right, then they were everlastingly right; and if they were, then, the other side was wrong, and everlastingly wrong; and the fancied political exigencies of this day, or sentiment, or special pleading, cannot change the fact." Otherwise, "the thousands of martyrs for the Union cause now in their graves are better off than their surviving comrades, who live to see this insult to American patriotism."[45]

Rear Admiral Foss exemplified the abiding obligation felt by Northern Civil War veterans toward their brothers who no longer walked the earth. As he mused,

> Imagine the return from the grave of the hundreds of thousands of dead Union veterans to receive three items of information:
>
> 1. During the Spanish-American war three ex-Confederate Generals—Wheeler, Fitzhugh Lee and Rosser—were given high rank and commissions in the U.S. Army over the heads of abler men who were officers of absolute loyalty and faithfulness for years.
> 2. This Government allows the battleship Mississippi to carry a silver service bearing a medallion likeness of that arch-traitor, Jefferson Davis.
> 3. Virginia proposes to put in the National Capitol a statue of R. E. Lee in rebel uniform, and Judge Torrance, Past Commander-in-Chief of the Grand Army of the Republic, publicly approves of it.
>
> Wouldn't those loyal Americans ask to be put back in their graves with a last look of contempt at their survivors who let such things be done by these later-day politicians and remain silent at such an insult to their memory?[46]

RECONCILIATION MARCHES ON: WHERE WOULD THE GAR STAND ON THE LEE STATUE?

As the 1910 national encampment approached, the Grand Army was clearly facing its most vital issue since refusing to draw a color line two decades earlier. The first attempt to secure an organizational protest against the Lee statue had failed, but there had been mitigating factors. In 1903, the statue was just a concept, and when the national encampment met, no one knew Lee would be clad in a full dress Confederate uniform. There was also the manner in which the Committee on Resolutions had conducted its business in San Francisco.

Past assistant adjutant general of the Department of Ohio H. W. Kasson recounted how John McElroy fought for and by 3:00 a.m. had won "the adoption of the simplest kind of a resolution of condemnation of that then incomplete statue of Lee . . . when he left the committee meeting, but awakened a few hours later to find that Grand Army men with 'business interests' had undone his work a brief half hour later."[47] Mrs. Isabel Worrell Ball of the Department of Potomac's WRC also believed that all efforts to secure the resolution "had been smothered, because . . . business interests of some of the richer men in the organization demanded care in offending the South."[48]

Now running for commander in chief, McElroy remained firmly against the Lee statue. Kasson added a candid assessment of the need for strong advocacy and leadership: "We are losing out all along the line. We are too old, too shattered, to keep up the battle individually, and as an organization we lag superfluous."[49] Unlike 1903, there was simply no way the Committee on Resolutions could forestall open debate on the Lee statue at the 1910 national encampment. Closely monitoring the controversy throughout the year, the *National Tribune* documented fervent, unremitting Union veteran opposition to the Confederate military leader's presence in Statuary Hall.

From January through the Grand Army's convening in Atlantic City on September 19, the newspaper published resolutions of protest from no less than 133 separate posts, five auxiliary groups (two WRCs; one Sons of Veterans Camp; one Ladies of GAR Circle; one unspecified), a joint meeting of numerous Chicago posts, and a New York County association with members from ten posts. In addition, seventy Union ex-servicemen expressed their outrage in the *Tribune* along with various veteran organizations (e.g., German American Veteran Association; Ex-Prisoners of War Association; Reunion of 127th Pennsylvania).[50]

Just as portentous for the Grand Army's conservative element were the furious sustained denunciations of past high-level officials who did not oppose the statue's inclusion in the Hall of Fame, the close attention being paid by veterans to the *National Tribune*'s coverage, and late-breaking developments just before the national encampment.

In the *Tribune*'s September 8 edition, Sergeant J. G. Maynard of Cole's Maryland Cavalry wrote that what "has pained me most is that any one of our Grand Army leaders should temporize with treason." By contrast,

> To my comrades of the rank and file I am grateful for their loyalty to principles, adherence to which during the war of the rebellion has brought only suffering since, at least to thousands who with pain-wracked bodies have to go on, tho a million of their comrades have passed on to the final muster.

> Yet among the thousands of protests that I have read in *The National Tribune* against the Lee statue, scarcely half a dozen have favored it, and of this tiny number I felt humiliated, wounded to the soul to read the names of men we have heretofore used to conjure with in the GAR.

Specifically calling out Burdett, Tanner, Torrance, and former Department of Ohio commander R. B. Brown, Maynard acidly concluded that he didn't "believe that these Past Commanders-in-Chief . . . represent for a single instant the views of the veterans who have given them higher honors than they will ever gain in any other way, and greater prominence than they ever achieved before or since. Indeed I believe that if the GAR could retrace its steps none of the four comrades who . . . approved the Lee statue could be elected Outside Guard of his Post."[51]

Maynard's views were greatly supported by three more departments (Kansas, North Dakota, and Vermont) adopting resolutions ("scathing," "unanimous," and "ringing," respectively) of protest to the Lee statue two weeks before the national encampment.[52] With these states joining the Departments of New York, Indiana, and Washington in formal opposition, the stage was now set for a showdown along the Jersey shore.

Before the Grand Army's arrival, another Northern ex-servicemen's organization conducted its annual encampment in Atlantic City. On September 15, the Union Veteran Legion declared its views on Lee's statue. The Legion expressed regret that the law creating Statuary Hall did not prohibit inclusion of someone "who had . . . participated in any movement calculated or intended to destroy the life of the Nation" and "failed to designate and define any source or power of censorship, of approval or dissent" regarding statues states might submit.

Specific to Lee, the veterans lamented that Virginia selected an individual who "devoted his great military genius to an effort to destroy" what other natives sons like Washington, Jefferson, and Marshall "periled life and fortune to build up and nurture." However "mistakenly enacted," Legion members, who had "risk[ed] life itself in support of the majesty of the law," chose not "to place ourselves in the position of rebelling against any law of the land, and particularly against a law which became a vital fact thru the signature of Abraham Lincoln."[53]

While the Grand Army spent its encampment's first few days in activities unrelated to Lee's statue, one of the affiliated organizations in attendance held its own annual meeting. On September 20, the National Association of Naval Veterans under newly elected Commodore William G. McEwan of the Left-Armed Corps adopted resolutions strongly opposing the location of Lee's statue. As recounted by the *Washington Herald*, "They declared that they have no objection to the statue of Lee in citizens' clothes, but they can see no justification for the placing of his image in Confederate uniform, bearing Confederate arms, in the halls of the National Congress."[54] Would the Grand Army follow suit?

The *Marion* (Ohio) *Daily Mirror* claimed that "the movement for a grand reunion of the blue and the gray at Gettysburg battlefield in 1913 has in a large measure softened those who were formerly most violent in their denunciations of the Lee statue."[55] The *Norwich* (Connecticut) *Bulletin* then confirmed what had been obvious for months: "If the most influential members of the Grand Army can prevent it, the present encampment will take no action on . . . Lee['s statue] being placed in the national capitol. Leading members of the Grand Army declare that they do not want to offend the soldiers of the Confederacy. 'Time is healing the wounds inflicted on both sides,' said one past national commander today, 'and there is no desire to reopen them.'"[56]

This was backed by the previously cited analysis of the eight months of *National Tribune*s published prior to the national encampment: while the protesting GAR post and auxiliary locations ranged throughout the North, not one former Confederate state was included.

But it was just as apparent that the rank and file and numerous commanders at post, department, and national levels harbored no such reservations and expected the Grand Army to take a stand consistent with its membership's wishes. For that to happen, the Committee on Resolutions would need to support a formal statement of protest.

When the committee met on the evening of Thursday, September 22, 1910, the clash between the conservatives led by Chairman Torrance and those seeking a resolution against the Lee statue was so acrimonious that it continued until 2 o'clock in the morning. After pondering numerous resolutions, the committee formally deliberated an omnibus declaration from the Department of Indiana that covered the entire issue, and requested congressional removal of Lee's statue from the Capitol. After intense disputation, the resolution was voted down by a narrow margin. Its chief advocate, William A. Ketcham, then informed Torrance that he would be presenting his state's resolution to the entire encampment as a minority report later that day.

The past commander in chief and his allies were wary of Ketcham, a former Indiana State attorney general—as the New York *Amsterdam Evening Recorder and Daily Democrat* reported, "The encampment is in control of conservative men and it is not expected that radical action will be taken on any subject. The leaders expect that some of the old solders who still have a lot of fighting spirit left in them will try to put through a resolution denouncing the placing of the Lee statue in the national capitol, but they hope to prevent the encampment from taking any action whatever."[57]

The committee's nasty debate was indeed a prelude to what took place during the general session on September 23. When it convened that afternoon, Ketcham was stunned by how few were in attendance; of the nearly nine hundred veterans present the day before, fewer than

250 remained. He immediately sought to postpone discussion of the Lee statue until the 1911 encampment on the grounds that such a small number of delegates could not provide a representative voice for the full Grand Army membership. Torrance agreed to a postponement (presumably to avoid any action by the encampment), but the motion was vociferously refused by those assembled.

After reading Indiana's resolution to the crowd and reporting that the committee's majority urged its defeat, Torrance yielded the floor to Ketcham, who presented the minority report recommending the resolution's adoption. While its authors empathized with admirers' desire to build local monuments to Confederates with celebrated battlefield or cabinet achievements, "we condemn the erection and maintenance of a monument to a tried, convicted and an executed felon [Henry Wirz, former Commandant of Andersonville Prison], as shocking to every enlightened sentiment and a reproach to those who fought for the cause to which they devoted themselves." In that vein, the report "demanded the removal of the Lee statue from Statuary Hall at Washington . . . and . . . removal from the battleship Mississippi of the . . . portrait of Jefferson Davis, and that these places should now and forever remain closed against embellishment by statues, portraits or other recognition of any one who did not win his honors by service on behalf and not against the country that is called upon to thus honor his memory."

Moving for the resolution's adoption, Ketcham castigated the Taft administration, pointedly stating that the Grand Army of the Republic hadn't "question[ed] . . . the President of the United States as to the rule of ethics or the rule of patriotism," nor asked for any "information from the Attorney General of the United States as to what ought to be the rule of patriotism." Rather, its members had "learned [their] lessons of patriotism in the furnace of war...burned down so deep into their natures that forty-five years have not lessened or diminished their ideals of patriotism. They did not need to go to Wall Street to learn what patriotism was . . . [thinking] they had a higher ideal of patriotism than could be obtained in [its] vicinity . . . I disagree, and it is my right to disagree, with the law officer of the Government."

He concluded with a devastating assessment of what this all meant for the GAR, in which he asked about its purpose, who it "represent[ed]," and whether he and his comrades had come to Atlantic City to sunbathe, "commune with one another and have a good time, and ask the Government of the United States to give us pensions and more pensions?" Ketcham spoke of visiting Statuary Hall with his son, and wondering what he could possibly tell him about the placement of a monument there memorializing an individual who had "pull[ed] down the American flag [and] . . . drape[d] this land in mourning and drench[ed] it in blood. . . . How am I to teach him the lessons of patriotism with an object lesson like that?"

Once the resolution was open for debate, what the *Washington Herald* termed a "sensational wrangle" began, with impassioned discussion keeping "the convention in an uproar for over three hours." The *Philadelphia Inquirer* similarly described the scene: "Feeling ran high and at one time the commander-in-chief was forced to direct the officer of the day to compel a comrade to take his seat."

According to Richmond's *Times Dispatch*, "The arguments were along the same lines as advocated by each side in the recent discussion throughout the country." In an excellent summary of the conservatives' position, it reported that the case they made was that "the bitterness engendered in the Civil War was disappearing and . . . sectional hatred should not be revived; that action adverse to the Lee statue would do more harm than good, especially to the GAR, and last, but not least, that the State of Virginia under the act of Congress of 1864, had the right to place in Statuary Hall the image of any man from that State whose memory it chose to perpetuate."

As expected, Torrance, Burdett, and Tanner took the lead in placing these views before the encampment, along with outgoing Commander in Chief Samuel R. Van Sant. Their opposition to any resolution was supported by D. Minor Steward of Tennessee, who feared Grand Army members in the South would bear the brunt of any backlash from a formal measure on the Lee statue. J. A. Prookshire of the Department of Louisiana and Mississippi endorsed this viewpoint, but another Union veteran who had resided below the Mason-Dixon line for decades decidedly did not. Past Georgia Department commander Albert E. Sholes expressed his belief that "the Grand Army should put itself on record as absolutely opposed to any act on the part of any State of this nation that shall encourage disloyalty in the generations that are to come after us."

Ketcham and his state's resolution were also staunchly supported by P. Coney of Kansas, newly elected Senior Vice Commander in Chief Charles Burrows from New Jersey ("Before you vote for this question, ask yourselves was I right or was I wrong? . . . ask it of the spirit of those comrades who went to their final rest on Southern battlefields. Comrades, loyalty is right forever and treason is wrong, eternally wrong"), Troy, New York judge Lew E. Griffith and others. Griffith made a powerful argument against Tanner's insistence that Wickersham's opinion had closed all legal challenges: "Acts of lawmakers must always be construed by the courts with reference to the conditions under which the laws were passed, and it is inconceivable that this act of Congress should have been turned as it had been by Virginia to something never contemplated by the lawmakers." Ketcham warned the encampment that adoption of the majority report would force between three to five thousand members of the Department of Indiana to leave the Grand Army. The *New York Tribune* further reported that he "attacked the policy of the delegates leaving the hall so often. He declared that there was never a chance to get the expression of the majority on any subject. He believed . . . the great majority of the Grand Army of the Republic would favor the minority report if they were there to hear it."

As darkness fell over the Atlantic Ocean, the exhausted and hungry assembly pressed for a deciding vote that would allow everyone to go to dinner. After a motion was made calling for indefinite postponement of any action regarding the placement of Robert E. Lee's statue in the national capitol, a voice vote was taken. Being too close to call, a rising vote then followed; with 133 ayes and 102 nays, the Grand Army of the Republic would not be taking any formal action against Lee's figure remaining in Statuary Hall. The newly elected senior officers were then inducted, and the 1910 annual encampment closed with the playing of "Taps."[58]

The funereal, poignant bugle call was a fitting conclusion to the Lee statue debate. The encampment's decision fatally compromised the Grand Army's prestige and moral authority, and helped propel the organization toward eventual insignificance.

Ketcham undoubtedly was right about the vote turning out differently with full GAR membership involvement, or if at least a sizable proportion of the delegates had been present that day. But they weren't, and a bare majority of the remaining Union veterans ultimately agreed with their conservative leadership—as the *Philadelphia Inquirer* reported, "Many of those who voted against the Lee resolution said that they felt the same about the matter as those who favored it, but they believed it was to the best interest of the country to take no action and drop the controversy."[59]

Apparently they were swayed by the arguments of past and soon-to-be former commanders in chief. Van Sant had urged the encampment, "'Let us do nothing here to-day to discredit the Grand Army of the Republic. Virginia . . . had the right to make her selection just the same as any other state.'"[60] Tanner, who had been unable to prevent the Department of New York from adopting a resolution of protest, had greater success in New Jersey, counseling his comrades as to the futility of such a gesture: "'Congress will never repeal that law, nor will it ever send that statue back to Virginia. It has never been accepted by Congress, and there isn't any likelihood that it ever will. But it is there, and it will certainly stay there, and so we may as well drop it.'"[61]

Torrance was dismissive of the situation's significance, calling it "a tempest in a teapot": "The Attorney-General . . . says [the statue] is properly there, and it is approved by President Taft . . . and there is not a newspaper of any importance in the land that condemns Virginia's action in the matter. We stand alone in our opposition."[62]

As a Grand Army resolution demanding removal of Lee's statue from the Hall of Fame stood little chance of spurring meaningful congressional action, almost everything Tanner said was true. But his recommendation to "'drop it,'" Van Sant's fears about sectional reconciliation, and Torrance's trivializing the issue while disdainfully disregarding (perhaps in personal response to its Grand Army coverage) the *National Tribune*'s staunch denunciation all poorly served the GAR, which ignored its membership's collective disgust over the bronze canonization of a man they unwaveringly considered a traitor and the embodiment of what they had fought against.

Whether or not an official protest would have made any difference was beside the point. No Americans had greater justification or gravitas to object to Lee's presence in Statuary Hall, and the nation's surviving citizen servicemen had made their emphatically negative views known through every possible avenue. By refusing to take a matching stand due to what was at best misguided patriotism, the Grand Army betrayed its own principles and tradition. Twenty years after rising to its greatest unified heights on the searing issue of race, that same association chose a course of inaction unworthy of the courage and commitment its members had conspicuously displayed for so long in war and peace.

Technically, the issue of Lee's statue was not dead, only postponed indefinitely. In November, Senior Vice Commander in Chief Burrows implored his comrades through the *National Tribune* to support a procedural change for the 1911 national encampment. Distressed by events in Atlantic City, he sought to have election of officers moved to the second day, "'in order that there may be a decent representation during the discussion of matters of far more importance.'" Specifically invoking what had happened regarding the Lee statue ("the matter . . . was really not decided at all"), the *Tribune* strongly agreed that "really important matters before the National Encampment [should not be] . . . relegated to the end of the last day."[63]

In February, the department that eight years earlier had been the Grand Army's first to adopt a resolution of protest against the Lee statue continued to agitate against its placement in the Capitol,[64] but this would be the last hurrah. At the national encampment held in late August at Rochester, New York, the resolution's fate remained the same despite officers being elected on the final day. As reported by the *Burlington Weekly Free Press*, "It was emphatically voted to indefinitely postpone consideration of a resolution calling upon Congress to remove the statue of Robert E. Lee . . . from the Hall of Fame at Washington."[65] Unlike the National Association of Naval Veterans,

Union Veteran Legion, Union Veterans' Union, and several of its own departments, the Grand Army as a whole never adopted any such resolution, no matter how mild.

Yet the same encampment voted down a resolution for the creation of a Lee monument at the national park at Vicksburg, Mississippi,[66] perhaps in part due to its being federal land, or Lee's noninvolvement in the fight for the strategic river stronghold. But the acrimony over Lee's presence in Statuary Hall did not automatically end with the Grand Army's refusal to take an opposing organizational position.

On Memorial Day 1911, amidst flag-festooned statues of Northern soldiers, a Capitol employee from Virginia adorned the Lee bronze with a floral wreath. The flowers went untouched until a Capitol policeman saw and immediately removed them, saying "that was not the time to decorate Lee's statue and other remarks of similar tenor." The *Times Dispatch* further reported that the story's getting out would almost certainly ensure the officer being fired for his "overzealousness."[67]

BETRAYAL, REMEMBRANCE, AND "THE UNFINISHED WORK"

Fifty years after cannon fire was directed at Fort Sumter, both betrayal and remembrance of why the Civil War had been waged were starkly evident. At the same national encampment in which it permanently tabled a resolution protesting the Lee statue, the Grand Army paid tribute to the most famous formerly enslaved individual in American history, along with the men of color who had served in Union blue.

Ceremonies were conducted at Frederick Douglass's grave monument, including placement of a wreath from black veterans, and throughout the encampment, AME Zion Church served as an open house and headquarters for African American comrades and Ladies of the GAR Douglass souvenirs were on sale, and the entire Thursday night program was "designated as Frederick Douglass camp fire and entertainment."

In its coverage, the influential African American *New York Age* reported with pride on the extensive participation of black veterans in the grand parade. Major Charles Douglass strode at the head of the Department of the Potomac looking "the picture of his illustrious father, with pure white hair, his shoulders erect, walking every inch a soldier, amids enthusiastic cheers and applause." Another black lumi-nary, Colonel James Lewis, led thirty-four of his comrades from the Department of Louisiana and Mississippi past William Howard Taft atop the reviewing stand.[68]

One month earlier, the president had attended and spoken at a very different Civil War–related gathering. The Manassas Peace Jubilee was organized by the GAR, United Confederate Veterans and Veterans Association of the Blue and the Gray and Their Sons to commemorate the fiftieth anniversary of the 1861 Battle of Bull Run. It was the first semi-centennial gathering of Union and Confederate survivors at the site in which they fought a major Civil War battle, and planning for the event was quite intricate.

Among the week-long festivities was dedication of a pavilion built by the United Daughters of the Confederacy at Groveton to memorial-ize the Yankee and Rebel dead from both Bull Run battles. In addition to those who fought at Manassas, the Veterans Association of the Blue and Gray and Their Sons assisted in the ceremony. Founded in 1906, the organization had included John F. Chase on its original Council of Administration, and his Left Armed Corps comrade Delmar R. Lowell was in Manassas as its Union representative and to deliver an address.[69]

The acknowledged highlight of the jubilee came before sixty thou-sand spectators, with accounts subsequently published throughout the country. Yankee and Rebel veterans advanced toward each other over the same ground upon which they had once clashed, the Richmond *Times Dispatch* capturing the extraordinary sight: "Three hundred and fifty ex-Confederates formed in a double line facing north, while a dozen yards away stood half that number Union veterans facing south. At a signal the veterans advanced with outstretched hands . . . Meeting, the veterans with clasped hands stood for five minutes grouped about the little blue flag, vowing eternal friendship and recounting incidents of 'fifty years ago.'"[70] The *Staunton* (Virginia) *Spectator and Vindicator* provided further detail: "When the two long lines met. . . . A mighty cheer went up, and many of the grizzled old soldiers wept."[71]

The veterans then joined a "love feast, commemorative of their reunion," in which they were "further regaled with an especially prepared series of motion pictures, showing stirring battle scenes and peaceful pictures of later days." An hour after everyone returned to the city, "forty-eight young women," each standing for a state, joined hands and sang "the Manassas national jubilee anthem, especially written for the occasion."[72]

Then it was President Taft's turn to speak to the cheering throng. Saying he was unsure as to "'whether peaceful means could have accomplished the result which we all now know was best,'" nonetheless the country "'developed a strength . . . of which the world did not know, and which we ourselves did not understand. We proved to the world our ability to fight out our difference to the death, and to reunite after the greatest civil war in history, to form the greatest nation in the world.'"

Continuing on the theme of coming together, Taft stated his "'greatest ambition as President . . . is to do everything that is sensible and reasonably possible to bring all of the sections of this country even closer together.'" Appealing to men who had known war, the President "'look[ed] to you veterans . . . to aid in the movement for peace.'" He ended with praise for the "beautiful sentiment" which had led to the Blue and Gray reunion.[73]

The Manassas Peace Jubilee was a rousing success, but there were discordant notes. Having seen the planned program, Fred Barger and his Lafayette Post comrades objected to use of the Confederate flag during the event, and its being blended with the Stars and Stripes. They sent copies of the resolutions adopted in protest to Taft, one of which read: "'That at this gathering . . . a most impressive ceremony would be to dig a grave, broad and deep, in the soil of that battlefield, and thereby publicly bury the Confederate flag. At such a ceremony it would be just and proper that the President of the United States should preside and the commander-in-chief of the Blue and Gray should participate.'" The Washington Times added the pertinent observation that many of the post's members had fought in both Bull Run battles.[74]

While the resolutions drew no official response, two days later the Times reported: "The old Confederate flag was not greatly in evidence today either at the battlefield or at Manassas courthouse. For every foot of Confederate colors in evidence, there were ten feet of federal symbol and emblem, and only the hard of heart would have denied the Confederates the presence of their ancient flag, more of a historical token than anything else nowadays."[75]

More conspicuous by their absence (provided anyone noticed) were African Americans. Union armies in 1861 and 1862 were exclusively white, so soldiers of color would not have been part of the re-enacted charge, nor the following "love feast"; however, not one newspaper mentioned the presence of blacks, veterans or otherwise, at any time during the jubilee.

Then there was the speech delivered by Virginia Governor William H. Mann, who had served in the state's Twelfth Infantry and was seriously wounded at Seven Pines. A half-century later, the Democrat "declared that the war was not fought on account of slavery, but to settle an inevitable question that must have brought on war at some time. Now there is an Indissoluble Union."[76]

Mann's ludicrous statement about the Civil War's causation, which apparently went unchallenged, was a prime example of reconciliatory cant seeking to recast the bloodiest four years in American history as rooted not in human slavery or white supremacy, but sectionalism. On that basis, the country could now extol the virtues of Yankee and Rebel alike without being troubled by deep ideological concerns or differences: "Governor Mann said that the deeds that were done during the Civil War raised the standard of manhood throughout the civilized world."[77]

The Blue and Gray organization's jubilee chairman, Reverend Delmar R. Lowell, surely knew better. As a 121st New York private, his right arm had been shattered by a Rebel bullet at Sayler's Creek, Virginia, a scant three days before Lee's surrender. Holder of a master's and doctorate, he had re-entered the US Army as a chaplain in 1890, retiring seven years later at fifty-three due to disability and, in 1904, was promoted one grade (to major) along with four hundred other Civil War veterans under a special act of Congress.[78] A well-connected Republican, Lowell was elected chaplain of both the Connecticut and US Houses of Representatives and, in 1892, GAR chaplain in chief; he also served as such for the Departments of Vermont and Connecticut.[79]

Beginning in 1905, the reverend became very involved in joint Union/Confederate initiatives. That year Lowell was one of the Grand Army presiding officers at a two-day meeting in Washington between high-level veterans of both sides that he officially opened; another Left-Armed Corps member, John Koster, also participated as former commander of the Department of New York. A major point of discussion was formation of "a great organization of the blue and the gray," with inspiration provided by distribution of a poem by Lucius Perry Hills:

We once were foes upon the tented field,
And faced each other in the deadly fight;
Each battled then for what he deemed the right.
As each one saw his duty there revealed,
And neither would his firm conviction yield:
Till smiling Peace dawned on the nation's sight.
And north and south both saw with glad delight
The brother-love which passion had concealed.[80]

The new Blue and Gray Association came to Atlanta in late March 1906 to attend a memorial for Joseph Wheeler at which GAR Commander in Chief Tanner spoke, followed by a two-day meeting and banquet; Lowell delivered an address during a working session.[81] In 1910, he presented a much more famous one, reading the Gettysburg Address during Grand Army Memorial Day services at Oakwood Cemetery in Syracuse, New York.[82] It is unknown whether Major Lowell thought of Lincoln's call for a "new birth of freedom" the following year while Governor Mann was insisting the Civil War had nothing to do with slavery.

For others in the Left-Armed Corps, no such question arises. When Rochester, New York, celebrated Washington's Birthday in 1911, a packed house in the city's Temple Theater watched a transfer of flags between students and Civil War veterans, one of whom then addressed the crowd:

"Fifty years ago this coming spring the Doctrine of State's Rights, promulgated by Senator Calhoun and others in Congress in defense

of human slavery, had ripened into the rebellion by the secession of a large number of the slave-holding states of this nation . . . Then it was that President Lincoln . . . called for the young men of the North to rally in defense of the flag, the same Old Glory you boys are now holding as standard bearers for the coming year."

"And the young men came from every farming community, every village, almost every manufacturing establishment, from the stores and counting houses, from the schools and colleges, pupils with their teachers, and kept coming as they were called year after year for four years, not for $13 or $16 per month pay, but to save the union of states, and never stopped to count the cost."[83]

In July 1913, at a semi-centennial commemoration reminiscent of Bull Run's two years earlier, another cohort member wrote his wife from a battlefield at which he had not fought:

"Yesterday I spent the day at the point where Pickett's charge culminated, a little spot of perhaps four acres on which was decided by a few hundred men the question whether this was one country or a divided one—whether this country should be free or slave—and in its decision hung the question of human slavery the world over."

"That momentous question was decided on this little spot in not exceeding ten minutes. If the confederates had won here, the union army would have been divided and probably beaten in detail and the whole north would have been open to Lee's army. If the union army succeeded as it did, it was the destruction of the confederates and human slavery. How little we realized at that time the tremendous issues at stake on this little spot and in the few minutes into which it was crowded."[84]

At the thirty-second annual reunion of his regiment in 1915, still another Bourne essayist powerfully conveyed the profound meaning Memorial Day held for Union veterans, and why he flatly opposed calls that it be revised to jointly pay homage to them and their Confederate counterparts:

"On Memorial day we are not living in the present. We live again in the days when our comrades were falling by our sides, and the irrepressible right and the stupendous wrong were contending on the battlefields, and not even the lapse of half a century can change the wrong to right, nor entitle it to any honor. That which was done can never be undone, and must remain a credit to one and a shame to the other until the end of time. Lives sacrificed cannot be restored and the responsibility must always remain with those who took them. It cannot be obscured under flags or wreaths or flowers."[85]

Alonzo Mabbett, William Bostaph, and Fred C. Barger had never forgotten why they lost the use of their right arms, or what their sacrifice, and those of comrades living and dead, truly signified for the United States. They and so many other Union veterans, white and black, personified the enduring power of soldiers' pride, and a warrior identity that fosters personal, professional, and civic responsibility and accomplishment decades removed from killing fields.

As the country followed a path of reconciliation that stripped the Civil War of its underlying ideology and racial foundation, those who defeated the Confederacy remembered the truth, and enhanced their victory by continuing to battle for freedom and equality for all Americans. Knowing time was running out, they sought to keep that obligation alive by inspiring new generations to continue the fight they had taken on as young men, and remained dedicated to for the rest of their days.

In Appreciation

A lifelong interest in the Civil War and its ongoing impact, coupled with growing up during the Vietnam era, choosing a career as a psychiatrist, and working with veterans, motivated my many years of researching and writing *One More War to Fight*. Along the way, I've been assisted by some very special people, whom I would like to thank.

First and foremost is my wife, the remarkable Dr. Virginia Streusand Goldman. No partner in life could have been more supportive of the time, effort, and commitment that this book required, nor provided greater editorial advice, unfailing faith in my endeavor, or unwavering love.

As described in the foreword and introduction, Dr. John R. Sellers brought the amazing Bourne Papers to my attention, kindling a burning desire to study the collection. Delighted when I published an article that investigated its autograph volumes, he was a steadfast proponent of my crafting books about the Left-Armed Corps. John and his devoted wife, Sylvia, became dear friends of ours, and we remember him with the utmost affection.

During his service as subject area expert for the US Civil War at the National Archives in Washington, DC, Michael P. Musick taught me how to access and use its invaluable pension and military service records.

Needing to learn how to write narrative nonfiction, I turned to a true master in the field. My close friend, the award-winning journalist and historian John C. (Jack) Waugh, generously conducted a one-student seminar that lasted until I was able to snatch the pebble from his hand. We take pleasure in reading everything the other writes, and any time we can speak or visit.

As being an author is an inherently lonely pursuit, it is essential to have family members who believe in what you're trying to accomplish. My mother, Mrs. Rita C. Goldman, and brother, Dr. Charles D. Goldman, are two of my biggest boosters, and I'm so grateful they're around to share in the joy of this book's release. The same holds for our niece, Rachel Heckel, and her husband, Donny, and with family not defined by blood, others who have been with me on this journey from the beginning, or for most of the road: my brother from medical school, Dr. William F. Alleyne II; my psychiatric mentor, Dr. Paul Kaufman; Dr. Joseph Engeln; Drs. Andrew D. Mosholder and Janet Harrison; Endre and Julie Krajcsovics; Dr. Matthew and Laurie Rudorfer; Hank and Jan Pohl; Teed Welch and Susan Brenner.

At Rowman & Littlefield, vice president and senior executive acquisitions editor Jon Sisk immediately "got" my work, found a reviewer whose comments contributed to *One More War to Fight* being enhanced through revision, and secured the use of Winslow Homer's magnificent painting for the cover. In preparing the book for publication, the contributions of assistant acquisitions editor Katherine Berlatsky and production editor Hannah Fisher were instrumental.

Concerning the academic history community, one individual stands out with respect to this particular volume. Dr. Eric Foner's pioneering research on Reconstruction inspired me to undertake *One More War to Fight*, and his encouragement early in the process was welcomed.

Above all, my obligation to the veterans of America's wars spanning World War II through the conflicts in Iraq and Afghanistan continues to mount. Like my decorated father-in-law, the late Alan L. Streusand, these men and women have responded emotionally and with great enthusiasm for both my approach and the Left Armed Corps. By sharing their experiences with grace and openness, they have enriched my understanding of what it means to go to war, and survive. I owe it to them and their predecessors to continue to tell their stories as honestly and accurately as I can, and through as much of their own words as possible.

Endnotes

Introduction

1. *New-York Tribune*, October 3, 1864; First Lieutenant Joseph J. Scruggs, Fifth USCT, Company E, diary entry for November 8, 1864, box 21, Civil War Times Illustrated Collection of Civil War Papers, 252–56, US Army Heritage and Education Center, Carlisle, PA; *Cleveland Morning Leader*, September 20, 1864.

2. Ora D. Walbridge, competition 1, file 24, Wm. Oland Bourne Papers, Manuscript Division, Library of Congress, Washington, DC (henceforth "WOB Papers").

3. Harold B. Simpson, "Murphy, Audie Leon (1924–1971)," accessed August 15, 2022, https://www.tshaonline.org/handbook/entries/murphy-audie-leon; Delaina Sepko, "Hollywood Fights Back," November 20, 2019, accessed July 7, 2021, https://blogs.bl.uk/sound-and-vision/2019/11/hollywood-fights-back.html.

Murphy is quoted verbatim from the recording of the full statement he made on the ABC broadcast, which was paid for and produced by the committee for the First Amendment in response to the House Committee on Un-American Activities (HUAC) hearings in late 1947.

As described on the US House of Representatives website, from its establishment in 1938, HUAC "rapidly became a soapbox from which New Deal programs were denounced and real and imagined communist subversives were routed out," with a "tendency to conduct witch hunts." Due to the efforts of committee member and "devout segregationist and anti-communist" John Rankin,* it became a permanent standing committee in 1945, and "At the height of the Cold War rivalry between the United States and the Soviet Union, HUAC's influence soared and contributed to a climate of domestic fear stoked by its sensational and often unsubstantiated investigations." ("The permanent standing House Committee on Un-American Activities," accessed August 15, 2022, https://history.house.gov/Historical-Highlights/1901

-1950/The-permanent-standing-House-Committee-on-Un-American-Activities/). For an excellent first-person account on the Committee for the First Amendment, HUAC, its chairman, Parnell Thomas, and McCarthyism, see Philip Dunne's *Take Two: A Life in Movies and Politics* (New York: McGraw-Hill Book Company, 1980), 190–220.

*The Democrat from Mississippi was also a notorious anti-Semite "who frequently denounced prominent Jewish organizations and individuals from the floor of Congress" (*JTA* [*Jewish Telegraphic Agency*] *Daily News Bulletin* 19[167] [August 28, 1952]: 4, accessed September 19, 2021, http://pdfs.jta.org/1952/1952-08-28_167.pdf?_ga=2.209349714.176527988.1632047840-857807900.1632047840).

4. Accessed May 9, 2020, https://www.npr.org/templates/story/story.php?storyId=3875422.

5. WOB Papers; Alfred J. Bollett, *Civil War Medicine: Challenges and Triumphs* (Tucson, AZ: Galen Press, Ltd., 2002), 159; James A. Chisman, (ed.), *76th Regiment Pennsylvania Volunteer Infantry (Keystone Zouaves): The Personal Recollections of Sergeant John A. Porter, Company B* (Wilmington, NC: Broadfoot Publishing Company, 1988), 78; *Soldier's Friend*, vol. I, no. 7, June 1865. A complete description of the origin, advertisement, administration, and judging of both Bourne handwriting contests (the second occurring in 1867) will be presented in a forthcoming book by the author.

6. Benjamin A. Gould, *Investigations in the Military and Anthropological Statistics of American Soldiers* (Cambridge, MA: Riverside Press, 1869); Frederick Phisterer, *Statistical Record of the Armies of the United States* (New York: Charles Scribner's Sons, 1883).

7. *Report of the Adjutant General of the State of Indiana*, vol. I (Indianapolis, IN: Alexander H. Connor, State Printer, 1869), 81.

8. E. D. Townsend, "November 30, 1865 Report on Veteran Reserves Corps," in Fred C. Ainsworth and Joseph W. Kirkley, *The War of the Rebellion: A Compilation of the Official Records of the Union and Confederate Armies*, Series III, vol. V (Washington, DC: Government Printing Office, 1900), 543.

9. Thomas M. O'Brien and Oliver Diefendorf, *General Orders of the War Department, Embracing the Years 1861, 1862 & 1863: Adapted Specially for the Use of the Army and Navy of the United States*, vol. II (New York: Derby & Miller, 1864), 120.

10. Townsend, "November 30, 1865 Report on Veteran Reserves Corps," 552; Fred Pelka (ed.), *The Civil War Letters of Colonel Charles F. Johnson, Invalid Corps* (Amherst: University of Massachusetts Press, 2004), 14; "General Orders, No. 111, Adjutant General's Office, March 18, 1864," in *History of the Fifth Massachusetts Battery: Organized October 3, 1861, Mustered Out June 12, 1865* (Boston, MA: Luther E. Cowles, 1902), 790.

11. Townsend, "November 30, 1865 Report on Veteran Reserves Corps," 553.

12. Townsend, "November 30, 1865 Report on Veteran Reserves Corps," 560.

13. Edward A. Pollard, *The Lost Cause: A New Southern History of the War of the Confederates* (New York: E. B. Treat & Co., 1866), 750–51.

14. *Memphis Daily Appeal*, June 23, 1869; *Memphis Daily Appeal*, June 26, 1869.

15. *World* (New York City), July 29, 1873; *Alexandria* (Virginia) *Gazette*, August 19, 1873; *Eastern State Journal* (White Plains, NY), August 22, 1873; *Memphis Daily Appeal*, August 23, 1873; *National Republican* (Washington, DC), October 10, 1876.

16. *Memphis Daily Appeal*, August 31, 1873.

17. *National Republican*, February 10, 1874.

Chapter 1

1. "Black Soldiers in the U.S. Military During the Civil War," accessed April 30, 2020, www.archives.gov/education/lessons/blacks-civil-war/.

2. Francis N. Thorpe, *The Constitutional History of the United States*, vol. 3, *1861–1895* (Chicago, IL: Callaghan & Company, 1901), 126–30; William MacDonald (ed.), *Select Statutes and Other Documents Illustrative of the History of the United States: 1861–1898* (New York: The MacMillan Company, 1909), 138; *Harper's Weekly Magazine*, January 23, 1864; *Harper's Weekly Magazine*, February 27, 1864, accessed April 30, 2020, http://13thamendment.harpweek.com.

3. MacDonald, *Select Statutes and Other Documents Illustrative of the History of the United States*, 139.

4. Dudley T. Cornish (1956), *The Sable Arm: Black Troops in the Union Army, 1861–1865* (Lawrence: University Press of Kansas, reprint 1987), 291.

5. William H. Thomas, competition 1, file 193, WOB Papers.

6. Gary W. Gallagher, *The Union War* (Cambridge, MA: Harvard University Press, 2011), 93.

7. Chandra Manning, *What this Cruel War was Over: Soldiers, Slavery and the Civil War* (New York: Alfred A. Knopf, 2007), 124.

8. Charles G. Halpine, *Baked Meats of the Funeral: A Collection of Essays, Poems, Speeches, Histories and Banquets by Private Miles O'Reilly, late of the (47th Reg't, New York Volunteer Infantry, 10th Army Corps* (New York: Carleton, 1866), 332.

9. Robert B. Roosevelt (ed.), *The Poetical Works of Charles G. Halpine (Miles O'Reilly): Consisting of odes, poems, sonnets, epics, and lyrical effusions, which have not heretofore been collected together. With a biographical sketch and explanatory notes* (New York: Harper & Brothers, 1869), 311; *New York Herald*, August 7, 1868.

10. Roosevelt, *The Poetical Works of Charles G. Halpine*, 311.

11. *New York Times*, August 4, 1868. Halpine's repeated use of "Nix-kom-heraus" in reference to African Americans was undoubtedly contemptuous. Readers of his time would likely have recognized the term as deriving from *nichts kommt heraus*, which translates to "'nothing comes out [of it]'"—see James E. Homans, *New American Encyclopedia of Social and Commercial Information* (New York: P. F. Collier & Son, 1908), 124.

12. "Literature of the Day," *Lippincott's Monthly Magazine* 4 (1869), 236.

13. *Republican Compiler* (Gettysburg, PA), September 18, 1865.

14. Webster Grim, *Historical Sketch of the Doylestown Democrat, 1816–1916: With Biographical Sketches of the Editors* (Doylestown, PA: Doylestown Publishing Company, 1916), 93; W. W. H. Davis, *History of the 104th Pennsylvania Regiment, from August 22nd, 1861, to September 30th, 1864* (Philadelphia, PA: Jas. B. Rogers, Printer, 1866), 181–82; 312.

15. *New York Herald*, March 1, 1865. Colyer would be removed from the position by Governor Fenton on September 1, 1865 due to the war's triumphant end, considerable decrease in associated "necessities," and necessity for "a corresponding reduction of employees, as well as expenses." In this letter to Colyer, Fenton clearly stated that his termination was "not caused by any dissatisfaction in the discharge of your official duties, nor by any lack of confidence in your zeal and integrity," and thanked him for his service on behalf of returning soldiers (*Albany* [NY] *Evening Journal*, September 4, 1865).

16. Vincent Colyer (New York Union League Club), *Report of Vincent Colyer, Superintendent, N.Y. State Soldiers' Depot in the City of New York: Presented to His Excellency Gov. Fenton, September 21, 1865* (New York: G. A. Whitehorne, 1865), 13, 18.

17. On May 3, 2020, a search of *Chronicling America*, the Library of Congress online database of US newspapers, for the term "Jew clothier" resulted in eighty-six hits from 1850–1914 that spanned the country. Almost all the references were used in a negative, overtly anti-Semitic connotation (frequently with thickly accented dialect), with the term often an identifier in lieu of an actual name.

18. *Soldier's Friend*, vol. I, no. 7, June 1865.

19. A. O. Abbott, *Prison Life in the South at Richmond, Macon, Savannah, Charleston, Columbia, Charlotte, Raleigh, Goldsborough, and Andersonville, during the Years 1864 and 1865* (New York: Harper & Brothers, 1865), 6.

20. Wm. Penn Sands, competition 1, file 6, WOB Papers.

21. John F. Huntington, competition 1, file 92, WOB Papers.

22. Ezra D. Hilts, competition 1, file 14, WOB Papers.

23. Ezra D. Hilts, competition 1, file 14, WOB Papers.

24. Rufus L. Robinson, competition 1, file 71, WOB Papers.

25. John Stewart, competition 1, file 93, WOB Papers.

26. Alexander Cameron, competition 1, file 103, WOB Papers.

27. Thomas T. Sanborn, competition 1, file 102, WOB Papers.

28. Henry T. Krahl, competition 1, file 120, WOB Papers.

29. Charles A. Edmonds, competition 1, file 51, WOB Papers.

30. Michael J. Fitz James, competition 1, file 144, WOB Papers.

31. Michael J. Fitz James, competition 1, file 144, WOB Papers.

32. William M. DeCamp, competition 1, file 147, WOB Papers.

33. William M. DeCamp, competition 1, file 147, WOB Papers.

34. William M. DeCamp, competition 1, file 147, WOB Papers.

35. In the *Loving v. Virginia* decision of June 12, 1967, the US Supreme Court unanimously held that "Virginia's statutory scheme to prevent marriages between persons solely on the basis of racial classifications" violated "the Equal Protection and Due Process Clauses of the Fourteenth Amendment," effectively putting an end to all race-based restrictions on marriage based on state laws (United States Supreme Court, LOVING v. VIRGINIA [1967], accessed April 30, 2020, http://caselaw.lp .findlaw.com/scripts/getcase.pl?court=US&vol=388&invol=1).

36. William M. DeCamp, competition 1, file 147, WOB Papers—his thoughts were remarkably similar to those expressed by Dr. Martin Luther King Jr. during his immortal "I Have a Dream" oration on August 28, 1963.

37. Henry C. Allen, competition 1, file 15, WOB Papers.

38. Henry C. Allen, competition 1, file 15, WOB Papers.

39. Manning, *What this Cruel War was Over*, 219. Brevet Brigadier General W. W. H. Davis was the highest ranking and most educated (prewar) member of the Left-Armed Corps, yet as shown in this chapter and throughout the book, his deep-seated anti-black bigotry marked him as a racial outlier among the 268 men who comprised the cohort.

40. *Soldier's Friend*, vol. II, no. 3, March 1866.

41. George P. Sanger (ed.), *The Statutes At Large, Treaties, and Proclamations of the United States of America from December 1863, to December 1865*, vol. XIII (Boston, MA: Little, Brown and Company, 1865), 507–8.

42. Sanger, *The Statutes At Large, Treaties, and Proclamations of the United States of America*, 508–9.

43. Oliver O. Howard, *Autobiography of Oliver Otis Howard*, vol. 2 (New York: The Baker & Taylor Company, 1908), 206–8.

44. W. E. B. Du Bois, "The Freedmen's Bureau," *Atlantic Monthly* 87(521) (March 1901): 354–65.

45. Du Bois, "The Freedmen's Bureau," 357.

46. Eric Foner, *Reconstruction: America's Unfinished Revolution: 1863–1877* (New York: Harper & Row, 1988), 142–43.

47. John Eaton and Ethel O. Mason, *Grant, Lincoln and the Freedmen: Reminiscences of the Civil War with Special Reference to the Work for the Contrabands and Freedmen of the Mississippi Valley* (New York: Longmans, Green, and Co., 1907), 238–41.

48. Eaton and Mason, *Grant, Lincoln and the Freedmen*, 240.

49. Paul A. Cimbala, *The Freedmen's Bureau: Reconstructing the American South after the Civil War* (Malabar, FL: Krieger Publishing Company, 2005), 11–12.

50. Cimbala, *The Freedmen's Bureau*, 13.

51. Cimbala, *The Freedmen's Bureau*, 19.

52. Cimbala, *The Freedmen's Bureau*, 23.

53. Foner, *Reconstruction*, 247–50.

54. Foner, *Reconstruction*, 249.

55. Cimbala, *The Freedmen's Bureau*, 23.

56. MacDonald, *Select Statutes and Other Documents Illustrative of the History of the United States*, 147.

57. MacDonald, *Select Statutes and Other Documents Illustrative of the History of the United States*, 147–49.

58. Cimbala, *The Freedmen's Bureau*, 24; "The Civil Rights Bill of 1866, April 09, 1866," accessed April 24, 2021, https://history.house.gov/Historical-Highlights /1851-1900/The-Civil-Rights-Bill-of-1866/; "39th Congress, 1st Session, HR 85," accessed April 24, 2021, http://blackfreedom.proquest.com/wp-content/uploads /2020/09/homestead4.pdf.

59. MacDonald, *Select Statutes and Other Documents Illustrative of the History of the United States*, 149–50.

60. MacDonald, *Select Statutes and Other Documents Illustrative of the History of the United States*, 150.

61. Du Bois, "The Freedmen's Bureau," 359.

62. Townsend, "November 30, 1865 Report on Veteran Reserves Corps," 543. The discharge status of VRC officers at war's end differed not only from that of their state regiment fellows, but also from the status of VRC enlisted personnel. As of June 17, 1865, "Enlisted men of the Veteran Reserve Corps who, if they had remained in the volunteer regiments from which they were transferred to the Veteran Reserve, would, under existing orders, now be entitled to muster out of service, will be so discharged, provided that no man shall be mustered out who desires to serve his full term" ("General Orders, No. 116, Adjutant General's Office, June 17, 1865," in Ainsworth and Kirkley, *The War of the Rebellion*, 55).

63. Cimbala, *The Freedmen's Bureau*, 19–21.

64. *Pamphlet Describing National Archives Microfilm Publication M1907, Records of the Field Offices for the State of Mississippi, Bureau of Refugees, Freedmen, and Abandoned Lands, 1865–1872* (Washington, DC: United States Congress and National Archives and Records Administration, 2004), 13, accessed September 17, 2021, https://www.archives.gov/files/research/microfilm/m1907.pdf; *Evening Star* (Washington, DC), March 4, 1868.

65. Charles W. Dodge, pension file #45499, Civil War and Later Pension Files; Records of the Department of Veterans Affairs, Record Group 15 (RG 15); National Archives Building, Washington, DC (NAB) (henceforth "RG 15, NAB"): George A. Otis (prepared under direction of Joseph K. Barnes), *The Medical and Surgical History of the War of the Rebellion*, part II, vol. II, *Surgical History* (Washington, DC: Government Printing Office, 1876), 969; "Records Relating to Indentures," *Records of the Assistant Commissioner for the State of North Carolina, Bureau Of Refugees, Freedmen, and Abandoned Lands, 1865–1870* (National Archives Microfilm Publication M843, roll 35), accessed April 30, 2020, http://freedmensbureau.com/ northcarolina/ncindentures2.htm.

66. *Pamphlet Describing National Archives Microfilm Publication M1909, Records of the Field Offices for the State of North Carolina, Bureau of Refugees, Freedmen, and Abandoned Lands, 1865–1872* (Washington, DC: United States Congress and National Archives and Records Administration, 2004), 8, 12, accessed May 26, 2021, https://www.archives.gov/files/research/microfilm/m1909.pdf.

67. National Archives Microfilm M1909.

68. *National Republican*, April 23, 1869.

69. *St. Paul Daily Globe*, March 29, 1897.

70. Guy V. Henry, *Military Record of Civilian Appointments in the United States Army*, vol. I (New York: D. Van Nostrand, 1873), 496.

71. *Index of Names and Subjects of General Orders, Quartermaster General's Office, 1867* (Washington, DC: Government Printing Office, 1868).

72. Accessed September 14, 2008, http://etext.lib.virginia.edu/etcbin/civwarlett -browse?id=B0812.

73. *St. Paul Daily Globe*, March 29, 1897.

74. *Daily Morning Call* (San Francisco), August 3, 1886.

75. Benjamin C. Cook, pension file #25924, RG 15, NAB: Deposition, June 3, 1891; Otis, *The Medical and Surgical History of the War of the Rebellion*, part II, vol. II, 771, 941.

76. *Pamphlet Describing National Archives Microfilm Publication M1913, Records of the Field Offices for the State of Virginia, Bureau of Refugees, Freedmen, and Abandoned Lands, 1865–1872* (Washington, DC: United States Congress and National Archives and Records Administration, 2006), 16, accessed April 30, 2020, http://www.archives.gov/research/microfilm/m1913.pdf.

77. *Journal of the Executive Proceedings of the Senate of the United States, from February 13, 1866, to July 28, 1866, inclusive*, vol. XIV, part II (Washington, DC: Government Printing Office, 1887), 957, 959.

78. *Message of the President of the United States and Accompanying Documents, to the Two Houses of Congress at the Commencement of the Second Session of the Fortieth Congress* (Washington, DC: Government Printing Office, 1867), 245.

79. "Records Relating to Murders and Outrages," *Records of the Assistant Commissioner for the State of Virginia, Bureau of Refugees, Freedmen, and Abandoned Lands, 1865–1869* (National Archives Microfilm Publication M1048, roll 59), accessed April 30, 2020, http://freedmensbureau.com/virginia/registeroutrages3.htm.

80. "Records Relating to Murders and Outrages."

81. "Records Relating to Murders and Outrages."

82. Elna C. Green, *This Business of Relief: Confronting Poverty in a Southern City, 1740–1940* (Athens: University of Georgia Press, 2003), 93.

83. Cimbala, *The Freedmen's Bureau*, 18.

84. Michael B. Chesson, *Richmond After the War, 1865–1890* (Richmond, VA: Virginia State Library, 1981), 94.

85. Chesson, *Richmond After the War*, 94–95.

86. *Staunton* (VA) *Spectator*, October 8, 1867.

87. Warren Ladd, *The Ladd Family: A Genealogical and Biographical Memoir of the Descendants of Daniel Ladd, of Haverhill, Mass., Joseph Ladd, of Portsmouth, R. I., John Ladd, of Burlington, N. J., John Ladd, of Charles City Co., VA., Warren Ladd, of New Bedford* (New Bedford, MA: Edmund Anthony & Sons, printers, 1890), 221–22.

88. William Augustus McNulty, competition 1, file 238, WOB Papers.

89. *Journal of the Executive Proceedings of the Senate*, 842.

90. Eugene Scheel, "The Reconstruction Years: Tales of Leesburg and Warrenton, Virginia," accessed April 30, 2020, www.loudounhistory.org/history/loudoun-cw-reconstruction-towns.htm.

91. Scheel, "The Reconstruction Years."

92. "Narrative Reports of Criminal Cases Involving Freedmen, March 1866—February 1867," *Records of the Assistant Commissioner for the State of Virginia, Bureau of Refugees, Freedmen, and Abandoned Lands, 1865–1869* (NARA Microfilm M1048, roll 59), accessed April 30, 2020, http://freedmensbureau.com/virginia/crimcases.htm.

93. "Narrative Reports of Criminal Cases Involving Freedmen."

94. "Narrative Reports of Criminal Cases Involving Freedmen," accessed April 30, 2020, http://freedmensbureau.com/virginia/crimcases4.htm.

95. "Narrative Reports of Criminal Cases Involving Freedmen."

96. *Message of the President of the United States and Accompanying Documents*, 245, 248.

97. William Augustus McNulty, pension file #34152, RG 15, NAB: Sworn Statement, January 18, 1868.

98. "Records Relating to Murders and Outrages," accessed April 30, 2020, http://freedmensbureau.com/virginia/registeroutrages4.htm.

99. *Journal of the Executive Proceedings of the Senate of the United States of America from March 5, 1869 to March 3, 1871, inclusive*, vol. XVII (Washington, DC: Government Printing Office, 1901), 560, 585, 940.

100. *The History of Fond du Lac County, Wisconsin* (Chicago, IL: Western Historical Company, 1880), 83; *Roster of Wisconsin Volunteers, War of the Rebellion, 1861–1865*, vol. I (Madison, WI: Democrat Printing Company, State Printers, 1886), 513.

101. J. A. Truesdell, comp., *The Blue Book of the State of Wisconsin* (Wisconsin: Wisconsin State Printing Board, 1880), 433.

102. Phineas P. Whitehouse to Mrs. Edna D. Cheney, March 11, 1867, *The Freedmen's Record*, vol. III, no. 3. *The Freedmen's Record* (originally called *The Freedmen's Journal*, but changed to the *Record* within a month due to another journal with the same name appearing simultaneously) was published monthly by the New-England Freedmen's Aid Society from January 1865 to April 1874 "to present information of the condition and progress of the Freedmen in the different departments of the South" and "indicate to the New-England public the most appropriate channel through which to pour their charities to the Freedmen" in service of "'the

industrial, social, intellectual, moral, and religious improvement of the Freedmen" (*Freedmen's Journal*, vol. I, no. 1, January 1865; *Freedmen's Record*, vol. I, no. 2, February 1865)—see also accessed August 25, 2021, https://www.accessible-archives.com/collections/african-american-newspapers/freedmens-record/.

103. Phineas P. Whitehouse to Miss Stevenson, Milton Society, November 8, 1867, *The Freedmen's Record*, vol. III, no. 11.

104. Du Bois, "The Freedmen's Bureau," 361. According to the American Freedmans Union Commission's December 1866 monthly journal, O. O. Howard reported that "1,386 teachers have been sustained, 760 of whom . . . were in the service of this Commission [which] . . . has sustained 301 schools and instructed 50,000 pupils"—among the New England Branch's teachers in Maryland who had been commissioned that year was Phineas P. Whitehouse. At the same time, the Commission was acutely aware of "WHAT REMAINS UNDONE": "DEDUCT the number of pupils, 90,398, taught by this Commission and the various missionary and denominational societies, from the estimate of colored children who are old enough to attend our school—800,000—and you will find that there are of these over 700,000 for whose mental improvement no opportunity has yet been provided!" (*American Freedman*, vol. I, no. 9, December 1866).

CHAPTER 2

1. W. E. B. Du Bois (1935), *Black Reconstruction in America: An Essay toward a History of the Part Which Black Folk Played in the Attempt to Reconstruct Democracy in America, 1860–1890* (New York: Atheneum, reprint 1977), 110.

2. *Constitution, By-Laws and Rules of Order of the Soldiers' and Sailors' National Union League, Washington, D.C.* (Washington, DC: Gideon & Pearson, printers, 1865), 3.

3. *Constitution, By-Laws and Rules of Order*, 3.

4. *Daily National Republican* (Washington, DC), October 21, 1865.

5. *New York Times*, December 3, 1865.

6. Robert B. Beath, *History of the Grand Army of the Republic* (New York: Bryan, Taylor & Co., 1889), 495.

7. *New York Times*, December 3, 1865.

8. *Daily National Republican*, October 21, 1865.

9. Beath, *History of the Grand Army of the Republic*, 495.

10. Marion M. Miller (ed.), *Great Debates in American History*, vol. 7, *Civil Rights*, Part I (New York: Current Literature Publishing Company, 1918), 449–50.

11. Miller, *Great Debates in American History*, 450.

12. *Western Reserve Chronicle* (Warren, OH), September 12, 1866.

13. Miller, *Great Debates in American History*, 452; *Evening Telegraph* (Philadelphia), September 1, 1866.

14. *Evening Telegraph*; *Philadelphia Inquirer*, August 31, 1866; A. H. Saxon, *P. T. Barnum: The Legend and the Man* (New York: Columbia University Press, 1989),

218–21. As to Barnum's participation in the Convention, the *Evening Telegraph* stated that he "is known to all the world as a general dealer in 'Humbugs,' but in politics he is a thorough radical, without a taint of his specialty in the showman's business."

15. *Western Reserve Chronicle*, September 12, 1866; *Evening Telegraph*.

16. Miller, *Great Debates in American History*, 452.

17. Miller, *Great Debates in American History*, 455.

18. Miller, *Great Debates in American History*, 455.

19. *Philadelphia Daily Evening Bulletin*, August 22, 1866.

20. *Philadelphia Daily Evening Bulletin*.

21. *Philadelphia Daily Evening Bulletin*.

22. *Albany* (NY) *Evening Journal*, August 2, 1866; *Democrat and Sentinel* (Ebensburg, PA), August 9, 1866.

23. *Brooklyn Daily Eagle*, August 24, 1866.

24. *New York Tribune*, August 21, 1866.

25. *New York Tribune*, August 25, 1866.

26. *Syracuse Daily Telegraph*, July 26, 1866.

27. Altina L. Waller, "Community, Class and Race in the Memphis Riot of 1866," *Journal of Social History* 18(2) (Winter 1984): 233–46.

28. Kevin R. Hardwick, "'Your Old Father Abe Lincoln Is Dead and Damned': Black Soldiers and the Memphis Race Riot Of 1866," *Journal of Social History* 27(1) (Autumn 1993): 109–28.

29. *Sun* (New York City), July 27, 1866.

30. Waller, "Community, Class and Race in the Memphis Riot of 1866," 233–46.

31. Hardwick, "'Your Old Father Abe Lincoln Is Dead and Damned,'" 109–28.

32. *Sun*, July 27, 1866.

33. Foner, *Reconstruction*, 262–63.

34. *Report of the Select Committee on the New Orleans Riot* (Washington, DC: Government Printing Office, 1867), 2–5.

35. *Report of the Select Committee*, 5–11.

36. *Report of the Select Committee*, 11–12.

37. *Report of the Select Committee*, 347–53; see also Joseph Wheelan, *Terrible Swift Sword: The Life of General Philip H. Sheridan* (Philadelphia, PA: Da Capo Press, 2012), 218–21.

38. *Daily Journal* (Ogdensburg, NY), August 28, 1866.

39. *New York Daily Tribune*, August 30, 1866.

40. *New York Daily Tribune*.

41. *New York Daily Tribune*, August 29, 1866.

42. *Albany Evening Journal*, September 1, 1866.

43. *New York Daily Tribune*, August 31, 1866.

44. *New York Daily Tribune*.

45. *New York Daily Tribune.*
46. "ROSS, Edmund Gibson, 1826–1907," accessed May 1, 2020, http://bioguide.congress.gov/scripts/biodisplay.pl?index=R000445.
47. *Western Reserve Chronicle,* September 12, 1866.
48. *Burlington* (VT) *Weekly Free Press,* October 5, 1866.
49. *Elk Advocate* (Ridgway, PA), September 27, 1866; Miller, *Great Debates in American History,* 455.
50. *Public Ledger* (Memphis, TN), September 18, 1866.
51. *Daily Phoenix* (Columbia, SC), September 27, 1866.
52. *Albany Evening Journal,* September 19, 1866.
53. *Fremont* (OH) *Journal,* September 21, 1866.
54. *Evening Telegraph,* September 19, 1866.
55. *Albany Evening Journal,* September 19, 1866.
56. *Burlington Weekly Free Press,* October 5, 1866.
57. Miller, *Great Debates in American History,* 456.
58. *Western Reserve Chronicle,* October 3, 1866.
59. *Burlington Weekly Free Press,* October 5, 1866.
60. *Western Reserve Chronicle,* October 3, 1866.
61. William Livingstone, *Livingstone's History of the Republican Party: A History of the Republican Party from its Foundation to the Close of the Campaign of 1900, including Incidents of Michigan Campaigns and Biographical Sketches,* vol. I (Detroit, MI: William Livingstone, 1900), 209: "Every State except Oregon was represented, and it is said that in an hour the Convention could have been turned into an army of 25,000 veterans."
62. *New York Times,* September 26, 1866; *Indianapolis Journal,* March 14, 1903; *Vermont Transcript* (St. Albans), September 21, 1866.
63. *Emporia* (KS) *News,* October 6, 1866.
64. *New York Times,* September 26, 1866.
65. Amos E. Hardy, competition 1, file 149, WOB Papers; Otis, *The Medical and Surgical History of the War of the Rebellion,* part II, vol. II, 623. As reported by Otis, Hardy's wound was so destructive (*"Shell fracture of head and surgical neck of right humerus, acromial process of scapula, and probably glenoid cavity"*) that his arm was amputated at the shoulder that day. At discharge eleven months later (August 31, 1865), his *"stump* [was still] *sensitive."*
66. *New York Times,* September 27, 1866.
67. *New York Times.*
68. Miller, *Great Debates in American History,* 457.
69. *Fremont Journal,* October 5, 1866.
70. Miller, *Great Debates in American History,* 458.
71. *Albany Evening Journal,* September 22, 1866.
72. *Western Reserve Chronicle,* October 3, 1866; *Burlington Weekly Free Press,* October 5, 1866.

73. John M. Williams, *The "Eagle Regiment," 8th Wis. Inf'ty Vols.: A Sketch of its Marches, Battles and Campaigns. From 1861 to 1865. With a Complete Regimental and Company Roster, and a Few Portraits and Sketches of Its Officers and Commanders* (Belleville, WI: "Recorder" Print, 1890), 80.

74. Williams, *The "Eagle Regiment,"* 74, 77.

75. *Western Reserve Chronicle*, October 3, 1866

76. *Burlington Weekly Free Press*, October 5, 1866

77. *Allegheny City Society*, accessed May 1, 2020, http://www.alleghenycity.org.

78. *Western Reserve Chronicle*, October 3, 1866.

79. *Lockport* (NY) *Daily Journal*, September 27, 1866.

80. *Burlington Weekly Free Press*, October 5, 1866.

81. *Western Reserve Chronicle*, October 3, 1866.

82. *Rochester* (NY) *Daily Union & Advertiser*, September 10, 1868. Concerning Grant's personal position on the administration's Reconstruction program, it is interesting that he took pains to respond to a claim that he agreed with it. As reported by the *Burlington Weekly Free Press* on October 5, 1866, Grant himself wrote to "a Mr. Kerr who in a recent speech, startled his hearers by the assertion that the general was a firm supporter of President Johnson and his 'policy,' as follows":

WASHINGTON, D. C., Sept. 19, 1866.

I see from the papers that you have been making a speech in which you pledge me to political party. I am further in the receipt of letter from Gen. Graham of Indiana, in which he says that his opponent for Congress had published an extract from a letter received from you, in which you pledged me to the support of President Johnson, and as opposed to the election of any candidate who does not support his policy. You, nor no man living, is authorized to speak for me in political matters, and I ask you to desist in the future. I want every man to vote according to his own judgment, without influence from me.

See also Beath, *History of the Grand Army of the Republic*, 26–27.

83. Beath, *History of the Grand Army of the Republic*, 26.

84. *Lockport Daily Journal*, September 27, 1866

85. *Lockport Daily Journal*.

86. *Albany Evening Journal*, September 24, 1866.

87. *Buffalo Daily Courier*, September 26, 1866.

88. Karl Marlantes, "Vietnam: The War That Killed Trust," *New York Times*, January 7, 2017.

89. *Buffalo Daily Courier*, September 26, 1866.

90. *Buffalo Daily Courier*.

91. Foner, *Reconstruction*, 267.

92. William H. Thomas, "Letter from the Fifth Regiment U.S.C.T.," *Christian Recorder* 5(44) (1865).

93. Thomas, "Letter from the Fifth Regiment U.S.C.T."
94. Thomas, "Letter from the Fifth Regiment U.S.C.T."

CHAPTER 3

1. Jonathan Shay, *Odysseus in America: Combat Trauma and the Trials of Homecoming* (New York: Scribner, 2002), 177.

2. James T. Bicknell, competition 2, file 56, WOB Papers.

3. John M. Palmer, *Personal Recollections of John M. Palmer: The Story of an Earnest Life* (Cincinnati, OH: The Robert Clarke Company, 1901), 1–90.

4. Palmer, *Personal Recollections of John M. Palmer*, 91–113.

5. Palmer, *Personal Recollections of John M. Palmer*, 222–23; *Broad Ax* (Chicago), August 5, 1916; "Gen. John M. Palmer's Bodyguard," *Journal of the Illinois State Historical Society* 10(3) (1917): 441.

6. *Broad Ax*.

7. Palmer, *Personal Recollections of John M. Palmer*, 113–221; *Indianapolis Journal*, September 26, 1900; *New York Times*, September 26, 1900.

8. Palmer, *Personal Recollections of John M. Palmer*, 222–23; "Gen. John M. Palmer's Bodyguard"; accessed May 2, 2020, www.nps.gov/civilwar/search-sold iers-detail.htm?soldier_id=cfd7dcd7-dc7a-df11-bf36-b8ac6f5d926a.

9. Palmer, *Personal Recollections of John M. Palmer*, 223.

10. Palmer, *Personal Recollections of John M. Palmer*, 223–26.

11. Palmer, *Personal Recollections of John M. Palmer*, 230–64.

12. Palmer, *Personal Recollections of John M. Palmer*, 264–66.

13. *Anderson* (Court House, SC) *Intelligencer*, November 8, 1866.

14. Palmer, *Personal Recollections of John M. Palmer*, 284–85; *Indianapolis Journal*, September 26, 1900.

15. *Burlington* (IA) *Daily Hawk*, January 23, 1876; *Quincy* (IL) *Herald*, August 7, 1890; *Buffalo Evening News*, August 8, 1890.

16. *Burlington Daily Hawk*; *Quincy Herald*; *Buffalo Evening News*; A. S. Chapman, "The Boyhood of John Hay," *The Century Magazine* 78(3) (1909): 444–54.

17. Chapman, "The Boyhood of John Hay," 444–54.

18. *Evening Star* (Washington, DC), September 27, 1901.

19. *Evening Star*; Chapman, "The Boyhood of John Hay," 444–54; Michael Burlingame (ed.), *With Lincoln in the White House: Letters, Memoranda, and Other Writings of John G. Nicolay, 1860–1865* (Carbondale: Southern Illinois University Press, 2000), 181.

20. Chapman, "The Boyhood of John Hay," 444–54; *Daily Evening Telegraph* (Philadelphia), April 7, 1871; *Evening State Journal* (Alexandria, VA), April 8, 1871; *Belmont Chronicle* (St. Clairsville, OH), April 20, 1871; *Emporia News* (KS), May 5, 1871; *Herald and Tribune* (Jonesborough, TN), May 18, 1871; *Marshall County Republican* (Plymouth, IN), June 15, 1871.

21. Burlingame, *With Lincoln in the White House*, 181; Chapman, "The Boyhood of John Hay," 444–54; *Burlington Daily Hawk*, January 23, 1876; *Quincy Herald*, August 7, 1890; *Buffalo Evening News*, August 8, 1890; "Gen. John M. Palmer's Bodyguard"; *Broad Ax*, August 5, 1916; *Omaha Daily Bee*, November 6, 1898.

22. John Hay, *Pike County Ballads and Other Pieces* (Boston, MA: James R. Osgood and Company, 1873), v (reprinting from *Harper's Weekly* acknowledged), 21–24.

23. *Quincy Herald*, August 7, 1890.

24. *Urbana* (OH) *Union*, April 12, 1871.

25. *Urbana Union*.

26. *Urbana Union*.

27. *Syracuse Journal*, April 8, 1871.

28. *Waverly* (NY) *Advocate*, June 23, 1871.

29. *New York Daily Tribune*, August 14, 1871.

30. *Utica* (NY) *Weekly Herald*, September 19, 1871.

31. *Wellington* (OH) *Enterprise*, January 9, 1884.

32. *Nashville Union and Dispatch*, December 7, 1867.

33. Foner, *Reconstruction*, 267–80; *Sun*, July 20, 1868; *Evening Telegraph*, July 21, 1868.

34. *Sun*, December 4, 1866.

35. *Evening Telegraph*, January 8, 1867; Donald R. Shaffer, "'I Would Rather Shake Hands with the Blackest Nigger in the Land': Northern Black Civil War Veterans and the Grand Army of the Republic," in Paul A. Cimbala and Randall M. Miller (eds.), *Union Soldiers and the Northern Home Front: Wartime Experiences, Postwar Adjustments* (New York: Fordham University Press, 2002), 442–62; Caroline E. Janney, *Remembering the Civil War: Reunion and the Limits of Reconciliation* (Chapel Hill: University of North Carolina Press, 2013), 117, 342.

36. *Evening Telegraph*, January 9, 1867; *Philadelphia Inquirer*, January 10, 1867.

37. *Evening Telegraph*; *Philadelphia Inquirer*.

38. *Soldier's Friend*, vol. IV, no. 7, July 1868.

39. John H. Holley, autograph book entry of April 13, 1865, WOB Papers; John H. Holley, pension file #65167, RG 15, NAB; John Henry Pinckney, autograph book entry of April 14, 1865, WOB Papers; John Henry Pinckney, pension file application #1134102, RG 15, NAB.

40. Foner, *Reconstruction*, 271–80.

41. Beath, *History of the Grand Army of the Republic*, 11–14, 34–36, 41–45.

42. Beath, *History of the Grand Army of the Republic*, 64–71.

43. Beath, *History of the Grand Army of the Republic*, 45, 68–71, 77–81.

44. Beath, *History of the Grand Army of the Republic*, 45, 77–81; *New York Tribune*, January 31, 1867.

45. *Weekly Caucasian* (Lexington, MO), September 12, 1866.

46. *New York Tribune*, July 2, 1867.

47. Thomas M. Hammond, "William H. Carney: 54th Massachusetts Soldier and First Black U.S. Medal of Honor Recipient," accessed May 5, 2020, https://www.historynet.com/william-h-carney-54th-massachusetts-soldier-and-first-black-us-medal-of-honor-recipient.htm; *New York Daily Tribune*, April 19, 1867; *Brooklyn Daily Eagle*, April 19, 1867.

48. *Philadelphia Inquirer*, November 11, 1867.

49. *Weekly Perrysburg* (OH) *Journal*, October 4, 1867.

50. Donald R. Shaffer, *After the Glory: The Struggles of the Black Civil War Veterans* (Lawrence: University Press of Kansas, 2004), 5.

51. *Republican Compiler*, August 30, 1867.

52. *Lancaster* (PA) *Intelligencer*, November 6, 1867.

53. *Lancaster Intelligencer*.

54. *Troy* (NY) *Daily Whig*, November 1, 1867.

55. *Troy Daily Whig*, February 26, 1868.

56. Foner, *Reconstruction*, 333–34; "The Impeachment of Andrew Johnson," PBS American Experience, accessed May 2, 2020, www.pbs.org/wgbh/americanexperience/features/general-article/grant-impeachment.

57. Foner, *Reconstruction*, 334–36; *National Republican*, February 25, 1868; Asher C. Hinds, *Hinds' Precedents of the House of Representatives of the United States, Including References to Provisions of the Constitution, the Laws, and Decisions of the United States Senate*, vol. III (Washington, DC: Government Printing Office, 1907), 863–68.

58. Foner, *Reconstruction*; Hinds, *Hinds' Precedents of the House of Representatives of the United States*, 870–901; PBS American Experience; *Evening Star*, April 25, 1868; *Green-Mountain Freeman* (Montpelier, VT), April 29, 1868.

59. *Evening Star*, April 27, 1868; *Evening Star*, May 12, 1868; *National Republican*, May 18, 1868.

60. *Nashville Union and Dispatch*, May 17, 1868; *New York Tribune*, May 18, 1868.

61. *Lowell* (MA) *Daily Courier*, May 20, 1868; *Troy Daily Whig*, May 20, 1868; *Troy Daily Whig*, May 30, 1868.

62. *Albany Evening Journal*, May 21, 1868.

63. *Troy Daily Whig*, May 30, 1868.

64. *Troy Daily Whig*.

65. *Cambria Freeman* (Ebensburg, PA), May 28, 1868.

66. *Cambria Freeman*.

67. *Cambria Freeman*, June 11, 1868.

68. *Lowell Daily Courier*, June 5, 1868.

69. *National Republican*, June 9, 1868.

70. *National Republican*, June 11, 1868.

71. *Albany Evening Journal*, June 19, 1868.

72. *Lowell Daily Courier*, June 20, 1868; *National Republican*, June 27, 1868.

73. *New York Tribune*, June 18, 1868.

74. *New York Tribune*.

75. *Philadelphia Inquirer*, June 23, 1868; *Nunda* (NY) *News*, June 27, 1868.

76. *Lowell Daily Courier*, June 20, 1868.

77. *Albany Evening Journal*, June 29, 1868.

78. *Western New-Yorker* (Wyoming County), June 25, 1868.

79. *Evening Telegraph*, July 2, 1868.

80. *Daily Ohio Statesman* (Columbus), July 7, 1868; *National Republican*, July 7, 1868.

81. *Daily Ohio Statesman*.

82. *National Republican*, July 7, 1868.

83. *Schoharie* (NY) *Union*, July 23, 1868.

84. *Schoharie Union*; *World* (New York City), September 24, 1867.

85. *Schoharie Union*.

86. Foner, *Reconstruction*, 339–41; *Lowell Daily Courier*, August 5, 1868; *Philadelphia Inquirer*, July 16, 1868; *Utica* (NY) *Morning Herald and Daily Gazette*, July 14, 1863; *New York Daily Tribune*, July 16, 1863; *Cleveland Morning Leader*, July 20, 1863; James D. Mccabe Jr., *The Life and Public Services of Horatio Seymour: Together with the Complete and Authentic Life of Francis P. Blair Jr.* (New York: United States Publishing Company, 1868), 98–99.

87. Foner, *Reconstruction*, 340; *Troy Daily Whig*, August 12, 1868; *Troy Daily Whig*, July 10, 1868; *Daily Union & Courier* (Rochester, NY), July 13, 1868.

88. George Wakeman, rep., *Official Proceedings of the National Democratic Convention, Held at New York, July 4–9, 1868* (Boston, MA: Rockwell & Rollins, printers, 1868), 154, 169–70.

89. *Lowell Daily Courier*, August 5, 1868.

90. *Brooklyn Daily Eagle*, July 27, 1868.

91. *Troy Daily Whig*, August 12, 1868.

92. *National Republican*, June 27, 1868; *Schoharie Union*, July 23, 1868; *Lowell Daily Courier*, August 5, 1868.

93. *Syracuse Journal*, August 12, 1868.

94. *New York Herald*, September 17, 1868.

95. *Philadelphia Inquirer*, September 15, 1868.

96. *Philadelphia Inquirer*.

97. *Gallipolis* (OH) *Journal*, May 12, 1864.

98. *Philadelphia Inquirer*, September 15, 1868; *Tiffin* (OH) *Weekly Tribune*, September 17, 1868; *White Cloud Kansas Chief*, October 15, 1868.

99. Wyn C. Wade, *The Fiery Cross: The Ku Klux Klan in America* (New York: Simon and Shuster, 1987), 31–46; Jerrold M. Packard, *American Nightmare: The History of Jim Crow* (New York: St. Martin's Press, 2003), 57–58; Harvey Fireside, *Separate and Unequal: Homer Plessy and the Supreme Court Decision that Legalized Racism* (New York: Carroll & Graf Publishers, 2004), 48–49.

100. Wade, *The Fiery Cross*, 40–41; Stanley F. Horn, *Invisible Empire: The Story of the Ku Klux Klan, 1866–1871* (Boston: Houghton Mifflin Co., 1939), 76, 172, 192–93, 245, 254, 316–17, 325.

101. Horn, *Invisible Empire*, 410–12, 414.

102. *New York Herald*, September 8, 1868.

103. *New York Herald*.

104. "The Birth of a Nation," accessed August 27, 2021, https://en.wikipedia.org/wiki/The_Birth_of_a_Nation; Eric M. Armstrong, "Revered and Reviled: D.W. Griffith's 'The Birth of a Nation,'" February 26, 2010, accessed August 27, 2021, https://web.archive.org/web/20100529224316/http://themovingarts.com/revered-and-reviled-d-w-griffiths-the-birth-of-a-nation/; Richard Corliss, "D. W. Griffith's The Birth of a Nation 100 Years Later: Still Great, Still Shameful," March 3, 2015, accessed August 27, 2021, https://time.com/3729807/d-w-griffiths-the-birth-of-a-nation-10/. Horrifyingly, the cinematic power of the Klan scenes in *The Birth of a Nation* is undeniable—as Corliss wrote: "The seductive artistry of Griffith's masterwork made his virulent, derisive depiction of blacks all the more toxic—one could say epidemic. This was not simply a racist film; it was one whose brilliant storytelling technique lent plausibility and poignancy to the notion of blacks as stupid, venal and brutal."

105. *New York Herald*, September 8, 1868.

106. *New York Herald*.

107. *New York Herald*.

108. *Syracuse Daily Journal*, July 9, 1868.

109. *Evening Telegraph*, September 25, 1868.

110. There were 6,900 attendees from Washington, DC (1,000), Albany (1,100), New York City (1,000), Delaware (500), Pennsylvania (2,700), and Massachusetts (600) alone (*Evening Star*, September 30, 1868; *Albany Evening Journal*, October 1, 1868; *Daily Ohio Statesman*, October 1, 1868). The modes of transportation were reported in the *Daily Register* (Hudson, NY) on October 1, 1868, and the "turnout" characterized by the *Evening Telegraph* on October 2, 1868.

111. *Evening Star*, October 1, 1868; *Daily Ohio Statesman*, October 1, 1868.

112. *Utica Morning Herald and Daily Gazette*, October 5, 1868.

113. *Evening Telegraph*, October 2, 1868; *Philadelphia Inquirer*, October 2, 1868.

114. Foner, *Reconstruction*, 341–45; *National Republican*, November 4, 1868.

CHAPTER 4

1. *Report of the Secretary of War, Part I in Message of the President of the United States and Accompanying Documents, to the Two Houses of Congress at the Commencement of the Third Session of the Fortieth Congress* (Washington, DC: Government Printing Office, 1868), 172.

2. *Evening Star*, March 4, 1868.

3. Wade, *The Fiery Cross*, 48.

4. Horn, *Invisible Empire*, 91.

5. *Report of the Secretary of War, Part I*, 175–76.

6. *Report of the Secretary of War, Part I*, 170–72.

7. *Report of the Secretary of War, Part I*, 172.

8. *Report of the Secretary of War, Part I*, 172–73.

9. *Report of the Secretary of War, Part I*, 174.

10. *Report of the Secretary of War, Part I*, 178; *Nashville Union and Dispatch*, July 14, 1868.

11. *Senate Journal of the Extra Session of the Thirty-Fifth General Assembly of the State of Tennessee. Convened at Nashville Monday, the Twenty-Seventh Day of July, 1868* (Nashville, TN: S.C. Mercer, Printer to the State, 1868), 153.

12. *Senate Journal of the Extra Session*, 153–54; Bureau of Refugees, Freedmen, and Abandoned Lands, 1865–1869. National Archives Microfilm Publication M999 Roll 34, "Affidavits Relating to Outrages March 1866–August 1868."

13. *Senate Journal of the Extra Session*, 154.

14. *Report of the Secretary of War, Part I*, 178–80.

15. *Report of the Secretary of War, Part I*, 179.

16. *Report of the Secretary of War, Part I*, 180.

17. *Report of the Secretary of War, Part I*, 181.

18. *Report of the Secretary of War, Part I*, 181–82.

19. *Report of the Secretary of War, Part I*, 182–86.

20. *Public Ledger*, August 22, 1868.

21. *Hickman* (KY) *Courier*, September 5, 1868.

22. *Jackson* (Court House, OH) *Standard*, September 3, 1868.

23. *Evening Telegraph*, September 9, 1868; *White Cloud Kansas Chief*, September 10, 1868; *Sunbury* (PA) *American*, September 12, 1868.

24. *Lowell Daily Courier*, September 17, 1868.

25. Wade, *The Fiery Cross*, 50–52.

26. Wade, *The Fiery Cross*, 48–52.

27. Foner, *Reconstruction*, 444–46; "Fifteenth Amendment," accessed May 2, 2020, https://memory.loc.gov/cgi-bin/ampage?collId=llsl&fileName=016/llsl016.db&recNum=1166.

28. "First Inaugural Address of Ulysses S. Grant, Thursday, March 4, 1869," accessed May 2, 2020, http://avalon.law.yale.edu/19th_century/grant1.asp.

29. "15th Amendment to the U.S. Constitution: Voting Rights (1870)," accessed May 2, 2020, https://www.ourdocuments.gov/doc.php?flash=false&doc=44.

30. Wade, *The Fiery Cross*, 82.

31. Wade, *The Fiery Cross*, 57

32. Horn, *Invisible Empire*, 295–96; *Evening Telegraph*, December 5, 1870; *St. Cloud* (MN) *Journal*, December 8, 1870; *New York Tribune*, March 11, 1871.

33. *St. Johnsbury* (VT) *Caledonian*, March 10, 1871.

34. Foner, *Reconstruction*, 454–55; Wade, *The Fiery Cross*, 82–83; "The Enforcement Acts of 1870 and 1871," accessed May 2, 2020, https://www.senate.gov/artandhistory/history/common/generic/EnforcementActs.htm; *An Act to enforce the Provisions of the Fourteenth Amendment to the Constitution of the United*

States, and for Other Purposes, accessed May 2, 2020, https://www.senate.gov/ artandhistory/history/resources/pdf/EnforcementAct_Apr1871.pdf.

35. Foner, *Reconstruction*, 455–56; Wade, *The Fiery Cross*.

36. Foner, *Reconstruction*, 456–59; Wade, *The Fiery Cross*, 93–107; Charles Lane, *The Day Freedom Died: The Colfax Massacre, the Supreme Court, and the Betrayal of Reconstruction* (New York: Henry Holt and Company, LLC, 2008), 1–5.

37. Foner, *Reconstruction*, 459.

38. Lane, *The Day Freedom Died*, 5.

39. Wade, *The Fiery Cross*, 109.

40. *Records of the Field Offices of the Freedmen's Branch, Office of the Adjutant General, 1872–1878* (Washington, DC: US Congress and National Archives and Records Administration, 2006), 1; "An Act to continue the 'Bureau for the Relief of Freedmen and Refugees, and for other Purposes, July 6, 1868," in George P. Sanger (ed.), *Public Laws of the United States of America, Passed at the Second Session of the Fortieth Congress, 1867–1868* (Boston, MA: Little, Brown and Company, 1869). 83–84.

41. "An Act relating to the Freedmen's Bureau and providing for its Discontinuance, July 25, 1868," in George P. Sanger (ed.), *Acts and Resolutions of the United States of America, Passed at the Second Session of the Fortieth Congress, December 2, 1867–November 10, 1868* (Washington, DC: Government Printing Office, 1868), 166–67.

42. *Records of the Field Offices of the Freedmen's Branch*; Alexander Shiras, *The National Bureau of Education, Its History, Work, and Limitations* (Washington, DC: US Government Printing Office, 1875).

43. Du Bois, "The Freedmen's Bureau," 354–65.

44. Henry, *Military Record of Civilian Appointments in the United States Army*, 276.

45. Foner, *Reconstruction*, 437; Lane, *The Day Freedom Died*, 9–12; *Intelligencer* (Gloversville, NY), May 1, 1873.

46. Lane, *The Day Freedom Died*, xviii, 143.

47. *Intelligencer*, May 1, 1873.

48. Lane, *The Day Freedom Died*, 110–17, 123–214.

49. Lane, *The Day Freedom Died*, 215–28; Foner, *Reconstruction*, 527–31.

50. Lane, *The Day Freedom Died*, 242–43; Foner, *Reconstruction*, 538–39; Fireside, *Separate and Unequal*, 59–64; "Ames, Adelbert: 1835–1933," accessed May 2, 2020, http://bioguide.congress.gov/scripts/biodisplay.pl?index=a000172.

51. Lane, *The Day Freedom Died*, 242–43; Foner, *Reconstruction*, 538–39; *New York Daily Tribune*, April 26, 1880.

52. *New York Daily Tribune*.

53. *New York Daily Tribune*; Foner, *Reconstruction*, 558; "The Birth of 'Jim Crow,'" accessed May 2, 2020, https://www.thirteen.org/wnet/slavery/timeline /1874.html, Thirteen/WNET New York reported that over twenty African Americans were killed in the "Clinton Massacre."

54. "Ames, Adelbert"; Fireside, *Separate and Unequal*, 59.

55. *New York Daily Tribune*, April 26, 1880.

56. *Evening Star*, September 20, 1875.

57. *Evening Star*.

58. *Knoxville* (TN) *Whig and Chronicle*, September 22, 1875; Lane, *The Day Freedom Died*, 243; Foner, *Reconstruction*, 560–61; *New York Daily Tribune*, September 17, 1875.

59. *Knoxville Whig and Chronicle*; Lane, *The Day Freedom Died*, 243; Foner, *Reconstruction*, 560–61; *New York Daily Tribune*.

60. "Bruce, Blanche Kelso, 1841–1898," accessed September 13, 2021, https://history.house.gov/People/Detail/10029#biography.

61. *New York Daily Tribune*, September 17, 1875.

62. *Public Ledger*, September 17, 1875; *Knoxville Whig and Chronicle*, September 22, 1875; *Philadelphia Inquirer*, September 17, 1875; *Daily Register*, September 28, 1875.

63. *Daily Graphic* (New York City), September 17, 1875.

64. *National Republican*, September 17, 1875.

65. *National Republican*, September 27, 1875.

66. Lane, *The Day Freedom Died*, 243; Foner, *Reconstruction*, 561–62; *New York Daily Tribune*, April 26, 1880.

67. Lane, *The Day Freedom Died*, 243–44; Foner, *Reconstruction*, 562; *New York Daily Tribune*; *Memphis Daily Appeal*, February 19, 1876; *Fairfield Herald* (Winnsboro, SC), February 23, 1876; *Evening Star*, March 14, 1876; *National Republican*, March 18, 1876; *Whig and Tribune* (Jackson, TN), March 18, 1876.

68. Lane, *The Day Freedom Died*, 229–46; Foner, *Reconstruction*, 530–31; Fireside, *Separate and Unequal*, 132; "United States Supreme Court: US v. CRUIKSHANK (1875)," accessed May 2, 2020, http://caselaw.lp.findlaw.com/scripts/getcase.pl?court=US&vol=92&invol=542.

69. Lane, *The Day Freedom Died*, 246–47; Foner, *Reconstruction*, 531; Fireside, *Separate and Unequal*, 133.

70. Lane, *The Day Freedom Died*, 247; Foner, *Reconstruction*, 563, 570–75; *New York Daily Tribune*, April 26, 1880.

71. *The Miscellaneous Documents of the Senate of the United States for the Second Session of the Forty-Forth Congress*, vol. VI, no. 3 (Washington, DC: Government Printing Office, 1877), 44–45.

72. *The Miscellaneous Documents of the Senate of the United States*, 45.

73. *The Miscellaneous Documents of the Senate of the United States*, 455–61.

74. *The Miscellaneous Documents of the Senate of the United States*, 462.

75. *The Miscellaneous Documents of the Senate of the United States*, 45.

76. Roy Morris Jr., *Fraud of the Century: Rutherford B. Hayes, Samuel Tilden, and the Stolen Election of 1876* (New York: Simon & Schuster, 2003), 3–4.

77. Morris, *Fraud of the Century*, 119; Lane, *The Day Freedom Died*, 247–48; Foner, *Reconstruction*, 574–80.

78. *New York Daily Tribune*, April 26, 1880.

79. Foner, *Reconstruction*, 582.

80. Lane, *The Day Freedom Died*, 248; Fireside, *Separate and Unequal*, 115, 175; "Politics and Race Relations in Reconstructed Louisiana," in *A Medley of Cultures: Louisiana History at the Cabildo*, 243–49, accessed May 2, 2020, www.crt.state.la.us /Assets/Museum/publications/A_Medley_Of_Cultures.pdf; *Wheeling* (WV) *Daily Intelligencer*, April 26, 1877.

81. *National Republican*, March 3, 1877.

82. *National Republican*, April 21, 1877.

83. *National Republican*; *Wheeling Daily Intelligencer*, April 26, 1877.

84. *Wheeling Daily Intelligencer.*

85. *Wheeling Daily Intelligencer*, March 24, 1877; *Cincinnati Daily Star*, March 30, 1877; *Columbian* (Bloomsburg, PA), March 30, 1877; *Wheeling Daily Intelligencer*, April 2, 1877; *National Republican*, April 3, 1877; *Memphis Daily Appeal*, April 6, 1877; *Anderson Intelligencer*, April 12, 1877.

86. *Green-Mountain Freeman*, April 18, 1877.

87. Lane, *The Day Freedom Died*, 249; Foner, *Reconstruction*, 582.

88. Foner, *Reconstruction*, 553–56; Packard, *American Nightmare*, 58–60; Fireside, *Separate and Unequal*, 20–21; *Pulaski* (TN) *Citizen*, February 11, 1875; *Lowell Daily Courier*, October 19, 1883.

89. Morris, *Fraud of the Century*, 3.

Chapter 5

1. *Proceedings of the Twenty-Third Annual Encampment of the Department of Ohio, Grand Army of the Republic, Held at Dayton, Ohio, April 24, 25 and 26, 1889* (LOC E462.1.O367), 27.

2. Frank Moore, *Memorial Ceremonies at the Graves of Our Soldiers: Saturday, May 30, 1868* (Washington City: Collected under Authority of Congress, 1869).

3. *Daily State Journal* (Alexandria, VA), October 4, 1871; *Daily State Journal*, September 23, 1872; *Daily State Journal*, October 19, 1872.

4. *Appendix to the House and Senate Journals of the Regular Session of the Twenty-Fifth General Assembly of the State of Missouri* (Jefferson City, MO: Ellwood Kirby, Public Printer, 1869), 63, 79–80.

5. *Appendix to the House and Senate Journals*, 80.

6. *Nashville Union and American*, June 1, 1869.

7. *Daily National Republican*, June 9, 1870; *Sun*, December 27, 1873.

8. *Daily National Republican*; *Gazette and Farmers' Journal* (Baldwinsville, NY), September 24, 1908.

9. Beath, *History of the Grand Army of the Republic*, 109, 112–13.

10. Shaffer, *After the Glory*, 7.

11. Barbara A. Gannon, *The Won Cause: Black and White Comradeship in the Grand Army of the Republic* (Chapel Hill: University of North Carolina Press, 2011), 3.

12. *Ottawa* (IL) *Free Trader*, June 26, 1869.

13. Senate Historical Office, "Senate Stories: Hiram Revels: First African American Senator," February 25, 2020, accessed 5/3/2020, https://www.senate.gov /artandhistory/senate-stories/First-African-American-Senator.htm.

14. *Evening Telegraph*, March 1, 1870.

15. *Cambria Freeman*, March 10, 1870.

16. *Cambria Freeman*, March 24, 1870.

17. *Buffalo Evening Courier and Republic*, November 16, 1870.

18. Shaffer, *After the Glory*, 4.

19. Gannon, *The Won Cause*, 5.

20. Gannon, *The Won Cause*, 228 (footnote 9, chapter 33).

21. Determination as to which Posts were integrated was made via author's personal knowledge based on research and Dr. Gannon's list of integrated Posts in her book, which was available online (http://woncause.com/appendices.php#o2, accessed October 10, 2018).

The Left-Armed Corps' Post membership was as follows:

New York: 42 (38 Posts)
Massachusetts: 20 (19 Posts)
Ohio: 18 (17 Posts)
Washington, DC/Dept. of Potomac: 16 (8 Posts)
Pennsylvania: 14 (10 Posts)
Illinois: 9
Indiana: 8
Michigan: 8
Connecticut: 6
Kansas: 6
Maine: 5
Minnesota: 4
Vermont: 4
Virginia: 4
California: 3
Missouri: 3
New Jersey: 3
Wisconsin: 3
Florida: 2
Iowa: 2
Oregon: 2
Utah: 2 (1 Post)
Arkansas: 1
Colorado: 1
Idaho: 1
Rhode Island: 1
South Carolina: 1

South Dakota: 1

West Virginia: 1

22. *National Tribune* (Washington, DC), August 26, 1909.

23. *Official Records of the Union and Confederate Navies in the War of the Rebellion*, Series I, vol. 21 (Washington, DC: Government Printing Office, 1906), 433; Frank M. Bennett, *The Steam Navy of the United States: A History of the Growth of the Steam Vessel of War in the U.S. Navy, and of the Naval Engineer Corps: Second Edition* (Pittsburgh, PA: Warren & Company, 1897), 440; *Register of the Commissioned and Warrant Officers of the Navy of the United States and of the Marine Corps to January 1, 1896* (Washington, DC: Government Printing Office, 1896), 104.

24. *National Tribune*, March 17, 1910; *Duluth Herald*, September 21, 1910; *The Tribune Almanac and Political Register, 1911* (New York: The Tribune Association, 1911), 417.

25. Roll of the Fortieth Annual Encampment, Department of Pennsylvania, GAR, Altoona, June 6 and 7, 1906; *Proceedings of the 50th Annual Encampment, Department of Pennsylvania, Grand Army of the Republic, held at Harrisburg, PA: June 8th and 9th, 1916* (Harrisburg, PA: Wm. Stanley Ray, State Printer, 1916), 182; *Proceedings of the 53d Annual Encampment, Department of Pennsylvania, Grand Army of the Republic: Lancaster, June 11th and 12th, 1919* (Harrisburg, PA: J. L. L. Kuhn, Printers to the Commonwealth, 1919), 148.

26. Stuart McConnell, *Glorious Contentment: The Grand Army of the Republic, 1865–1900* (Chapel Hill: University of North Carolina Press, 1992), xiv.

27. *Soldier's Friend*, vol. IV, no. 2, February 1868.

28. Beath, *History of the Grand Army of the Republic*, 531–32.

29. Harrison O. Thomas, pension file #21443, RG 15, NAB; Otis, *The Medical and Surgical History of the War of the Rebellion*, part II, vol. II, 965; Harrison Otis Thomas, competition 1, file 78, and competition 2, file 58, WOB Papers; William H. Ward (ed.), *Records of Members of the Grand Army, with a Complete Account of the Twentieth National Encampment* (San Francisco, CA: H.S. Crocker & Co., 1886), 403–4.

30. Thomas pension file, including Questionnaires completed on May 8, 1898 and March 15, 1915; Henry D. Coolidge & Edward A. McLaughlin, *Commonwealth of Massachusetts Manual for the Use of the General Court* (Boston, MA: Wright & Potter Printing Company, State Printers, 1891), 477; *National Tribune*, June 30, 1910; 1910 census, Brockton, Massachusetts; *Early History of the Department of Massachusetts, GAR, from 1866 to 1880 Inclusive* (Boston, MA: E.B. Stillings & Co., 1895), 5–6.

31. *Utica* (NY) *Daily Press*, May 26, 1897; *Utica* (NY) *Herald Dispatch, August 8, 1908; National GAR Records Program—Historical Summary of Grand Army of the Republic (GAR) Posts by State: NEW YORK*, accessed May 3, 2020, http://www .suvcw.org/garrecords/garposts/ny.pdf.

32. Georgia Drew Merrill (ed.), *The History of Androscoggin County Maine* (1891), chapter X, accessed May 3, 2020, http://genealogytrails.com/maine/ androscogginco/andro_history_part_ten_d_two.html.

33. Beath, *History of the Grand Army of the Republic*, 503–4.

34. Herbert T. O. Blue, *History of Stark County, Ohio* (Chicago, IL: S.J. Clarke Publishing Company, 1928), 499; Ohio Historical Society Archives, *MSS 715 Grand Army of the Republic, Ohio Department Records*, box 4; T. D. McGillicuddy (comp.), *Proceedings of the Annual and Semi-Annual Encampments of the Department of Ohio, Grand Army of the Republic for the First Fourteen Years of Its Existence* (Columbus, OH: The F. J. Heer Printing Co., 1912), 54, 56, 141.

35. Military Order of the Loyal Legion of the United States, accessed May 3, 2020, www.suvcw.org/mollus/mollus.htm.

36. McConnell, *Glorious Contentment*, xiii–xiv.

37. Earl J. Hess, *The Union Soldier in Battle: Enduring the Ordeal of Combat* (Lawrence: University Press of Kansas, 1997), 158–77.

38. Eric T. Dean Jr., *Shook Over Hell: Post-Traumatic Stress, Vietnam, and the Civil War* (Cambridge, MA: Harvard University Press, 1997), 214.

39. Brian M. Jordan, *Marching Home: Union Veterans and Their Unending Civil War* (New York: Liveright Publishing Corp., 2015), 151–69; Shaffer, *After the Glory*, 67–95; David Blight, *Race and Reunion: The Civil War in American Memory* (Cambridge, MA: Harvard University Press, 2002), 98–170.

40. Foner, *Reconstruction*; Henry Louis Gates Jr., *Stony the Road: Reconstruction, White Supremacy, and the Rise of Jim Crow* (New York: Penguin Press, 2019).

41. Foner, *Reconstruction*, 586.

42. Emma Lou Thornbrough, *The Negro in Indiana: A Study of a Minority* (Indianapolis, IN: Indiana Historical Bureau, 1957), 255.

43. Thornbrough, *The Negro in Indiana*, 255–56, 272.

44. David O. Mull, competition 1, file 249, WOB Papers; 1870 census, Franklin Township, Franklin County, Ohio; David O. Mull, pension file #46524, RG 15, NAB; Harriet Mull (widow), pension file #311111, RG 15, NAB: Affidavit, January 23, 1891.

45. *Annual Report of the Board of Education of the Columbus Public Schools, for the School Year Ending August 31, 1884* (Columbus, OH: Gazette Printing House, 1884), 196, 198; *Annual Report of the Board of Education of the Columbus Public Schools, for the School Year Ending August 31, 1885* (Columbus, OH: The Lutheran Book Concern, 1885), 34; *Annual Report of the Board of Education of the Columbus Public Schools, for the School Year Ending August 31, 1886* (Columbus, OH: The Lutheran Book Concern, 1886), 50; *Annual Report of the Board of Education of the City of Columbus, for the School Year Ending August 31, 1890* (Columbus, OH: Nitschke Bros., 1890), 67; James U. Barnhill, *History of the Schools of Columbus, Ohio* (Columbus, OH: James U. Barnhill, 1892), 75; Harriet Mull pension file: Edward S. Wilson, MD, Affidavit, January 7, 1891.

46. Barnhill, *History of the Schools of Columbus*, 74.

47. Christopher K. Hays, "Way Down in Egypt Land: Conflict and Community in Cairo, Illinois, 1850–1930" (PhD diss., University of Missouri-Columbia, 1996:

Ann Arbor, MI: UMI Company, 1997; Illinois State Historical Library, Springfield, IL), 352.

48. *Cairo* (IL) *Bulletin*, January 21, 1875.

49. *Cairo Bulletin*.

50. *Cairo Evening Bulletin*, February 1, 1869; *Cairo Evening Bulletin*, July 21, 1869; *Cairo Daily Bulletin*, September 15, 1870; *Cairo Daily Bulletin*, December 22, 1870.

51. *Cairo Evening Bulletin*, February 1, 1869.

52. *Cairo Daily Bulletin*, September 15, 1870.

53. *Cairo Daily Bulletin*, April 13, 1870.

54. *Cairo Daily Bulletin*, September 10, 1871; *Cairo Daily Bulletin*, December 20, 1871; *Cairo Daily Bulletin*, December 22, 1871.

55. Hays, "Way Down in Egypt Land: Conflict and Community in Cairo," 357–58.

56. *Cairo Bulletin*, November 16, 1873; *Cairo Bulletin*, July 22, 1874; *Cairo Bulletin*, July 3, 1874.

57. *Cairo Bulletin*, September 27, 1876; *Cairo Bulletin*, September 28, 1876; *Cairo Bulletin*, October 1, 1876; *Cairo Bulletin*, February 21, 1877; *Cairo Bulletin*, March 21, 1877.

58. *Cairo Bulletin*, March 29, 1877.

59. Giles W. Shurtleff, Letters of June 17, 1877, and August 9, 1877, in American Missionary Association Manuscripts, Microfilm Ohio Roll 21, Amistad Research Center, Tulane University, New Orleans, LA.

60. *Cairo Bulletin*, August 9, 1877.

61. *Cairo Bulletin*, December 5, 1877; *Cairo Bulletin*, December 6, 1877.

62. *Cairo Bulletin*, March 31, 1878.

63. Hays, "Way Down in Egypt Land: Conflict and Community in Cairo," 357–58; William B. Neff (ed.), *Bench and Bar of Northern Ohio: History and Biography* (Cleveland, OH: The Historical Publishing Co., 1921), 131; Cyrene E. Margolis, *Stark County, Ohio Civil War Veterans: A History of Those Who Served* (Knoxville, TN: Tennessee Valley Publishing, 2002), 187–88.

64. "Brooklyn NY History," accessed May 3, 2020, http://www.brooklynonline.com/history.

65. *National Republican*, September 14, 1875; *Evening Star*, September 14, 1875; *Sun*, September 14, 1875.

66. *Sun*.

67. H. H. Proctor. "Self-Supporting Church. The First Congregational Church, of Atlanta, Ga.," *The American Missionary* 90(1) (March 1898): 35; Allison Dorsey, *To Build Our Lives Together: Community Formation in Black Atlanta, 1875–1906* (Athens: University of Georgia Press, 2004), 59; *New York Evening Post*, August 3, 1887.

68. *New York Evening Post*.

69. *Fort Worth Daily Gazette*, July 20, 1887.

70. *Fort Worth Daily Gazette*; *Alexandria Gazette*, July 27, 1887; *Austin* (TX) *Weekly Statesman*, July 28, 1887.

71. *Austin Weekly Statesman*; *New York Tribune*, July 30, 1887.

72. *Albany Evening Journal*, July 30, 1887.

73. *New York Tribune*, August 3, 1887.

74. *New York Evening Post*, August 3, 1887.

75. *New York Evening Post*, August 16, 1887.

76. *Albany Evening Journal*, August 23, 1887.

77. *Albany Evening Journal*.

78. *Lowell Daily Courier*, August 9, 1887; *Lowell Daily Courier*, August 29, 1887.

79. *Troy* (NY) *Daily Times*, September 1, 1887; *Austin Weekly Statesman*, September 1, 1887.

80. Edgar J. Wiley, comp., *Catalogue of the Officers and Students of Middlebury College in Middlebury, Vermont, and of Others who Have Received Degrees, 1800–1915* (Middlebury, VT: Published by Middlebury College, 1917), 223; Evarts B. Kent, pension file #44812, RG 15, NAB.

81. *Morning News* (Savannah, GA), August 20, 1887.

82. *Burlington Weekly Free Press*, September 2, 1887.

83. *Burlington Weekly Free Press*.

84. *Lockport Daily Journal*, September 2, 1887.

85. *Evening Star*, September 23, 1887; *New York Evening Post*, September 23, 1887; *Burlington Weekly Free Press*, September 30, 1887.

86. *New York Evening Post*, October 3, 1887; *New York Evening Post*, October 26, 1887.

87. *New York Evening Post*, September 23, 1887.

88. *Burlington Weekly Free Press*, September 30, 1887.

89. *Seventy-Fifth Anniversary: General Catalogue of Oberlin College, 1833–1908* (Oberlin, OH: Published by Oberlin College [Press of O. S. Hubbell Printing Co., of Cleveland] 1909), Int. 38, 771; Henry Robert Burke, "John Newton Templeton – First African-American Graduate of Ohio University," 1999, accessed May 7, 2021, http://lestweforget.hamptonu.edu/page.cfm?u uid=9FEC4DF3-B710-52F7-18FFD0C8B2E59FE6; "OHIOtrivia, February 2019," accessed May 7, 2021, https://www.ohio.edu/alumni/newsletter-images /OHIOAlumni/2019/February2019/OA_February2019TRIVIA.html; Stephen Middleton, *The Black Laws in the Old Northwest: A Documentary History* (Westport, CT: Greenwood Press, 1993), xv–xvi, 3–7; Joseph W. Tannehill, *Ohio Interrogation Points* (Columbus, OH: F. J. Heer Printing Company, 1917), 33–34.

90. Middleton, *The Black Laws in the Old Northwest*, 7; Tannehill, *Ohio Interrogation Points*, 33–34.

91. *Marietta* (OH) *Semi-Weekly Register*, June 3, 1887.

92. *Burlington Weekly Free Press*, September 30, 1887; *New York Evening Post*, September 23, 1887; *Freeman* (Fremont, OH), February 2, 1850; *Spirit of Democracy* (Woodsfield, OH), February 27, 1850; Kate Rousmaniere, "School Segregation in Oxford Ohio: The Perry Gibson Case of 1887," January 2003, accessed May 3, 2020, www.units.miamioh.edu/eduleadership/faculty/kate/oxford/deseg.html; *New York Evening Post*, September 21, 1887.

93. *Burlington Weekly Free Press*, September 30, 1887; *New York Evening Post*, September 23, 1887; *Wichita Daily Eagle*, November 17, 1887; *Iola* (KS) *Register*, November 18, 1887; Kim C. Warren, *The Quest for Citizenship: African American and Native American Education in Kansas, 1880–1935* (Chapel Hill: University of North Carolina Press, 2010), 104–5, 111–14.

94. *Burlington Weekly Free Press*.

95. *Albany Evening Journal*, January 30, 1888.

96. *Bennington* (VT) *Banner*, April 19, 1888.

97. *Bennington Banner*.

98. *New York Tribune*, July 25, 1880.

99. Samuel W. Durant, *History of Ingham and Eaton Counties Michigan, with Illustrations and Biographical Sketches of their Prominent Men and Pioneers* (Philadelphia, PA: D. W. Ensign & Co., 1880), 585; *Portrait and Biographical Album of Ingham & Livingston Counties, MICHIGAN* (Chicago, IL: Chapman Bros., 1891), 411–12.

100. "Views of Leading Colored Men, on the Results of the Election," *Southern Workman*, February 1885, 23.

101. *St. Paris* (OH) *New-Era*, August 20, 1883; *Buffalo Evening News*, August 20, 1883; *Cortland* (NY) *News*, August 20, 1883; *Evening Star*, July 31, 1883; *National Republican*, May 31, 1883; *Washington Times*, October 7, 1911—at the time of his decision, Mills was the Department of the Potomac's Judge Advocate.

102. *Buffalo Evening News*.

103. *Daily Globe* (St. Paul, MN), October 16, 1883; Fireside, *Separate and Unequal*, 20–21.

104. *Daily Globe*; Fireside, *Separate and Unequal*, 20–21; *New York Daily Tribune*, October 16, 1883. "Jim Crow" refers to a general pattern of discrimination against African Americans based on actual laws, such as "black codes" in many Northern states throughout the nineteenth century, or the systematic use of discriminatory local and state statutes across the Lower South that affected every aspect of black life well into the second half of the twentieth century, or social practice.

The term is usually attributed to a racist minstrel show tune, "Jump Jim Crow," sung decades before the Civil War. The April 28, 1837, edition of the *Vermont Phoenix* of Brattleboro reported that "The negro song of *Jim Crow* is being arranged by the London musicians for a superb quadrill [*sic*] and gallopade at Almack's." Four weeks later the *North Carolina Standard* in Raleigh quoted the *New York Express*: "The astonishing popularity of that doggerel song, Jim Crow, shows what curious materials the world is made of. We have heard it sung in all corners of ways and bye-ways in the U.

States, from Maine to Louisiana, and now it is versified to fit English politicians, as appears in the article below, from that grave journal, the London Times."

JIM CROW'S TRIP TO DOWNING-STREET

I cam, good folk, from Downing-street,
A little time ago—
And ebery man dere wheel about,
And jump Jim Crow.
Wheel about and turn about,
And do jis so;
Ebery Whig can wheel about, and jump Jim Crow.

Dere's many oder litel men,
Whose name I do not know,
But all of dem can wheel about,
And jump Jim Crow.
Wheel about, and turn about,
And do jis so;
No nigger like de Ministers can jump Jim Crow.

—May 24, 1837.

105. *New York Evening Post*, October 16, 1883; *New York Age*, May 20, 1922; *Lockport Daily Journal*, April 10, 1880.

106. *Memphis Daily Appeal*, October 17, 1883.

107. *Easley* (SC) *Messenger*, October 19, 1883.

108. *Memphis Daily Appeal*, October 17, 1883.

109. *New York Daily Tribune*, October 17, 1883.

110. *Sun*, October 23, 1883.

111. *Daily Los Angeles Herald*, October 18, 1883.

112. *Emporia* (KS) *Weekly News*, October 18, 1883.

113. *National Republican*, October 23, 1883.

114. *National Republican*; *Evening Times* (Washington, DC), July 21, 1899; *Appeal* (St. Paul, MN), July 29, 1899.

115. *World*, November 18, 1883; *National Republican*, November 19, 1883.

116. *World*; *National Republican*.

117. *Vermont Phoenix* (Brattleboro), November 23, 1883.

118. "Current Topics," November 17, 1883, in Irving Browne, cond., *The Albany Law Journal: A Weekly Record of the Law and the Lawyers*, vol. XXVIII (July, 1883, to January, 1884) (Albany, NY: Weed, Parsons and Company, 1884), 381; *Washington Critic*, August 6, 1887.

119. Packard, *American Nightmare*, 60.

120. *Rome* (NY) *Daily Sentinel*, January 19, 1884; *Omaha Daily Bee*, March 4, 1884; *Anderson Intelligencer*, March 13, 1884.

121. *Omaha Daily Bee; Intelligencer; Iola Register*, March 14, 1884; "Ex parte Yarbrough, 110 U.S. 651 (1884)," accessed May 3, 2020, https://supreme.justia.com /cases/federal/us/110/651/case.html.

122. John D. Smith, *Black Judas: William Hannibal Thomas and The American Negro* (Athens: University of Georgia Press, 2000), 162.

123. *Cleveland Gazette*, January 30, 1886.

124. *Stark County* (OH) *Democrat*, August 5, 1886.

125. *Massillon* (OH) *Independent*, August 20, 1886.

126. *Cleveland Gazette*, December 4, 1886.

127. Gannon, *The Won Cause*, 6, 85.

128. Gannon, *The Won Cause*, 92–93, 105.

129. Gannon, *The Won Cause*, 5; Shaffer, *After the Glory*, 157.

130. Gannon, *The Won Cause*, 25; Shaffer, *After the Glory*, 157.

131. *Daily Morning Call* (San Francisco), August 3, 1886.

132. Gannon, *The Won Cause*, 25.

133. *Proceedings of the Twenty-Second Annual Encampment of the Department of Ohio, Grand Army of the Republic, Held at Toledo, Ohio, April 25th, 26th and 27th, 1888* (LOC E462.1.O367), 131–32, 134, 138; *Cleveland Gazette*, May 5, 1888.

134. *Proceedings of the Twenty-Third Annual Encampment of the Department of Ohio*, 67–68.

135. *National Tribune*, June 13, 1889.

136. Gannon, *The Won Cause*, 5; Shaffer, *After the Glory*, 152–56.

137. *Utica Morning Herald*, August 4, 1885; *New York Tribune*, August 8, 1885. They were not the only members of a minority to honor Grant—according to the *Philadelphia Inquirer*'s August 22, 1885, edition, "'Among the touching sights of the great Grant funeral procession,' says the *Independent*, 'were the Jewish rabbis, who could not ride on their Sabbath, and who walked the whole distance, some Christian ministers keeping them company by turns.'"

138. Accessed September 6, 2021, http://chroniclingamerica.loc.gov/lccn/ sn82016187. While the background information for the *National Tribune* on the Library of Congress *Chronicling America* website states that the publication evolved into "the official paper of the Grand Army of the Republic," the newspaper steadfastly refuted this. In its August 11, 1910 edition, the issue was directly addressed in an excellent piece that nowadays would be called a mission statement:

> The National Tribune has, whenever occasion arose, emphatically denied that it was an organ of the Grand Army of the Republic or that the Order was in any way responsible for what appeared in its columns. The National Tribune is a thoroly [*sic*] independent paper and expresses only the opinions and beliefs of the editor and owners. It has no financial or other allegiance to any order, party, syndicate or association of men whatever outside of its little circle of stockholders. There is no more independent paper in the United States than The National Tribune. While a large proportion of its subscribers and supporters are GAR men, yet it has very many thousands who do not

belong to the Order and who are too young to have been in the war, and this proportion is constantly increasing as the people generally become aware of its fair, independent spirit and the value of the reliable, impartial news from the National Capital that it contains. From the very first The National Tribune has declined to be considered the organ of the Grand Army of the Republic, believing that it could be of much more service to the Order and to the veterans and their widows by occupying an independent position. It is an organ only of the great body of patriotic people of the country, and its first object, intention and purpose is to voice their wishes and feelings on everything that concerns the prosperity and advancement of our country. It is the only paper in the country that devotes itself to steady and unflinching support of the principles for which the war was fought, to a proper conservation of the results gained at such a terrible price of life and health, and it is the only one which constantly stands on guard to prevent any invasion or nullification of those results. It is the only paper that devotes itself to keeping alive the memories of the inestimable services which the veterans rendered the country in its hour of mortal peril and to properly reminding the people of this country how much they owe the men who gave lavishly of their young health and strength to saving the Nation. It is the only paper that tells the stories of the great battles, the appalling slaughter, the breaking marches and trials of camp and picket life, truthfully, accurately and in a way to secure conviction. This far it is an organ of the GAR and no farther.

139. *National Tribune*, August 22, 1889.

140. *Troy Daily Times*, November 7, 1889.

141. *Fair Play* (Ste. Genevieve, MO), January 25, 1890.

Chapter 6

1. *Iola Register*, August 21, 1891.

2. *Sun*, January 5, 1890; Shaffer, *After the Glory*, 145; *Omaha Daily Bee*, January 6, 1890.

3. *Wichita Eagle*, August 3, 1887.

4. *St. Paul Daily Globe*, December 10, 1889; *Sun*, December 12, 1889; *New York Herald*, December 12, 1889.

5. *St. Paul Daily Globe*; *New York Tribune*, December 11, 1889.

6. *New York Tribune*; *News and Citizen* (Morrisville and Hyde Park, VT), December 19, 1889.

7. *New York Herald*, December 12, 1889.

8. "Lancaster Daily Intelligencer (Lancaster, PA)," accessed May 3, 2020, https://chroniclingamerica.loc.gov/lccn/sn83032300/; *Lancaster Daily Intelligencer*, December 11, 1889.

9. *Sun*, December 12, 1889.

10. *New York Herald*, December 12, 1889.

11. *Kansas City* (MO) *Sun*, August 1, 1914; "The Colonel: James Lewis, Sr.," accessed 5/3/2020, http://www.creolegen.org/2012/06/20/the-colonel-james-lewis-sr.

12. *National Tribune*, December 19, 1889.

13. *Sun*, January 6, 1890; *Pittsburg Dispatch*, January 6, 1890; *Omaha Daily Bee*, January 6, 1890; *Fort Worth Daily Gazette*, July 15, 1887; *Emporia Weekly News*, August 8, 1889; *New York Evening Post*, July 18, 1914; *Kansas City Sun*, August 1, 1914.

14. *Washington* (DC) *Bee*, January 11, 1890.

15. *Sun*, February 13, 1890.

16. *Gazette and Farmers' Journal*, January 30, 1890.

17. *Syracuse Weekly Express*, February 27, 1890.

18. *Evening Star*, July 16, 1890; *Duluth Evening Herald*, July 29, 1890; *Buffalo Courier*, August 4, 1891; B. N. Adams, comp., *Unofficial Proceedings in Connection with the Twenty-Forth National Encampment, Grand Army of the Republic, Held in Boston, Week August 11–16, 1890, issued under the direction of the Executive Committee* (Boston, MA: E. B. Stillings & Co., Printers, 1891), 126, 161.

19. *National Tribune*, August 21, 1890.

20. *National Tribune*, October 23, 1890.

21. *National Tribune*, March 17, 1892; *Buffalo Courier*, August 4, 1891; *Rochester* (NY) *Democrat and Chronicle*, August 5, 1891.

22. *Rochester Democrat and Chronicle*.

23. *New York Herald*, August 5, 1891.

24. *New York Evening Post*, August 5, 1891.

25. *Statesman* (Yonkers, NY), August 6, 1891.

26. *Statesman*.

27. *Journal of the Twenty-Fifth National Encampment, Grand Army of the Republic, Detroit, Mich., August 5th, 6th and 7th, 1891* (Rutland, VT: The Tuttle Company, Printers, 1891), 50–52; *New York Evening Post*, August 6, 1891.

28. *Journal of the Twenty-Fifth National Encampment*, 52.

29. *Brooklyn Daily Eagle*, August 6, 1891; *Wheeling Intelligencer*, August 7, 1891.

30. *Brooklyn Daily Eagle*; *Wheeling Intelligencer*.

31. *Journal of the Twenty-Fifth National Encampment*, 10, 14, 176. The five committee members were William Warner of Missouri, John P. Rea of Minnesota, W. S. Decker of Colorado, Henry E. Taintor of Connecticut, and Lucius Fairchild of Wisconsin. Fairchild (1886), Rea (1887), and Warner (1888) were all past commanders in chief, and Taintor was commander of the Department of Connecticut in 1887—see also McConnell, *Glorious Contentment*, 217.

32. *Journal of the Twenty-Fifth National Encampment*, 249–50; *Rock Island* (IL) *Daily Argus*, August 7, 1891.

33. *Journal of the Twenty-Fifth National Encampment*, 251.

34. *Journal of the Twenty-Fifth National Encampment*, 252–54.

35. *World*, August 7, 1891; *Rock Island Daily Argus*, August 7, 1891.

36. *Journal of the Twenty-Fifth National Encampment*, 254–55.

37. *Evening Star*, August 7, 1891.

38. *Journal of the Twenty-Fifth National Encampment*, 37, 256; *Evening Star*.

39. *Journal of the Twenty-Fifth National Encampment*, 21, 256–57.
40. *Evening Star*, August 7, 1891.
41. *Journal of the Twenty-Fifth National Encampment*, 42, 258.
42. *Journal of the Twenty-Fifth National Encampment*, 259–62.
43. *Journal of the Twenty-Fifth National Encampment*, 18, 262.
44. *Journal of the Twenty-Fifth National Encampment*, 261–63.
45. *Evening Star*, August 7, 1891.
46. *Evening Star*.
47. *Journal of the Twenty-Fifth National Encampment*, 263–64.
48. *World*, August 7, 1891.
49. *Evening World*, August 7, 1891.
50. *New York Herald*, August 8, 1891.
51. *Omaha Daily Bee*, August 10, 1891; *Worthington* (MN) *Advance*, August 13, 1891; *St. Johnsbury Caledonian*, August 13, 1891; *Hartford* (CT) *Post*, cited by *Iola Register*, August 21, 1891.
52. *Evening Herald* (Shenandoah, PA), August 22, 1891.
53. *National Patriotic Order Sons of America*, accessed May 3, 2020, http://www.nationalposofa.org.
54. *Pittsburg Dispatch*, August 27, 1891; *Fort Worth Gazette*, August 27, 1891.
55. *Pittsburg Dispatch*; *Fort Worth Gazette*.
56. *National Tribune*, September 3, 1891.
57. *Washington Bee*, September 5, 1891.
58. *Sacramento Daily Record-Union*, August 8, 1891.
59. *Appeal* (St. Paul, MN), August 15, 1891.
60. *National Tribune*, August 20, 1891.
61. *Stark County Democrat*, September 10, 1891.
62. *Washington Bee*, August 22, 1891.
63. *Washington Bee*, September 19, 1891.
64. *Appeal*, September 12, 1891.
65. *Stark County Democrat*, August 20, 1891; *Iron County Register* (Ironton, MO), August 20, 1891.
66. *World*, cited by *Iola Register*, August 21, 1891.
67. *Sun*, August 10, 1891.
68. *Rock Island Daily Argus*, September 8, 1891; *Wellington* (OH) *Enterprise*, September 9, 1891; *Appeal*, September 12, 1891.
69. *Daily Argus*; *Appeal*.
70. *Brenham* (TX) *Weekly Banner*, September 17, 1891.
71. *Evening Star*, September 21, 1892.
72. *Warrensburgh* (NY) *News*, January 7, 1892.
73. *Brooklyn Standard-Union*, February 6, 1892.
74. *National Tribune*, March 17, 1892; *Evening Star*, September 21, 1892 (NB: Palmer's entire commander in chief address to the 1892 National Encampment was printed in this edition).

75. *Evening Star.*
76. *Evening Star, Rochester Democrat and Chronicle,* May 20, 1892.
77. *Elmira* (NY) *Gazette and Free Press,* May 3, 1892; *Evening Star.*
78. *National Tribune,* June 9, 1892; *Evening Star.*
79. *Lowell Daily Courier,* June 4, 1892.
80. *Wichita Daily Eagle,* May 13, 1892; *Evening Star,* September 21, 1892.
81. *Evening Star.*
82. *Times* (Amenia, NY), December 1, 1892.
83. Shaffer, *After the Glory,* 145–49.
84. Shaffer, *After the Glory,* 150.
85. McConnell, *Glorious Contentment,* 216–18.
86. *National Tribune,* April 24, 1890.
87. *National Tribune,* October 23, 1890.
88. *National Tribune,* November 6, 1890. Though he didn't mention it, Goodrich knew first-hand how well black soldiers had acquitted themselves during the Civil War. In 1864 he had transferred from the 115th New York to serve as a second lieutenant in Thomas W. Higginson's First South Carolina (later reclassified as Thirty-Third USCT), the first regiment composed entirely of freedmen (*Annual Report of the Adjutant-General of the State of New York, For the Year 1903: Registers of the One Hundred and Fourteenth, One Hundred and Fifteenth, One Hundred and Sixteenth, One Hundred and Seventeenth, One Hundred and Eighteenth, One Hundred and Nineteenth and One Hundred and Twentieth Regiments of Infantry* (Albany, NY: Oliver A. Quayle, State Legislative Printer, 1904), 221, accessed May 11, 2021, https://museum.dmna.ny.gov/application/files/2115/ 5309/5400/115th_ Infantry_CW_Roster.pdf; *New York Tribune,* January 23, 1893).
89. *National Tribune,* May 19, 1892.
90. *St. Paul Daily Globe,* November 26, 1892.
91. *National Tribune,* April 13, 1893.
92. *National Tribune,* April 6, 1893.
93. *National Tribune,* September 3, 1896.
94. *National Tribune.*
95. *Times,* December 1, 1892.

Chapter 7

1. "United States Supreme Court, Plessy v. Ferguson (1896), No. 210," accessed 5/4/2020, http://caselaw.lp.findlaw.com/scripts/getcase.pl?court=US&vol =163&invol=537
2. *Syracuse Daily Journal,* June 23, 1887.
3. *Syracuse Daily Journal, Buffalo Evening News,* January 13, 1899. Depew would become a Senator from New York in 1899.
4. G. G. Benedict, *A Short History of the 14th Vermont Reg't* (Bennington, VT: Press of C. A. Pierce, 1887), 29–32; Carol Reardon, *Pickett's Charge in History and Memory* (Chapel Hill: University of North Carolina Press, 1997), 92.

5. Andrew E. Ford, *The Story of the Fifteenth Regiment Massachusetts Volunteer Infantry in the Civil War, 1861–1864* (Clinton, MA: Press of W. J. Coulter, 1898), 37–39, 153–54; Steve Light, "The Great Cause," May 16, 2013, accessed May 4, 2020, http://battlefieldbackstories.blogspot.ca/2013/05/the-great-cause.html—see also Reardon.

6. *Lancaster Daily Intelligencer*, July 6, 1887.

7. *Troy Daily Times*, July 5, 1887.

8. *Post* (Ellicottville, NY), July 4, 1888; *Butler* (PA) *Citizen*, July 13, 1888; *Burlington Weekly Free Press*, July 20, 1888; *Albany* (NY) *Times*, July 6, 1888.

9. *Daily Graphic*, August 11, 1886.

10. *Salt Lake Herald*, July 3, 1888

11. *Daily Graphic*, August 11, 1886.

12. *Poughkeepsie Daily Eagle*, September 1, 1892; *Rock Island Daily Argus*, September 1, 1892; *Saratogian* (NY), September 8, 1892.

13. *Salt Lake Herald*, July 4, 1888.

14. *Salt Lake Herald*.

15. *Salt Lake Herald*.

16. *Salt Lake Herald*.

17. *Burlington Weekly Free Press*, July 20, 1888. As detailed by black Union veteran and GAR Judge Advocate George W. Williams, "During the winter of 1863–64 a large number of Negro troops were at persistent drill in Maryland, under Burnside, and in Virginia, under Butler." They would make their field debut in February 1864, and "By the spring of 1864 a numerous force of Negro troops had been added to [the Army of the Potomac], and an active and brilliant military career opened up to them" (*A History of the Negro Troops in the War of the Rebellion, 1861–1865* [New York: Harper & Brothers, 1888], ix–x, 231–56).

18. William H. Powell (ed.), *Officers of the Army and Navy (Volunteer) Who Served in the Civil War* (Philadelphia, PA: L.R. Hamersly & Co., 1893), 322.

19. *Butler Citizen*, July 13, 1888.

20. Powell, *Officers of the Army and Navy*, 127; *National Tribune*, July 15, 1897; *Salt Lake Tribune*, May 30, 1909. Gobin would rise even further in the GAR, becoming its commander in chief in 1897 (*National Tribune*, September 2, 1897).

21. *Butler Citizen*, July 13, 1888.

22. Powell, *Officers of the Army and Navy*, 100.

23. *Butler Citizen*, July 13, 1888.

24. *Butler Citizen*. When the *Bellows Falls* (VT) *Times* considered Longstreet's "nomination and confirmation . . . as Surveyor of the Port of New Orleans" on June 25, 1869, it reported the former Confederate general "has doubtless been called upon to endure much opposition and obloquy from his late associates in the rebel army, and from others who refuse to be comforted and reconstructed. He is called a traitor to the lost cause."

In its January 4, 1904, obituary, the New York *Commercial Advertiser* quoted Longstreet on his postwar views: "'the surrender of my sword was my reconstruction.

I looked upon the 'Lost Cause' as a cause totally, irrevocably lost. I adopted the principles of the Republican party, and threw myself into sympathy with the government into which I had been received as a member. Of course, by this action I sacrificed the esteem of the southern people.'"

The newspaper noted that Longstreet's joining an 1870 New Orleans procession of African Americans celebrating the Fifteenth Amendment's ratification "particularly enraged the south," and he "was ostracized for accepting Republican office," including his New Orleans post, "internal revenue collector" in 1878 and "postmaster" in 1879, the last two positions coming after his having moved to Georgia.

25. *Proceedings of the Twenty-Third Annual Encampment of the Department of Ohio*, 38.

26. *Proceedings of the Twenty-Third Annual Encampment of the Department of Ohio*, 38.

27. *Michigan at Gettysburg, July 1st, 2nd and 3rd, 1863: Proceedings Incident to the Dedication of the Michigan Monuments upon the Battlefield of Gettysburg, June 12th, 1889* (Detroit, MI: Winn & Hammond, 1889), 88.

28. *Michigan at Gettysburg, July 1st, 2nd and 3rd, 1863*, 89–90.

29. *Michigan at Gettysburg, July 1st, 2nd and 3rd, 1863*, 93.

30. *Twenty-Seventh Annual Report of the Superintendent of Public Instruction, State of New York* (1881), 187; *Rochester City Directory 1880*, 479, accessed May 4, 2020, www.libraryweb.org/rochcitydir/images/1880/1880stats.pdf; *Publications of Rochester Historical Society*, vol. I (Rochester, NY: Rochester Historical Society, 1892), 80; *Rochester Historical Society Publication Fund Series*, vol. VIII (Rochester, NY: Rochester Historical Society, 1939), 131.

31. *Rochester Democrat and Chronicle*, February 23, 1890.

32. *Western Kansas World* (WaKeeney), December 19, 1885; *Western Kansas World*, March 3, 1894.

33. *Western Kansas World*, May 30, 1891.

34. Blight, *Race and Reunion*, 2, 95, 104–5.

35. Eric Foner, "Ken Burns and the Romance of Reunion," in Robert B. Toplin (ed.), *Ken Burns's the Civil War: Historians Respond* (New York: Oxford University Press, 1996), 113.

36. Shaffer, *After the Glory*, 169.

37. Andre Fleche, "'Shoulder to Shoulder as Comrades Tried': Black and White Union Veterans and Civil War Memory," *Civil War History* 51(2) (2001): 175–201.

38. Fleche, "'Shoulder to Shoulder as Comrades Tried,'" 175–201.

39. M. Keith Harris, "Slavery, Emancipation, and Veterans of the Union Cause: Commemorating Freedom in the Era of Reconciliation, 1885–1915," *Civil War History* 53(3) (2007): 264–90.

40. Caroline E. Janney, "The Civil War at 150: Memory and Meaning," *Common-Place* 14(2) (2014), accessed August 23, 2014, www.common-place.org/vol-14/no-02/janney/#.VFCLvWfYHyg; Janney, *Remembering the Civil War*, 9.

41. Hess, *The Union Soldier in Battle*, 160, 168–69.
42. *National Tribune*, July 28, 1892.
43. *Wichita Daily Eagle*, May 13, 1892.
44. *Morning Call* (San Francisco), March 11, 1894.
45. *Morning Call*.
46. *Morning Call*; *New York Tribune*, August 3, 1863; *Daily Morning and Journal Courier* (New Haven, CT), June 25, 1904
47. *Sun*, July 21, 1895
48. Fireside, *Separate and Unequal*, 1–8, 22–28, 115–41, 184–219, 241–45.
49. Fireside, *Separate and Unequal*, 221–30; *New York Evening Post*, May 18, 1896.
50. Fireside, *Separate and Unequal*, 221–25; *Weekly Messenger* (St. Martinville, LA), May 23, 1896; *Roanoke Daily Times*, May 19, 1896.
51. Fireside, *Separate and Unequal*, 225–26; *New York Daily Tribune*, May 19, 1896; *Princeton* (MN) *Union*, May 21, 1896.
52. Fireside, *Separate and Unequal*, 226–28; *Evening Star*, June 24, 1896; *Iowa State Bystander* (Des Moines), August 7, 1896.
53. Packard, *American Nightmare*, 78.
54. *Utica* (NY) *Observer*, December 12, 1971; *Iowa State Bystander*, September 14, 1894; *St. Paul Daily Globe*, June 28, 1895. In 1895 Wells married Chicago attorney and civil rights activist Ferdinand L. Barnett, a forty-one–year-old widower with two sons. Several years earlier Barnett had hired his future wife for his paper, *The Conservator*.
55. Packard, *American Nightmare*, 56–57, 232–33; Fireside, *Separate and Unequal*, 241–44; *Newtown* (NY) *Register*, March 23, 1899.
56. Patrick J. Kelly, "The Election of 1896 and the Restructuring of Civil War Memory," *Civil War History* 49(3) (2003): 254–80.
57. Kelly, "The Election of 1896 and the Restructuring of Civil War Memory," 254–80.
58. Blight, *Race and Reunion*, 347–54; Janney, *Remembering the Civil War*, 222–25; *Evening Star*, April 12, 1898; *Evening Times*, May 7, 1898; *San Francisco Call*, February 17, 1898.
59. *Lexington* (VA) *Gazette*, May 4, 1898; *Evening Star*, June 15, 1898; *National Tribune*, July 21, 1898.
60. *Washington Times*, January 26, 1906.
61. Anthony L. Powell, "An Overview: Black Participation in the Spanish-American War," accessed May 4, 2020, www.spanamwar.com/AfroAmericans.htm; Marvin Fletcher, "The Black Volunteers in the Spanish-American War," *Military Affairs* 38(2) (April 1974): 48–53; "Buffalo Soldiers and the Spanish-American War," accessed May 4, 2020, www.nps.gov/prsf/historyculture/buffalo-soldiers-and-the-spanish-american-war.htm; *Rochester Democrat and Chronicle*, July 17, 1894; Blight, *Race and Reunion*, 347–54; Janney, *Remembering the Civil War*, 225–27; *Salt Lake Herald*, May 18, 1898; *Evening Star*, April 23, 1905; *Appeal*, October 8, 1898.

62. *Sun*, May 1, 1898; Powell, "An Overview: Black Participation in the Spanish-American War"; *Broad Ax* (Chicago), September 7, 1918. The four black regiments of Army Regulars that emerged from the original six segregated units formed under Congressional action in 1866 were called "Buffalo Soldiers," a term the soldiers themselves rarely used, but of which they were proud. According to the National Park Service, the sobriquet most likely originated with the Cheyenne due to perceived similarity between African American soldiers' hair and buffalo fur. Given the veneration accorded buffalo by Native Americans, the term was one of respect and fitting, as the Buffalo Soldiers became adversaries to be contended with and feared: "The Buffalo Soldiers." Accessed May 4, 2020, www.nps.gov/prsf/historyculture/buffalo-soldiers.htm.

63. *Sun*.

64. Kelly, "The Election of 1896 and the Restructuring of Civil War Memory," 254–80.

65. Fletcher, "The Black Volunteers in the Spanish-American War," 48–53; Powell, "An Overview: Black Participation in the Spanish-American War"; Blight, *Race and Reunion*, 351–53; Janney, *Remembering the Civil War*, 226–29; *Broad Ax*, September 7, 1918; *New York Tribune Illustrated Supplement*, August 1898; *New Haven Morning Journal and Courier*, September 10, 1898. On July 31, 1898 the *New York Tribune* reported that six black non-commissioned officers (two in the Ninth Cavalry and four in the Twenty-Fifth Infantry) "who rendered particularly gallant and meritorious service in the face of the enemy in the actions around Santiago on July 1 and 2 have been appointed second lieutenants in the two colored immune regiments recently organized under special act of Congress . . . These two negro regiments were in the thick of the fiercest fighting at El Caney and San Juan and won high praise for their courage and efficiency. The 9th Cavalry was also with the Rough Riders at La Quasina."

66. *National Tribune*, September 22, 1898.

67. *World*, August 22, 1898; James N. Leiker, *Racial Borders: Black Soldiers along the Rio Grande* (College Station: Texas A&M University Press, 2010), 104.

68. Leiker, *Racial Borders*, 104.

69. Leiker, *Racial Borders*, 189–90; *Iowa State Bystander*, January 27, 1905; *New York Herald*, August 20, 1899; Herschel V. Cashin, Charles Alexander, William T. Anderson, Arthur M. Brown, and Horace W. Bivins, *Under Fire with the Tenth United States Cavalry* (New York: F. Tennyson Neely, 1899), xiii–xiv, 277–79; *New York Times*, September 9, 1917.

70. *National Tribune*, July 23, 1891.

71. *Evening Bulletin* (Maysville, KY), July 8, 1897; *Caucasian* (Clinton, NC), July 8, 1897.

72. *Alexandria Gazette*, September 16, 1897; *Austin Weekly Statesman*, September 23, 1897; *Evening Bulletin* (Honolulu, HI), September 23, 1897; *Evening Star*, October 4, 1897; *Richmond Planet*, October 9, 1897. The *Richmond Planet* was "founded by 13 former Richmond slaves" in 1882, and "initially edited by Edmund

Archer Randolph, the first African American graduate of Yale Law School. Two years later, 21-year-old John Mitchell, Jr., succeeded Randolph and continued as editor for the next 45 years, until 1929" (accessed August 30, 2021, https://chroniclingamerica.loc.gov/lccn/sn84025841/).

73. *Salt Lake Herald*, February 24, 1898; *Wichita Daily Eagle*, February 23, 1898; *Sun*, February 24, 1898; Donna Tracy, "Lake City remembers postmaster's lynching with historical marker," *Lake City* (SC) *News & Post*, October 9, 2013, accessed May 4, 2020, www.scnow.com/newsandpost/news/article_9407d6dc-30dc-11e3-a206 -0019bb30f31a.html.

74. *Salt Lake Herald*; *Daily Eagle*; Tracy.

75. *Appeal*, March 5, 1898.

76. *Alexandria Gazette*, March 21, 1898.

77. *Iowa State Bystander*, May 6, 1898.

78. *Evening Herald*, June 29, 1898; *True Democrat* (Bayou Sara, LA), July 9, 1898; *Evening Star*, August 1, 1898.

79. *Washington Times*, December 30, 1898.

80. *Washington Times*, January 18, 1899; *Manning* (SC) *Times*, April 5, 1899; *Evening Star*, April 8, 1899; *Evening Star*, April 10, 1899.

81. *Evening Star*, April 10, 1899; *Washington Times*, April 14, 1899; *Evening Times*, April 22, 1899; *Iowa State Bystander*, April 28, 1899.

82. *Evening Times*; *Iowa State Bystander*.

83. *Iowa State Bystander*.

84. *Watchman and Southron* (Sumter, SC), May 3, 1899; see also Blight, 349.

85. *Evening Times*, May 8, 1899.

86. *Appeal*, May 27, 1899.

87. *Gold Leaf* (Henderson, NC), September 1, 1898 (contains Norfolk *Virginian-Pilot* reprint); *Tazewell* (VA) *Republican*, October 27, 1898; *Rock Island Argus*, October 25, 1898.

88. *Appeal*, May 27, 1899. This description of a fictional event grimly foreshadowed what took place twenty-two years later in Tulsa, Oklahoma. Over May 31– June 1, 1921, "Black Wall Street," the "thriving business district and surrounding residential area" of the Greenwood District, a nationally known "affluent African American community," was the focus of a white citizens' riot that began with questionable accusations against a young black man who had ridden in an elevator with a white woman.

When the violence ended twenty-four hours after it began, "35 city blocks lay in charred ruins, over 800 people were treated for injuries and contemporary reports of deaths began at 36. Historians now believe as many as 300 people may have died." Exactly as *The Appeal* had predicted, "twenty-four hours afterward" Greenwood no longer "had a place on the map," and was "merely a pile of ashes and rubbish": "1921 Tulsa Race Massacre," accessed May 4, 2020, https://www.tulsahistory.org/exhibit /1921-tulsa-race-massacre/#flexible-content.

89. *Kansas City* (MO) *Journal*, July 29, 1899.

90.   *Appeal*, December 30, 1899.

91.   *Rochester Democrat and Chronicle*, September 16, 1891.

92.   *Rochester Democrat and Chronicle*; *Washington Herald*, February 15, 1913; *Annual Report of the Adjutant-General of the State of New York, For the Year 1903: Registers of the One Hundred and Twenty-first, One Hundred and Twenty-second, One Hundred and Twenty-third, One Hundred and Twenty-fourth, One Hundred and Twenty-fifth, One Hundred and Twenty-sixth and One Hundred and Twenty-seventh Regiments of Infantry* (Albany, NY: Oliver A. Quayle, State Legislative Printer, 1904), 1160, accessed May 11, 2021, https://museum.dmna.ny.gov/application/files/1615/5309/8777/127th_Infantry_CW_Roster.pdf; accessed 5/4/2020, www.nps.gov/civilwar/search-battle-units-detail.htm?BattleUnitCode=UUS0103RI00C; *Albany Evening Journal*, September 22, 1866.

93.   *Rochester Democrat and Chronicle.*

94.   *Rochester Democrat and Chronicle*, September 16, 1891; *Washington Herald*, February 15, 1913; *Daily Dispatch* (Richmond, VA), March 14, 1865.

95.   *Saint Paul Daily Globe*, April 11, 1881; *Saint Paul Daily Globe*, December 22, 1881; *Evening Star*, December 14, 1905; *New York Tribune*, December 15, 1905. Herman Haupt graduated from West Point at eighteen in 1835 (George G. Meade was a classmate), but soon left the military. Expertise in bridge building and tunneling enabled his rise through the ranks at the Pennsylvania Railroad, with Haupt eventually becoming a director and chief engineer, and also serving as the Hoosac Tunnel project's chief engineer.

When he joined the Union military effort at the personal request of Secretary of War Stanton, his engineering and logistical genius soon became apparent. Originally a civilian employee, he eventually was commissioned a brigadier general. Abraham Lincoln was among his greatest admirers—after he saw what Haupt and his men had constructed in just nine days, the astonished President told a friend: "'I have seen the most remarkable structure that human eyes ever rested upon. That man, Haupt, has built a bridge across Potomac Creek, about four hundred feet long and nearly a hundred feet high, over which loaded trains are running every hour, and, upon my word . . . there is nothing in it but bean-poles and corn-stalks.'"

Haupt continued as the Union military railroad superintendent until September 1863, when he resigned—see O. E. Hunt, "Federal Military Railroads," in O. E. Hunt (ed.), *The Photographic History of the Civil War in Ten Volumes: Volume Five: Forts and Artillery* (Springfield, MA: Patriot Publishing Co., 1911) and *National Tribune*, October 10, 1907.

96.   Henry A. Castle, *History of St. Paul and Vicinity: A Chronicle of Progress and a Narrative Account of the Industries, Institutions, and People of the City and Its Tributary Territory*, vol. II (Chicago, IL: The Lewis Publishing Company, 1912), 571; *The United Service: A Monthly Review of Military and Naval Affairs: Volume I* (Philadelphia, PA: L.R. Hamersly & Co., 1889), 111; *Saint Paul Daily Globe*, March 29, 1897; *Omaha Daily Bee*, September 5, 1896; *Saint Paul Daily Globe*, April 14, 1897; *Saint Paul Daily Globe*, March 30, 1897; *Saint Paul Daily Globe*, March 31, 1897.

97. *Saint Paul Daily Globe*, August 4, 1897.
98. *Saint Paul Daily Globe*, May 11, 1898.
99. *Saint Paul Daily Globe.*
100. *Washington Times*, December 30, 1898.
101. *Richmond Dispatch*, May 31, 1900. McKinley knew all about war and Antietam, still the single deadliest day in American history. As a sergeant in the Twenty-Third Ohio commanding the Commissary Department, on his own initiative he provided "'hot coffee' and 'warm food'" to his regimental comrades despite coming under fire: "Monument to William McKinley," accessed May 4, 2020, www.nps.gov/anti/learn/historyculture/mnt-mckinley.htm.
102. *National Tribune*, August 22, 1901.
103. "Virginia Constitution, 1902," accessed May 8, 2021, http://vagovernment matters.org/primary-sources/517; A. E. Dick Howard, "Opinion/Commentary: Virginia's 1902 Constitution: Era of disenfranchisement," *Daily Progress*, January 3, 2021, accessed May 8, 2021, https://dailyprogress.com/opinion/columnists/opin ion-commentary-virginias-1902-constitution-era-of-disenfranchisement/article _09596440-49e5-11eb-aa32-63e9371c0bdf.html.

Chapter 8

1. *New York Daily Tribune*, June 4, 1869.
2. Ladd, *The Ladd Family*, 222–23; *Executive Documents of the House of Representatives for the Third Session of the Forty-Sixth Congress, 1880–'81*, vol. 19, nos. 12 and 13 (Washington, DC: Government Printing Office, 1881), 252, 609; *Journal of the Executive Proceedings of the Senate of the United States of America: Fifty-Second Congress from December 7, 1891, to March 3, 1893, also Fifty-Third Congress, Special Session from March 4, 1893, to April 15, 1893*, vol. XXVIII (Washington, DC: Government Printing Office, 1909), 52; *Journal of the Executive Proceedings of the Senate of the United States of America: Fifty-Fifth Congress from March 15, 1897, to March 3, 1899*, vol. XXXI, Part I (Washington, DC: Government Printing Office, 1909), 584; *Washington Times*, April 15, 1902; *National Tribune*, March 7, 1907; 1910 census, Summerville, Dorchester County, South Carolina.
3. *Evening Times*, August 7, 1889; *Rock Island Daily Argus*, August 10, 1889; *Newberry* (SC) *Herald and News*, August 15, 1889; *National Tribune*, March 9, 1893.
4. *Evening Times*; *Newberry Herald and News*; *Somerset* (PA) *Herald*, August 14, 1889.
5. Beath, *History of the Grand Army of the Republic*, 139.
6. *Charleston Daily News*, June 25, 1868.
7. *Daily Phoenix* (Columbia, SC), May 17, 1870; *Charleston Daily News*, May 25, 1870.
8. *Charleston Daily News*, May 31, 1870; *St. Johnsbury Caledonian*, September 15, 1882; Linda Welch, "David T. Corbin," accessed May 4, 2020, http://ver montcivilwar.org/units/3/obits.php?input=1430; *New York Herald*, February 3,

1879; *New York Tribune*, February 3, 1879; Douglas R. Egerton, *The Wars of Reconstruction: The Brief, Violent History of America's Most Progressive Era* (New York: Bloomsburg Press, 2014), 268; Walter Allen, *Governor Chamberlain's Administration in South Carolina: A Chapter of Reconstruction in the Southern States* (New York: G. P. Putnam's Sons, 1888), 192–219; 229–36; Foner, *Reconstruction*, 544; *Utica* (NY) *Daily Observer*, June 11, 1872; *New York Daily Tribune*, December 25, 1875; *Syracuse Morning Standard*, August 22, 1876. In December 1875, Whipper would be elected by the general assembly as judge for the First Circuit in Charleston, but Republican Governor Daniel Chamberlain adamantly refused to sign the commission. He considered Whipper to be "Ignorant of law, ignorant of morals, a gambler by open practice, an embezzler of public funds, he is as unfit for judicial position as any man whom by any possibility you could name."

There was basis for the governor's appraisal, as Whipper reportedly lost $27,000 at faro to a black member of Columbia's City Council in 1872, and as secretary of the Sinking Fund Commission in 1871 and 1872 had received but not turned over to the State $19,550 in money and securities. This he acknowledged to an 1873 special committee of investigation: "I have not made a settlement with the Treasurer of the Commission as Secretary. All moneys received by me and the State bonds are yet in my hands." Threatening to take his seat on the bench by force in August 1876, he made no such effort after Chamberlain swore to use all his legal power and authority against both the attorney and anyone "aiding or abetting W. J. Whipper in his . . . unlawful attempt."

9. *Charleston Daily News*.

10. *Charleston Daily News*, May 26, 1871; *Charleston Daily News*, May 30, 1872.

11. *Daily Phoenix*, February 28, 1873; *Edgefield* (SC) *Advertiser*, March 13, 1873.

12. "Beaufort National Cemetery, Beaufort, South Carolina," accessed May 4, 2020, http:///www.nps.gov/nr/travel/national_cemeteries/South_Carolina/Beaufort_National_Cemetery.html; "Beaufort National Cemetery," accessed May 4, 2020, https://www.battlefields.org/visit/heritage-sites/beaufort-national-cem etery; *Jamestown* (NY) *Daily Journal*, June 10, 1873.

13. *Jamestown Daily Journal*; *Daily Phoenix*, August 13, 1868; *Charleston Daily News*, February 1, 1871; *Daily Phoenix*, July 4, 1868.

14. Susan Trail, "Commemoration and the Problem of Reconciliation: The Creation of Antietam National Cemetery," *Catoctin History* (Fall/Winter 2005), 2–9.

15. Trail, "Commemoration and the Problem of Reconciliation," 2–9; *Philadelphia Inquirer*, January 28, 1868; *Documents of the Senate of the State of New York: Ninety-First Session—1868*, vol. VII (Albany, NY: Printing House of C. Van Benthuysen & Sons, 1868), 8.

16. *Philadelphia Inquirer*; *Documents of the Senate of the State of New York*, 35–48.

17. *Philadelphia Inquirer*; *Documents of the Senate of the State of New York*, 8, 35–48; "Covode, John: 1808–1871," accessed May 8, 2021, https://history .house.gov/People/Detail/11480#biography; *Alexandria Gazette*, February

24, 1868; *Philadelphia Inquirer*, February 11, 1871; *4th Cavalry/64th Regiment Pennsylvania Volunteers*, accessed May 4, 2020, www.pa-roots.com/pacw/cavalry /4thcav/4thcavorg.html.

18. *Documents of the Senate of the State of New York*, 8, 35–48; *Documents of the Senate of the State of New York: Ninety-First Session—1868*, vol. I (Albany, NY: Van Benthuysen & Sons' Printing House, 1868), 17–18.

19. *Hudson* (NY) *Daily Star*, 1868.

20. *New York Daily Tribune*, June 4, 1869.

21. *New York Daily Tribune*.

22. *New York Tribune*, May 14, 1873; John Niven, ed., *The Salmon P. Chase Papers, Volume 5: Correspondence, 1865–1873* (Kent, OH: Kent State University Press, 1998), 306–8.

23. *Daily Phoenix*, May 16, 1873.

24. *Anderson Intelligencer*, June 17, 1880; J. Michael Martinez, *Carpetbaggers, Cavalry, and the Ku Klux Klan: Exposing the Invisible Empire during Reconstruction* (Lanham, MD: Rowman & Littlefield Publishers, Inc., 2007), 163–99.

25. *Anderson Intelligencer*.

26. *Anderson Intelligencer*, *Roanoke Daily Times*, July 9, 1896; "Smalls, Robert: 1839–1915," accessed May 4, 2020, https://history.house.gov/People/Detail/21764.

27. Benjamin C. Cook, pension file #25924, RG 15, NAB; *Staunton Spectator*, December 14, 1869; *Daily State Journal*, April 28, 1871; 1880 census, Richmond, Henrico County, Virginia.

28. Accessed May 4, 2020, www.google.com/patents/US135525; *Daily State Journal*, February 3, 1873; *Daily State Journal*, February 22, 1873.

29. *Daily State Journal*, September 23, 1872; *Daily State Journal*, October 17, 1872; *Daily State Journal*, July 26, 1872.

30. *Journal of the Executive Proceedings of the Senate of the United States of America, from March 21, 1879 to March 3, 1881, inclusive*, vol. XXII (Washington, DC: Government Printing Office, 1901), 442; *Daily Dispatch* January 8, 1881; *Daily Dispatch*, February 22, 1881.

31. *National Tribune*, July 29, 1882; *National Tribune*, May 17, 1883; *National Tribune*, February 7, 1884; *National Tribune*, July 31, 1884.

32. *Wichita Eagle*, July 24, 1887; *Daily Dispatch*, May 15, 1884; Ainsworth R. Spofford, ed., *American Almanac and Treasury of Facts, Statistical, Financial, and Political, for the Year 1886* (New York: The American News Company, 1885), 152; *Richmond Dispatch*, January 13, 1885; *Richmond Dispatch*, June 14, 1885; *Daily Morning Call*, August 3, 1886. At the time ex-President Grant remained crippled by a serious hip injury sustained in a fall on the ice in front of his Manhattan home on Christmas Eve (*New York Tribune*, December 28, 1883; *West-Jersey Pioneer* [Bridgeton], January 3, 1884; *Brooklyn Union*, May 30, 1884).

33. *Wichita Eagle*, October 10, 1886; *Daily Times* (Richmond, VA), November 10, 1886.

34. *Abilene* (KS) *Reflector*, November 18, 1886.

35. *Wichita Eagle*, July 30, 1887.

36. *Wichita Eagle*, January 19, 1889.

37. *Richmond Dispatch*, January 10, 1888; *Richmond Dispatch*, January 3, 1893; *Richmond Dispatch*, January 18, 1896.

38. *Richmond Dispatch*, June 18, 1897; *Evening Star*, September 17, 1897; *Richmond Dispatch*, October 14, 1897; *Richmond Dispatch*, February 2, 1898; *Evening Star*, February 23, 1898.

39. *Richmond Dispatch*, May 18, 1898; 1900 census, Richmond, Henrico County, Virginia; *Times Dispatch* (Richmond, VA), March 5, 1906.

40. *Richmond Dispatch*, January 6, 1900; *Richmond Times*, March 8, 1900.

41. *Richmond Times*, September 16, 1900.

42. *Richmond Times*, April 17, 1902; *Richmond Times*, May 25, 1902.

43. *Times Dispatch*, March 5, 1906; Cook pension file: Death Certificate; Affidavit of Lee W. Staton, MD, January 13, 1908.

44. *Times Dispatch*; *Auburn* (NY) *Citizen*, March 8, 1906; *National Tribune*, May 17, 1906.

45. *Indianapolis Journal*, May 26, 1890; United Service Publishing Co., comp., *In and about Vicksburg: An Illustrated Guide Book to the City of Vicksburg, Mississippi* (Vicksburg, MS: Gibraltar Publishing Co., 1890), 263–64; *Attica* (NY) *News*, November 12, 1891.

46. *National Tribune*, September 19, 1895.

47. *National Tribune*, September 3, 1896.

48. *Syracuse Daily*, July 21, 1898.

49. *Evening Times*, August 6, 1898; *Philadelphia Inquirer*, August 7, 1898.

50. *Alexandria Gazette*, August 9, 1898; *Scranton Tribune*, August 9, 1898; *Richmond Dispatch*, August 9, 1898.

51. *Richmond Planet*, August 13, 1898.

52. *Staunton Spectator and Vindicator*, August 18, 1898.

53. *Iowa State Bystander*, August 19, 1898.

54. *Iowa State Bystander*.

55. *National Tribune*, March 24, 1898.

56. *New York Press*, May 30, 1897; *Evening Times*, May 27, 1897; *National Tribune*, July 29, 1897; *Buffalo Evening News*, August 24, 1897; *Journal of the Thirty-First National Encampment of the Grand Army of the Republic, Buffalo, New York, August 25th, 26th, and 27th, 1897* (Lincoln, NE: State Journal Company, Printers, 1897), 267–69; *New York Tribune*, May 11, 1900; Bob Janiskee, "Pruning the Parks: Castle Pinckney National Monument (1933–1956)," October 13, 2009, accessed May 4, 2020, https://www.nationalparkstraveler.org/2009/10/pruning-parks-castle-pinckney-national-monument-1933-19564731.

57. Bruce E. Baker, *What Reconstruction Meant: Historical Memory in the American South* (Charlottesville: University of Virginia Press, 2007), 82.

58. *Evening Times*, June 17, 1899; see also Baker, *What Reconstruction Meant*, 82.

59. *Richmond Dispatch*, May 31, 1900; *Semi-Weekly Messenger* (Wilmington, NC), June 1, 1900.

60. *Journal of the Thirty-Fourth National Encampment of the Grand Army of the Republic, August 29th and 30th, 1900, Chicago, Illinois* (Philadelphia, PA: Town Printing Company, 1901), 181–82.

61. *Journal of the Thirty-Sixth National Encampment of the Grand Army of the Republic, Washington, D.C., October 9th to 10th, 1903* (Minneapolis, MN: Kimball & Storer Co., 1903), 83–86.

CHAPTER 9

1. William H. Thomas, *The American Negro: What He Was, What He Is and What He May Become* (New York: The Macmillan Company, 1901).

2. *New York Tribune*, January 5, 1901; *Post-Standard* (Syracuse, NY), February 16, 1901.

3. Smith, *Black Judas*, 124, 137–38.

4. "Views of Leading Colored Men, on the Results of the Election," *Southern Workman*, February 1885, 23(2). The legal definition of *particeps criminis* is "one who takes part in a crime," i.e., "accomplice" ("Particeps criminis," *Merriam-Webster.com Legal Dictionary*, Merriam-Webster, accessed June 12, 2021, https://www.merriam -webster.com/legal/particeps% 20criminis).

5. John D. Smith, "The Lawyer vs. the Race Traitor: Charles W. Chestnutt, William Hannibal Thomas, and *The American Negro*," *The Journal of The Historical Society*, vol. III, no. 2 (Spring 2003): 225–48.

6. *New York Tribune*, January 5, 1901; *New York Times*, January 12, 1901.

7. *Saint Paul Globe*, March 3, 1901.

8. *Saint Paul Globe*; *Colored American* (Washington, DC), February 2, 1901.

9. *New York Tribune*, April 13, 1901.

10. *Colored American*, April 13, 1901.

11. *Washington Times*, April 20, 1901.

12. Smith, "The Lawyer vs. the Race Traitor," 225–48.

13. *St. Louis Republic*, March 17, 1901; *Florida Star* (Titusville), March 29, 1901; *Washington Bee*, April 16, 1898; *Post-Standard*, April 30, 1904; *Colored American*, February 2, 1901.

14. *St. Louis Republic*.

15. *Florida Star*, March 29, 1901.

16. *Buffalo Courier*, April 6, 1901.

17. *Seventh Report of the Class of 1890 of Harvard College, 1920: Thirtieth Anniversary* (Concord, NH: The Rumford Press, 1921), 65–66 (see also www.web dubois.org/wdb-about.html#autobiog, accessed May 4, 2020); Rebecca Cooper, "W. E. B. DuBois in Philadelphia," accessed December 19, 2014, www47.homep age.villanova.edu/charlene.mires/tours/dubois.htm (see also http://www.webdubois .org/wdb-phila.html#dbinphila, accessed May 8, 2021); "The W. E. B. Du Bois

Lectures," accessed May 5, 2020, www.hup.harvard.edu/collection.php?cpk=1011; *Colored American*, June 7, 1902; *Yale* (MI) *Expositor*, June 15, 1900.

18. *Buffalo Courier*, April 6, 1901; W. E. Burghardt Du Bois (ed.), *The College-Bred Negro: Report of a Social Study Made Under the Direction of Atlanta University; Together with the Proceedings of the Fifth Conference for the Study of the Negro Problems, Held at Atlanta University, May 29–30, 1900* (Atlanta: Atlanta University Press, 1900), 111–12.

19. Du Bois, *The College-Bred Negro*, 114.

20. *Appeal*, June 15, 1901; Smith, "The Lawyer vs. the Race Traitor," 225–48.

21. *Broad Ax*, October 19, 1901.

22. *Broad Ax*.

23. W. E. B. Du Bois, *The Philadelphia Negro: A Social Study* (New York: Schocken Books Inc., 1967; first published in 1899), 328, 351; *McCook* (NE) *Tribune*, January 12, 1900.

24. Cooper, "W. E. B. DuBois in Philadelphia"; "Nation's Premier Civil Rights Organization," accessed May 5, 2020, https://www.naacp.org/nations-premier-civil-rights-organization; accessed May 5, 2020, www.webdubois.org/wdb-sources.html.

25. *The Monument to Robert Gould Shaw: Its Inception, Completion and Unveiling, 1865–1897* (Boston, MA: Houghton, Mifflin and Company, 1897), 41–53, 71–95; *Exercises at the Dedication of the Monument to Colonel Robert Gould Shaw and the Fifth-Fourth Regiment of Massachusetts Infantry, May 31, 1897* (Boston, MA: Municipal Printing Office, 1897); "Robert Gould Shaw and the 54th Regiment," accessed May 5, 2020, www.nps.gov/boaf/historyculture/shaw.htm.

26. *National Tribune*, October 7, 1897; "Port Hudson State Historic Site," accessed May 8, 2021, https://www.lastateparks.com/historic-sites/port-hudson-state-historic-site.

27. M. E. Hall, "Vergennes," *The Midland Monthly* 4(2) (1895): 130–36.

28. *Evening Star*, April 15, 1899; *Washington Times*, April 23, 1899. Five years later, the formal program with which the Royal Arcanum feted its twenty-fifth anniversary featured piano selections from "Carmen," along with "some coon songs . . . [that] made a great hit." Cohort member Jared D. Terrill, one of several former grand regents, was on the reception committee (*Evening Star*, April 30, 1904); whether or not he helped plan the evening, it is alarming that a fraternal benevolent society thought such entertainment was suitable.

As the Jim Crow Museum of Racist Memorabilia at Ferris State University reported in its online article, "What Were Coon Songs?" (accessed May 5, 2020, https://www.ferris.edu/HTMLS/news/jimcrow/question/2005/may.htm), some blacks composed songs that were equally debasing of African Americans as those of white songwriters. Authors Richard A. Reublin and Robert L. Maine of the Parlor Songs Association, Inc., go on to say that "In their time, coon songs spoke volumes about white attitudes towards African Americans. Unfortunately, in many cases they also spoke volumes about some black composers' sense of personal pride and self image. They are an historical document that clearly shows white attitudes and the terribly oppressive social world that African Americans had to cope with."

29. *Evening Star*, April 12, 1898.

30. *Washington Times*, May 24, 1897.

31. *Colored American*, March 10, 1900.

32. *Minneapolis Journal*, September 6, 1904.

33. *Minneapolis Journal*.

34. *Brooklyn Daily Eagle*, May 2, 1905.

35. *Brooklyn Daily Eagle*, May 14, 1905.

36. *New York Press*, June 18, 1905.

37. Joseph B. Foraker, *Notes of a Busy Life*, vol. 2 (Cincinnati, OH: Stewart and Kidd Company, 1916), 231–33; *Broad Ax*, September 1, 1906; John D. Weaver, *The Brownsville Raid* (College Station: Texas A&M University Press, 1992), 15–16, 18, 281; *Evening Star*, February 11, 1907; *Evening Star*, February 13, 1907; *Utica Daily Press*, October 10, 1899; *Brownsville* (TX) *Daily Herald*, August 14, 1906; *Brownsville Daily Herald*, September 11, 1906; *Washington Herald*, April 7, 1910.

38. Weaver, *The Brownsville Raid*, 15–16, 78–102, 281; Foraker, *Notes of a Busy Life*, vol. 2, 232–34, 247; *Evening Star*, November 22, 1906; *New York Age*, November 22, 1906.

39. *Salt Lake Herald*, November 30, 1906.

40. *Commoner* (Lincoln, NE), December 7, 1906.

41. Foraker, *Notes of a Busy Life*, vol. 2, 234–35; "Foraker, Joseph Benson (1846–1917)," accessed May 8, 2021, https://bioguideretro.congress.gov/Home/MemberDetails?memIndex=f000253; Joseph B. Foraker, *Notes of a Busy Life*, vol. 1 (Cincinnati, OH: Stewart and Kidd Company, 1917), 15–16, 32–35, 70–71.

42. *Bismarck* (ND) *Daily Tribune*, December 20, 1906.

43. *Bismarck Daily Tribune*; Foraker, *Notes of a Busy Life*, vol. 2, 239–47.

44. Foraker, *Notes of a Busy Life*, vol. 2, 249–58.

45. *National Tribune*, February 21, 1907.

46. Foraker, *Notes of a Busy Life*, vol. 2, 260–98.

47. *New York Tribune*, December 15, 1908.

48. *Broad Ax*, December 17, 1908.

49. *Broad Ax*.

50. *Broad Ax*; Hammond, "William H. Carney: 54th Massachusetts Soldier and First Black U.S. Medal of Honor Recipient"; *New York Age*, December 17, 1908; *New York Evening Post*, December 19, 1908.

51. Foraker, *Notes of a Busy Life*, vol. 2, 351–52; *Washington Times*, January 2, 1909; "The Constitution, Amendments 11–27," accessed May 8, 2021, https://www.archives.gov/founding-docs/amendments-11-27.

52. *Washington Herald*, January 6, 1909; *Los Angeles Herald*, January 13, 1909.

53. *Marion* (OH) *Daily Mirror*, January 28, 1909; *Sun*, January 29, 1909; *Washington Herald*, February 24, 1909; *Broad Ax*, March 6, 1909; *Nashville Globe*, March 5, 1909; Weaver, *The Brownsville Raid*, 282–83; "Aldrich, Nelson Wilmarth:

1841–1915," accessed May 6, 2020, http://bioguide.congress.gov/scripts/biodisplay .pl?index=A000083. Aldrich was the grandfather of another Republican leader, New York governor and vice president of the United States, Nelson Aldrich Rockefeller.

54. Foraker, *Notes of a Busy Life*, vol. 2, 313–14.

55. *Nashville Globe*, March 5, 1909.

56. *Washington Herald*, March 7, 1909; Foraker, *Notes of a Busy Life*, vol. 2, 320; *Broad Ax*, March 13, 1909.

57. *Washington Herald*, October 22, 1909.

58. *Los Angeles Herald*, March 30, 1909; *Washington Herald*, April 16, 1909; *Washington Herald*, April 30, 1909; *Evening Star*, July 28, 1909; accessed May 6, 2020, https://history.army.mil/books/Sw-SA/Dickinson.htm.

59. *Evening Star, 61st Congress, 2d Session, 1909–1910: House Documents*, vol. 13 (Washington, DC: Government Printing Office, 1909), 57–58.

60. *61st Congress, 2d Session, 1909–1910: House Documents*, 57–58.

61. *Brownsville Daily Herald*, November 18, 1909.

62. *Salt Lake Herald-Republican*, November 28, 1909.

63. *Hawaiian Star* (Honolulu, HI), April 6, 1910; *Washington Herald*, April 7, 1910; *Garland* (UT) *Globe*, April 16, 1910.

64. *61st Congress, 3d Session, December 5, 1910–March 4, 1911: Senate Documents*, vol. 85 (Washington, DC: Government Printing Office, 1911), 67–68.

65. *Sun*, June 27, 1916.

66. Foraker, *Notes of a Busy Life*, vol. 2, 326–27.

67. John D. Weaver's book, *The Brownsville Raid*, was first published in 1970, and spurred interest in the case. After the army agreed to its being reopened in 1972, Lieutenant Colonel William Baker, who had come to the Pentagon to work in the brand-new Army Equal Opportunity Program, asked to be assigned to the inquiry. His contribution proved to be vital, and in September, secretary of the Army Robert F. Froehlke pronounced the unprecedented mass punishment "a gross injustice" and ordered the discharges of all 167 men to be reversed to honorable. In its coverage, the *New York Times* further reported that army officials stated that no effort would be undertaken to find out whether there were any surviving members of the group, and "that the action ruled out any back pay and allowances for their descendants."

As it turned out, two of the men were still alive. Edward Warfield of Los Angeles had been among the fourteen troopers designated for re-enlistment, unlike Dorsie W. Willis of Minneapolis. On February 12, 1973, in an emotional ceremony at his church on his eighty-seventh birthday, Mr. Willis, whose dishonorable discharge and banning from any other federal service had forced him to earn a living shining shoes for the next fifty-nine years, received his honorable discharge. After US representative Augustus F. Hawkins (D., California) introduced a bill calling for Willis and the other soldiers' descendants to be compensated for the injustice they had undergone, a hearing was held in the House on June 14. Mr. Willis was in attendance, as was his senator, Hubert H. Humphrey, who testified along with Representative Hawkins, and promised that an accompanying bill would be brought before the Senate.

The former vice president proved as good as his word—on August 4, the Senate passed his bill to award $25,000 to Mr. Willis as compensation, which was received by the veteran on January 10, 1974. While expressing his gratitude for the check as "'a great birthday present,'" he pointedly noted that "'it comes too many years too late.'"

At his death on August 24, 1977, Dorsie W. Willis "was buried at the U.S. Military Cemetery at Fort Snelling, Minnesota with full military honors."

New York Times, September 29, 1972; *New York Times*, February 12, 1973; *New York Times*, June 15, 1973; *New York Times*, August 5, 1973; *Gettysburg Times*, October 3, 2018; *New York Times*, October 8, 2018; "Dorsie Willis, Brownsville Massacre Survivor," accessed June 3, 2021, https://digitalcommons.chapman.edu/upi_african_american/50/; "Dorsie Willis (1886–1977)," Harry Lembeck, May 29, 2015, accessed June 3, 2021, https://www.blackpast.org/african-american-history/willis-dorsie-1977/.

68. Weaver, *The Brownsville Raid*, 273–77; David L. Lewis, *W.E.B. Du Bois: A Biography* (New York: Henry Holt and Company, L.L.C., 2009), 228–30; *Washington Bee*, October 24, 1908. The *Evening Star* reported on November 22, 1906, that Republican Representative Olcott of New York "would have undoubtedly been defeated by negro votes if the storm had broken in time," and that "the efforts of Booker Washington [were required] in person to save Olcott." More than two weeks after the cashiering of the black troops was made public, Washington still "has not yet been heard from upon the subject . . . and it is not known whether he feels aggrieved or not at the administration's repayment of his efforts in Olcott's behalf."

69. *Washington Herald*, November 2, 1910; Eliot McCormick, "Fight City Legends: The Galveston Giant," April 1, 2020, accessed May 6, 2020, https://www.thefightcity.com/jack-johnson-the-galveston-giant/; *Vermont Watchman* (Montpelier), November 3, 1910; Louis R. Harlan and Raymond W. Smock (eds.), *The Booker T. Washington Papers*, vol. 10, *1909–1911* (Champaign-Urbana: University of Illinois Press, 1981), 76.

70. *New York Tribune*, November 5, 1910; *Washington Times*, March 20, 1912; *Broad Ax*, November 16, 1912.

71. *Salt Lake Herald*, August 13, 1909; *Omaha Daily Bee*, August 14, 1909; *National Tribune*, August 19, 1909; *Salt Lake Herald-Republican*, August 18, 1909; *Salt Lake Tribune*, August 24, 1909; *Ogden* (UT) *Standard*, August 24, 1909. Bostaph's nomination and election to the Grand Army's second highest office was not without controversy. As the *Salt Lake Herald* reported on August 13, the "utmost harmony" that prevailed when all the other officers were elected was decidedly not the case with senior vice commander. As soon as Bostaph's name was presented as Utah's candidate, Department of Pennsylvania Commander Robert B. Beath rose in protest against the GAR tradition of filling the office with an individual from the hosting state. Classifying his opposition as long-standing and principled, Beath said that it was not meant as any reflection on Bostaph's capacity for the office.

James Tanner, while lauding "the war record and the civil career of the candidate named," supported Beath's position, saying that "the department of Utah was small and that the delegates should consider the possibility of this department's candidate having to assume the duties of commander-in-chief." In its August 14 coverage, the *Omaha Daily Bee* reported that it was Beath who contended that "the smaller departments might not always be able to supply a man capable of acting as commander in the event of the disability of the commander-in-chief."

In any case, Beath's and Tanner's opposition went for naught, with the *Bee* calling their stab at ending the Grand Army's practice "ineffectual," and the home state *Herald* reporting that their contentions "seemed not to be popular with the delegates as a whole, as there were no other nominations made. Utah's candidate was therefore declared elected unanimously."

In its coverage on August 19, the *National Tribune* reported Beath's protestations but omitted Tanner's agreement, only citing the latter's praise of Bostaph's "high character and qualifications." Ascending to the podium amid cheers, the newly elected senior vice commander, despite the patronizing and rather insulting comments of both men, was noted as gracious in his acceptance remarks.

72.   See Michael Korda, *Clouds of Glory: The Life and Legend of Robert E. Lee* (New York: HarperCollins Publishers, 2014) for one of the more recent, in-depth studies.

73.   Joshua Lawrence Chamberlain, *The Passing of the Armies: An Account of the Final Campaign of the Army of the Potomac, Based Upon Personal Reminiscences of the Fifth Army Corps* (Gettysburg, PA: Stan Clark Military Books, 1994), 246.

74.   Alice R. Trulock, *In the Hands of Providence: Joshua L. Chamberlain and the American Civil War* (Chapel Hill: University of North Carolina Press, 1992), 9–10.

75.   Chamberlain, *The Passing of the Armies*, 248–49.

76.   Ulysses S. Grant, *Memoirs and Selected Letters: Personal Memoirs of U.S. Grant* (Garden City, NY: Library of America, 1990), chapter LXVII, 490; "Ulysses S. Grant," accessed May 13, 2022, https://www.battlefields.org/learn/biographies/ulysses-s-grant.

77.   Alan T. Nolan, *Lee Considered* (Chapel Hill: University of North Carolina Press, 1991), 150

78.   Elizabeth Brown Pryor, *Reading the Man: A Portrait of Robert E. Lee Through His Private Letters* (New York: Viking Penguin, 2007), 399.

79.   *Soldier's Friend*, vol. II, no. 3, March 1866. The entire preample and resolutions read as follows:

"*Whereas*, Robert E. Lee, late general-in-chief of the rebel army, has recently been in this city, we, the members of the Soldiers' and Sailors' National Union League, representing, as we believe, the sentiments of all truly *loyal* Americans, and more than half a million of the nation's defenders, embrace the opportunity to resolve—

First: That while we will abide by the decisions of the military authority of the country, and cheerfully support the military honor, we can not but lament that Robert E. Lee has been placed by the liberality of our Government beyond the jurisdiction of the military tribunals of the land, before which he could have been summoned to answer to the charge of treason, and received the reward of a traitor.

Second: While we can fraternize with the deluded masses of the Confederate army, we charge Robert E. Lee with treachery to God for wantonly violating the obligation of his oath, and we brand him as a traitor to his country, whose flag he dishonored and whose confidence he betrayed, and as an enemy of the race he labored to destroy, and we commit him, with all his crimes, to posterity, as an object of execration, and as a warning to tyrants who would wrest from a people the natural right of liberty.

Third: We protest against any act whereby the said Lee shall hold, occupy, or enjoy any portion of the estate seized by the Federal authority by virtue of the confiscation act. We have periled our lives for our country's honor and our nation's flag, and we will perish rather than surrender at any time to any person the graves of our honored dead.

The last demand we make in the name of the defenceless heroes who perished at Andersonville, Belle Isle, and Libby, and whose sufferings demanded the commiseration of mankind, and would have been mitigated by Robert E. Lee, had not his humanity and loyalty been entombed in the same sepulcher."

80. Thomas L. Connelly, *The Marble Man: Robert E. Lee and His Image in American Society* (Baton Rouge: Louisiana State University Press, 1977), 98–99.

81. *National Tribune*, September 19, 1889. At the current time, Lee's birthday is a public holiday in two southern states, Alabama and Mississippi, and a third (Georgia) observes it on the Friday after Thanksgiving, although there is no longer any specific reference to Lee. The state of Virginia celebrates Lee-Jackson Day, which commemorates the Army of Northern Virginia's commander and his most trusted lieutenant, "Stonewall" Jackson, on the Friday prior to Martin Luther King Day: accessed May 8, 2021, https://www.officeholidays.com/holidays/usa/robert-e -lees-birthday.

82. *National Tribune*.

83. *New York Herald*, January 25, 1903; *Philadelphia Inquirer*, January 26, 1903; *Montour American* (Danville, PA), June 17, 1909.

84. *Anderson Intelligencer*, March 4, 1903.

85. *Anderson Intelligencer*, *Washington Times*, June 14, 1901; *Manning Times*, June 26, 1901.

86. *National Tribune*, October 16, 1902.

87. David G. Smith, "Race and Retaliation: The Capture of African Americans during the Gettysburg Campaign," in Peter Wallenstein and Bertram Wyatt-Brown (eds.), *Virginia's Civil War* (Charlottesville: University of Virginia Press, 2005), 137–51; Stephen W. Sears, *Gettysburg* (New York: Houghton Mifflin Company, 2003), 111–12.

88. "About the National Statuary Hall Collection," accessed May 6, 2020, www .aoc.gov/capitol-hill/national-statuary-hall-collection/about-national-statuary-hall -collection; *New York Tribune*, August 1, 1910.

89. *Washington Times*, January 20, 1903.

90. *Richmond Times*, January 20, 1903.

91. *National Tribune*, January 22, 1903.

92. *Richmond Dispatch*, January 23, 1903; *Alexandria Gazette*, January 23, 1903; *National Tribune*, January 29, 1903; H. Spalding, "Jacques Marquette, S. J.," in *The Catholic Encyclopedia*, vol. 9 (New York: Robert Appleton Company, 1910), accessed May 8, 2021, https://www.newadvent.org/cathen/09690a.htm.

93. *National Tribune*, February 5, 1903.

94. *National Tribune*, February 12, 1903.

95. *National Tribune*.

96. *Evening Star*, February 13, 1903.

97. *Times Dispatch*, February 22, 1903.

98. *Times Dispatch*, March 5, 1903; *Evening Star*, March 5, 1903.

99. *Times Dispatch*, March 17, 1903; *National Tribune*, March 19, 1903.

100. *Evening Star*, March 7, 1903. Curtis would go on to be elected to four terms as a senator from Kansas, then vice president of the United States under Herbert Hoover: "CURTIS, Charles: 1860–1936," accessed September 2, 2021, https://bioguide.congress.gov/search/bio/C001008; "MILLER, James Monroe: 1852–1926," accessed September 2, 2021, https://bioguide.congress.gov/search/bio/M000733; "COOPER, Henry Allen: 1850–1931," accessed September 2, 2021, https://bioguide.congress.gov/search/bio/C000752.

101. *National Tribune*, March 12, 1903. Lacey joined the Third Iowa in May 1861, and went on to serve as a sergeant major and lieutenant with the Thirty-Third Iowa before his promotion to assistant adjutant general—after studying law he became a member of the bar in 1865: "LACEY, John Fletcher: 1841–1913," accessed September 2, 2021, https://bioguide.congress.gov/search/bio/L000010; Weeks was already an attorney when he enlisted in the Fifth Michigan Volunteer Infantry as a first sergeant, then served as a first lieutenant, adjutant and captain in the Twenty-Second Michigan before being "appointed assistant inspector general of the Third Brigade, Second Division, Reserve Corps, Army of the Cumberland, in 1863; was mustered out in December 1863"; "WEEKS, Edgar: 1839–1904," accessed September 2, 2021, https://bioguide.congress.gov/search/bio/W000243.

102. *National Tribune*; MAYNARD, Harry Lee: 1861–1922," accessed September 2, 2021, https://bioguide.congress.gov/search/bio/M000283.

103. *National Tribune*, April 16, 1903.

104. *Times Dispatch*, March 19, 1903; *Times Dispatch*, April 29, 1903.

105. *National Tribune*, February 19, 1903; *Washington Times*, March 15, 1903; *National Tribune*, March 19, 1903; *Columbus* (NE) *Journal*, April 8, 1903; *National Tribune*, April 23, 1903; *Times Dispatch*, May 21, 1903; *National Tribune*, May 28,

1903; *National Tribune*, June 11, 1903; *National Tribune*, June 25, 1903; *National Tribune*, July 9, 1903.

106. *Washington Times*, May 10, 1903.

107. *Guthrie* (OK) *Daily Leader*, June 11, 1903.

108. *Minneapolis Journal*, July 9, 1903.

109. *Washington Times*, October 18, 1903.

110. *Saint Paul Globe*, October 17, 1903.

111. *Washington Times*, October 18, 1903.

112. *National Tribune*, November 12, 1903.

113. "WARNER, Vespasian: 1842–1925," accessed May 6, 2020, http://bioguide.congress.gov/scripts/biodisplay.pl?index=W000158.

CHAPTER 10

1. *Jamestown Evening Journal*, June 30, 1915.

2. *National Tribune*, August 5, 1909; *National Tribune*, August 19, 1909; *National Tribune*, March 17, 1910; *National Tribune*, April 28, 1910.

3. *National Tribune*, December 16, 1910.

4. *Elmira* (NY) *Star-Gazette*, January 13, 1910.

5. *National Tribune*, January 27, 1910.

6. *National Tribune*, January 13, 1910.

7. *National Tribune*, January 27, 1910.

8. *National Tribune*, March 17, 1910.

9. *National Tribune*, April 14, 1910.

10. *Daily Long Island Farmer* (Jamaica, NY), March 31, 1910.

11. *National Tribune*, March 31, 1910.

12. *National Tribune*.

13. *National Tribune*, March 10, 1910.

14. *National Tribune*, April 28, 1910.

15. *National Tribune*.

16. *National Tribune*, March 31, 1910; "Captain Henry Wirz," accessed May 8, 2021, https://www.nps.gov/ande/learn/historyculture/captain_henry_wirz.htm.

17. *National Tribune*, April 28, 1910.

18. *Troy Times*, April 13, 1910.

19. *National Tribune*, April 28, 1910.

20. *New York Tribune*, June 23, 1910.

21. *New York Press*, June 24, 1910; *New York Tribune*, June 24, 1910.

22. *New York Press*; *National Tribune*, June 16, 1910.

23. *National Tribune*, July 7, 1910.

24. *National Tribune*, July 21, 1910.

25. *Buffalo Courier*, August 1, 1910; *New York Tribune*, August 1, 1910.

26. *New York Tribune*.

27. *National Tribune*, August 4, 1910.

28. *National Tribune*, August 11, 1910

29. *National Tribune.*

30. *New York Evening Post*, August 13, 1910.

31. *New York Evening Post.*

32. *Brooklyn Daily Standard Union*, August 17, 1910.

33. *Daily Standard Union.*

34. *National Tribune*, August 4, 1910.

35. *National Tribune*, August 25, 1910.

36. *National Tribune*, September 1, 1910.

37. *National Tribune.*

38. *National Tribune*, August 4, 1910.

39. *National Tribune*, August 18, 1910.

40. *National Tribune*, August 25, 1910.

41. *National Tribune*, September 15, 1910.

42. *National Tribune*, September 1, 1910.

43. *National Tribune.*

44. *National Tribune.*

45. *National Tribune.*

46. *National Tribune.*

47. *National Tribune*, September 8, 1910.

48. *National Tribune*, February 23, 1911.

49. *National Tribune*, September 8, 1910.

50. *National Tribune*: January 20, 1910; January 27, 1910; February 3, 1910; March 17, 1910; March 24, 1910; March 31, 1910; April 14, 1910; April 28, 1910; May 5, 1910; May 12, 1910; May 19, 1910; May 26, 1910; June 16, 1910; June 23, 1910; June 30, 1910; July 7, 1910; July 14, 1910; July 21, 1910; August 4, 1910; August 11, 1910; August 18, 1910; August 25, 1910; September 1, 1910; September 8, 1910; September 15, 1910.

51. *National Tribune*, September 8, 1910.

52. *National Tribune.*

53. *National Tribune*, October 20, 1910.

54. *Democratic Banner* (Mt. Vernon, OH), September 20, 1910; *Salt Lake Tribune*, September 21, 1910; *Washington Herald*, September 21, 1910.

55. *Marion Daily Mirror*, September 21, 1910.

56. *Norwich* (CT) *Bulletin*, September 23, 1910.

57. *Amsterdam* (NY) *Evening Recorder and Daily Democrat*, September 23, 1910; *National Tribune*, September 29, 1910; *Times Dispatch*, September 24, 1910. Ketcham was among the thirty-eight charter members ("some of the greatest names in Indiana's legal history") who organized the Indianapolis Bar Association in November 1878, and was elected attorney general of Indiana in 1894 and 1896 as a Republican ("Proceedings of the Mid-Winter Meeting," *Indiana Law Journal* 18[3] [1943]: article 3, 215; *Indianapolis News*, December 27, 1921).

58. *National Tribune*; *Times Dispatch*; *Philadelphia Inquirer*, September 24, 1910; *Journal of the Forty-Fourth National Encampment of the Grand Army of the Republic at Atlantic City, New Jersey, September 22d and 23d, 1910* (Minneapolis, MN: Press of Byron & Willard Co., 1910), 311–27; *Washington Herald*, September 24, 1910; *National Tribune*, May 21, 1891; *Deseret Evening News* (Salt Lake City, UT), September 24, 1910; *New York Tribune*, September 24, 1910; *Troy Times*, September 24, 1910. William A. Ketcham did not resign from the GAR—in fact, he served as its National Judge Advocate from 1915 through 1920, when he was elected commander in chief. He completed his term before dying six days shy of his seventy-sixth birthday on December 27, 1921 (*Indianapolis News*; *Journal of the House of Representatives of the Commonwealth of Massachusetts, 1921* [Boston, MA: Wright & Potter Printing Co., State Printers, 1921], 684; *Journal of the Eighty-Third National Encampment of the Grand Army of the Republic: Indianapolis, Ind., August 28 to September 1, 1949* [Washington, DC: United States Government Printing Office, 1949], 8).

59. *Philadelphia Inquirer*.

60. *Troy Times*, September 24, 1910; *Journal of the Forty-Fourth National Encampment of the Grand Army of the Republic*, 318.

61. *New York Tribune*, September 24, 1910.

62. *Journal of the Forty-Fourth National Encampment of the Grand Army of the Republic*, 323.

63. *National Tribune*, November 24, 1910.

64. *National Tribune*, February 23, 1911.

65. *Burlington* (VT) *Weekly Free Press*, August 31, 1911. In April 2020, the Virginia General Assembly approved

An Act to establish the Commission for Historical Statues in the United States Capitol to provide for the replacement of the Robert E. Lee statue in the National Statuary Hall Collection at the United States Capitol, to recommend to the General Assembly as a replacement a statue of a prominent Virginia citizen of historic renown or renowned for distinguished civil or military service to be commemorated in the National Statuary Hall Collection, and to provide for the selection of a sculptor for the new statue; and to provide for submission of the Commonwealth's request to the Joint Committee of Congress on the Library for approval to replace the Robert E. Lee statue in the National Statuary Hall Collection at the United States Capitol.

The commission in July having voted unanimously to recommend the statue's removal, and the Virginia Museum of History and Culture having accepting ownership upon its removal at the commission's request, Virginia Governor Ralph Northam announced on December 21, 2020, that Lee's statue was "removed from the United States Capitol overnight." Five days earlier, the commission "voted to recommend civil rights icon Barbara Rose Johns to represent Virginia in the National Statuary Hall Collection," replacing the Lee statue: accessed September 20, 2021, https://lis.virginia.gov/cgi-bin/legp604.exe?201+ful+CHAP1099+pdf, https://www.governor.virginia.gov/newsroom/all-releases/2020/july/headline-859644-en.html, https://www.dhr.virginia.gov/wp-content/uploads/2020/08/VMHC-Letter-to-DHR-August-18-2020.pdf, https://www.governor.virginia.gov/newsroom/all-releases/2020/december/headline-890324-en.html and https://www.governor.virginia.gov/newsroom/all-releases/2020/december/headline-890268-en.html.

66. *Burlington Weekly Free Press.*

67. *Times Dispatch,* June 2, 1911.

68. *New York Age,* August 31, 1911.

69. *Bismarck Daily Tribune,* July 21, 1911; *Washington Times,* July 19, 1911; *Semi-Weekly Messenger,* April 3, 1906; *Times Dispatch,* July 21, 1911; *Topeka State Journal,* July 21, 1911; *Alexandria Gazette,* July 20, 1911; *Evening Star,* July 20, 1911; *Washington Times,* July 21 and 22, 1911; *Washington Herald,* July 21, 1911; *New York Times,* July 22, 1911; *The Christian Advocate* 86(6) (September 7, 1911): 1201–2.

70. *New York Times; Times Dispatch,* July 22, 1911; *Evening Standard* (Ogden, UT), July 21, 1911.

71. *Staunton Spectator and Vindicator,* July 28, 1911.

72. *Times Dispatch,* July 21, 1911.

73. *Times Dispatch,* July 22, 1911.

74. *Washington Times,* July 19, 1911.

75. *Washington Times,* July 21, 1911.

76. *Times Dispatch,* July 22, 1911; "Gov. William Hodges Mann," accessed May 6, 2020, https://www.nga.org/governor/william-hodges-mann.

77. *Times Dispatch.*

78. William H. Taylor, *Taylor's Legislative Souvenir of Connecticut, 1901–1902: Portraits and Sketches of State Officials, Senators, Representatives, Etc.* (Putnam, CT: Published by W. H. Taylor, 1901), 193; *New York Times,* November 23, 1902; *Evening Star,* May 26, 1904; *New York Times,* July 22, 1911; *Washington Evening Star,* February 2, 1912; *Washington Times,* February 2, 1912.

79. Taylor, *Taylor's Legislative Souvenir of Connecticut,* 193; *Syracuse Journal,* March 6, 1908; *Syracuse Journal,* August 19, 1909; *Washington Herald,* February 2, 1912.

80. *Evening Star,* April 10, 1905; *Evening Star,* May 11, 1905.

81. *Times Dispatch,* March 26, 1906.

82. *Post-Standard,* May 30, 1910.

83. *Rochester Democrat and Chronicle,* February 23, 1911.

84. *Ogden Standard,* July 11, 1913.

85. *Jamestown Evening Journal,* June 30, 1915.

Index

Abbott, A. O., 20

Ackerman, William K., 150

Adams, R. N., 246

African Methodist Episcopal Church (AME): Brownsville Affray and, 290, 297; Douglass, F., and, 341; GAR and color line, 196; on Harlan and *Plessy v. Ferguson*, 227; on lynching, 242

Albany Evening Journal: on Cleveland Soldiers' Convention, 57; on education, 154–55, 160; on election of 1868, 94, 95; on Forrest, 59–60; on Ulster County (NY) Soldiers' Conventions, 66

Albany Law Journal, 168

Alcorn (Senator), 103

Alexander, Charles, 235–36

Alexandria Gazette, 240, 310

Alger, Russell A., 186; Department of Louisiana and Mississippi and, 184; Gray and, 182, 184; Spanish-American War and, 231

Allen, Henry C., 27–28, 33

Amalgamated Council of Trades, 199

AME. *See* African Methodist Episcopal Church

American Missionary Association, 152, 156

The American Negro (Thomas, W.), 275–79, 281

American Protestant Association (APA), 310

Ames, Adelbert: as Governor of Mississippi, 122, 123–25, 127–28

amputation, 36. *See also* Left-Armed Corps

Amsterdam (NY) *Evening Recorder and Daily Democrat*, 335

Anderson, Robert, 252

Anderson (Court House, SC) *Intelligencer*, 308

Andersonville Prison, 57, 258, 318, 321, 336

Anthony, James H., 321–22

Antietam monument, 247–48, 390n101

Antietam National Cemetery, 257–59

Conservative Convention
of Soldiers and Sailors and,
93; GAR and, 139; on Lee,
R., 308; in MOLLUS, 143;
Pennsylvania Democratic
Soldiers' Convention and, 51
Dean, Eric T., Jr., 143
DeCamp, William M., 25–27
Decker, W. S., 189, 190, 191
Declaration of Principles, GAR,
84, 86
Decoration Day: at Beaufort
National Cemetery, 262–63,
271–72; at Florence National
Cemetery, 271
DeKlyne (Deputy Marshal), 120
Democratic party: "Banty Tim"
and, 80; Bryan and, 229;
Clinton Massacre and, 123;
Colfax Massacre and, 120,
122–27; Davis, W., of, 19;
education and, 155; in election
of 1866, 51, 64, 66; in election
of 1868, 93–100; in election of
1876, 130; in election of 1884,
162; GAR and, 144; Hayes
and, 130–33; Left-Armed
Corps and, 161–62; Lost
Cause and, 213; Memphis,
Tennessee massacre and, 54;
Ulster County (NY) Soldiers'
Convention and, 66. *See also*
specific individuals
Department of California/
California and Nevada, 140

Department of Connecticut, 140,
173, 188, 344, 381n31
Department of Delaware, 173
Department of Florida, 140,
204–5
Department of Georgia/Georgia
and South Carolina, 140, 252–
53, 272, 338
Department of Idaho, 140
Department of Illinois, 85, 140,
173
Department of Indiana, 85, 173,
206, 333, 335, 338
Department of Iowa, 85, 173
Department of Kansas, 173, 333
Department of Kentucky, 190
Department of Louisiana and
Mississippi, 179–87, 191–93,
199–203, 206, 337, 342
Department of Massachusetts,
142, 173, 203
Department of Michigan, 140,
141
Department of Minnesota, 85,
173
Department of Missouri, 173, 189
Department of New York, 140,
173, 345; Lee, R., and, 322–24,
333, 339
Department of North Dakota,
333
Department of Ohio, 135, 140,
142–43, 173–74, 188, 218
Department of Pennsylvania, 141,
173, 217

251–52; as US deputy marshal monitoring voting, 129–30

Ladies of GAR Circle, 332; Douglass, F., and, 341

Lancaster (PA) *Daily Intelligencer*, 213; on election of 1868, 88–89, 92–93; on GAR, 180–81

Lane, Charles, on Reconstruction, 118–19; on Colfax Massacre, 121

Lane, James H., 48

Latonia (NH) *Democrat*, 176

Lee, Arthur, 42–43

Lee, Fitzhugh, 284–85; in Spanish-American War, 230, 232, 331

Lee, Robert E., 5, 9, 94, 98; birthday as public holiday, 400n81; equestrian statue at Gettysburg, 307–8; GAR and, 307–8, 313–15, 318–41; National Statuary Hall and, 309–15, 317–41, 404n65; regarded by others, 304–15, 318–41; Soldiers' and Sailors' National Union League on, 306, 399n79; in Southern Historical Society, 9

Lee statue. *See* National Statuary Hall, and *Evening Star*, 312

Left-Armed Corps, ix, 3, 6–8, 135, 219–20; advocate for equality, 20–28, 136–37, 144; all Union veterans and, 11–12; black suffrage and, 83; commemoration of Civil War dead and, 266, 271–72; Freedmen's Bureau and, 35–44; GAR and, 140–44, 302–4; Jim Crow and, 136–37, 144, 161–62; National Statuary Hall and, 321–22; Pittsburgh Soldiers' and Sailors' Convention (1866) and, 58, 61; Republican party and, 144, 161; Southern Loyalists' Convention, 49; VRC and, 35–44; Washington, G., and, 345–46. *See also* Allen; Anthony; Barger; Bates, D.; Bicknell; Bostaph; Bourne; Broshears; Byers; Cameron, A.; Chase, J.; Cook; Dake; Davis, W.; DeCamp; Dodge; Edmonds; Farley; Fitz James; Gelray; Hall; Hardy; Haskell; Hilts; Huntington; Jones, W. J.; Kent; Koster; Krahl; Ladd; Lowell; Mabbett; MacNulty, W.; McEwan; Mull; Pinn; Reynolds; Robinson; Sanborn; Sands; Seage, R.; Smith, A.; Stewart; Terrill; Thomas, H.; Thomas, W.; Walbridge; Warren, W.; White, G.; Whitehouse; Wise, E.

Leiker, James N., 235

Lewis, James: Davis, J. funeral and, 181; GAR and, 182, 185–86, 187, 342; Spanish-American War and, 231

Lexington (VA) *Gazette*, 230

on education, 153, 154, 157–58; on GAR, 186

New York Herald: on Davis J. funeral, 180, 181; Forrest interview, 101–2; on GAR, 186, 193

New York Independent, 194–95

New York Press, 288

New York Soldiers' Depot, 19–20

New York Times: Dudley and, 48; on Brownsville Affray, 397n67; on Halpine, 353n11; on Thomas, W., 276; on Twenty-Fifth Infantry, 387n65

New York Tribune: on call for National Convention of Conservative Soldiers and Sailors, 94; on commemoration of Civil War dead, 261; on GAR, 87; on Haupt, 389n95; on Johnson, A., impeachment, 91; on National Statuary Hall, 322, 338; on call for Pittsburgh Soldiers' and Sailors' Convention, 52; on *Plessy v. Ferguson*, 227; on Thomas, W, 277

Nicholls, Francis T., 131

Nicolay, John G., 77

Ninth Cavalry, 233

Ninth Regiment, VRC, 8

Nolan, Alan T., 305

Northam, Ralph, 404n65

North Carolina Standard, 377n104

Northcott, H. S., 191

Norwich Bulletin, 334

O'Beirne, James R., 96

Odysseus in America (Shay), 73

Ogden (UT) *Standard*, 302

Olcott (Representative), 398n68

"Old Abe," 63–64, 91, 207

Olin, William M., 295

Oliver, Robert Shaw, 299

Omaha Daily Bee, 182, 194, 398n71

O'Neall, Joseph W., 135, photo of, *210*, 218

103rd USCT, 244

113th USCT, 292

115th New York, 383n88

121st New York, 25, 344

127th New York, 244

Otis, George A., 361n65

Ottawa (IL) *Free Trader*, 138

Packard, Jerrold M.: on Jim Crow, 169, 227–28

Packard, Stephen B.: Colfax Massacre and, 120, 121; Hayes and, 131, 132

Palmer, Betty, 74

Palmer, John: GAR commander in chief, 200–3

Palmer, John M., 73–77; "Banty Tim" and, 77; education and, 148; GAR and, 85; in Republican party, 73–74; Lincoln, and, 73–74, 75; photo of, *72*

Patriotic Order Sons of America, 195–96

Patton, William W., 168–69

Peace Convention, 74

Twenty-Fifth Infantry, 231–32, 387n90; Brownsville Affray and, 5, 288–302

Twenty-Fourth Infantry, 233, 285–86

Twenty-Fourth VRC, 35–36, 37

Twenty-Second Iowa, 26

Twenty-Second Massachusetts, 73

Twenty-Second Michigan, 401n101

Twenty-Seventh USCT, 70

Twenty-Third Ohio, 390n101

Twyman, P. A., 243

Union Herald (Columbia, SC), 251

Union Veteran Legion: Broshears at, 285; National Statuary Hall and, 314–15, 334, 341

Union Veterans' Union: denounces color line in any patriotic organization, 196; National Statuary Hall and, 311, 341

United Colored Democracy, 301

United Confederate Veterans: Castle Pinckney and, 271; Manassas Peace Jubilee and, 342

United Daughters of the Confederacy, 342

United States Colored Troops (USCT): 129, 185; 103rd, 244; 113th, 292; Fifth, 11, *14*, 69, 70, 83, *134*, 275; Fourth, 83; Third Heavy Artillery, 53, 75;

Thirty-Eighth, 83; Thirty-Fifth, 39; Thirty-First, 254; Thirty-Third, 383n88; Twenty-Second, 35; Twenty-Seventh, 70

United States Sanitary Commission, 6–7

Up from Slavery (Washington, B.), 278–79

Urbana (OH) *Union*, 80

USCT. *See* United States Colored Troops

US v. Cruikshank, 128

Valentine, Edward V., 313

Vallandigham, Clement L., 98–99

Van Sant, Samuel R., 337, 339

Veazey, Wheelock G., 187, 188–89, 193, 198

Vermont Phoenix (Brattleboro), 168

Vermont Soldiers' Convention, 61

Veteran Reserve Corps (VRC), ix, 8, 22; Corbin in, 254; discharge status of officers, 356n62; Freedmen's Bureau and, 33–44; Left-Armed Corps and, 35–44

Veterans Association of the Blue and Gray and Their Sons, 342

Veterans' Reserve (Forty-Fourth US Infantry), 36

Vicksburg Massacre, 122

Vietnam War, 6, 68

Virginian-Pilot (Norfolk), 242

voting. *See* black suffrage

VRC. *See* Veteran Reserve Corps

About the Author

Dr. Stephen A. Goldman is a psychiatrist and international consultant with decades of experience in academic and clinical medicine, public health, and medical product safety. A Life Fellow of the Academy of Consultation-Liaison Psychiatry and Distinguished Life Fellow of the American Psychiatric Association, he has innovatively linked having treated and worked with combat veterans with in-depth study of the Civil War, Reconstruction, and race. The only physician to serve on the Abraham Lincoln Institute Board of Directors, his thought-provoking findings have been welcomed on television, radio, podcasts, and in other venues. Recipient of the New York University School of Medicine Alex Rosen Award for Excellence in Medicine and the Humanities, Dr. Goldman and his wife live in Montgomery County, Maryland.